DEATH on the NILE

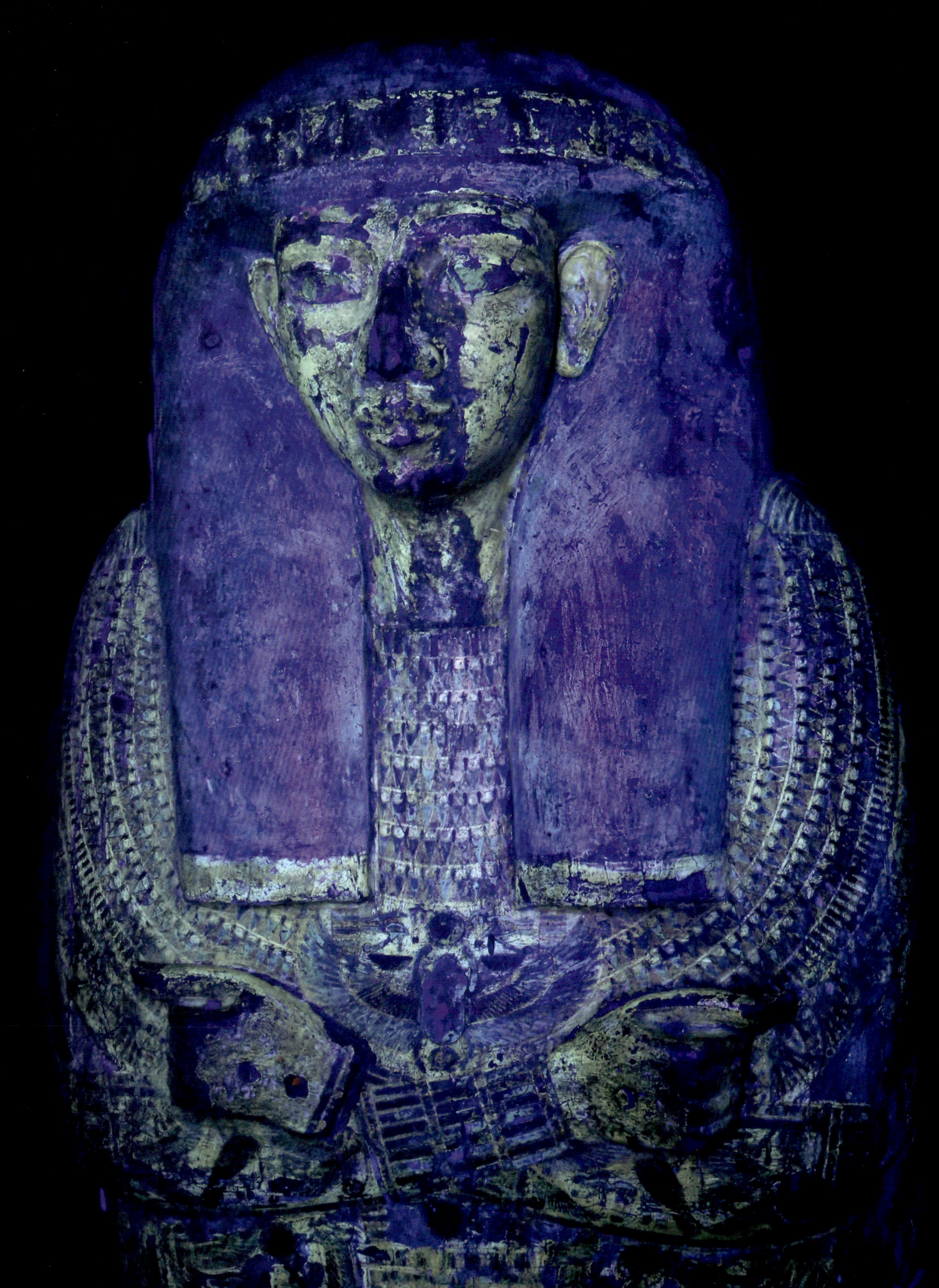

DEATH on the NILE

Uncovering the Afterlife of Ancient Egypt

Foreword by Tim Knox

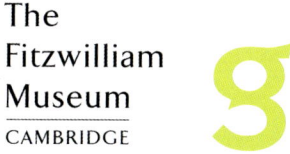

The Fitzwilliam Museum in association with D Giles Limited, London

© 2016 The Fitzwilliam Museum

First published in 2016 by GILES
An imprint of D Giles Limited
4 Crescent Stables, 139 Upper Richmond Road,
London SW15 2TN, UK
www.gilesltd.com

British Library Cataloguing in Publication Data.
A catalogue record for this book is available from
the British Library.

ISBN (hardover): 978-1-907804-71-1
ISBN (softcover): 978-1-910731-03-1

All rights reserved

No part of the contents of this book may be reproduced,
stored in a retrieval system, or transmitted in any form
or by any means, electronic, mechanical, photocopying,
recording, or otherwise, without the written permission of
the Syndics of The Fitzwilliam Museum and D Giles Ltd.

For The Fitzwilliam Museum
Curators and Editors: Julie Dawson and Helen Strudwick
Production Editor: Helen Strudwick
Photographs are by Michael Jones, Amy Jugg, Andrew
Norman, Jaymes Sinclair and Katie Young

For D Giles Limited
Copy-edited and proof-read by Jodi Simpson
Designed by Alfonso Iacurci
Produced by GILES, an imprint of D Giles Limited, London
Printed and bound in China

All measurements are in centimetres and millimetres
Height precedes width precedes depth

Front cover: The inner coffin of Nespawershefyt
(Fitzwilliam Museum, E.1.1822): top, the weighing of
Nespawershefyt's heart from the coffin box; bottom,
Nespawershefyt's face from the lid.
Back cover: The coffins of two men named Nebamun
and Ipuky during funeral rituals, as depicted in their
joint tomb at Thebes (fig. 35).
Frontispiece: Outer coffin lid of Nespawershefyt (cat. 26).
Original pistacia resin varnish over parts of the painted
surface fluoresces greenish-yellow under ultraviolet light.
Page 6: Carpenters at work, depicted in the tomb of Ipuy
(TT217 at Thebes).

CONTENTS

6	Director's Foreword Tim Knox	113	Catalogue Helen Strudwick and Julie Dawson
8	Curators' Acknowledgements Julie Dawson and Helen Strudwick	115	Introduction
		118	Early burial practices
13	Egyptian Coffins at the Fitzwilliam Museum: The Formation of the Collection Helen Strudwick	124	Funerary gods and beliefs
		136	Late Old Kingdom to early Middle Kingdom
		150	The dead become Osiris
		167	Decorated anthropoid coffins
29	Coffins of the Middle Kingdom: Their Origins and Development Wolfram Grajetzki	178	Economic and political influences
		202	Objects buried with Nakhtefmut
		207	Objects found on Nakhtefmut's body
49	Coffins from the New Kingdom to the Roman Period John H. Taylor	214	Later nested coffins
		227	Later coffins
75	Egyptian Coffins: Materials, Construction and Decoration Julie Dawson, Jennifer Marchant and Eleanor von Aderkas with contributions from Caroline R. Cartwright and Rebecca Stacey		
247	Glossary		
251	Picture Credits		
252	Map and Dates		
253	Index		

Director's Foreword
Tim Knox

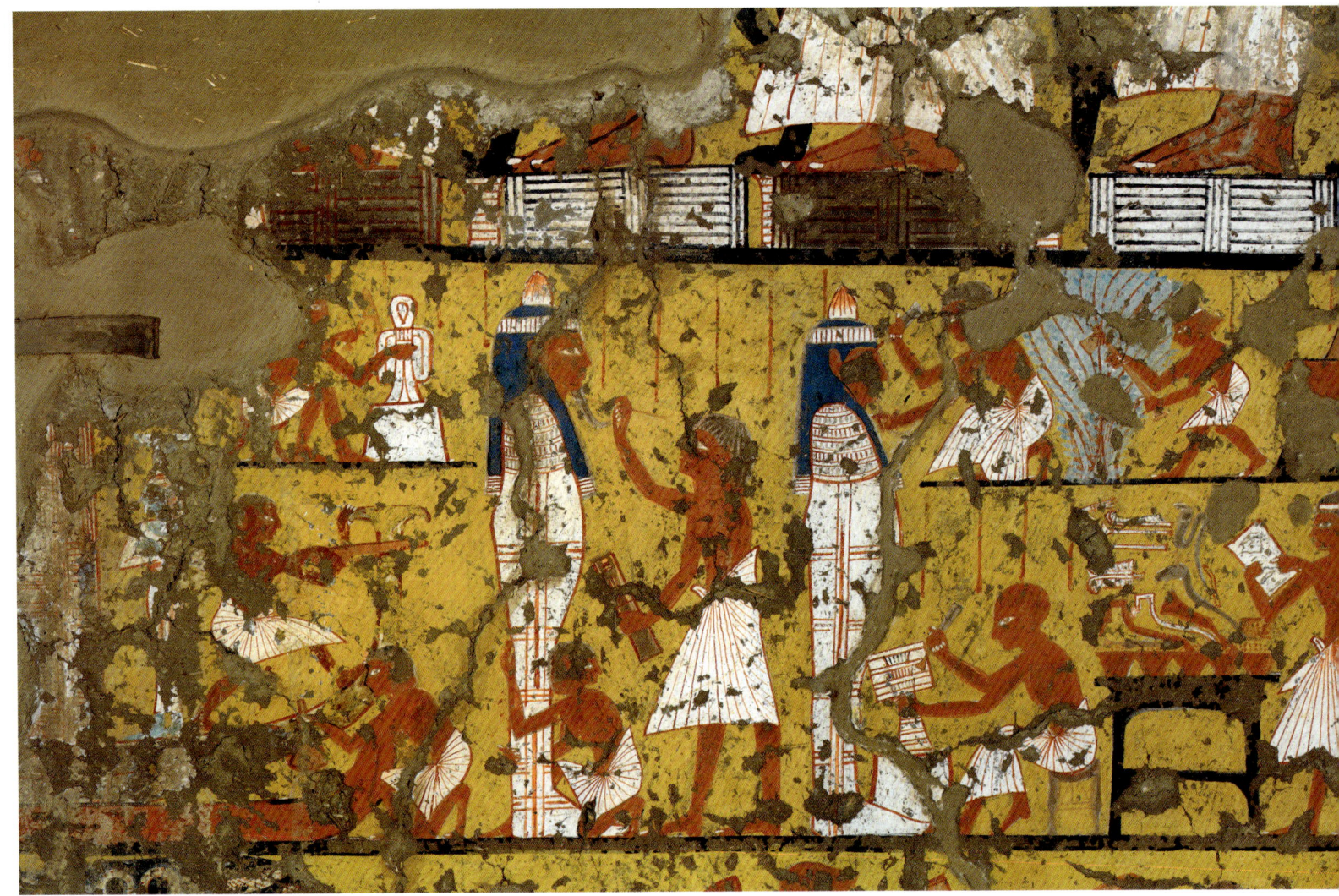

A brightly coloured scene from the tomb of Ipuy at Thebes, dating to about 1280–1215 BC, shows the preparation of items of burial equipment, such as furniture, ritual objects and a funerary mask. We see tools, including saws and chisels, and there is a pot of some substance – probably glue – being heated, while a figure on all fours, with his hand in front of his face, tends the fire underneath the pot. In addition, two coffins can be seen, being worked on by craftsmen, one using a chisel to finish off the shape of the head of a coffin, while another uses a long paintbrush to add the finishing touches to a beard.

This scene presents us with an excellent opportunity to see into the world of the people who worked in the ancient Egyptian funerary industry. This is important because it is all too easy to be so overwhelmed by the richly decorated remains from this part of the ancient world that one forgets to think about the craftsmen who

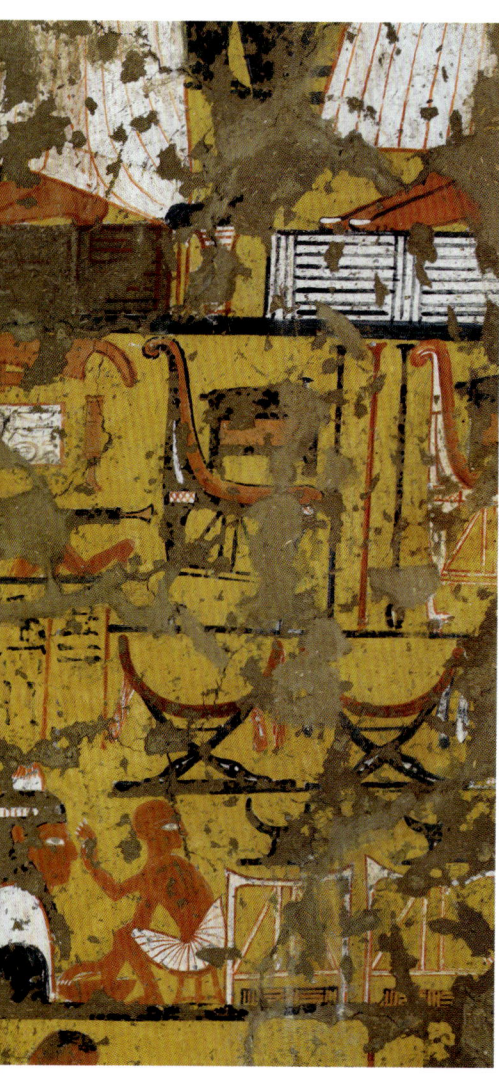

Carpenters at work, depicted in the tomb of Ipuy (TT217 at Thebes). From the left, working with an adze on a decorative element for a shrine and (below) a shrine within a barque, all mounted on a sledge, with men using saws and chisels; a coffin being painted; a coffin, with a man using a chisel; two registers of figures: at the top, felling a tree; a large container being heated over a fire and a man tending it on all fours, with a group of tools above him; in the register below: working with a chisel on a decorative element for a shrine; a table with objects used in a funeral ritual called Opening the Mouth and Eyes, and a man with a papyrus checking everything is there; working on a funerary mask.

created the masterpieces displayed in museum collections around the world. In the past, many scholars have studied the belief systems of the ancient Egyptians, including how they are presented on objects found in their burials. This has, of course, included studies of coffins and their decoration and inscriptions.

Here at the Fitzwilliam Museum, the Antiquities Department has been carrying out an extensive research project on its own collection of ancient Egyptian coffins since 2006. In addition to Egyptologists studying the decorative motifs and inscriptions, a team of research scientists and conservators has been using the most up-to-date imaging and analytical techniques to investigate the construction of these objects. This builds on and enhances the work of other institutions around the world involved in similar work, and it forms a key contribution to the global study of these ancient artefacts.

The University of Cambridge is internationally recognised for the high quality of its research. It is natural, therefore, that this research is published and disseminated. The results of the work of the coffins project team will be presented in an extensive catalogue, giving scholars around the world in-depth information about every aspect of the history, iconography, inscriptional information and construction of the Fitzwilliam Museum's extensive coffin collection. As we celebrate our bicentenary year, it is highly appropriate that we share the fruits of this internationally important project with a wider audience through this exhibition, giving visitors an opportunity to preview the results of these studies.

We are indebted to The Monument Trust for their support for our exhibitions programme, including the exhibitions for our bicentenary year, of which *Death on the Nile* is one. We also thank Mathew Pritchard and the Estate of Agatha Christie for generously allowing us to borrow the name of his grandmother's celebrated book as a perfect title for our exhibition. The Museum is also very grateful for the support of the British Museum and the Louvre for their generous loans to the exhibition, and to the UK Government Indemnity Scheme (GIS), administered by Arts Council, which makes borrowing these important artefacts possible.

Visitors to *Death on the Nile* will encounter many old favourites from the Fitzwilliam's collection, such as the coffins of Nespawershefyt and the cartonnage mummy case of Nakhtefmut. But here they can be explored in new ways to discover, for example, fingerprints left behind by people moving a coffin lid before the varnish had dried, or to spot the disagreement between the person who carved a hieroglyph and the artist who applied the paint over it. These details flesh out the people who created such beautiful works of art and further bring to life the vivid image of the craftsmen shown in Ipuy's tomb.

Like these workers, the Antiquities Department team continue to busy themselves with working on the coffins in their charge and, in the process, add to the sum of global knowledge about these important artefacts and the people for whom and by whom they were made.

Curators' Acknowledgements

Julie Dawson and Helen Strudwick

'Death on the Nile' has its origins in work associated with the refurbishment of the Fitzwilliam Museum's galleries in 2004-6 and preparatory work for a full scholarly catalogue of the Museum's ancient Egyptian coffin collection and associated material. A generous grant from the Getty Foundation enabled the initial investigation and conservation programme during that period, with additional support from the Heritage Lottery Fund, the Isaac Newton Trust and the Aurelius Charitable Trust for upgrading our facilities and equipment. Since that time, detailed study of the coffins has continued in the background, while other projects pressed for attention, and is now progressing towards completion; the full catalogue will appear after this exhibition.

During this project, colleagues around the world have been generous in sharing information about their work on Egyptian coffins. Amongst these, from the Egyptological world, first and foremost we are indebted to Wolfram Grajetzki and John Taylor, both acknowledged experts in this area, who have both been invaluable in sharing their expertise over the last few years. We have also been fortunate enough to persuade them each to contribute a chapter to this book. John was also extremely helpful in securing the loans for the exhibition from the British Museum, and Hélène Guichard similarly supported our request to borrow the coffin of Madja (cat. 22) from the Louvre. It would be hard to overestimate the contribution of Caroline Cartwright and Rebecca Stacey of the British Museum, who have undertaken, respectively, the identification of all the coffin woods and the original resins associated with the objects and thus greatly deepened our understanding of the technology of the objects. Their work has fed into the catalogue entries and they have both contributed sections to the chapter 'Egyptian Coffins: Materials, Construction and Decoration' in this book. We are particularly grateful to Caroline also for helping us review the CT scans of the inner coffin of Nespawershefyt (cat. 26). Her expertise and profound knowledge of the structure and behaviour of the woods were critical to understanding the features observed. We record here also our gratitude to David Saunders who, as Keeper of Conservation and Scientific Research at the British Museum when this project began, supported his colleagues' participation in the research.

We must add a special word of thanks to our colleague Jennifer Marchant (Conservator of Antiquities) who has been the backbone of the second phase of the investigation project, collating the earlier results, setting up and carrying out a great deal of the new work, and supervising the antiquities conservation laboratory and its interns. Her unstinting support, organisation and cheerful determination have been crucial. Eleanor von Aderkas joined the project in 2014 to carry on the examination and analysis of the painted surfaces started by Abigail Granville. Jennifer and Eleanor are co-authors of 'Egyptian Coffins: Materials, Construction and Decoration' and have contributed to the catalogue entries. We owe both of them and Abigail our profound gratitude for their dedication and expertise, and we thank the Thriplow Charitable Trust for supporting the pigment analysis.

It has been a great privilege to collaborate with Geoffrey Killen and Elsbeth Geldhof who, from their respective areas of expertise (ancient Egyptian woodworking and the decoration techniques used on Egyptian coffins), have both assisted with the catalogue and created the replicas shown in the exhibition. They have enriched the project with their mixture of scholarship and craft skill, together with their limitless enthusiasm.

We have benefitted from discussion of our investigative work with colleagues at home and abroad, especially those institutions that are part of the Vatican Coffin Project. We are also grateful to Asja Müller and Fruzsina Bartos, who have generously shared aspects of their own research with us.

Several conservators have contributed their skills to the project from the start in 2004. In particular we must mention the following, all of whom worked on principal objects in the exhibition and whose results have fed into the catalogue entries: Lucy Skinner (cats 26 and 43), who was also overall project conservator from 2005 to 2006; Sophie Rowe (cats 22 and 53); Christina Rozeik (cats 32 and 34–39); Julie Unruh (cat. 43); Lucy Wrapson (cat. 54); and also Deborah Walton. Tom Bilson investigated and conserved the mummy shroud (cat. 52) as a student project at the Textile Conservation Centre. A succession of conservation interns has been involved since the beginning, developing their practice in new areas while giving us the benefit of their hard work, fresh ideas and enthusiasm: Emily Brown, Julie Chang, Nicole Doub, Pia Edqvist, Kathryn Etre, Bryony Finn, Carmen Li, Sophia Oelman, Eri Ohara Anderson, Flavia Ravaioli, Tom Riddolls, Sarah Stannage, Margreta Sonnenwald, Cathy Tully and Alexandra Zappa. We are grateful to the Heritage Lottery Fund (through the Institute for Conservation internship scheme) and the Marlay Group of the Fitzwilliam Museum for supporting an internship each.

In addition to the analysts already mentioned, we are indebted to the following experts for their generous assistance with the identification of a variety of materials: Ruth Siddall (University College London), Janet Ambers (British Museum), Alan Clapham (Worcestershire Archaeology), Catherine Higgett and David Peggie (National Gallery), and Marc Walton (formerly of the Getty Conservation Institute). We owe a particular debt of gratitude to Trevor Emmett, now retired from the Life Sciences Department, Anglia Ruskin University, but continuing his many analytical collaborations with the Fitzwilliam and a great friend of and contributor to this project. Paola Ricciardi (Fitzwilliam Museum) and Spike Bucklow (Hamilton Kerr Institute) have been constant sources of help and advice for the analytical work. Chris Hurst and Chris Titmus (both of the Hamilton Kerr Institute) assisted with imaging and X-ray work.

CT scanning is a technique widely used in the examination of mummies, but thus far is much less frequently applied to understanding the internal structure of wooden coffins. Tom Turmezei (Wellcome Trust PhD Clinical Fellow, Cambridge University Engineering Department, and Honorary Consultant Radiologist, Addenbrooke's Hospital, Cambridge), who had already tackled the challenges involved in CT scanning artists' mannequins for the Fitzwilliam's 'Silent Partners' exhibition, acceded readily to our request for assistance. The fantastic results of the exercise feature in this book and in the exhibition. To our immense appreciation of Tom's expertise and enthusiasm we must add also our thanks to staff of the Radiology Department at Addenbrooke's Hospital (especially James Brennan, Hilary Charlesworth and Arnel Ramosa) for generously facilitating the visit of the inner coffin of Nespawershefyt (cat. 26) to the scanner in 2015. Alessia Amenta shared information from the CT scanning undertaken in the Vatican Coffin Project. In 2005, the cartonnage of Nakhtefmut (cat. 32) and the Roman-Egyptian red shroud mummy (cat. 54) were scanned. On that occasion Halina Szutowicz and Barbara Housden undertook the work. We are indebted to them and also to Nagui Antoun, who very kindly retrieved files from that session for us. Corinne Duhig examined the scans of the mummy in 2005, and Bob Loynes has recently carried out further investigation as part of his own research and also produced images for inclusion in the book and the exhibition.

Producing an exhibition catalogue always relies heavily on the work of photographers. At the Fitzwilliam Museum, we are fortunate to be able to call upon a team of people who are prepared to squeeze themselves into tiny or awkward spaces in order to take the ideal photograph of a small drip of paint or a damaged, but therefore particularly fascinating, surface on a coffin, as well as creating beautiful images of spectacular objects, with equal professionalism. Our thanks go to them all: Mike Jones, Amy Jugg, Andrew Norman, Jaymes Sinclair and Katie Young, and also Lynda Clark. Steven Snape ransacked the Garstang Archive in Liverpool for us in order to retrieve photographs from John Garstang's excavations at Beni Hasan (fig. 8, p. 20), while Catharine Roehrig kindly searched out the image of Wah wrapped up in his mummy wrappings from the archives at the Metropolitan Museum of Art in New York (fig. 89, p. 151).

We have received so much assistance from colleagues in the Fitzwilliam Museum that it is almost impossible to thank everyone without running the risk of omitting someone. Nevertheless, certain people stand out, of whom the first is Lucilla Burn, now combining the roles of both Keeper of Antiquities and Assistant Director (Collections) of the Museum but still finding the time to read the manuscript of this book and to be unstinting in sharing her wise counsel on the exhibition. Past and present technicians from the Antiquities Department, Bob Bourne, Louise Jenkins, Rob Law and Charis Millet, have responded to repeated requests for coffins to be moved around or measured with good humour and their characteristic care of the objects. Meghan Strong and Samantha Oxford volunteered at the Museum for a large part of the genesis of the exhibition.

Early in the project, members of the Museum's maintenance department agreed to act as a sounding board for ideas for the exhibition and to read sections of this book. They are Ron Considine, Peter Cornwall, Darren Potter, Alan Shinn and Colin Yaxley. We are very grateful for their comments and for sparing time to be involved.

We are grateful to the Director, Tim Knox, and to Ian McClure and Rupert Featherstone, former and current directors of the Hamilton Kerr Institute and Assistant Directors (Conservation), Fitzwilliam Museum, for their constant support. Our particular thanks also go to Mella Shaw, who, with the assistance of David Evans, led the planning and installation of the exhibition and without both of whom it would simply not have happened; to David Packer and Liz Woods, our registrars; to Allison Kingsbury, Facilities Manager; to Phil Wheeler, Security Manager; to Anna Lloyd-Griffiths, Secretary to the Keepers; and to members of the Museum's Marketing and Press, Education, Information and Communications Technology, and Visitor Services teams.

Allison McCormick, with help from Pat Barylski, from D Giles Limited has steered us through the process of producing material for this book; we are very grateful for her patience and kindness.

Finally, we cannot end without thanking two people, Craig Hartley and Nigel Strudwick, for their very particular support, their forbearance over the last few months, their constant wise advice and assistance, and their many suggestions for improvements to this book.

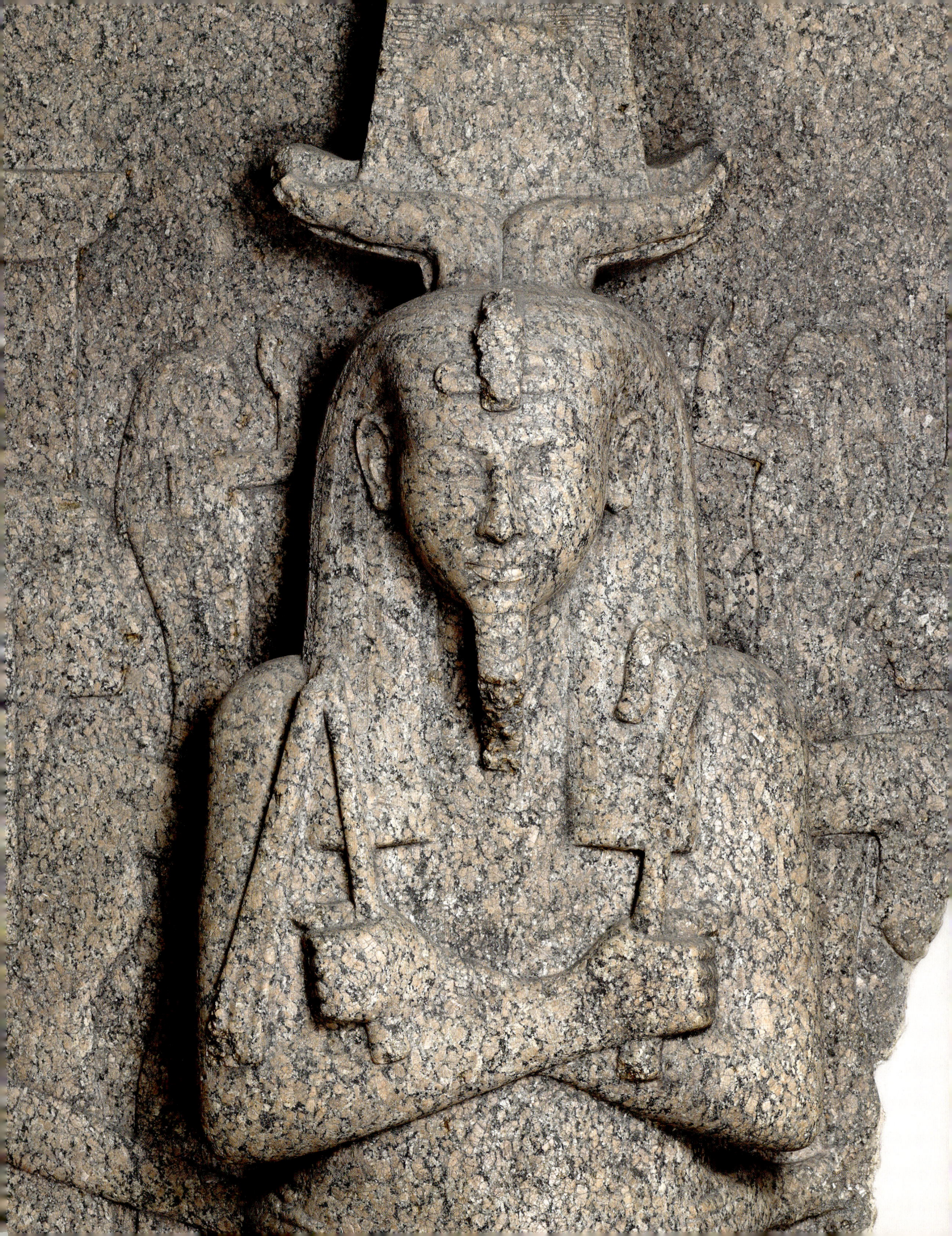

EGYPTIAN COFFINS AT THE FITZWILLIAM MUSEUM

The Formation of the Collection

Helen Strudwick

When the Fitzwilliam Museum was founded in 1816, Western interest in ancient Egypt was still in its infancy. Until Napoleon's expedition set off to Egypt in 1798, the country was very little known and Egyptian artefacts were regarded as strange leftovers from a culture that was inferior to the classical world of Greece and Rome. The first objects of ancient Egyptian origin came to the Museum in 1822, in the form of an elaborate set of coffins made for a man named Nespawershefyt (fig. 2). They were a gift from two young Cambridge alumni, Barnard Hanbury and George Waddington. These two friends had become interested in new discoveries from Egypt, as revealed in the volumes of the *Description de l'Égypte*, published between 1809 and 1829. Together Hanbury and Waddington journeyed up the Nile as far as Ethiopia and back, buying a number of antiquities as they went, of which one was the coffin set of Nespawershefyt.

The year 1822 was important generally for Egyptology; it was in September 1822 that Jean-François Champollion published his first theories about the ancient Egyptian hieroglyphic script. Within a relatively short time, inscriptions on monuments in Egypt, as well as on objects like Nespawershefyt's coffins, could be read, at least to a limited extent. From this time onwards, antiquities from Egypt acquired a much greater value, both monetarily (because people wanted to acquire them) and in terms of the information that they would yield about the lives of the Egyptians. The subject of Egyptology was born.

The following year, in 1823, the famous adventurer and explorer Giovanni Battista Belzoni came to Cambridge. He was trying to secure funds for an expedition in hopes of winning a prize of 10,000 francs for being the first Westerner to reach the fabled city of Timbuktu (in West Africa). Shortly after his visit, he presented the newly established Fitzwilliam Museum with the lid

Fig. 1
Detail of the sarcophagus lid of Ramesses III (fig. 3)

Fig. 3
Sarcophagus lid of king Ramesses III (1183–1151 BC) E.1.1823, Fitzwilliam Museum

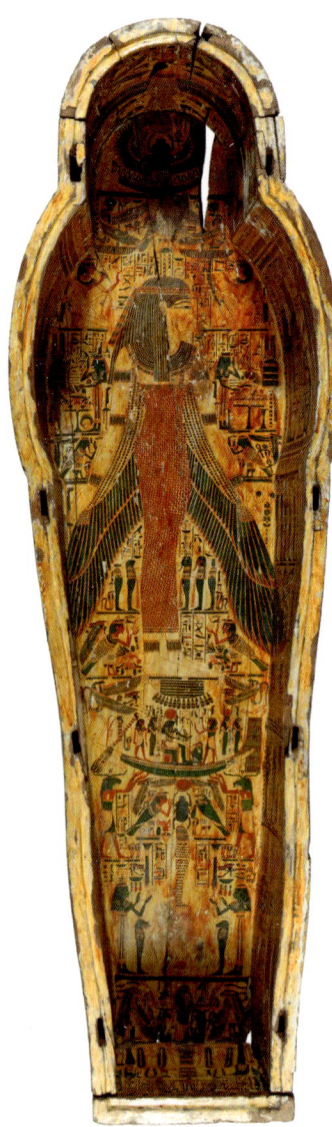

Fig. 2
The inner coffin box of Nespawershefyt (cat. 26), decorated with a large winged figure of the Goddess of the West

of the sarcophagus of Ramesses III (figs. 1 and 3), which he had retrieved with some difficulty from the king's tomb in the Valley of the Kings in March 1817. 'It cost much trouble, as may be supposed, to remove a heavy piece of granite from those abysses,' Belzoni wrote in his account of his second trip to Egypt, 'through a place scarcely high enough to allow a man to sit on the ground, up an uneven and craggy ascent, by the assistance of people, strangers to every sort of order, and who had to contend with the dust that rose under the feet, and the excessive heat from the number of labourers.' Shipping it to Britain must have been fraught with problems too, although Belzoni was well known for his ability to transport large antiquities to Europe. Eventually, as the *Cambridge Chronicle* of 4 April 1823 reported, it arrived at the Museum 'after considerable difficulty'. It has been suggested by Janine Bourriau (former Keeper of Antiquities) that Belzoni may have been prompted to give the lid to the Museum because he hoped that he would receive an honorary degree from Cambridge University in return. However, he died later the same year while en route to Timbuktu.

In the period following the deciphering of hieroglyphs, the frenzy for acquiring Egyptian antiquities, which had begun in the wake of Napoleon's Egyptian expedition, intensified, and many sites that had been untouched up to that time were ransacked for treasures for the European market. Many of the objects acquired at that period were in almost pristine condition. People like Belzoni shipped large collections of objects to European cities (especially Berlin, Paris, Turin and London), where they were viewed with intense interest in museums including the Louvre and the British Museum. Many young British travellers on the Grand Tour took in Egypt on their journeys and brought home souvenirs in the form of substantial collections of artefacts, some of which they passed on to British museums. This is precisely what Hanbury and Waddington had done in 1822, and a second coffin that they had acquired in Egypt – a large granite sarcophagus belonging to a man named Hunefer (fig. 4) – was given to the Museum in 1835, two years after Hanbury had died.

Egypt came to be a fashionable place to visit for those who could afford it. In 1868, the then Prince of Wales (later Edward VII) and his wife included Egypt in a tour of the eastern Mediterranean and, while in Luxor, received an extraordinary gift of twenty coffins (and sets of coffins), all said to come from a single pit on the west bank of the Nile. When the prince returned to Britain, the coffins were distributed to museums around the country, with the Fitzwilliam receiving the coffins of Pakepu (fig. 5). It is not clear whether a mummy was found inside the coffins, but, in the account of her travels in Egypt with the prince and his wife, the Honourable Mrs William Grey recorded that she could not 'bear the idea of disturbing, and still less of removing these corpses, especially when you see, from the careful way in which they are wrapped up, and the very out-of-the-way places chosen for their family tombs, that their wish was to remain

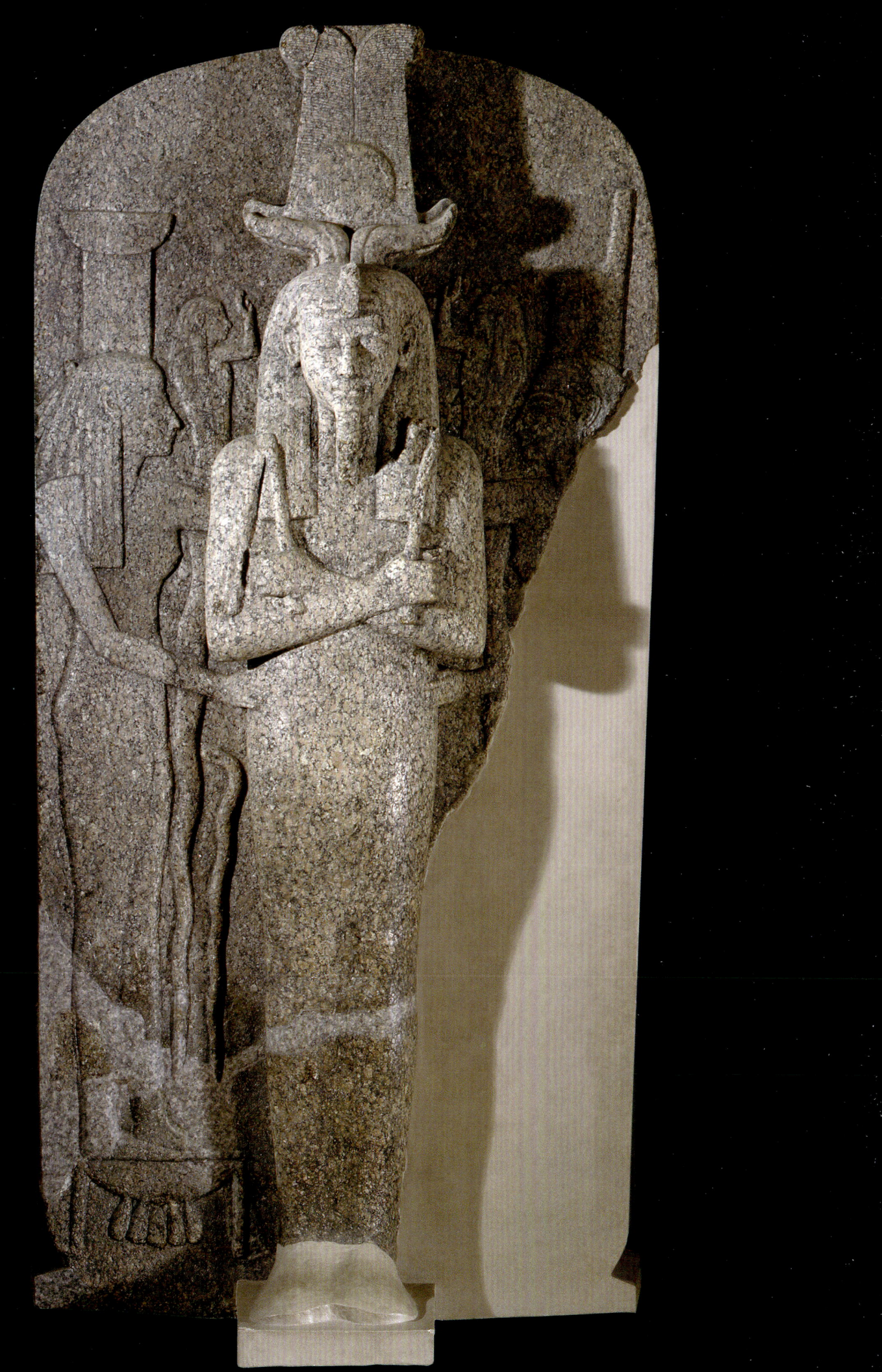

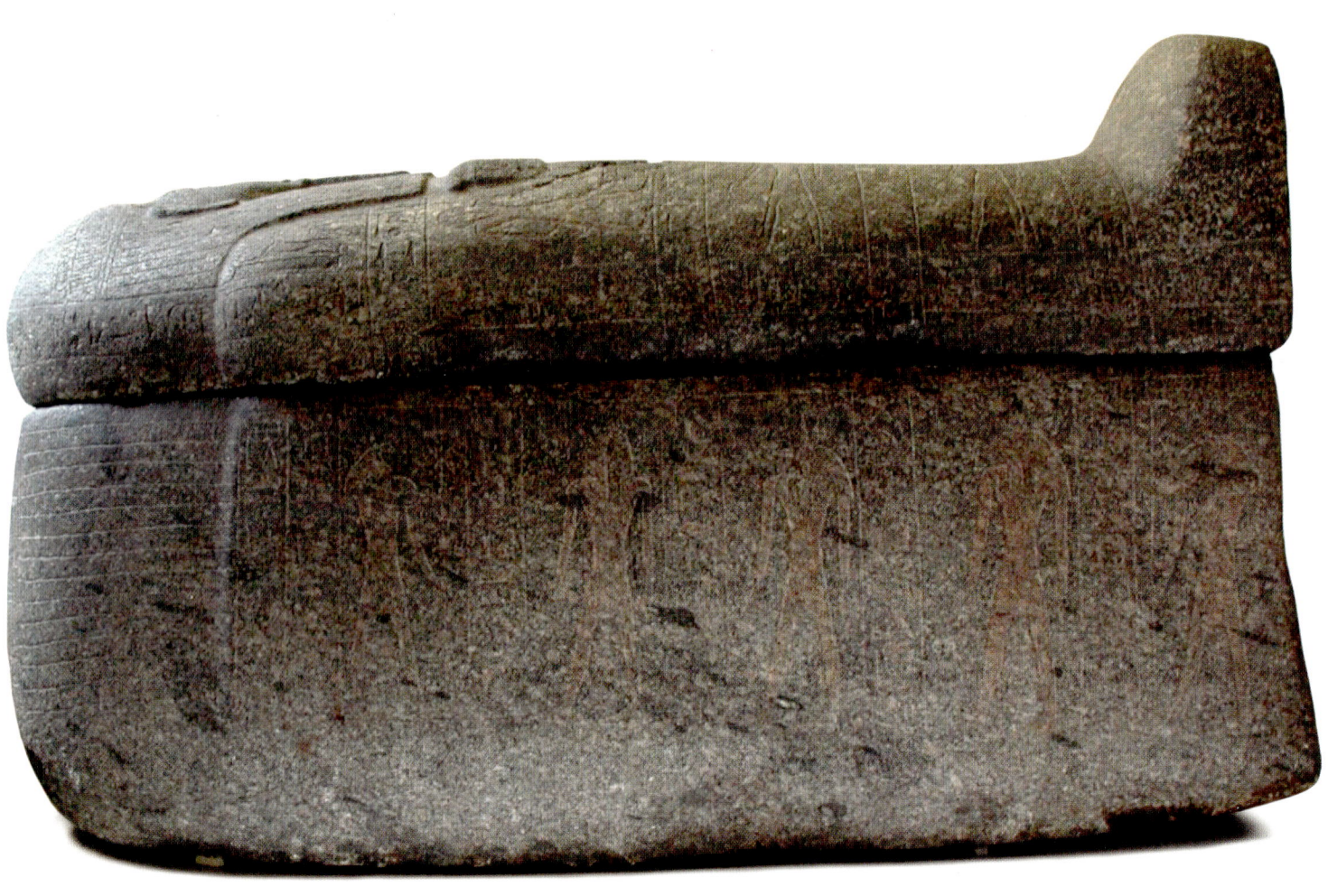

Fig. 4
Granite sarcophagus of Hunefer, about 1225 BC (Fitzwilliam Museum, E.1.1835)

there undisturbed forever'. Clearly, many of the coffins she saw were found with mummies still inside, but there is no record that a body was received with Pakepu's coffins when they arrived in Cambridge.

A further ten coffins, said to have been found in the same pit, were transported to a new museum in Cairo that had been established by the French scholar Auguste Mariette. He was the first director of the Service des Antiquités, an organisation set up in 1858 to control unregulated excavations in Egypt. According to a law of 1838, no artefacts could leave Egypt. The Service des Antiquités sought to enforce that, although obviously exceptions were made for important visitors, such as the Prince of Wales, and it was still legal to buy antiquities in shops and take them home as souvenirs of one's travels. However, a system of compensating excavators for their work in Egypt was introduced in 1884, granting to the excavators any antiquities not required for the museum in Cairo, especially duplicate objects, subject to the approval of the Egyptian authorities. This system came to be known as division (or *partage* in French). Over time, it became a formalised part of the permit granted by the service that excavators received a half share of the finds from each season's excavations; but this division excluded unique or particularly significant objects, and also all objects from intact tombs. This affected many major museums in Britain and the United States that had become partners in previously unregulated excavations on the basis that they would receive the finds into their collections. The restrictions of the division system meant that spectacular items had to remain in Egypt.

The Fitzwilliam was never a major partner in excavations in Egypt, but it did support the work of the famous archaeologist William Matthew Flinders Petrie, subscribing to his excavations and, in return, receiving items from his share of the division. In this way, too, the Museum supported the work of the Egypt Exploration Fund (EEF), today known as the Egypt Exploration Society (EES), as well as two organisations set up by Petrie: the Egyptian Research Account (ERA) and the British School of Archaeology (BSA).

It was in the course of ERA excavations at the Ramesseum in Luxor, in 1896, that James Quibell came upon a small shaft, cut in the ground, containing two coffins that had clearly been robbed at some point in the past. Below them, however, he found more coffins, this time undisturbed, including the complete burial of a priest named Nakhtefmut. Quibell's description of the discovery is vivid, though not as detailed as a modern excavation report would be. It does, however, describe the relative positions of the objects found around the coffins and other finds in the shaft, as well as the position of the amulets and other items found on Nakhtefmut's body. The mummy case was inside three coffins, nested together like Russian dolls, but Quibell's report does not reveal what happened to them. The majority of the finds from the burial, including Nakhtefmut's striking cartonnage mummy case (cat. 32), came to the Fitzwilliam Museum that year.

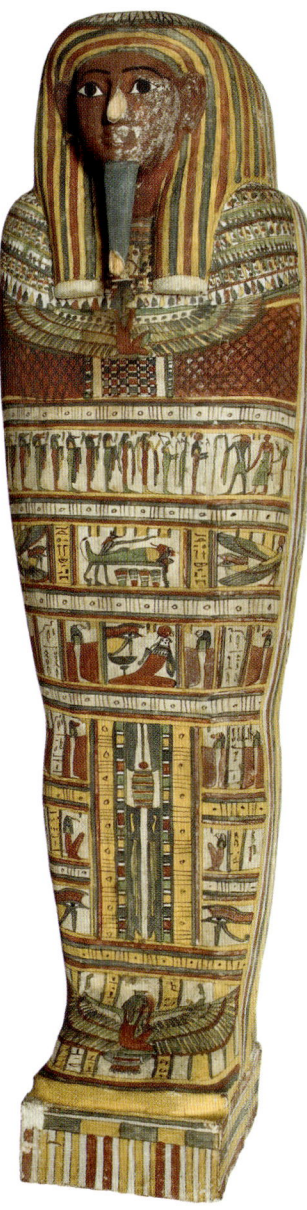

Fig. 5
Inner coffin of Pakepu (cat. 43)

From that division, the Museum also received a second cartonnage case, made for a priest named Hor (fig. 6), which came from a disturbed burial. The coffin had become rather mis-shapen after the mummy was removed, and the face, which was gilded, had been torn off, causing further damage. Recent conservation work has managed to restore the original shape of the cartonnage.

In 1900, while the ERA was excavating at Abydos under John Garstang, they found a disturbed pit tomb containing the remains of a burial that included a rectangular coffin, decorated with scenes of a funeral procession, with a figure of a mourning woman bent over with grief. After division with the Egyptian government, the coffin was allocated to the excavators, who gave it to the Fitzwilliam, where it is now known as the coffin of the mourning women (cat. 21, fig. 7). From excavations in 1903, carried out by the EEF at el-Hiba, the Museum received a Roman mummy, wrapped in a red shroud and with a portrait panel (cat. 54). In 1911, two more objects dating to the Roman period came to the Museum from EEF excavations, this time at Hawara: a cartonnage mask and footcase (cat. 55), found on a mummy not buried in a tomb but placed in a chamber above ground, along with four more mummies. The roof of the chamber had apparently fallen in and covered them.

The mechanism by which excavation finds were shared between interested parties is well illustrated by an example of the distribution of artefacts from Garstang's excavations in the winter of 1902–3 at Beni Hasan. The site had been known for a long time thanks to the existence of a number of tombs, decorated with lively scenes, belonging to local governors of this region during the Middle Kingdom (about 2050–1790 BC). Garstang was interested in finding the burials of the less important people at the site (fig. 8), and created an excavation committee

Fig. 6
Cartonnage mummy case of Hor after conservation (Fitzwilliam Museum, E.8.1896)

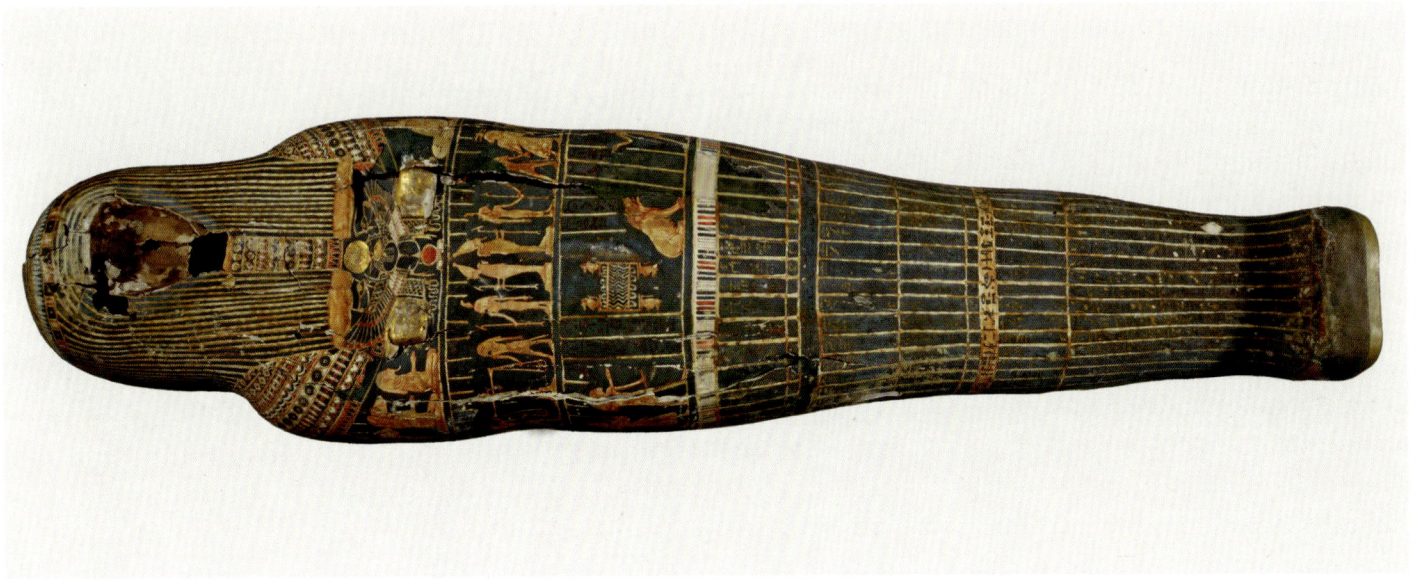

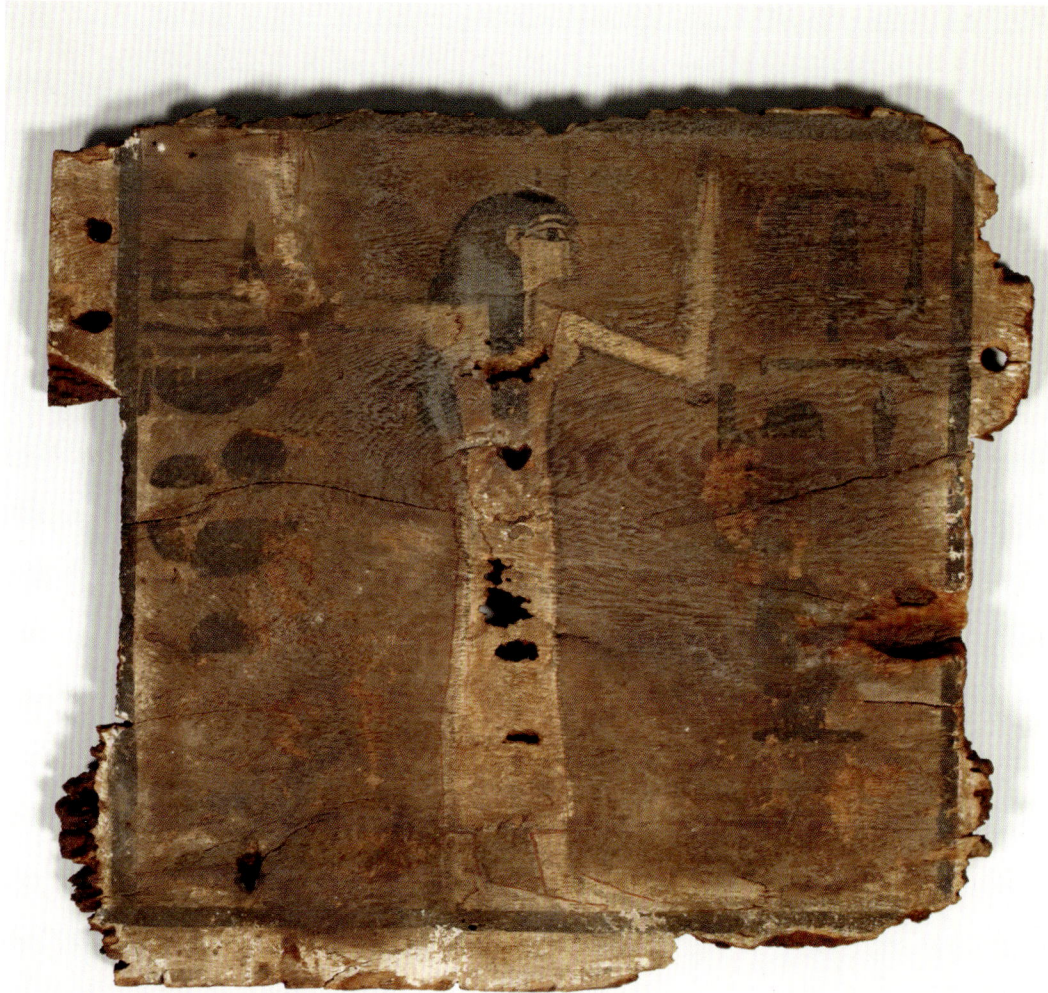

Fig. 7
Foot end of the coffin of the mourning women (cat. 21)

and syndicate to fund his explorations. He succeeded in obtaining the necessary money, and his excavations were very fruitful: in 1907, after further work at Beni Hasan, he published a book entitled *The Burial Customs of Ancient Egypt as Illustrated by Tombs of the Middle Kingdom; Being a Report of Excavations Made in the Necropolis of Beni Hasan during 1902–3–4*.

The Fitzwilliam Museum's director at the time, M. R. James, was a member of Garstang's syndicate, holding shares both as an individual and in partnership with three other people. On 20 July 1903, James received a letter from Garstang inviting him to attend a meeting of the Beni Hasan Excavation Committee in order to share out the finds from the 1902–3 season. The objects were to be displayed at the Society of Antiquaries in London, for viewing by the shareholders, before the meeting at the same place two days later. Garstang had grouped the objects into eight shares of approximately equal value; on the day,

Helen Strudwick

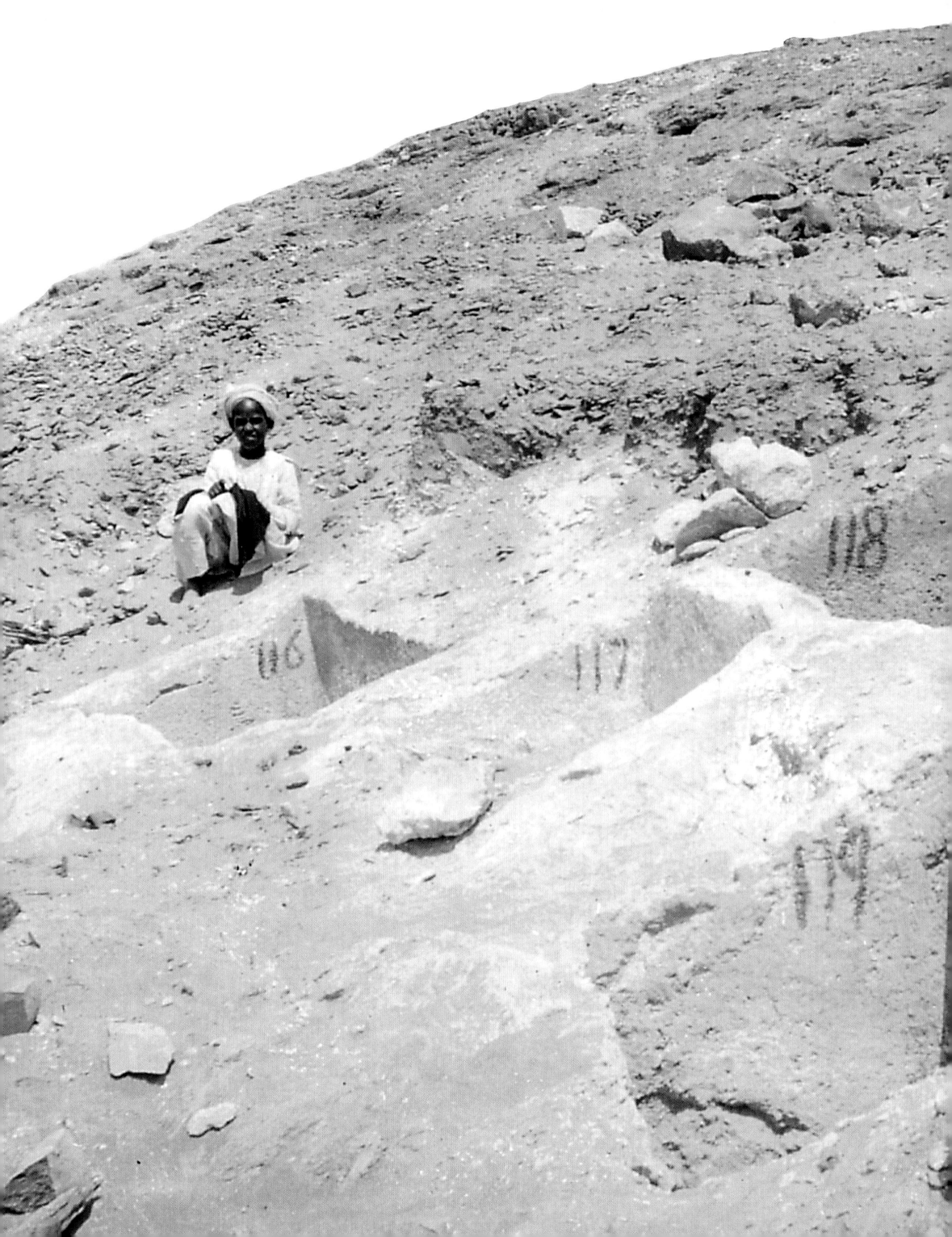

Fig. 8
Burial pits at Beni Hasan. Photograph taken by Garstang during the 1902–3 season. Garstang Archive, University of Liverpool

lots were cast to establish the order in which shareholders made their selection. James seems to have been fourth to choose and opted for 'The complete tomb deposit of Khety', which consisted of a coffin (cat. 11) and the group of models of daily life that were found with it (cat. 12). After all the choices had been made, one share remained, which went to James and his three partners. This included the coffins of a warrior named Userhet, whose inner coffin came to the Fitzwilliam (cat. 20) while the outer coffin went to the University of Liverpool, where it is now displayed in the Garstang Museum.

In the same letter of 20 July 1903, there is mention of finds 'distributed previously by arrangement', although the nature of the arrangement is not explained. Several other coffins from this season of Garstang's excavations are now in the Museum's collection, including the coffin of Nakht (cat.15) and the cartonnage mask of Tjay (cat. 18). Since they do not appear in the list for consideration by Garstang's syndicate members, they must have been among the finds 'distributed previously'. Additionally, in the Fitzwilliam's archives is a letter dated 17 July 1903 from an architect called Edward Towry Whyte, written to M. R. James, offering the Museum 'a wooden coffin from the Garstang find at Beni Hasan'. In a second letter from Whyte, dated 20 July, he explains that the coffin was given to him by F. G. Hilton Price, the director of the Society of Antiquaries at the time and also a syndicate member. From the dates of Whyte's letters, it appears that this coffin too was one of the finds distributed 'by arrangement' before the syndicate chose their share.

James obviously accepted the offered coffin and it was sent to the Museum on 29 July 1903, Whyte writing a third letter to James, saying, 'I did not pay carriage as I have a strong idea that much greater care is taken of a thing when that is not done'. The coffin (fig. 9) is in fact made up of parts of the coffins of two individuals named Senuitef and Warethotep. In his first letter, Whyte says, 'it came to me in planks and I have put it together with deal pins so that it can be easily taken to pieces again'. It seems likely that the coffin was found in pieces, and it may be that Garstang's workmen confused planks from two coffins during excavation.

In 1926, the Museum received the remains of a coffin discovered by Petrie, working for the BSA and ERA, at Abydos (cat. 44). It had been made for a distinguished local dignitary called Irethereru, who lived around 740–600 BC. The coffin was originally box-shaped, but with four corner posts and a vaulted lid. It now exists only as a number of pieces of acacia wood, with a white paste fill in the incised hieroglyphs. Although Petrie described it as being complete, it is clear that only a small proportion of the original, very large coffin was recovered. This was the last significant coffin from Egypt to come into the Museum's collections.

One hundred years after Champollion announced the deciphering of hieroglyphs, archaeology in Egypt was changed forever by the discovery of the tomb of Tutankhamun in the Valley of the Kings in November 1922. The excavators, Lord Carnarvon and Howard Carter, were expecting to receive the usual half share of the finds, and they intended to share these with the Metropolitan Museum of Art, New York, which was providing additional resources to help with the scale of the task of recording and conserving the objects found there. However, at almost the same moment as the discovery was made, meetings were being held between Western excavators and the Service des Antiquités about a proposed change in the law relating to divisions of antiquities, which would drastically reduce the share of finds allocated to excavators. The EES's *Journal of Egyptian Archaeology* for April 1923 reported that the 'danger has luckily been averted for the time being owing to representations made to the Egyptian Government by a large number of learned societies', but this situation was only temporary. After Lord Carnarvon's death in 1923, Carter

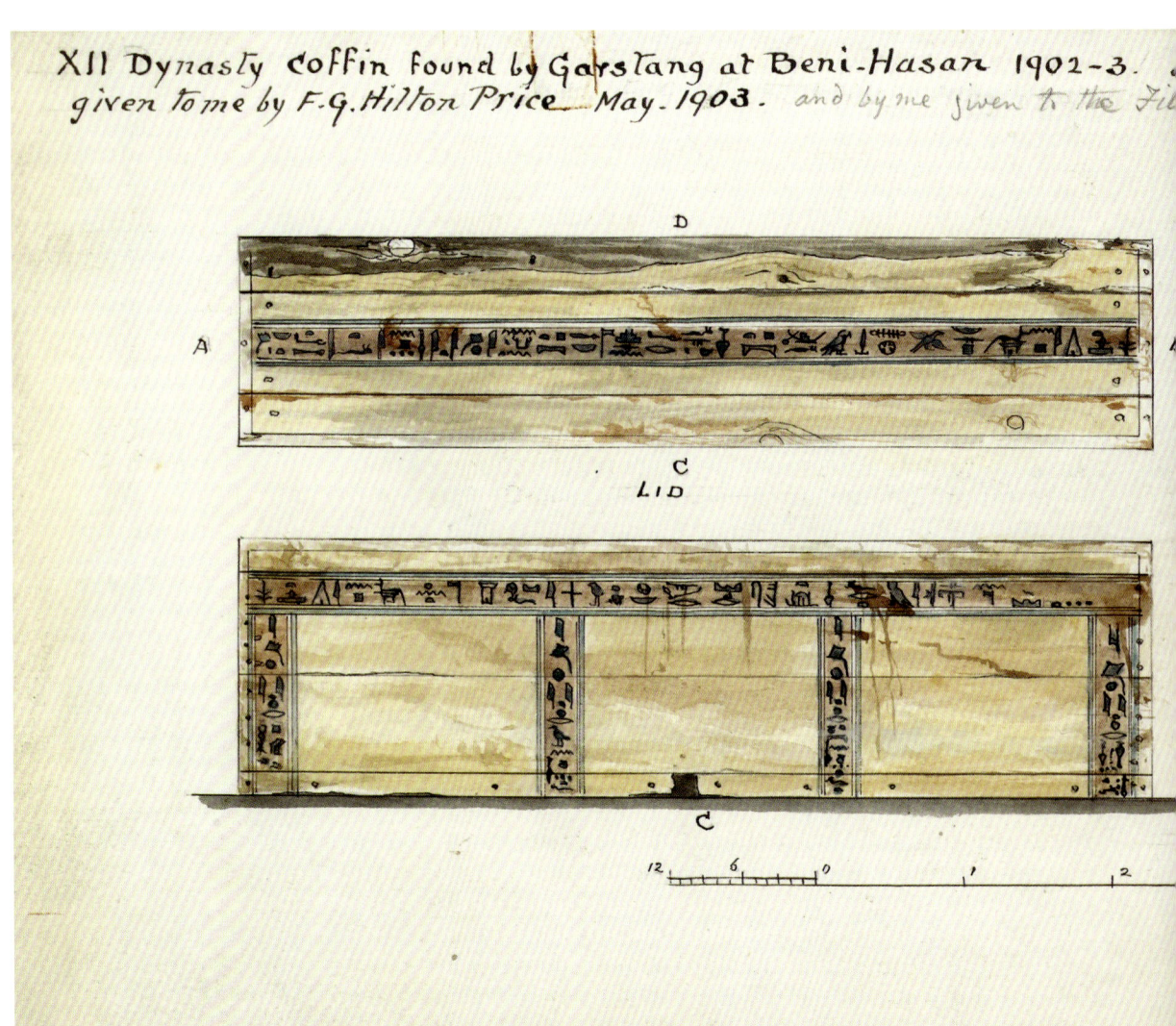

Fig. 9
Whyte's drawing of a wooden coffin (Fitzwilliam Museum, E.70.1903) from Garstang's excavations at Beni Hasan in 1902–3

had had to deal, on his own, with the authorities, and they were becoming increasingly reluctant to allow any of the finds from Tutankhamun's tomb to leave Egypt. Carter was no diplomat and wrangled bitterly with the Egyptian government. Ultimately, Lady Carnarvon and he agreed to sign a new contract to work on the tomb that took away any right to a share of the finds; in 1925, the Egyptians brought in a law that eliminated almost completely the system of division. It was finally abolished in 1983.

Henceforth, foreign explorations in Egypt were conducted for the purpose of expanding knowledge rather than acquiring antiquities, and museums outside Egypt no longer received large and spectacular finds, such as coffins, directly from excavations. Their collections of Egyptian objects did continue to increase, but from this point onwards principally through gifts and bequests. At the Fitzwilliam, such bequests included objects from Edward Towry Whyte, who had

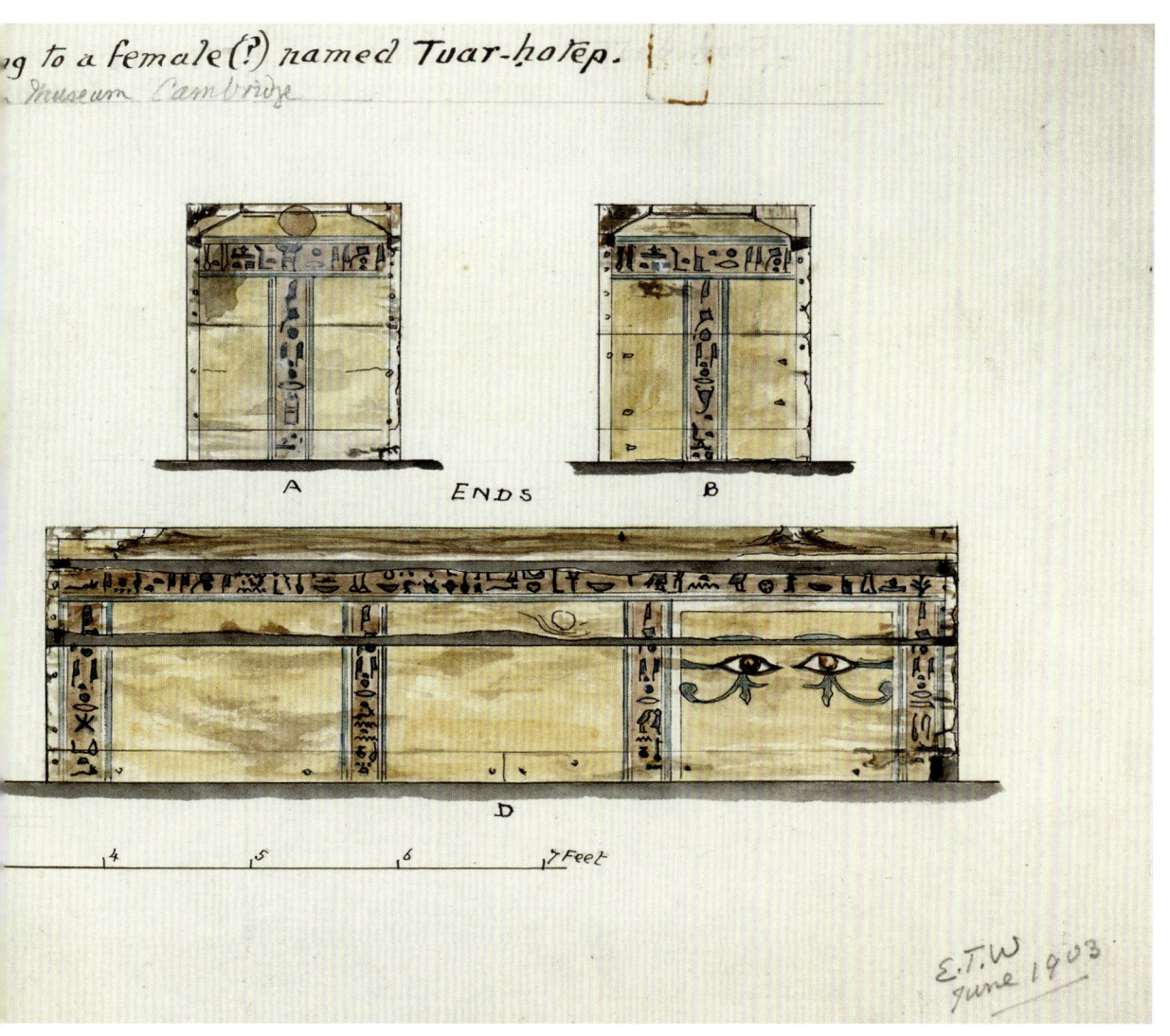

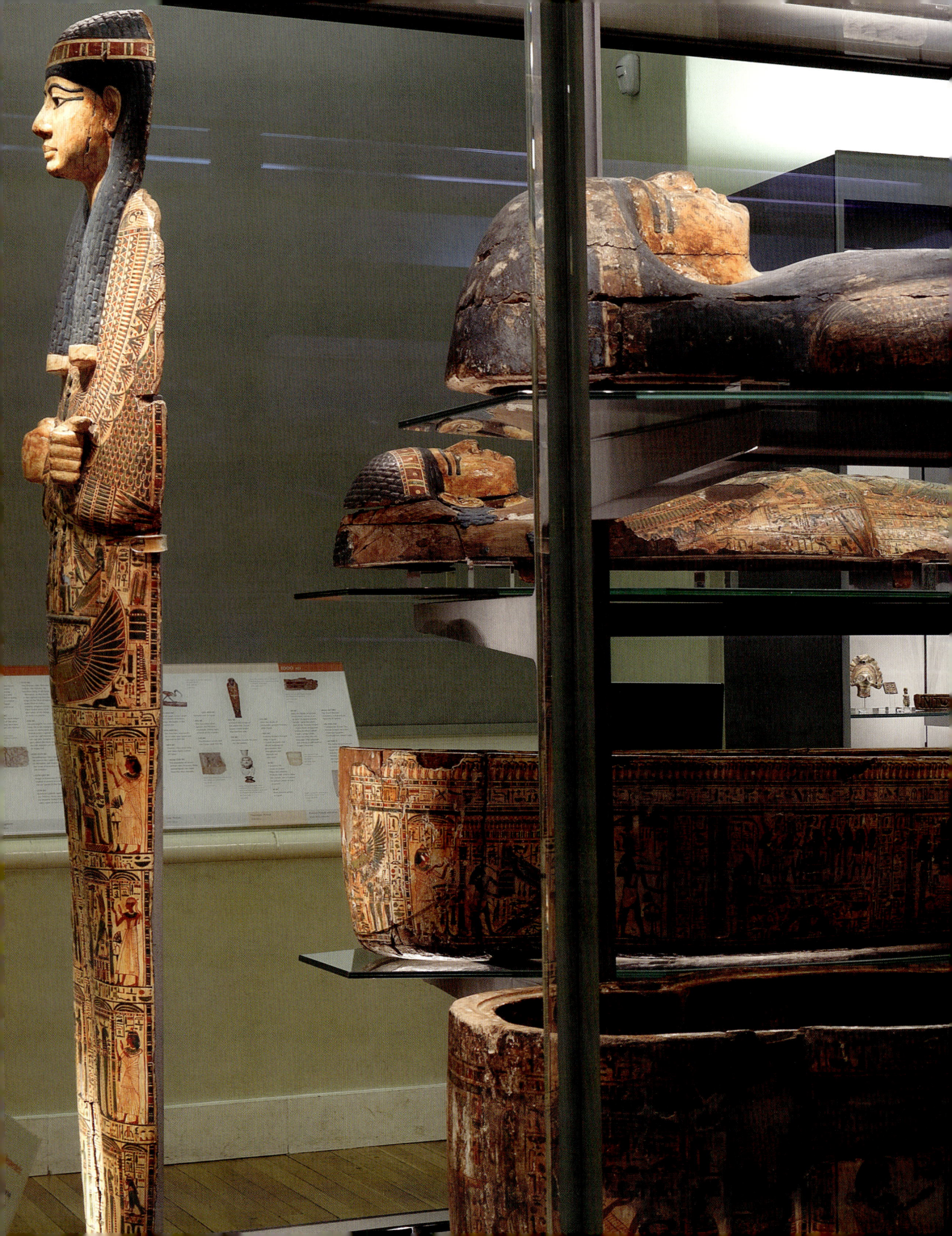

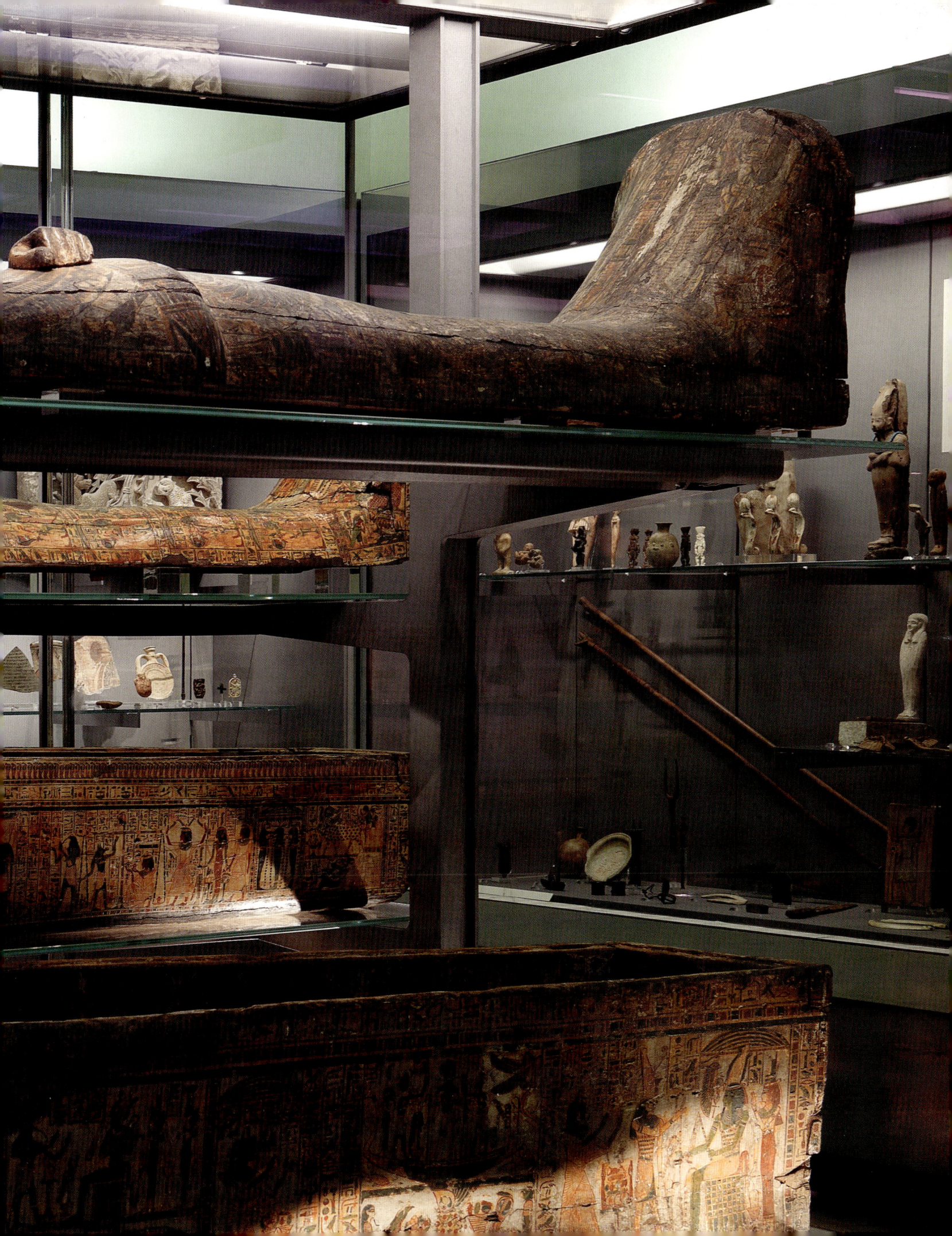

Fig. 10 (previous page) The coffins of Nespawershefyt (cat. 26) on display in the Egyptian galleries at the Fitzwilliam Museum

written, in one of his 1903 letters to M. R. James: 'I am an old Pembroke man and am interested in the Museum as from it I got my first Knowledge of Antiquities.' When he died in 1932, he left over 450 objects from his collection of Egyptian artefacts to the Museum.

In 1901, the Syndicate of the Fitzwilliam Museum recognised the importance of the Egyptian collections and agreed that two rooms should be allocated for their display, which should be in chronological order. In order to achieve this, they allocated £30 towards the costs of setting up the new displays, including buying two new display cases. Since then, the display of coffins from ancient Egypt has been a spectacular feature of the galleries on the lower floor. The sarcophagus lid of Ramesses III was for many years displayed lying on its back (fig. 11), as the centrepiece of the gallery, but in 1968 it was raised into its now vertical position in the centre of Gallery 20. In 2005–6, the Egyptian galleries were redisplayed, with Ramesses remaining in the same place and the Museum's first ancient Egyptian acquisition, the coffin set of Nespawershefyt, in a central position in Gallery 19, where it forms an important focus for the Museum's education programme (fig. 10).

Reading list

Adkins, Lesley and Roy. *The Keys of Egypt: The Race to Read the Hieroglyphs*. London: HarperCollins, 2000.

Drower, Margaret. *Flinders Petrie: A Life in Archaeology*. London: Gollancz, 1985.

James, T. G. H. *Excavating in Egypt: The Egypt Exploration Society 1882–1982*. London: British Museum 1982.

James, T. G. H. *Howard Carter: The Path to Tutankhamun*. London and New York: Keegan Paul International, 1993.

Thompson, Jason. *Wonderful Things: A History of Egyptology*. vol. 1, *From Antiquity to 1881*. Cairo: American University in Cairo Press, 2015.

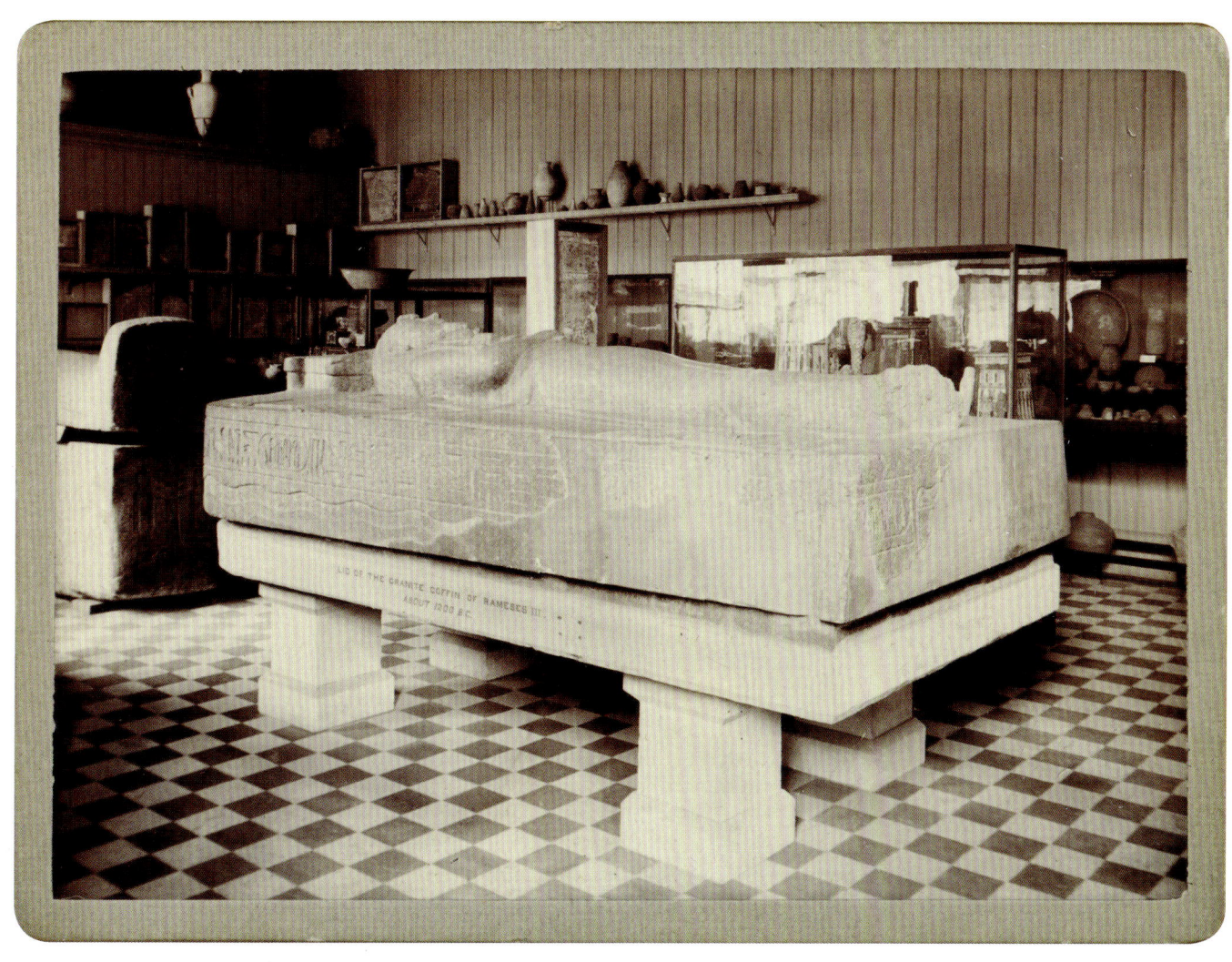

Fig. 11
Egyptian antiquities displayed at the Fitzwilliam Museum in 1925, centred around the sarcophagus lid of Ramesses III. The feet of Hunefer's sarcophagus are visible at the left.

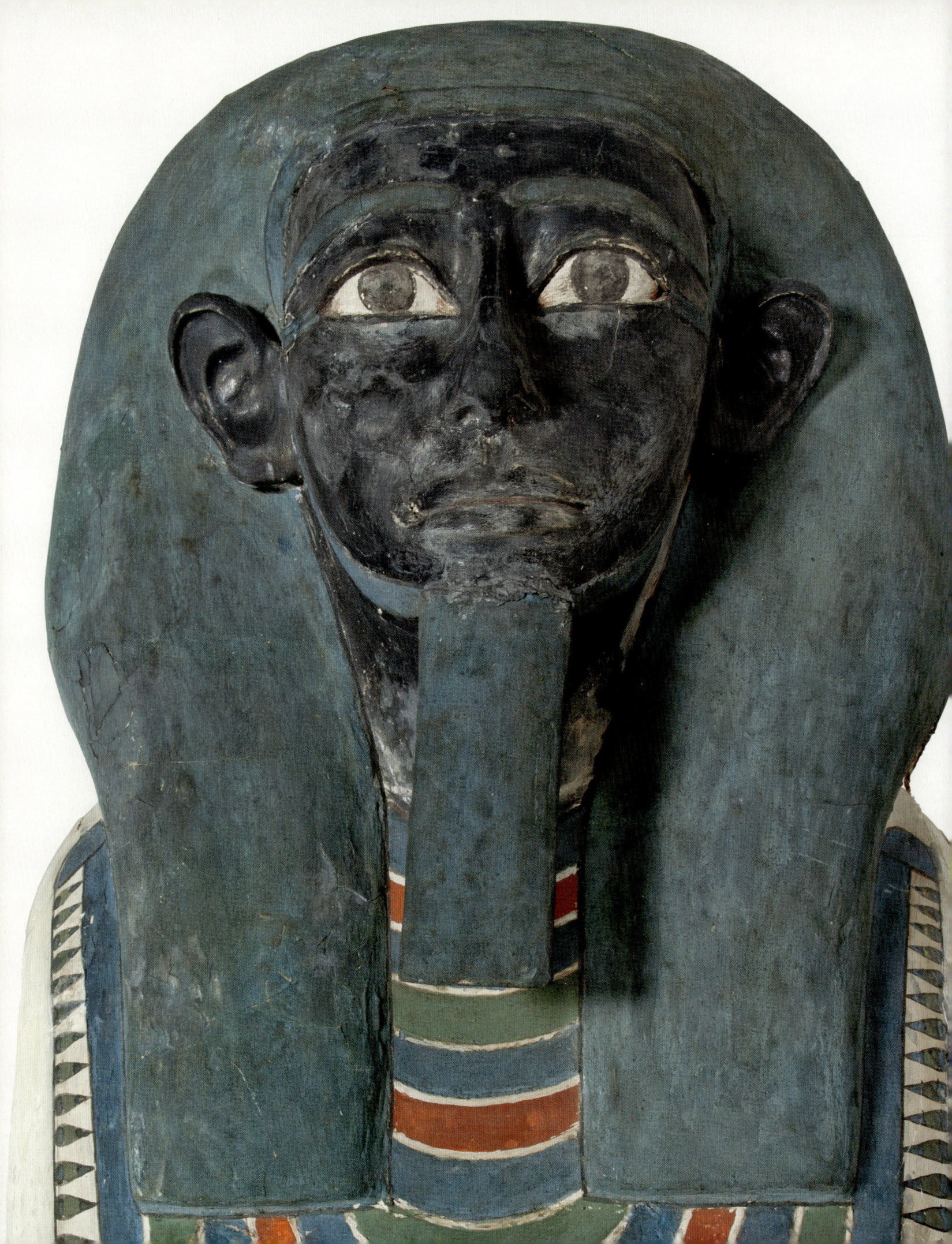

COFFINS OF THE MIDDLE KINGDOM
Their Origins and Development

Wolfram Grajetzki

In prehistoric Egypt, until about 3200 BC, the deceased were usually placed in simple holes in the ground, wrapped in a mat or an animal skin. Sometimes the dead were equipped with personal adornments, as well as pottery vessels to provide a symbolic supply of food for eternity placed around the body, suggesting that the afterlife was seen as an extension of their life on earth. The essentials for life were placed next to the deceased in the graves. However, because written sources are missing, it is very hard to form a real understanding of the Egyptians' religious beliefs at that period.

Over time, burials became more complex. Already by around 3500 BC, the first underground chambers lined with mud bricks were built, and the first coffins appear. Most often these are simple wooden boxes in which the deceased was placed on his or her left side, often in a contracted position, as if sleeping. Wealthy people were often wrapped in linen. These are the first signs of embalming and mummification. Coffins were not inscribed, but the outside was often fashioned in an imitation of the niches of a palace façade. Especially in the Archaic Period, around 3000 BC, the burial chambers of the rich were filled with many objects of daily life. The underworld was most likely still seen as an extension of the world of the living.

In the Fourth and Fifth Dynasties, the classic period of what is known as the Old Kingdom, the world of burials changed; far less energy was devoted to the underground parts of a tomb. Kings were buried in huge pyramids, while high officials had free-standing or rock-cut tombs. These buildings had offering chapels, often decorated with scenes showing the deceased and his family, as well as work on the tomb owner's estate. The whole focus of the tomb was the chapel above ground, where rituals for the deceased were performed. In stark contrast, the equipment placed underground in the burial chamber was limited to a few pottery vessels and model tools. Even coffins were common only for the wealthiest people, and most of them were not decorated at all. Few of them bear an inscription, often simply listing the titles and the name of the

Fig. 12
Detail of the anthropoid coffin of Userhet (cat. 20)

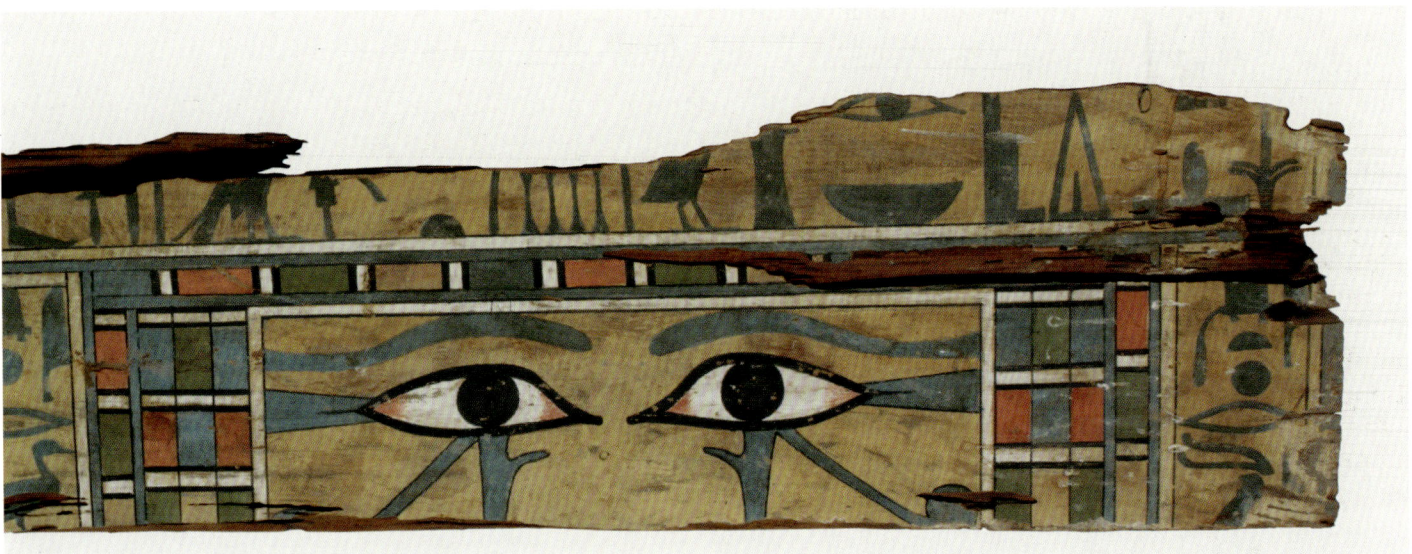

Fig. 13
Eye-panel from the coffin of Senumutef, about 1850–1790 BC
(Fitzwilliam Museum, E.69.1903)

deceased. Burial chambers were not decorated. Apart from a few coffins and the occasional inscribed object, the underground burial chamber was basically text free. Mummification was further developed, with the deceased being wrapped in linen. There is evidence that internal organs were removed from the body, and the first canopic jars, in which the organs were placed, appear at this time. In some cases the body was covered with paste and the whole body, especially the face, realistically modelled. As in earlier periods, the deceased were often placed on their left side in a slightly contracted sleeping position.

At the end of the Old Kingdom, the underworld god Osiris first appears in Egyptian sources. According to Egyptian myth, in the ancient past Osiris ruled as king over Egypt, but was killed by his brother Seth, his body dismembered and the body parts scattered all around the country. Isis, Osiris's wife and sister, reassembled his body, and his son Horus came and awakened him; Osiris then became ruler of the underworld. The life of Osiris was closely identified with the life of the Egyptian king, who was king on Earth and after death became the king of the afterlife. Many inscriptions in the royal pyramids relate to Osiris and the identification of the king with that god. However, Osiris was not only important for the king; as ruler of the underworld, Osiris also secured the eternal food supply for the non-royal deceased and protected their afterlife. This is frequently expressed in offering formulas on coffins or in inscriptions in tomb chapels.

It is probably no accident that, at about the time that Osiris appears in ancient Egyptian texts, the underground part of Egyptian tombs received more attention. Additional objects were placed in the burial chambers, many of them items used in rituals associated with mummification. On the interior walls of the pyramids of kings and queens, long religious inscriptions – known to Egyptologists as the Pyramid Texts – which ensured that the king was

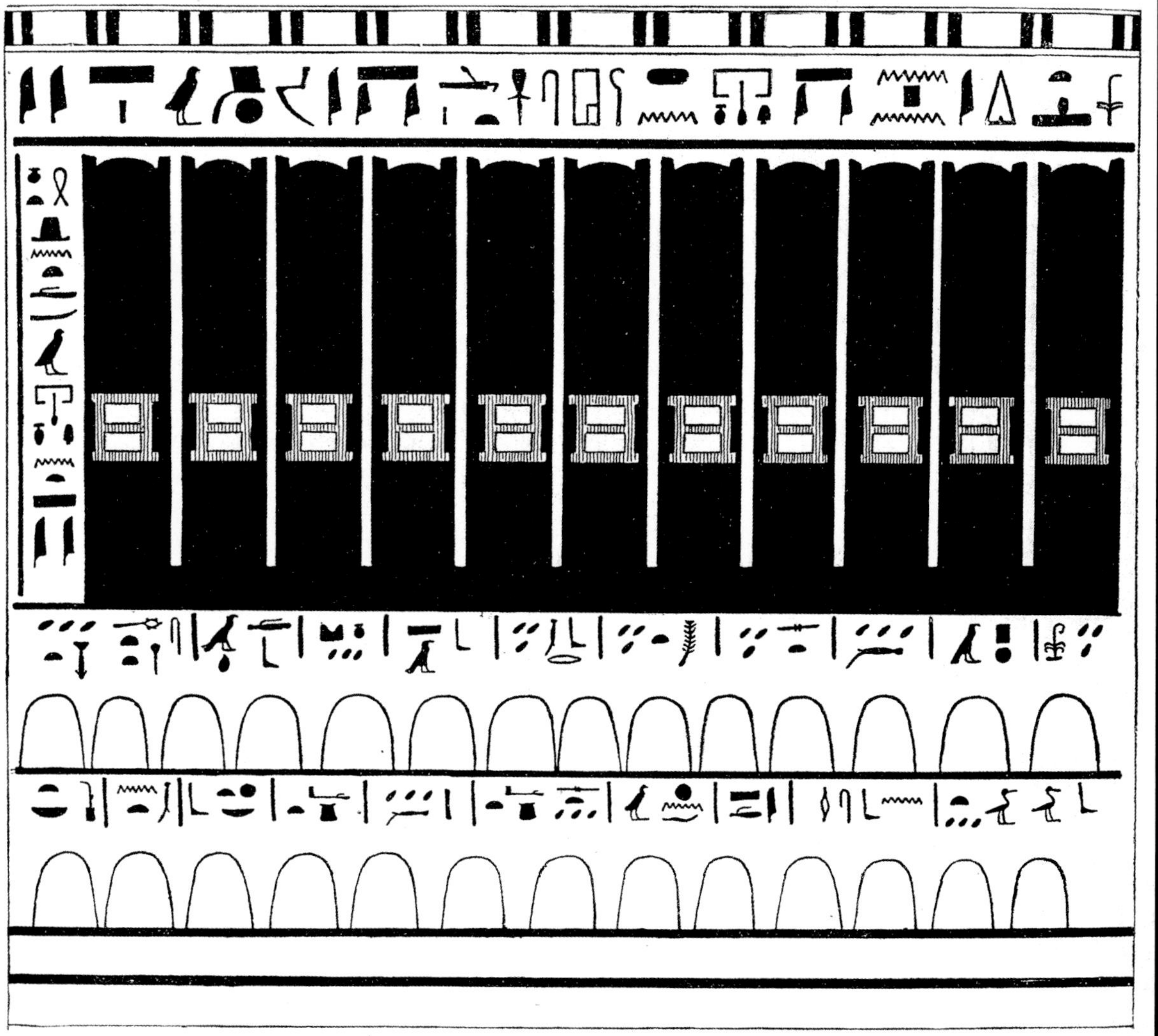

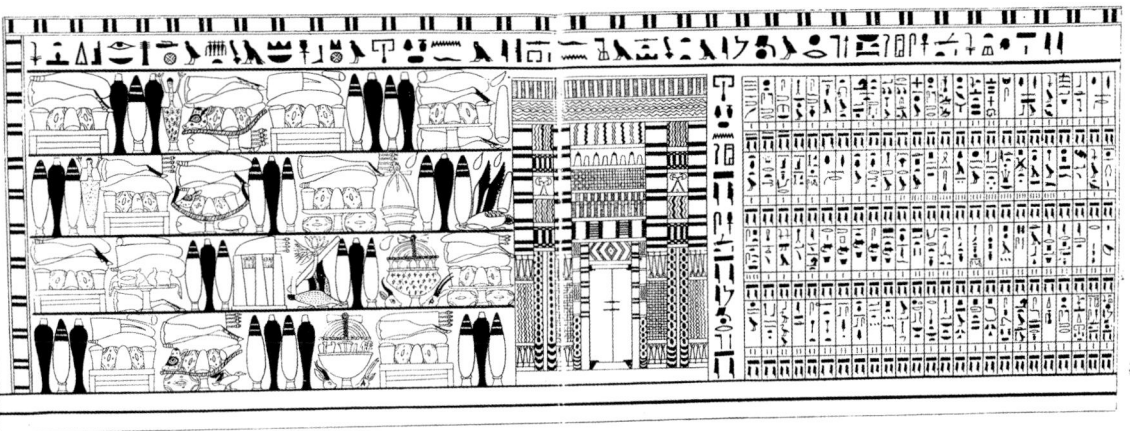

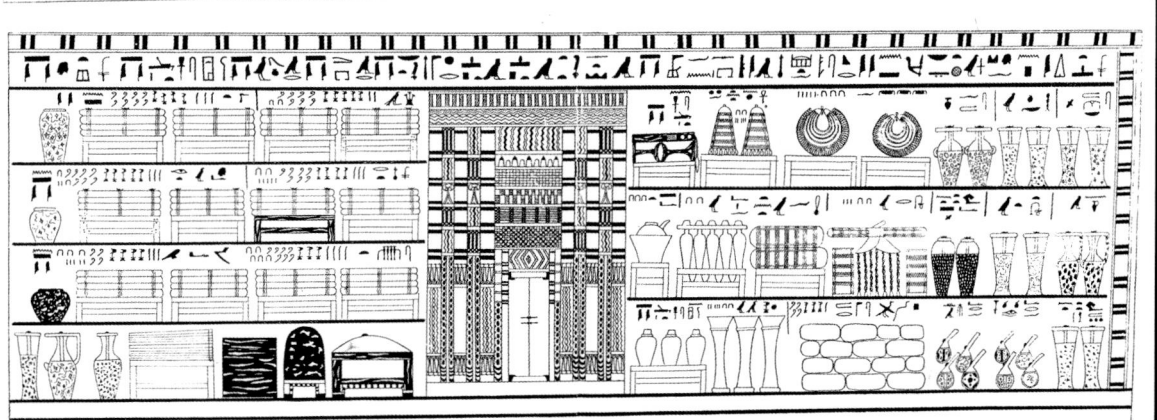

Decorated walls from the burial chamber of the official Shy, late Old Kingdom, about 2200 BC. The foot end (fig. 14) shows a granary. The other walls (fig. 15) include depictions of two false doors and many offerings and ritual objects. A long offering list is shown at top right.

transformed into Osiris began to appear. However, the texts of the kings and queens are very much part of the world of gods and goddesses. The king also travelled up to the northern sky to become one of the 'imperishable stars' (the circumpolar stars which never go below the horizon). The king was already a god on Earth, and now became a god in the underworld.

In contrast to royalty, the afterlife of officials was primarily concerned with securing an eternal food supply, providing a safe journey into the underworld and performing the correct rituals around mummification. These concerns had perhaps already been important, but they were now for the first time clearly expressed in pictures and writings placed in the tomb. Burial chambers of officials were often decorated. Texts and pictures became part of the burial chamber. There are depictions of objects, many perhaps related to rituals connected with the burial itself. Food offerings are often shown, and one list names about a hundred such offerings (figs. 14 and 15).

Around this time, coffins received more attention too, and a standard type developed. As before, the deceased was placed within the coffin on his or her left side with the head to the north, looking therefore to the east. Correspondingly, the coffin had two *wedjat* eyes (fig. 13) on its front side enabling the deceased to see the rising sun every morning. The four outer walls of the coffin were each decorated with one text line (see cat. 3), with an additional text line on the lid. These texts are most often offering formulae providing the deceased with everlasting rituals, the main aim of which was to secure a supply of food for eternity. The interiors of coffins were sometimes decorated too. This decoration was copied from the burial chambers of officials. Often on the inner foot end there is a depiction of a granary; the inner left side has a long offering list next to the depiction of offerings; and on the inner right side there are burial goods, most of them used in rituals rather than in daily life. Longer texts on late Old Kingdom and First Intermediate Period coffins are very rare (fig. 16).

During the First Intermediate Period (about 2170–2010 BC), Egypt disintegrated into several smaller political units. However, burial customs did not change very much. Coffin decoration remained basically the same, although many regional centres developed their own style, making it possible today to distinguish these local variations. Even the way of writing hieroglyphs on coffins varied from cemetery to cemetery. Evidently, different local workshops were operating in the politically and culturally fragmented country. In southern Egypt especially, figures were added to the outside of the coffin in scenes reflecting daily life. On coffins made for women, the owner is sometimes shown with a mirror and servants helping her with her hair. On men's coffins, there are offering bearers supplying the deceased with food.

The period known as the Middle Kingdom started around 2010 BC. At that time, local kings in the South, who had been ruling from Thebes from about

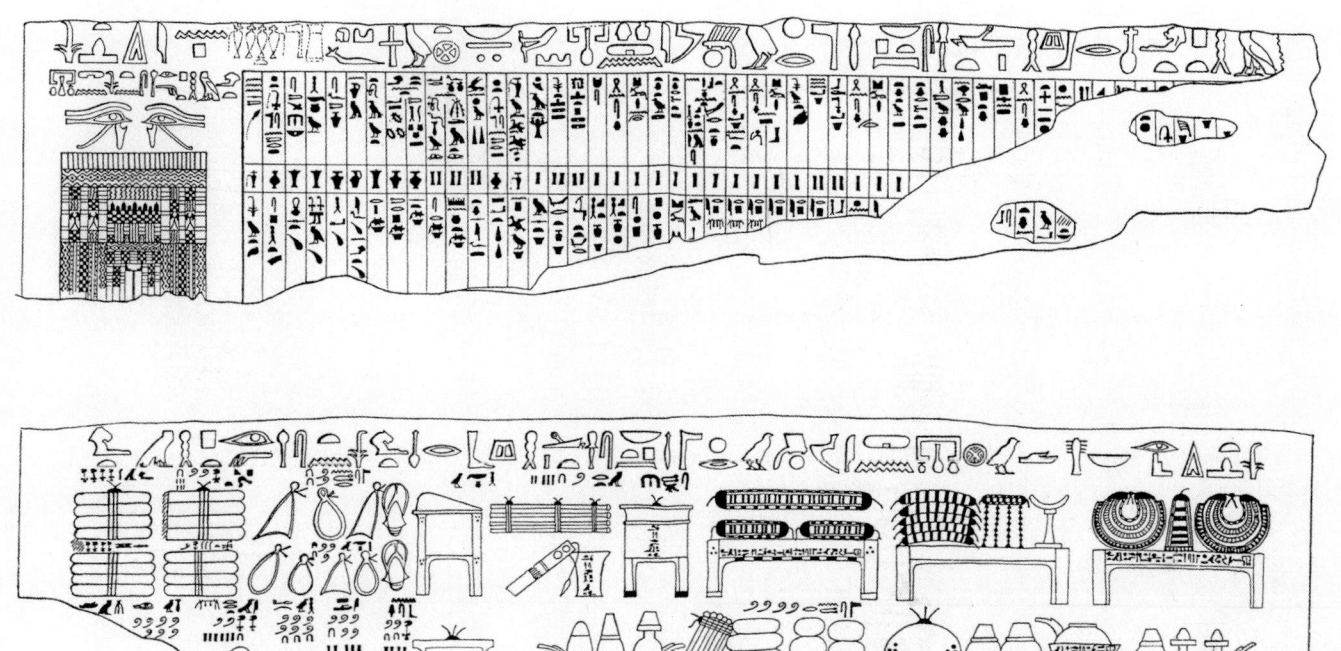

Fig. 16
Interior of the coffin of Ptahemhat. The inside walls are decorated in a similar way to a burial chamber. There is a false door (top left), with a long offering list to the right, and many offerings and objects used in rituals (bottom).

2120 BC onwards, managed to unite the country, although this left them with the problem of reorganising political structures. One important point was keeping the provinces under control; to this end, new, loyal governors were placed all around the country, each with his own court.

The governors were buried in splendid rock-cut tombs, often decorated with paintings and reliefs presenting the life and rituals of the local courts, each of which was in many ways a copy of the royal one. Local governors had officials running the province and their estates: 'stewards' oversaw different tasks; 'treasurers' were responsible for incoming goods at the governor's palace; 'overseers of fields' looked after the governor's fields; and 'physicians' took care of the wellbeing of the governor and his family. These local administrators were buried next to the governors they served, so as to be close to their master for all eternity. Most of the burials of local governors were looted early on (although there are a few well-preserved ones), as their monumental offering chapels were always visible and therefore easy targets for tomb robbers. In contrast, the burials of lower officials were often simple shaft tombs with a small chamber at the bottom and little tomb architecture above ground. Most probably these graves were no longer visible after just one or two generations and thus less of a target for tomb robbers. Even if these tombs were looted, robbers took only the more valuable objects, such as metal items and personal adornments. The

Fig. 17
The mask of Tjay (cat. 18), as it was found. The photograph shows that, at the point of discovery, this fragile object was in a state of collapse. It seems likely that only the section that survives today was actually removed from site.

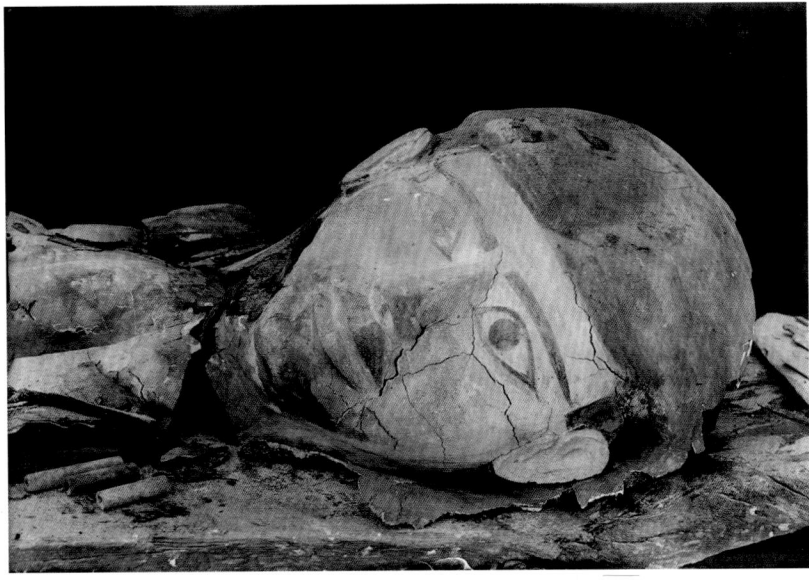

wooden coffins often remained in the burial chamber until their discovery during excavations at the beginning of the twentieth century. Indeed, the examples found in these local cemeteries today form the core group of coffins known from Middle Kingdom burials. Regrettably, however, these burial grounds were excavated too early in the history of Egyptian archaeology or were the target of half-official or even totally illegal excavations. The well-preserved coffins and equipment recovered from these tombs were sold on the art market and are now spread around collections all over the world, but most often very little is known about the tombs in which they were found.

The only cemetery known to have survived in a better state of preservation is close to Beni Hasan, the name of a modern village in Middle Egypt. The site is well known for its decorated rock-cut tombs of local governors. The ancient towns serving the cemetery were called Herwer and Menatkhufu, although their locations in the region around Beni Hasan are not precisely known. The existence of the decorated rock-cut tombs here has been known for a long time, and individual scenes depicted in tombs were already recorded and published in the early nineteenth century. However, it was only at the end of that same century that the Egyptologist Percy Newberry systematically recorded almost all of the tomb scenes and published them in several volumes. A few years later, from 1902 to 1904, John Garstang excavated several more cemeteries in the region, but especially those in front of the governors' tombs. He found about a thousand smaller burials, many of them belonging to lower officials; some of them were even found intact. These provide the largest corpus of excavated Middle Kingdom coffins. Most of the burials were arranged in a similar way. First there was the coffin, or in wealthier burials a set of inner and outer coffins. Placed next to them were wooden models showing food production, offering bearers and boats. These were model depictions of the official's estate (fig. 18). Also next to the coffin were pottery vessels to secure an eternal supply of food. Placed on top of the coffin was a wooden headrest and wooden sandals, objects relating to funerary rituals. The deceased was wrapped in linen, but rarely properly mummified. Often a mask was placed over the head (fig. 17). The body was decorated with personal adornments, most importantly a broad collar, as well as armlets and anklets. Most of the objects, including the personal adornments, were especially made for the burial; items obviously used during a person's lifetime are surprisingly rare.

Garstang's excavations were published in 1907 in a single volume. However, the report does not reach the standards expected today and even falls short of those of its time. Only a few tombs are described in detail. One chapter is devoted to the coffins, but only a few examples out of perhaps several hundred coffins and coffin fragments are shown. The objects, including the coffins, were distributed to museums around the world, the Fitzwilliam among them.

The coffin and models from the tomb of Khety (cats. 11 and 12), dating to about 2010–1950 BC, the early Middle Kingdom, is a perfect example of a tomb group of its time. The exterior of the coffin is inscribed all around with a single line of text and another line on the lid. The texts on the long sides of the coffin contain offering formulas: that on the front is concerned with an eternal provision of food, achieved by means of a 'voice offering', words that were spoken at a ritual during the funeral, which caused the dead to receive food for all eternity; the prayer on the rear side of the coffin is for a 'good burial', to make sure that the appropriate burial equipment was used. Writing appropriate spells or prayers on the coffin meant that essential offerings and rituals would be performed forever, ensuring a good burial for all eternity. The inscription on the lid seems mainly to be concerned with a successful journey to the underworld.

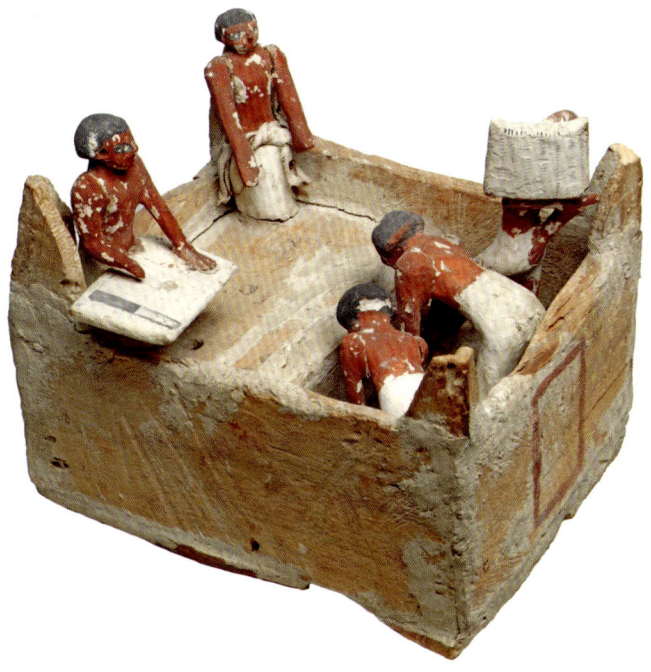

Fig. 18
Model granary from the tomb of Khety (cat. 12)

Altogether, the whole tomb group of Khety, including the texts on the coffin and the wooden models, is very much concerned with the wellbeing of the deceased. The provision of food expressed by the texts on the coffin is also represented in the wooden models (fig. 18), and perhaps by dishes placed in the tomb chambers. The model boats, typical of tombs of the period, enabled the deceased free movement. It is noticeable that, in this burial, there was little direct contact with any gods. The gods provided food and a good burial, but were set very much apart from the world of the deceased. The afterlife was still seen as extension of life on Earth.

The coffin of Khety has a rather simple decorative scheme, identical to earlier coffins, dating from the late Old Kingdom and First Intermediate Period. Other Middle Kingdom coffins show more text bands and further decoration. Indeed, coffins in the Twelfth Dynasty (about 1975–1790 BC) underwent a rapid development; Khety's coffin type marks the beginning of this process. Early in this period, text columns were added on the outer sides of the coffins, in which the deceased is often said to be 'revered by' certain gods that helped with the mummification of Osiris (fig. 19). A little later, a painted 'false door' – an interface between the worlds of the living and the dead – under the *wedjat* eyes was added on the front. In the mid-Twelfth Dynasty, coffins were often painted on all sides with a palace façade and with a false door on the front.

As in the late Old Kingdom, the interiors of coffins were often decorated with a frieze of objects showing items most likely used in the embalming chamber for preparing the deceased for the afterlife, as well as objects used

Fig. 19
Coffin of Senuitef (Fitzwilliam Museum, E.70.1903), found at Beni Hasan, tomb 65. The coffin is decorated on the long sides with a line of text at the top, but with four additional vertical text columns. At the head end there are *wedjat* eyes.

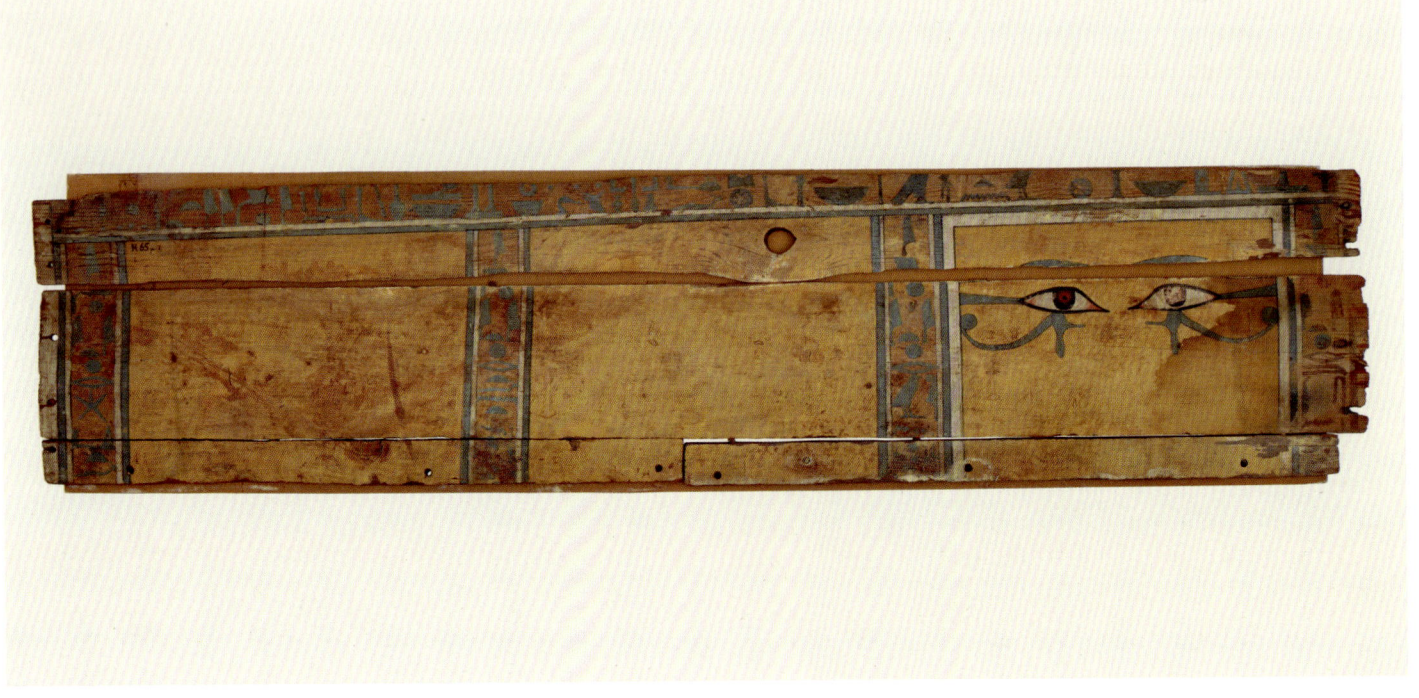

36 Coffins of the Middle Kingdom

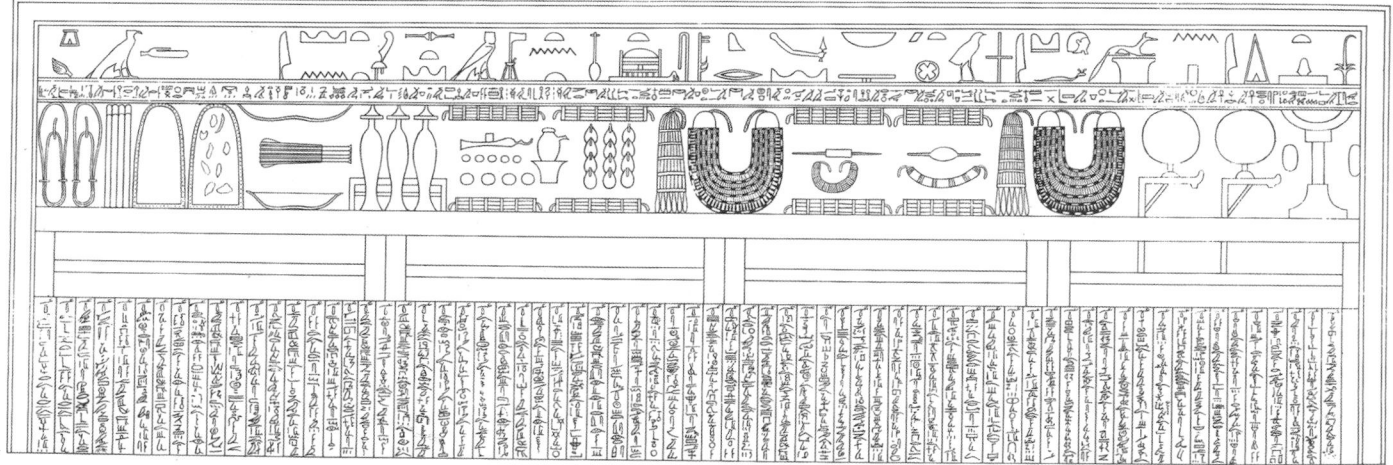

Fig. 20
Interior of the coffin of Dagi, showing a range of items in the 'frieze of objects'. Many of them are also familiar as burial goods, such as the mirrors and headrest (right), and also personal adornments.

in other rituals (fig. 20). Many of them were also found in the burials, such as personal adornments, a mirror, sandals (placed in the tombs as wooden models), a headrest, staves and weapons (figs. 21–23). A typical feature of Middle Kingdom coffins is the use of longer religious texts. These are written in columns on the inner sides of the coffins, most often below the friezes of objects, and are also placed on the underside of the lid and on the bottom. These texts are spells, some already known from the Pyramid Texts of the Old Kingdom, but there are also many new inscriptions on coffins, referred to as Coffin Texts in Egyptology; more than one thousand spells are known so far, and with almost every coffin discovered, new ones are found. However, several spells were used in certain places and times and are therefore found on many coffins all over the country, while others are typical of particular places and appear less frequently. For example, at Deir el-Bersha, several coffins are decorated with the Book of the Two Ways – an illustrated guide for the deceased to find his or her way around in the underworld, with a map and longer texts providing explanations and spells to say at certain places (fig. 24).

One example of a coffin fragment with Coffin Texts (cat. 14) belongs to a woman and most probably comes from Asyut, south of Beni Hasan. The woman's name is lost, but in the text the coffin owner is addressed as 'she'. Parts of several texts are preserved on the fragment (fig. 26). Coffin Text spell 203 is one example, mainly concerned with the condition of the deceased in the underworld. The emphasis is on the supply of food and a wish not to be turned upside down. The deceased does not want to eat excrement but bread and beer. Spell 204 is shorter, but basically addresses the same concerns. A similar fear is again expressed in spell 574, while spell 210 is, according to its heading, mainly concerned with the question of avoiding work in the underworld. Although these spells and the text programme on this small piece of wood are fragmentary, one major theme is evident: achieving a good 'life' in the afterlife for the deceased, one that includes

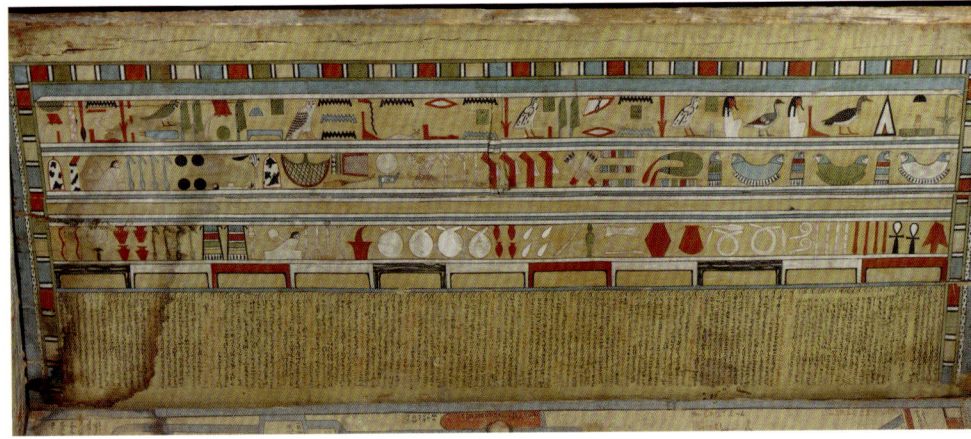

Fig. 24
Interior of the coffin of Gua (British Museum, EA30839). The bottom is painted with the Book of the Two Ways, a guide to the underworld.

Fig. 21
Outer coffin of Sen (British Museum, 30841), found at Deir el-Bersha. The interior decoration includes shields covered with hides, bead necklaces, two bows, a mirror, some vessels, *was*-sceptres and items of linen.

Fig. 22
Outer coffin of Sen (British Museum, 30841). At centre left is a row of five granaries.

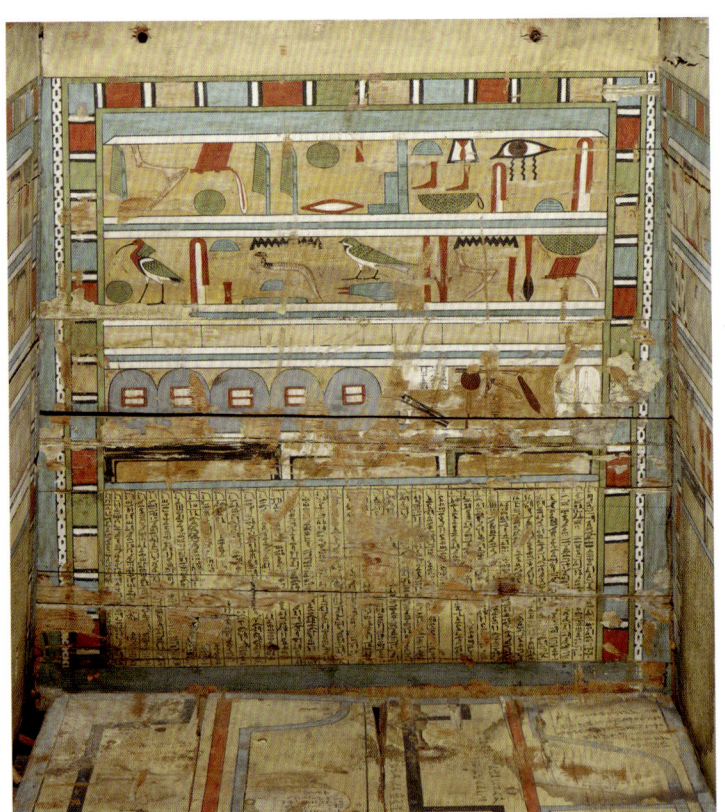

Fig. 23
Long side of the outer coffin of Sen (British Museum, 30841). At the head is a 'false door' (a doorway painted on to the coffin to allow the deceased's spirits to come and go) and offerings.

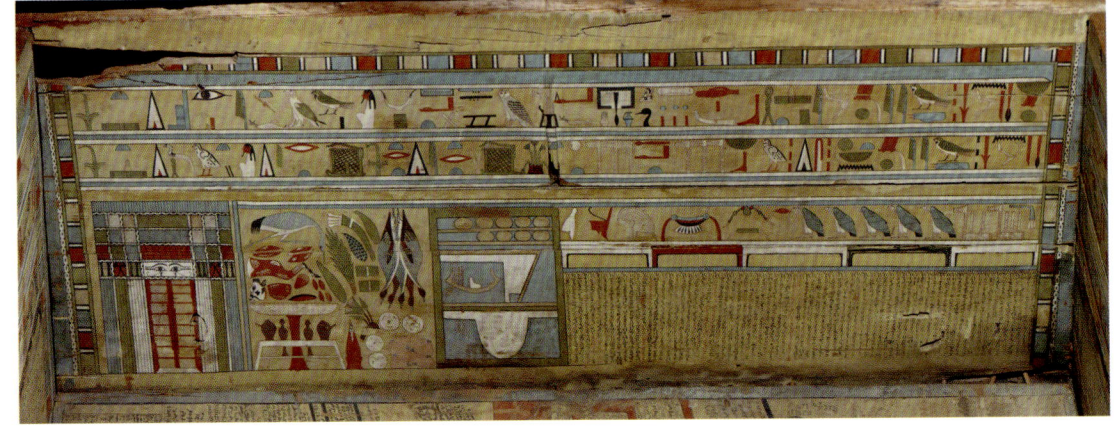

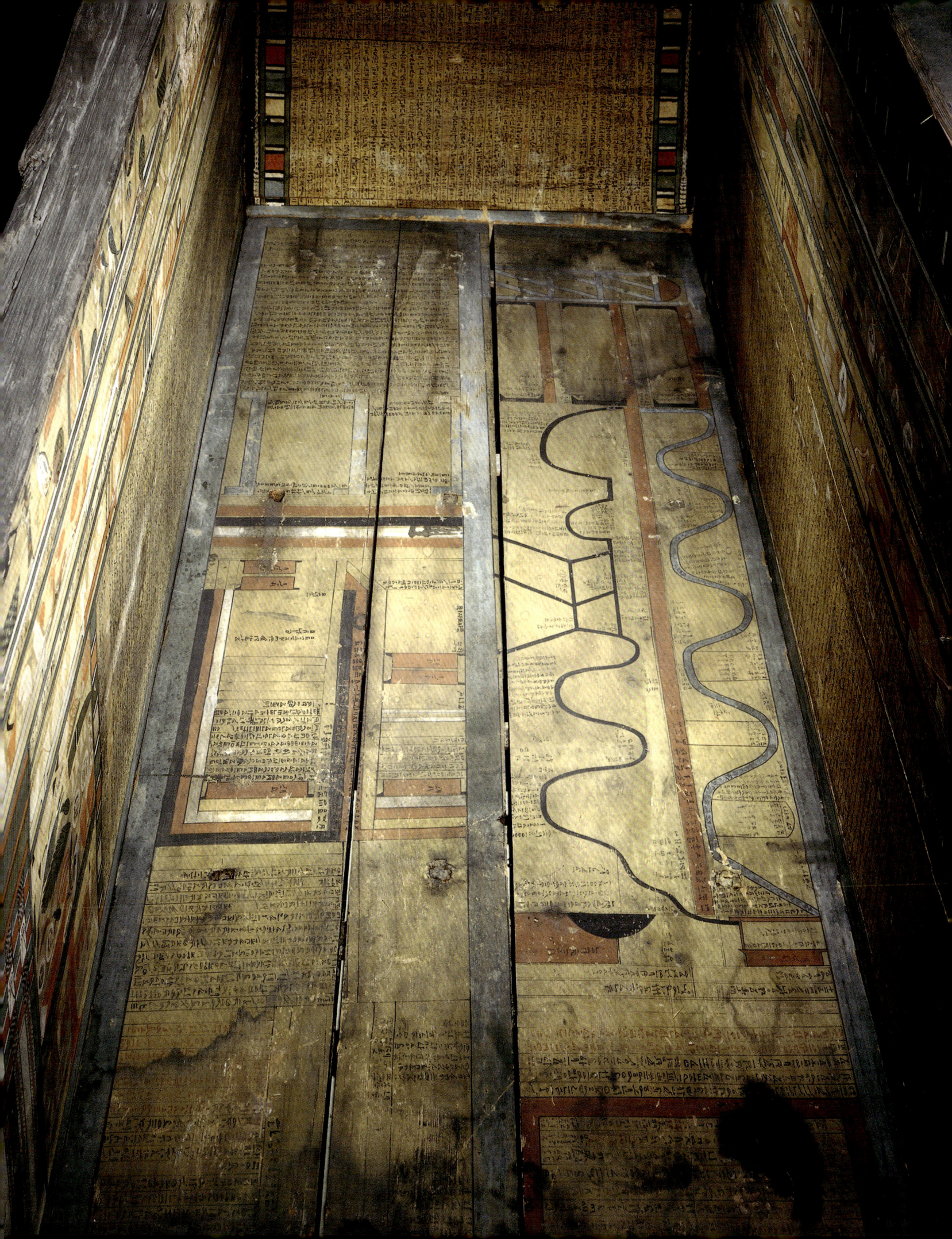

Fig. 25
Foot end of the coffin of Ankhef (British Museum, EA46631), with figures of two of the children of Horus (later known as the Sons of Horus; cat. 17)

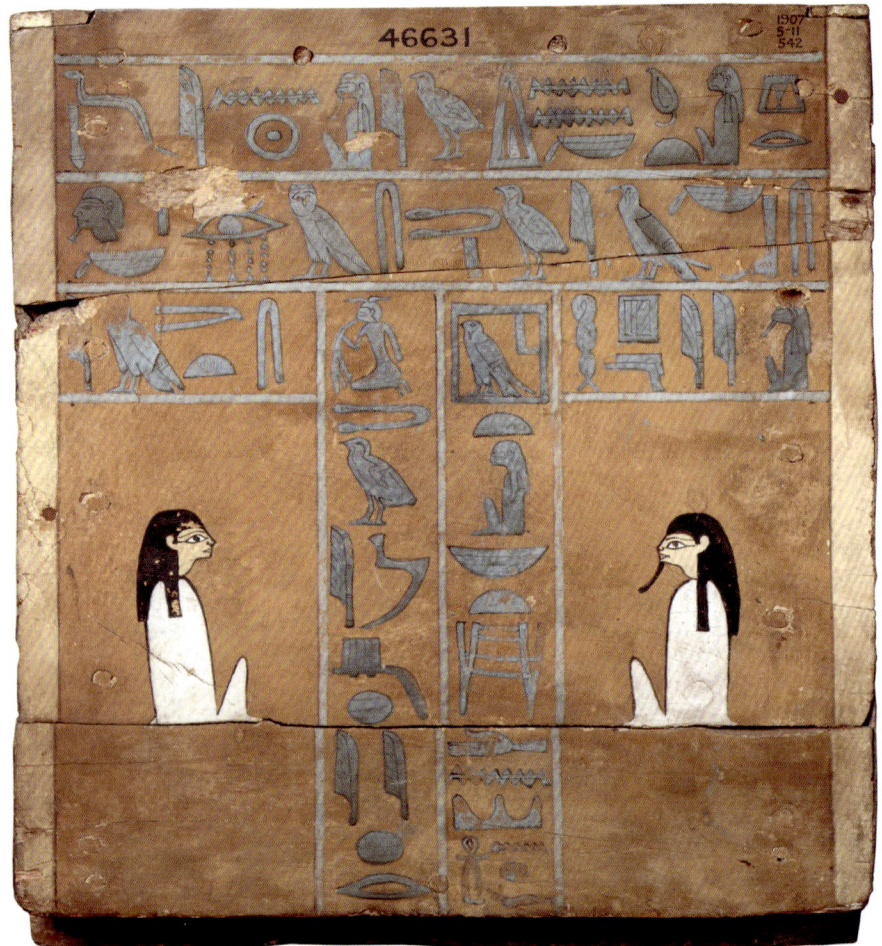

food and freedom from the burden of work. The short formulae on the outside of this coffin fragment seem to confirm the status of the dead woman in her life; she wanted to be 'honoured by her whole town'. This wish would already have been very important in her earthly existence, and by placing it on her coffin, she ensured that her social position remained unaltered in the afterlife. As reflected in these short inscriptions, the deceased was still a human being in the underworld and thus was faced with the same problems as in the real world.

A different coffin tradition can be recognised at Asyut. A line of governors, who belonged to the most powerful and wealthiest officials in the country, already ruled there during the First Intermediate Period and in the Middle Kingdom. The cemeteries around these governors' tombs are among the largest of the Middle Kingdom, but over the last hundred years few systematic excavations have been conducted there. Most coffins from Asyut were discovered during illegal digs, and the objects found were sold to museums and private collections. In the First Intermediate Period, a style of coffin developed at Asyut that was different from coffins from other places. Rather than having only single lines of text on the outside of the coffin, the inscriptions are most often doubled or even tripled.

Another typical feature on the exteriors is the depiction of daily life scenes, funerary rituals or offerings to the deceased. Coffins from other cemeteries are decorated on the inside and, unlike the coffins from Asyut and some other Upper Egyptian sites, they rarely show human figures. It was probably deemed too dangerous for humans to be depicted too close to the body of the deceased. For the ancient Egyptians, the depiction of a person was considered almost to be that person, and evidently was not wanted within the coffin. Placing the human figures on the coffin's exterior took away much of this danger, but also gave the opportunity to show important rituals with human figures. While the objects depicted on coffins from most other places appear as static items, on coffins from Asyut (and a few other places) the objects are shown in active roles. One perfect example is the coffin fragments of the 'master physician' Wepwawetemhat, showing offering bearers bringing animals to the deceased (fig. 27). Another special feature of coffins from Asyut is the depictions of gods on the short ends (fig. 25); on the foot end of the coffin of Ankhef, the four children of Horus take care of the mummy. This is the first time in ancient Egyptian history that depictions of deities appear on private monuments.

There are indications that private individuals in the Middle Kingdom took over the idea of becoming Osiris, something reserved in the Old Kingdom for the king. Indeed, already in the First Intermediate Period there are inscriptions where the deceased is called 'Osiris', but these are exceptions. Only during the Twelfth Dynasty (1975–1790 BC) did it become more common. In the Fitzwilliam Museum this is clearly expressed on the coffin of 'lady of the house' Nakht (cat. 15), dating from about 1915–1870 BC. The entire textual programme on Nakht's coffin is similar to earlier examples; the long text bands on the front and back express a wish for the eternal supply of food and for a good burial. However, the coffin displays several innovations, demonstrating the arrival of new religious beliefs during the Twelfth Dynasty. The coffin is decorated all around with a palace façade. This design goes back to the Archaic Period (about 3030–2700 BC) or even earlier, appearing as a decoration on the coffins of that time, and also as an architectural feature on the large free-standing tombs in the area around

Fig. 26
Detail of hieroglyphs from Coffin Texts painted on the interior of the coffin of an unknown woman (cat. 14)

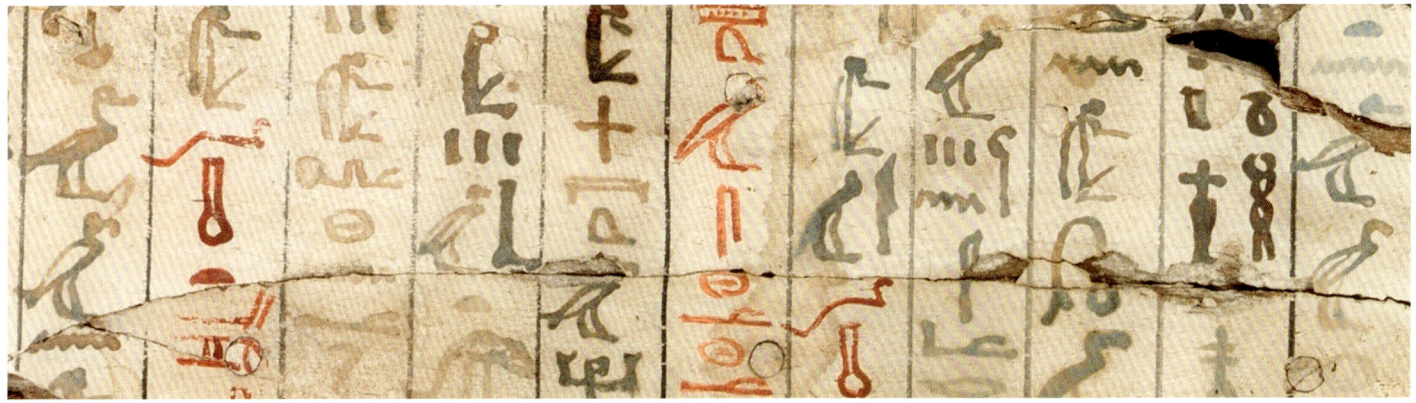

Memphis. The palace façade is also part of the hieroglyph of the Horus name, the oldest title of Egyptian kings and the most important expression of royalty. The motif appears sporadically throughout the Old Kingdom (about 2700–2170 BC) as a decoration on coffin exteriors, but does not occur with any frequency in the First Intermediate Period and early Middle Kingdom. In the mid-Twelfth Dynasty, however, an increasing number of coffins were decorated with a palace façade, while other royal symbols, including crowns, the royal uraeus, the royal vulture, royal staves and weapons (fig. 28), began to be shown in the friezes of objects. At the same time, certain Coffin Texts became more popular. One example is Coffin Text spell 397, dealing with the journey into the underworld to Osiris. It seems the deceased was not becoming a king, as the royal symbols might imply, but was identified with, and coming close to, Osiris, the king of the underworld.

Another innovation of the Twelfth Dynasty is the development of anthropoid (human-shaped) coffins. Mummy masks covering the head of the dead had already been used earlier, in the First Intermediate Period. They were made of cartonnage and showed the deceased as a mummy with a long wig, a beard and a broad collar. In the mid-Twelfth Dynasty, these masks were extended over the whole body to form anthropoid coffins. The first coffins of this new type were frequently made of thin wood or of a wooden frame covered with cartonnage and therefore have often not survived well; only about a dozen examples are preserved (fig. 29). Decoration is most often simple: several of the coffins are not even inscribed; others bear a single line of text down the front. The body is often only coloured black or white, but a few are painted all over with a floral pattern. The head is covered with a long wig and, on some coffins,

Fig. 27
Detail of a fragment of the coffin of Wepwawetemhat (cat. 13), showing a bull being brought as an offering to the deceased

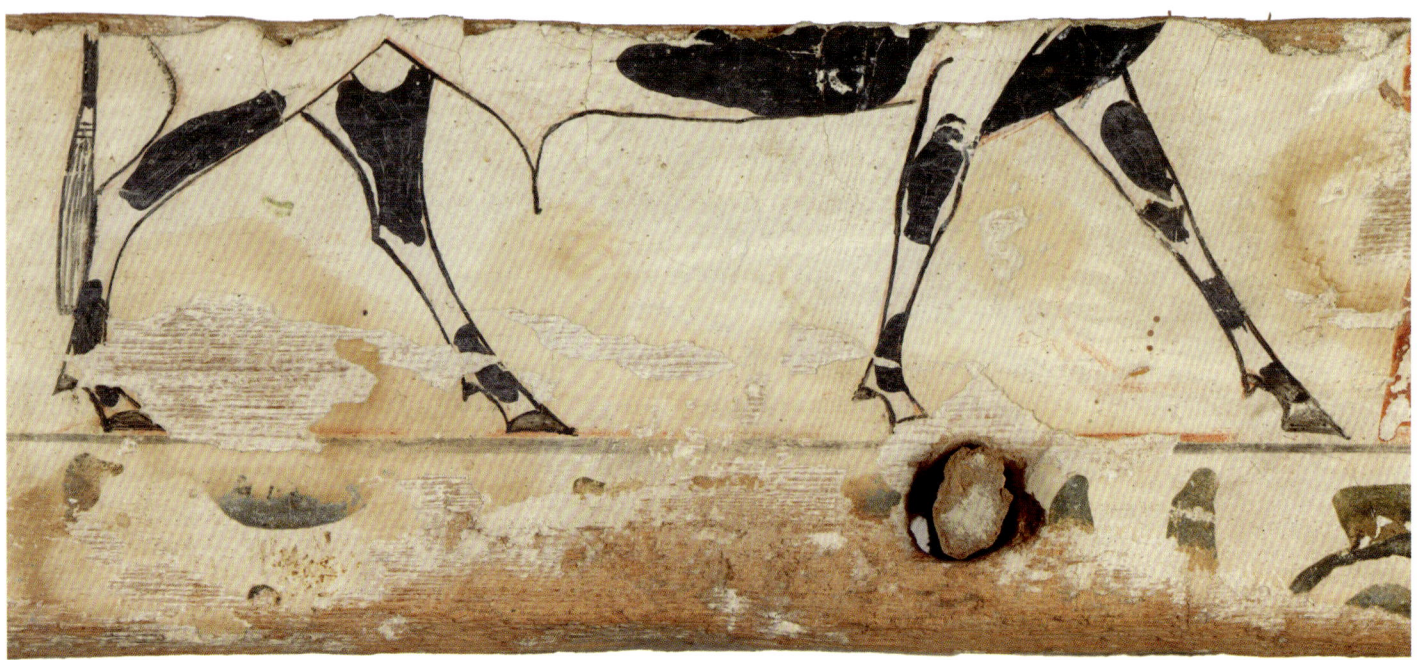

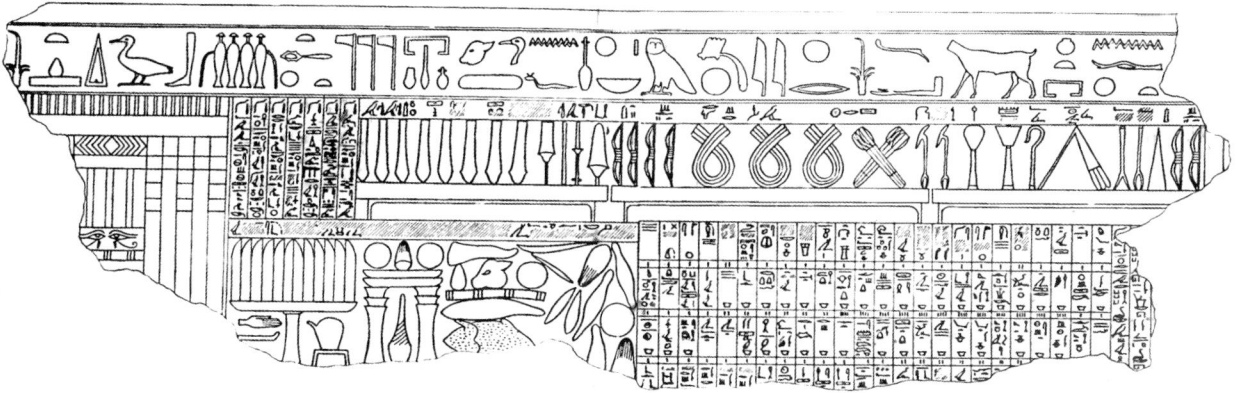

Fig. 28
Coffin of Nakht, found at el-Lisht. The frieze shows a number of royal insignia, such as a mace, a flail, a *heqa*-sceptre and two *was*-sceptres.

a headdress resembling a *nemes*, a royal crown not normally worn by officials or any non-royal people.

These early anthropoid coffins were always part of a coffin set and were placed in an outer rectangular box coffin, lying on their left side as if they were mummies; evidently they were at first not seen as proper coffins, but rather as some kind of extra mummy cover or as a more stable type of mummy bandaging. Not all burials, even those of high-status people, had an anthropoid coffin. It seems they were not thought to be essential as the outer rectangular coffin was. A good example of this is the burial of the Thirteenth Dynasty king Hor (about 1775 BC), whose tomb was found largely intact. His mummy was placed within a coffin set, comprising an outer undecorated sarcophagus and an inner wooden coffin decorated with gold foil. The mummy of the king was adorned with a mask, but it was not placed in an anthropoid coffin.

The later Twelfth Dynasty, from about the reign of Sesostris III (about 1870 BC) onwards, saw further changes in burial customs and also in the political landscape of Egypt. The local governors lost power and resources. As a result, they no longer built huge, decorated rock-cut tombs or maintained local courts on the scale of the early Middle Kingdom. It seems that local workshops making coffins and other funerary products no longer had enough wealthy customers and therefore stopped working or at least operated on a much more reduced scale than before. While about a thousand decorated coffins dating to the early Middle Kingdom have survived, so far fewer than thirty coffins are known that date to the late Middle Kingdom. The only places with a substantial funerary industry were those cemeteries with a royal presence: Thebes, Abydos and the Memphis-Fayum region. High-quality coffins were still produced here, and these regions were the centres of development for the next two hundred years. At first the outside of coffins changed little, but decoration on the inside disappeared. There were no Coffin or Pyramid Texts, nor were there friezes of objects. This is in stark contrast to earlier developments and is not yet fully understood. Furthermore, coffin decoration developed differently in northern and southern Egypt. In the northern Egyptian

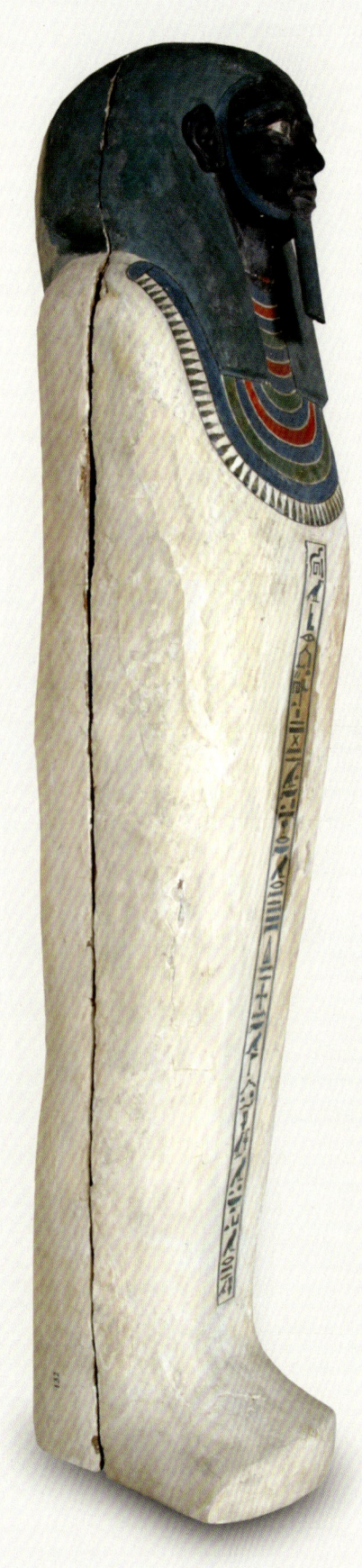

Fig. 29
Anthropoid coffin of Userhet (cat. 20). In this example, the box and the lid were each hollowed out from a single large piece of sycamore fig wood.

cemeteries of the royal residences at Dahshur and el-Lisht, coffin design remained conservative. In the Thirteenth Dynasty (about 1790–1650 BC), coffins with more inscriptions were preferred, but far fewer were used than on early Middle Kingdom coffins, and texts were no longer placed on the inside of the coffin but on the outside only. These new texts are often already close to the later collections of spells now known as the Book of the Dead (fig. 30). In southern Egypt, more columns of text were added to the outside decoration, with up to nine columns on the long side of the coffin. On the foot and head ends of some coffins, the figures of Isis and Nephthys are painted, protecting the mummy.

At the end of the Thirteenth Dynasty (around 1650 BC), Egypt entered its darkest age, now known as the Second Intermediate Period. In the North, the country was ruled by people from the Levant, who brought their own distinctive culture, known as Hyksos in later sources. During the same period, Egypt was attacked from the South by the powerful Kerma Empire, and the country was in permanent conflict with its neighbours. Egypt became divided, with one dynasty ruling in Thebes and another in Abydos, both rather weak. In this troubled time, Egyptian royal courts had only restricted resources. Even the burials of the kings were modest. In Thebes they were buried under small pyramids, while in Abydos they did not have pyramids at all. Private officials, even wealthy ones, often reused older shafts or were simply buried in the ground.

A number of important developments can be seen in burial customs at this time, especially at Thebes. Only a few burial goods, specially made for the tomb, appear, of which the most important was apparently the coffin. Canopic containers were still used in royal burials, but were rare in burials of the highest officials. Other burial goods were mainly taken from daily life, including vessels for the eternal food supply. Burials of women often contained jewellery,

Fig. 30
Two vignettes from the much later Book of the Dead of Ramose (Fitzwilliam Museum, E.2.1922; see cat. 9)

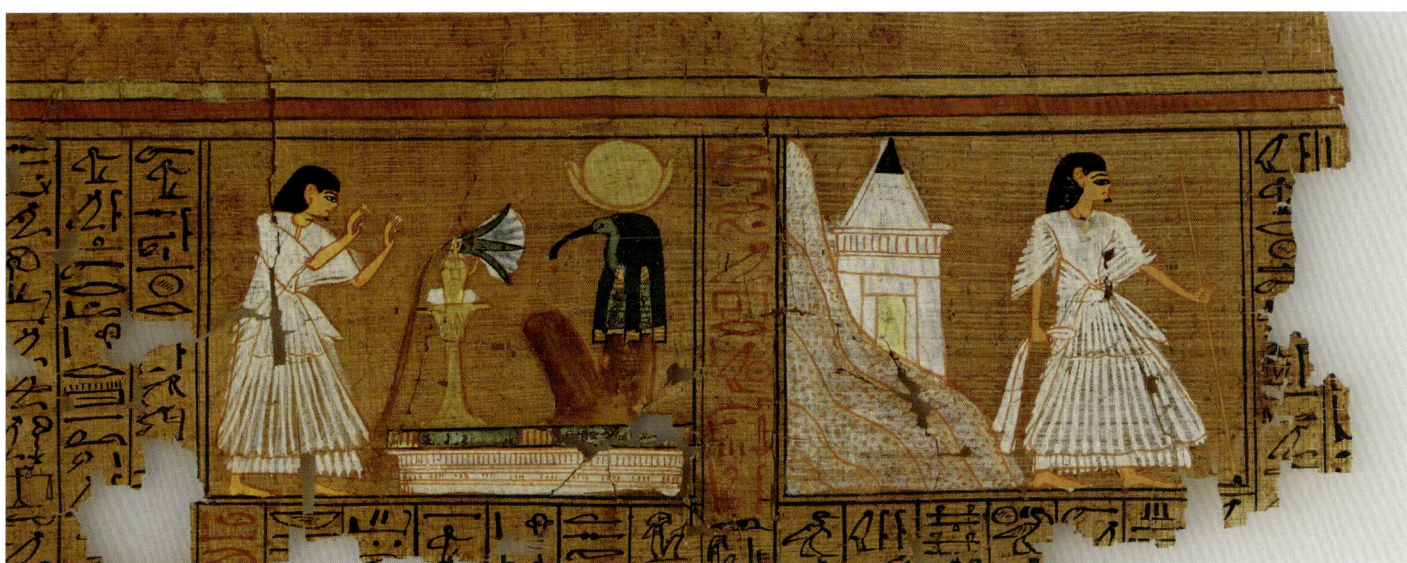

Wolfram Grajetzki

confirming their social status. Rectangular coffins following Middle Kingdom traditions were still produced, but inscriptions were few and are often so garbled that it is impossible to read them.

A fundamental change in coffin shape and design took place. At the highest social level, anthropoid coffins became important and were now placed into the burial without an outer rectangular coffin. These coffins were decorated all over with a feather design and are today called *rishi* coffins, after the Arabic word *risha*, meaning 'feather' (see, for example, fig. 92 on p. 167). They were given this name by early excavators in the nineteenth century, when the first coffins of this type were found at Thebes. Aside from the feather design, another typical feature of *rishi* coffins is their construction: they are frequently cut from a single log of wood, while later anthropoid coffins are often constructed from many different pieces. In general, *rishi* coffins closely conform to the tradition of Middle Kingdom anthropoid coffins. The deceased wears a *nemes*-like headdress, and often there is just one text line on the front. The decoration is otherwise rather simple, with no indication of modelled hands on the front (unlike later coffins). The foot end often features depictions of Isis and Nephthys, as on Middle Kingdom box coffins. *Rishi* coffins were still in use in the early Eighteenth Dynasty but were gradually replaced by other types of anthropoid coffins.

The *rishi* coffin developed at Thebes, while in other parts of the country rectangular coffins in the Middle Kingdom tradition were still produced. Inscriptions on these coffins are rare, and the decoration is often eclectic, with elements borrowed from the earlier Middle Kingdom. One important innovation is the location of the *wedjat* eyes at the head end. During this period, one eye was painted on each long side, rather than two on the left side, the change in decoration apparently a response to changes in burial customs. During the late Middle Kingdom and Second Intermediate Period, the dead were no longer laid on their left sides but placed on their backs. The new position might have been influenced by the rising popularity of *rishi* coffins and the practicality of laying them flat, as they were not placed inside an outer rectangular coffin as earlier anthropoid coffins had been.

Burial equipment and coffins at the beginning of the New Kingdom (about 1550 BC) were still very much in the tradition of the Second Intermediate Period. Rectangular and *rishi* coffins were still used, though it is often hard to date single examples to one period or other, and it is clear that workshops did not change their style with the new political situation. One example is a coffin from Abydos in the Fitzwilliam Museum (fig.31). In the early Eighteenth Dynasty, *rishi* coffins were apparently rarely used at Abydos, but coffins in the tradition of the late Middle Kingdom were still produced. The Fitzwilliam example is decorated on the outside with figures showing mourners and offering bearers. There are also several text columns, sadly not mentioning the coffin owner. The high number

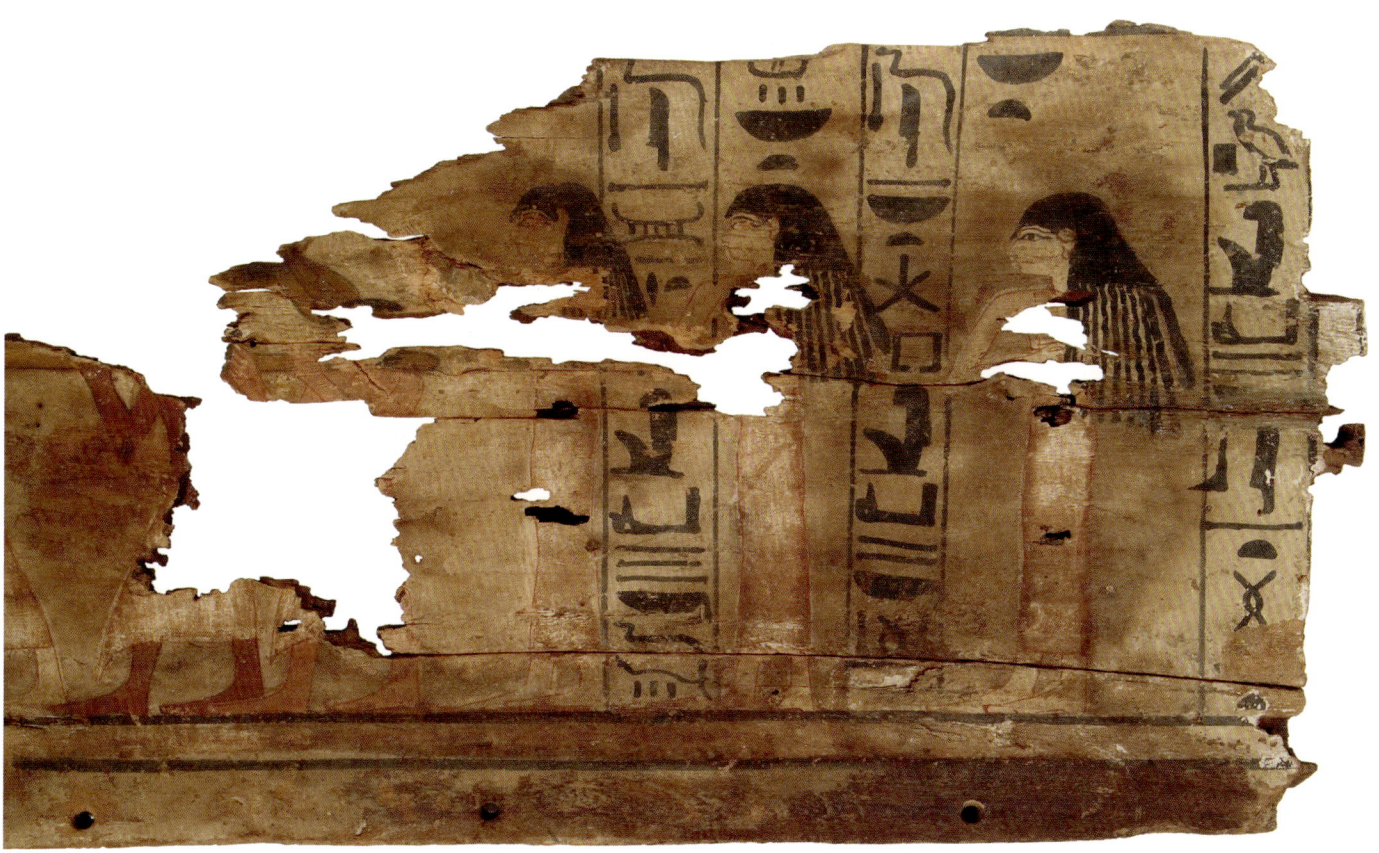

Fig. 31
Detail of the coffin of the mourning women (cat. 21), from Abydos, showing women in the funeral procession. The figures are interspersed with columns of text.

of text columns is certainly influenced by late Middle Kingdom and Second Intermediate Period coffins, which have a similar high number of columns of inscriptions. Depictions on the short ends show Isis and Nephthys, protectors of the deceased, who already appeared in this position on Middle Kingdom coffins.

Further reading

Grajetzki, Wolfram. *Burial Customs in Ancient Egypt: Life in Death for Rich and Poor*. London: Duckworth, 2003.

Miniaci, Gianluca. *Rishi Coffins and the Funerary Culture of Second Intermediate Period Egypt*. GHP Egyptology 17. London: Golden House Publications, 2011.

Willems, Harco. *Historical and Archaeological Aspects of Egyptian Funerary Culture*. Culture and History of the Ancient Near East. Leiden: Brill, 2014.

Willems, Harco. *Chests of Life: A Study of the Typology and Conceptual Development of Middle Kingdom Standard Class Coffins*. Mededelingen en verhandelingen van het Vooraziatisch-Egyptisch Genootschap 'Ex Oriente Lux' 25. Leiden: Ex Oriente Lux, 1988.

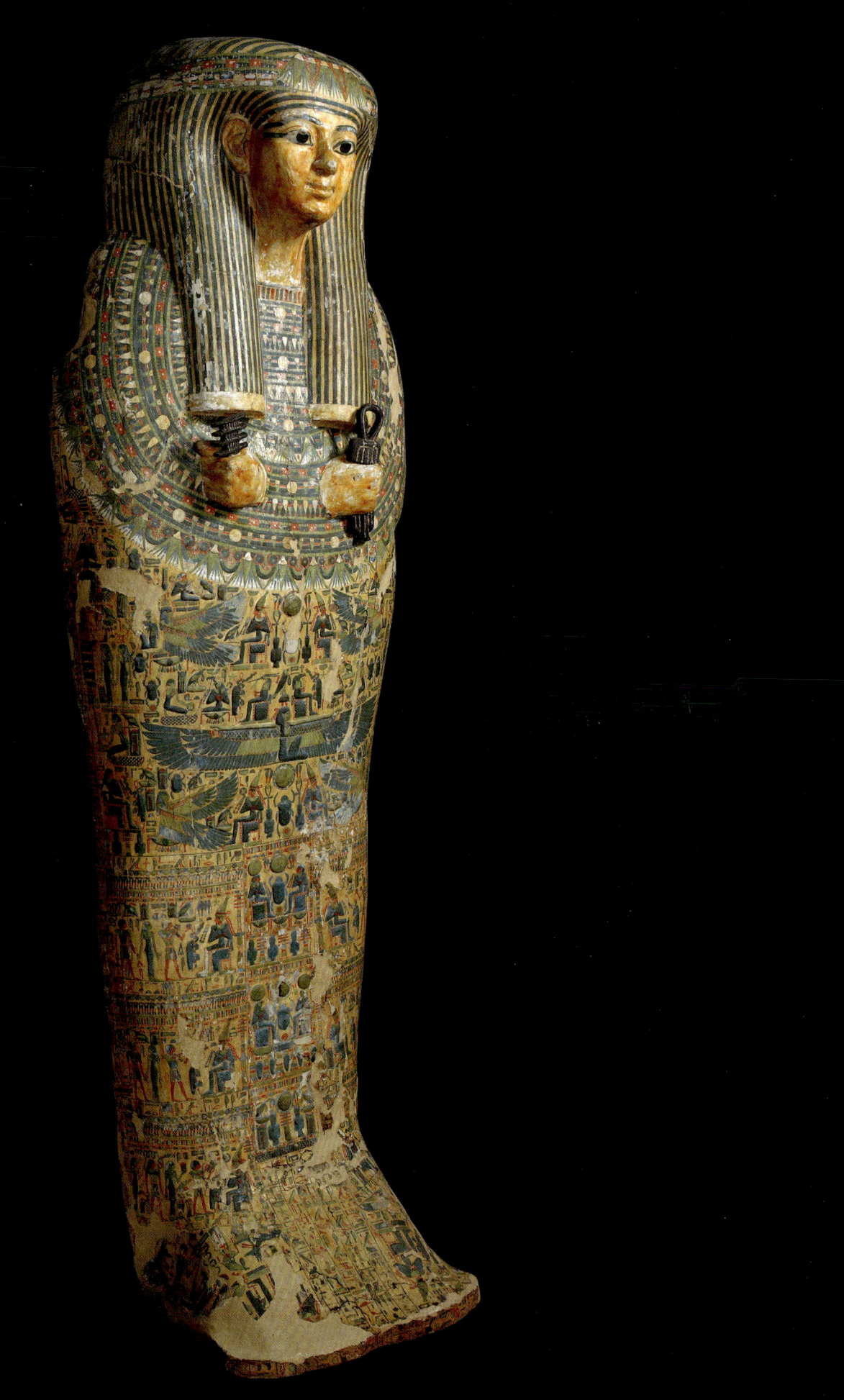

COFFINS FROM THE NEW KINGDOM TO THE ROMAN PERIOD

John H. Taylor

The reign of Ahmose, founder of the Eighteenth Dynasty (about 1550–1290 BC), was marked by the expulsion of the Hyksos, the repressing of the hostile Nubian kingdom and the restoration of centralised government in Egypt under a native ruler. The expansionist military exploits of Ahmose and his successors established Egypt as a world power and ushered in the phase of her greatest prosperity, now known as the New Kingdom (about 1550–1070 BC). In burial practices and in the function and design of coffins there were significant developments during this 500-year period, but these emerged gradually.

The clearest picture of trends in mortuary practices in this period comes from Thebes, the chief cult centre of Amun-Re, 'king of the gods', and the burial place of the pharaohs and many of their most senior officials. The burials of the kings became increasingly elaborate from reign to reign. The cult of each dead ruler was maintained in a temple that was physically separated from the burial place. The royal tomb was no longer capped by a pyramid but comprised a sequence of passages and chambers hewn into the rock in the Valley of the Kings, their walls and ceilings decorated with texts and images from the Books of the Underworld. These compositions (the books of Amduat, Gates, Caverns, Day and Night and others) traced the course of the sun god Re's nightly journey through the underworld, during which he was rejuvenated through a momentary merging with the body of Osiris (the two gods being regarded as complementary aspects of a single divine entity). The burial chamber represented the location of this crucial reanimation and the mummy of the king lay there encased in multiple containers – shrines, sarcophagi of stone and (as the intact tomb of Tutankhamun revealed) up to three anthropoid coffins, two made from gilded and inlaid wood and a third of solid gold. These coffins were great works of craftsmanship which represented the deceased ruler transformed into the guise of Osiris and enfolded in the protective wings of goddesses.

Fig. 32
Outer coffin of Bakenmut in the form of *sah* (British Museum, EA24792)

In the tombs of private individuals, the mortuary cult chapel and the burial chamber were still in close physical proximity. The chapel decoration focused on the provisioning of the dead (via a stela and a statue) and on the material adjuncts of a 'good burial', which were represented in images of the funeral procession. Other depictions reflected the owner's role in life, and were designed to confirm and perpetuate his or her social status beyond the threshold of death. The rock-cut burial chamber (usually without decoration, as in earlier periods) was stocked with material provisions – food, drink, clothing, household furniture – and also with magical images and texts to ensure transition into the afterlife. A new repertoire of spells had now taken the place of the older Coffin Texts: the spells for Going Forth by Day (known today as the Book of the Dead). The words were written on papyrus rolls and illustrated with equally powerful images (or 'vignettes'), and selected extracts were also placed on coffins. The form and decoration of non-royal coffins reflected the priorities of equipping the dead with magical forces to bring about their resurrection and safe passage into the afterlife. There was a strong perception that the dead person must be made self-sufficient to undertake this perilous journey.

At the beginning of the New Kingdom the decline of rectangular coffins continued, and the anthropoid coffin became the dominant form. The *rishi* type survived until the reign of Tuthmosis III (about 1480–1425 BC), but even before this, changing concepts had led to the development of a new type. The great rise of the anthropoid coffin can probably be explained by the increasing importance that was attached to identifying the deceased with Osiris. The shape and colouring of the coffin from the Eighteenth Dynasty onwards played a crucial role in promoting this identification. As the early anthropoid coffins of the Middle Kingdom (about 2010–1790 BC) show, the prototype image, both for Osiris and for the transfigured dead, was that of the *sah* – the body wrapped in pure white cloth, denoting the divine character of the person and expressing the regenerative transformation which they were believed to be undergoing. Another distinctive feature of the *sah* image was the depiction of the forearms and hands, folded crosswise on the breast. They were not always represented on the early coffins, but became increasingly usual over time. In the New Kingdom, the typical headdress of coffins was no longer the *nemes*, with its ambiguous royal associations, but the striated tripartite wig which all divinities are depicted wearing.

The early anthropoid coffins of the New Kingdom have a white-coloured background with a predominantly blue wig (see cat. 22), elements of the idealised divine image which can be traced back to the Middle Kingdom. Early in the reign of Tuthmosis III, a different colour scheme was adopted – a black background, shining with gold (real gold or yellow paint as a cheaper substitute) (see cat. 24). In the symbolic language of colour, black represented the fertile silt from which vegetation sprang, hence rebirth. This association of the colour was linked with Osiris, who was sometimes described as 'the black one'. Allusions to rebirth were also made by placing the deceased under the protection of Nut, mother of Osiris according to the cosmogony of Heliopolis and by extension the divine mother of all mortals. This relationship with Nut as eternal mother is among the most persistent themes of Egyptian coffin decoration; her image was painted on the lid, either in the form of a vulture or a female figure with outspread wings (see cat. 16), and she is addressed in an often-repeated text inscribed in the centre of the lid, in which the deceased calls on the goddess to descend and shield him or her, and to place him or her 'among the imperishable stars'. The new visual manifestation of the immortal dead that the anthropoid coffin enshrined was also applied to other kinds of funerary image, such as *shabti* figures and the miniature coffins which contained them.

Although rectangular coffins were now rarely used, some of their key design features were retained and transferred on to the surfaces of the anthropoid coffin. The grid pattern of text bands was adapted to the curved surfaces of the coffin, now reflecting the arrangement of the binding tapes which held the outer shroud of the mummy in place. But although older motifs were blended with the new physical form, there was a change of emphasis in the underlying meaning. The older concept which had linked the coffin with ideas of the house or tomb, and with provisioning and freedom of movement, was now no longer so influential, and hence some of the familiar features of rectangular coffins which expressed these ideas disappeared or were reduced in prominence. Offering lists, offering tables

Fig. 33
Spell 151 from the Book of the Dead of Muthetepti
(British Museum, EA10010)

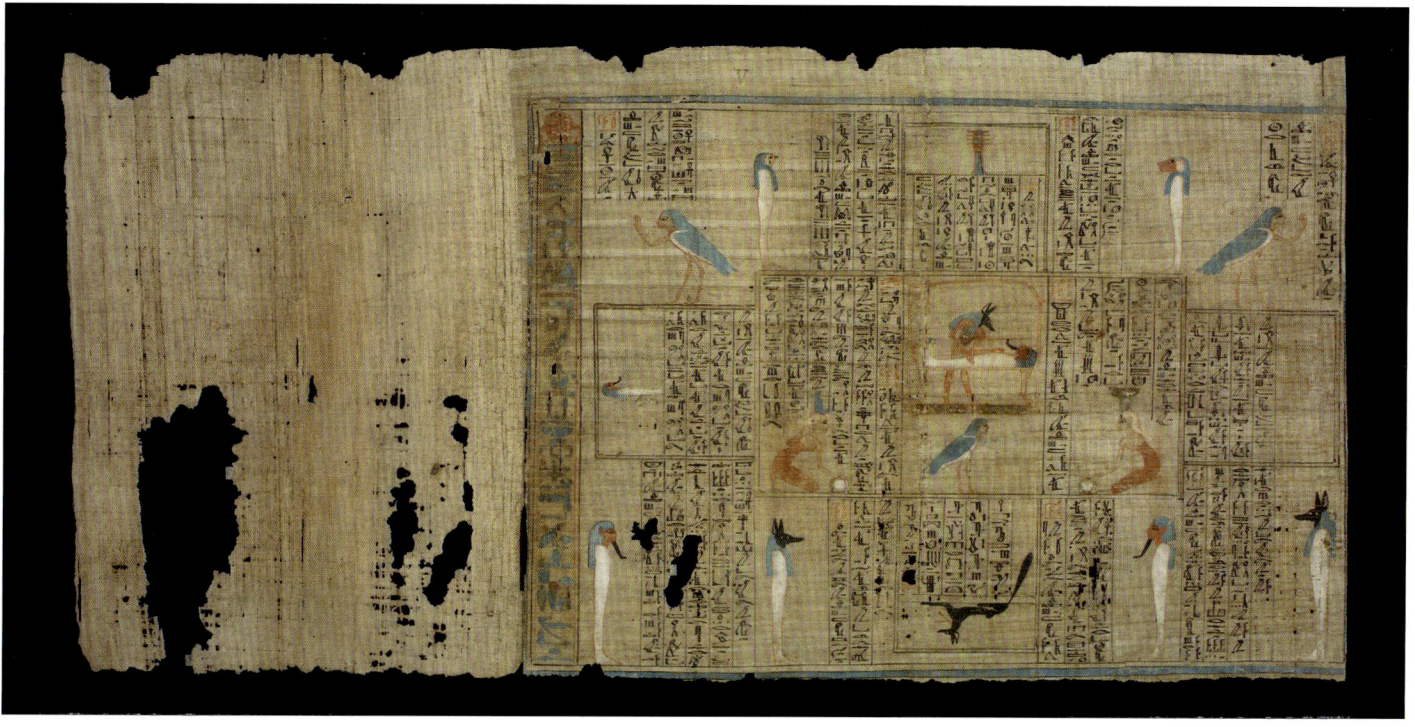

Fig. 34
The outer coffin of Henutmehyt (British Museum, EA48001), with representations of the jackal-headed god Anubis flanked by two of the Sons of Horus and two images of Thoth as an ibis-headed god

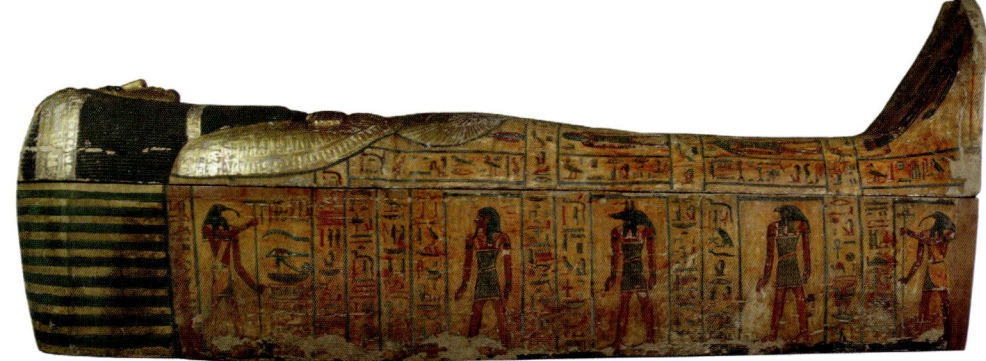

and object friezes no longer appeared, while the false door and the motif of the pair of eyes were simplified in form and reduced to secondary locations on anthropoid coffins. Surface decoration concentrated instead on the magical protection and resurrection of the Osiris-deceased.

The concept of the protective environment had a long history. It was already manifested on coffins of the Middle Kingdom through the inclusion of speeches by deities, which reflected rituals concerned with the embalming and resurrection of the deceased as Osiris. This idea was now developed, and found expression in a series of magical utterances and images, which were synthesised and incorporated into a text known today as spell 151 of the Book of the Dead. The vignette which accompanies these texts is a remarkable 'diagram' of the burial chamber of the tomb, with the deceased in the form of the mummified Osiris lying on a bier in the centre (fig. 33). The embalmer god Anubis stands at his side, having completed the preservation and purification of the body of the deceased, who is in a state of potential resurrection. All around are protective forces, to keep at bay the destructive agents of the god Seth, to ensure the physical integrity of the mummy and to facilitate its transformation into a fully resurrected being, freed from the confining wrappings. Isis and Nephthys kneel at the foot and head of the bier and the four Sons of Horus are positioned at the sides, together with four protective emblems. Each deity and emblem is accompanied by the words of a speech; they form a protective cordon around the deceased. In the Eighteenth and Nineteenth Dynasties it is clear that this sacred environment was held to be so important that it was magically realised by disposing the main elements of spell 151 on the surface of the coffin, turning a two-dimensional picture into a three-dimensional reality, and forging a direct conceptual link between the mummy inside the coffin and Osiris (fig. 34). For this reason, Isis and Nephthys are regularly painted at the foot and head of the coffin, while on each side of the case containing the body are two of the sons of Horus and a figure of Anubis, their speeches occupying the adjacent columns of inscription. The protective emblems are omitted; instead, on many coffins, the decorative scheme is completed by two figures of the god Thoth located on each side. These figures belong to another text from the Book of the Dead, spell 161, which alludes to the physical uniting of the deceased's body parts and the triumph of the sun god Re over his enemy Apophis. After this victory, during Re's nocturnal journey through the underworld, Thoth opens the sky to enable the sun god to ascend to the heavens, a journey in which the deceased can also take part.

The creation of this ideal environment in the tomb was the end point of a sequence of rituals which were enacted between death and burial. Aspects of this lengthy process were prominently depicted in images on the walls of tomb chapels and on papyri. From these depictions we learn that the coffin played a key role in the transference of the deceased from one world to the next. On the day of burial the coffin was transported to the tomb under a catafalque mounted on a sledge. It was then set upright at the entrance to the tomb, where, under the life-giving solar rays, it was the focus of a public display of lamentation by the dead person's family (fig. 35). Here took place the all-important ritual known as the Opening of the Mouth and Eyes, a symbolic reanimation of the mummified body. This was actually performed on the mummy, but in formal depictions it is often the anthropoid coffin that is receiving the ritual, indicating that the coffin had come to be regarded as the external form of the reborn deceased. Indeed, as a substitute body, or receptacle for the spirit, the anthropoid coffin itself underwent an Opening of the Mouth at the completion of the manufacturing process in the craftsman's workshop. When the rituals at the tomb were completed, the mummy in its coffin was placed in a recumbent position in the burial chamber; in this dark and usually unadorned space, the iconography on the coffin surface magically generated the required sacred environment.

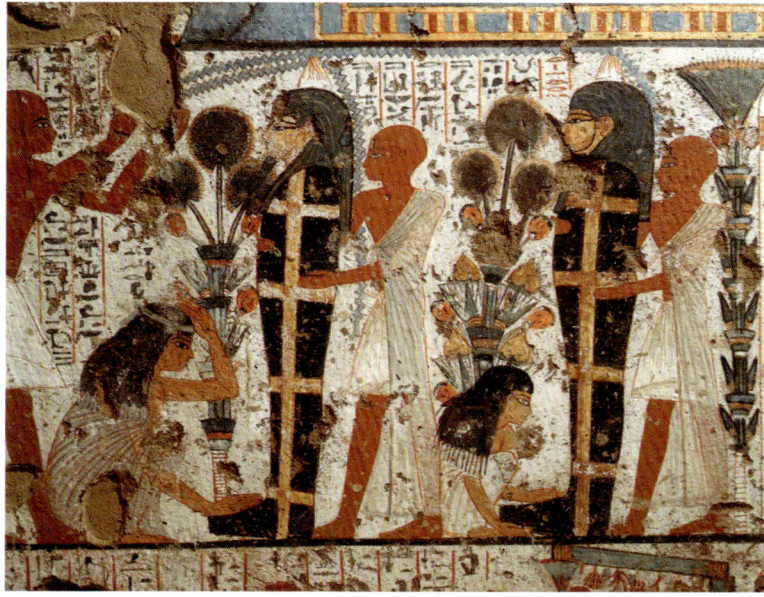

Fig. 35
Wall painting from the tomb of Nebamun and Ipuky at Thebes, showing mourners with two coffins during funeral rituals

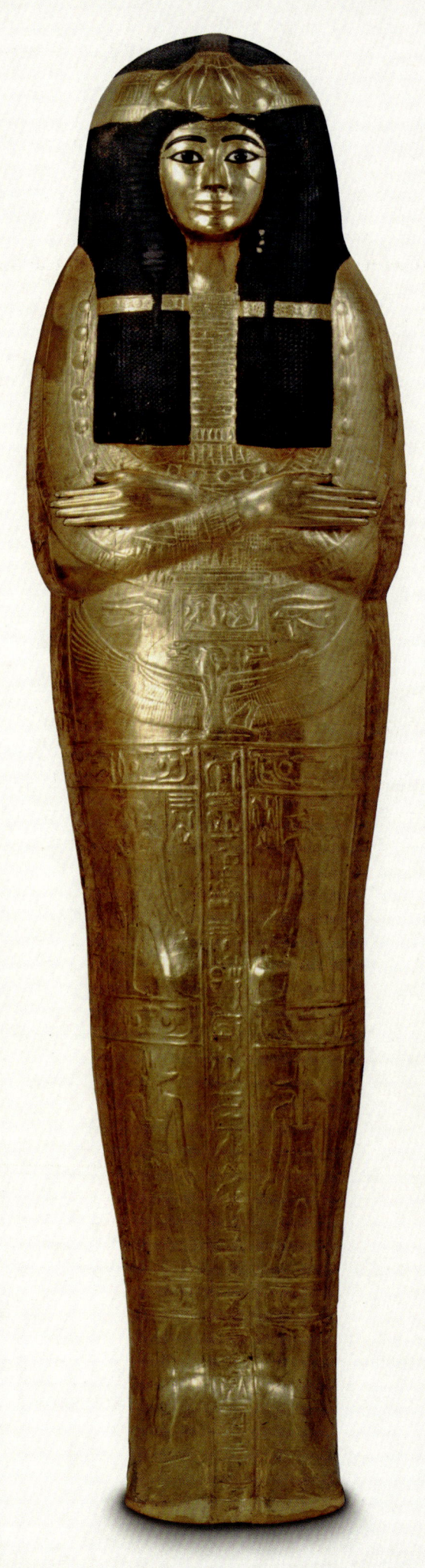

Fig. 36
The gilded inner coffin of Henutmehyt (British Museum, EA48001)

The coffin, then, acted as an interface between two worlds. It represented the actual form of the divine deceased, but through the images and texts on its surface it was also a part of the surrounding environment, the sacred space in which the deceased existed for eternity. The virtue of placing magical texts and images on the coffin is explained in the rubric to spell 72 of the Book of the Dead: 'As for him who knows this book on earth, or it is put in writing on the coffin, it is my word that he shall go out into the day in any shape that he desires.' Moreover, the function of the coffin as a point of contact between worlds is hinted at in several New Kingdom sources: wall paintings of funeral ceremonies show a dead man's coffin being embraced by his widow and, in a remarkable literary text, the scribe Butehamun writes a letter to the coffin of his dead wife Ikhtay: 'O noble chest of the Osiris, the chantress of Amun, Ikhtay, who rests under you. Listen to me, send the message and say to her, since you are close to her: "How are you doing? How are you?" It is you [the coffin] who shall say to her: "Woe, you are not sound," so says your brother, your companion...' Here the coffin is defined as a means of communication between the living and the dead; perhaps as an idealised image of the dead person it shared something with statues and ancestor busts as a focus for contact.

The reign of Akhenaten (about 1352–1336 BC) was marked by a radical and dislocating shift in the long-established pattern of Egyptian religious practice, as the king sought to reject the plurality of the ancient gods and to replace their cults with the worship of the sun in the form of the shining solar disc (Aten). In this phase, when the royal residence was relocated to el-Amarna, traditional concepts of afterlife were overturned; the deceased was not resurrected as Osiris but simply continued to live in another sphere of existence by the power of the sun and by receiving offerings. However, centuries-old tradition was strong; recent excavations in the cemetery of the lower-status inhabitants at el-Amarna have recovered coffins from this period showing that they continued to be made in anthropoid form with the same basic surface treatment and the same colouring (black and yellow) as before. While traditional texts and images of gods were replaced by repetitive scenes of the deceased offering to the Aten – in which the deceased was now more often depicted as a living person, not as a *sah* – a jackal-headed god appears on one coffin from this cemetery, showing that even at Amarna, adherence to ancient belief was not easily eradicated.

Akhenaten's revolution was deeply unpopular, and after his death the old traditions of cult and divine worship were restored. His innovations, however, did leave marks on religion, iconography and written language. Soon after the end of the Amarna phase, innovations in coffins are seen (some of which may have had their origins before the reign of Akhenaten). The exterior colouring changed from the contrasting black and gold (or black and yellow) to a polychrome decoration on a yellow background. The yellow was symbolically

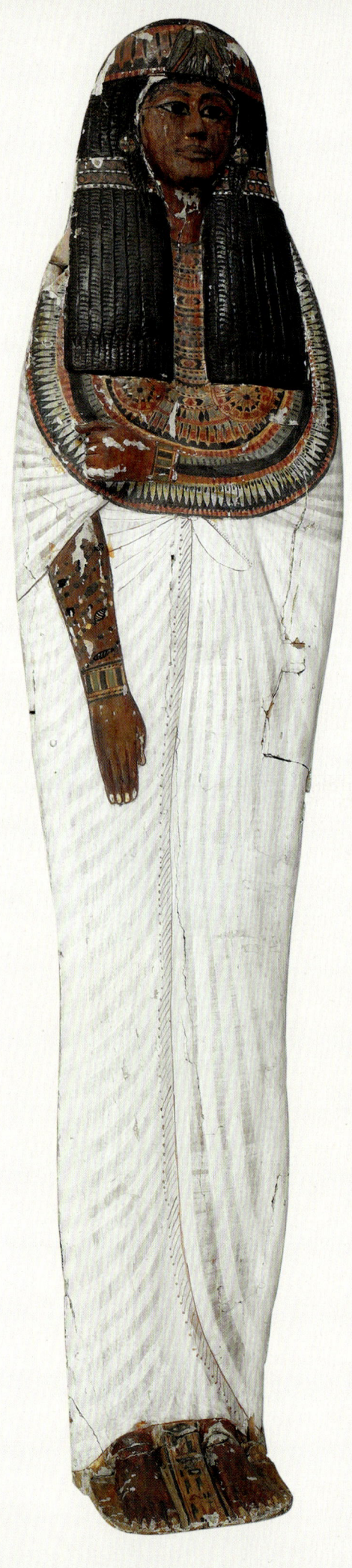

Fig. 37
A mummy board showing its owner, Iineferti, in a fringed garment of fine linen, with an elaborate collar and headdress (Metropolitan Museum of Art, New York, 86.1.5c)

associated with the rays of the sun, and the underlying concept is that of the deceased revivified by the life-giving solar rays. This idea was not in itself new but was now given greater emphasis, and the dazzling effect of the coffins was enhanced by the use of a shiny yellowish varnish on the painted surfaces. This varnish, shown by analysis to consist of pistacia resin, was also used as incense in temple ritual; its Egyptian name, *senetjer*, 'that which makes divine', may point to a second function in the funerary sphere, to confer godlike qualities on the deceased. For persons of high status, gold leaf was applied to the coffin, either to the face or, more rarely, over the whole surface (fig. 36).

The first two centuries of production of these so-called yellow coffins correspond to the Nineteenth and Twentieth Dynasties (about 1290–1070 BC), a time of change in Egypt's prosperity and international prestige, as the strong rule of Sety I and Ramesses II was succeeded by a descent into weakening royal power and economic instability. There is no evidence for a decline in the production of coffins, but, perhaps as a consequence of the persistence of this economic stress, comparatively few examples have survived from this period (for reasons, see below). However, it is known that a 'complete' assemblage comprised two anthropoid coffins, an inner (*wet*) and an outer (*wet aa*), inside which a human-shaped cover or 'mummy board' lay over the wrapped body. These mummy boards were of two main types. Earlier examples were in two parts – a mask, extended to include the depiction of the crossed arms, and a cover for the legs, representing the interconnecting text bands of the *sah* image, sometimes with figures of gods in openwork in the intervening spaces. These perforated covers enhanced the polychrome effect by allowing the outer mummy shroud (sometimes dyed a bright reddish colour) to appear through the apertures.

The second type of mummy board was radically different. It was a full-length image of the owner, represented as if alive, with hands and feet exposed, dressed in the elaborate headdress and garments that were worn on festal occasions, a costume which was associated with ritual (fig. 37). These images of 'daily life' occasionally appeared on the lid of the inner coffin, but more typically the lids depicted the owner in the traditional Osirian *sah* form. It has been conjectured that the 'daily life' mummy boards and lids are representations of the *akh* – the transfigured state which the deceased sought to attain at the end of the journey, after obtaining release from the mummy wrappings. The contrast between this image and that of the tightly bound and restricted *sah* – of the outer and inner coffin lids – is striking, and was evidently intended to emphasise that the deceased underwent transformation.

The gender of the coffin owner became more clearly marked in this period, with distinctively male and female types of headdress and different positions for the hands: clenched fists for men, fingers extended for women. Masculinity was also emphasised by the inclusion of a carved wooden beard, attached to the chin by means of a tenon. Representing a deceased male as Osiris was relatively straightforward, but since women were also equated with the god, and yet wished to retain their personal identity – including gender – the craftsmen who made the coffins were presented with a paradox. A solution sometimes adopted in this period was to equip women's coffins with indications of dual gender. This was reflected through the use of a reddish skin colouring (usually more appropriate to males in Egyptian artistic conventions), and the substitution of masculine for feminine grammatical forms in the inscriptions.

The ideal magical equipment that was thought necessary for resurrection was elaborate and costly, and was certainly not available to everyone; there is some evidence that access to certain rituals or items of equipment might have been restricted on grounds of status, but little can be said of this. Therefore people and/or their relatives had to choose how to use their resources, and that choice would affect the appearance of the coffin. There were clearly standard patterns, but no two coffins are identical; some were prefabricated and sold off the shelf, while others were commissioned, involving negotiations with craftsmen. From the New Kingdom, documents survive that relate to this process. They come almost entirely from Deir el-Medina (the community of specialist craftsmen who built and decorated the royal tombs) and record prices for making and decorating coffins of different types; costs varied according to the value of the materials used, the complexity of the decoration, the craftsmen's level of skill and the time required; the resulting agreement would determine the end product. The quality of coffins would have been a clear indication of the wealth and status of the deceased – and would have been apparent to the whole community at the funeral, when the coffin was visible. It also confirmed the social position of the dead in the afterlife, and hence there was a motivation for people to obtain the best work they could afford. It should be remembered that the majority of the population would have been too poor to afford a coffin of any kind; for those who could not aspire to wood, coffins were made from cheaper materials such as clay or basketry, usually without any decoration; another inexpensive solution was to wrap the body in a mat made of bundles of reeds or palm ribs.

The strong centralised government and internal cohesion of Egyptian society in the New Kingdom is reflected also in the funerary sphere. There is a notable uniformity in the conceptual role and style of coffins throughout the country, with strong similarities between those found in the Memphite area (close to present-day Cairo), in Middle Egypt, at Thebes, and even in cemeteries in Nubia, far beyond Egypt's southern frontier. In contrast, the 350 years of the Third Intermediate Period (about 1070–715 BC) that followed were marked by political disunity and economic stress. As the country became divided into smaller kingdoms and principalities, the personal authority of the ruler was eroded and access to material resources became more restricted, with a decline in the production of large temples and tombs. These changes had a direct impact on burial practices, which had to respond to the prospect of a more uncertain long-term provision for the dead. The personal and perpetual link between a deceased person and their 'house of eternity' was now broken. Few new tombs were constructed, and old sepulchres were more intensively reused, so the sacred environment formerly provided by the tomb decoration was either unavailable or had to be shared with others in communal burials. In consequence, the coffin now assumed the role of the deceased's personal cosmos to a greater extent than ever before.

During the first part of this phase, the Twenty-first Dynasty (about 1070–945 BC) the outward form of coffins remained little altered, with persons of high status having an outer and inner anthropoid coffin, decorated in polychrome on a yellow background and highly varnished (see fig. 32). However, the content of the decoration reflected the changes that were in progress. The mummy board remained a standard element of the assemblage, but, like the coffin lids, it now depicted the deceased in the mummified form of the *sah*. The image of the deceased as *akh*, which had been popular in the Nineteenth Dynasty, disappeared or was reduced to a much less conspicuous form.

Although the deceased was still identified with Osiris, the coffin's role in realising the protected space around the bier, as represented in spell 151 of the Book of the Dead, was superseded by different concepts. The iconography of the coffin surfaces now became sharply focused on the process of rebirth through the complementary relationship between Osiris and the sun god Re, a concept which had informed the decoration of royal tombs in the New Kingdom and which now became the key to immortality for the king's subjects as well. The coffins are covered with images of the solar disc, the scarab beetle, and the sun god in falcon-headed and ram-headed form, besides many depictions of Osiris

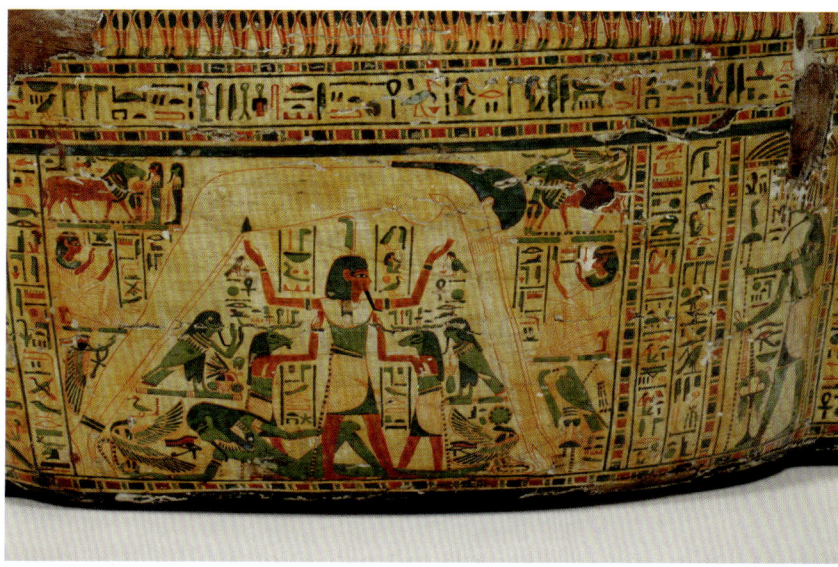

Fig. 38
Detail from the inner coffin of Nespawershefyt (cat. 26). The arched form of Nut, the sky goddess, is held above the earth, Geb, by the god of the air called Shu

and his entourage of deities. Some scenes were drawn from older models, while others were newly created. Among those which recur most frequently are the creation of the universe through the separation of Geb and Nut, symbolising the eternal renewal of the creative cycle (fig. 38); Osiris enthroned on a stepped mound; Osiris on a bed, awakening to new life; the Hathor cow emerging from the slopes of the western mountain; and the tree-goddess 'lady of the sycamore', feeding the deceased. These and other scenes are repeated in varying positions on the sides of the coffin cases, and much the same repertoire of images also appears on funerary papyri of the same period. In order to make the most effective use of space, the interior surfaces of the coffin case (and often the back of the mummy board) were also painted, often with a large *djed*-pillar (a symbol of Osiris) or a figure of the Goddess of the West (a form of Hathor) on the floor (see fig. 2), and rows of divine figures representing the many different incarnations of the sun god on the side walls. There is much repetition, but there is also a clear effort to condense magically charged meaning into a small compass: spells and prayers are reduced to brief incipits (opening words), and complex images are simplified, or merged, blending two or more scenes into a single new composition.

In contrast to the relatively slow pace of evolution in the prosperous New Kingdom, the Twenty-first Dynasty (about 1070–945 BC) was a period of concentrated inventiveness in funerary iconography. It is striking that this development occurred within a context of severe economic strain, which perhaps itself gave impetus to the search for new ways of expressing ideas in a concise form. Another effect of this stress was a shortage of the resources which rulers had traditionally relied upon to demonstrate their authority and integrity. The army commanders who ruled southern Egypt from Thebes, using the title of high priest of Amun, were constrained to dismantle the royal burials of the New Kingdom, turning the gold-stocked tombs in the Valley of the Kings into a 'bank' to support a weak economy and to stabilise their own authority. Ancient royal coffins were appropriated and stripped of gold, and some were reconditioned and used again for members of the new ruling families. This recycling of coffins was not an isolated phenomenon. Good-quality wood, suitable for the construction of coffins, was always a scarce commodity in Egypt. A high proportion of the coffins which were provided for burials at Thebes in this period show clear signs of having been used before. On some, the painted and varnished surface conceals an earlier layer of decoration which has been covered over (see, e.g., cat. 25). Inscriptions frequently were altered to place a new name over that of a previous owner and, where the sex of the second occupant differed from that of the first, the visible marks of gender – style of headdress, position of hands and presence or absence of false beard – were also altered. Radiography is revealing that in some instances old wooden coffins were completely dismantled and their components used to build new ones (see cat. 26).

In circumstances such as these, one could no longer confidently expect that one's body would remain forever in the same coffin, nor could one even be sure of having a permanent resting place. Coffins and mummies of royal persons were moved from tomb to tomb in the Theban necropolis and grouped together in caches, perhaps for ease of protection as the threat of robbery and state-authorised asset stripping prevailed. The mummies of members of priestly families were also gathered into communal tombs, a process which reached its culmination in the tenth century BC (end of the Twenty-first and beginning of the Twenty-second Dynasty). Several of these group burials have been discovered at Thebes, the largest being the Bab el-Gasus at Deir el-Bahri, which contained the remains of 153 members of the clergy of Amun in single and double coffins.

In the second half of the tenth century BC, the interior surfaces of the coffins began to be decorated in a manner that reflected a closer affinity with the architectural space of the tomb. At the same time, the external image of the deceased on the lid was more emphatically 'mummified': the collar, composed of many rows of flower petals and buds, grew larger, covering the arms so that only hands protruded, and a red leather band (or *stola*; see cat. 37), an element of the mummy trappings which equated the deceased with Osiris, was painted on the breast as well. This was, however, the final stage in the evolution of the yellow-varnished coffins; they ceased to be produced in the reign of Osorkon I (925–890 BC), being replaced by coffins of a distinctly different style. The wooden coffins continued in anthropoid shape but were much simpler in design, representing the shrouded body with only the head emerging, the arms and hands commonly omitted. Below a small decorative collar there was usually a central line of inscription, sometimes flanked by large figures of deities but often without any other decoration. An assemblage might include one, two or (rarely) three such coffins, but the mummy board was now discontinued, and the innermost covering of the body was a closely fitting envelope or case made of cartonnage.

These cartonnage cases were made according to a sophisticated process (see also pages 92-93), whereby layers of linen soaked in glue or gum were moulded around a mummy-shaped core of mud and straw. The core was then removed, leaving a hollow shell into which the wrapped body was inserted and secured by means of string passed through a series of holes along the rear flaps. A wooden footboard was pegged or tied into place to seal the case completely, and the outer surface was brilliantly decorated with religious scenes and texts on a layer of fine paste (fig. 39). Modern experimentation aimed at replicating the constructional technique has suggested that the fabric of the case would have hardened quickly, making it impossible to remove it from the mummy without damage, and it may be no accident that the introduction of these cartonnages coincides with an end to the practice of recycling coffins, which had been prevalent throughout the previous centuries. By eliminating the possibility of reusing the cartonnage,

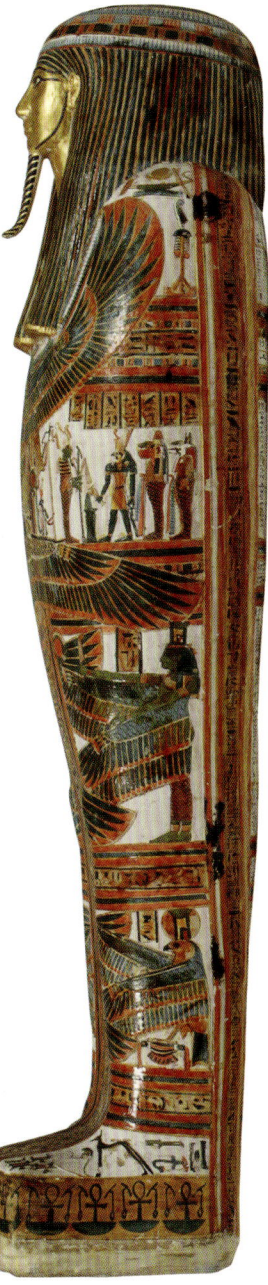

Fig. 39
The brightly coloured cartonnage mummy case of Nakhtefmut (cat. 32)

one could ensure that the magically charged iconography and text on its surface would continue to function for the wellbeing of the deceased, even if the outer wooden coffins should be taken away.

The cartonnage case was simultaneously the outer surface of the mummy and the innermost layer of the coffin ensemble. Its decoration was markedly different from that of the yellow-varnished coffins. The themes of resurrection and solar-Osirian unity were still represented, but now through more generic images, painted on a larger scale. The cartonnage of Nakhtefmut, priest of Amun, discovered in a cemetery at the Ramesseum temple at Thebes, perfectly illustrates the typical decoration (cat. 32; see fig. 39). The striated divine headdress and curled beard indicate that Nakhtefmut is in *sah* form, and the gilded face adds confirmation of his divine status. The front of his body is completely enfolded in the protective wings of deities; on the torso are two large falcons representing different manifestations of the sun god (the upper one with the head of a ram), and lower down, Isis and Nephthys are represented twice – first in human shape and then as kites (*djerty*), the bird forms which they assumed as mourners for their dead brother Osiris. Across the breast, the gods Horus and Thoth honour Osiris in two forms, in mummified human shape and as his fetish, the emblem of his cult centre at Abydos. The sun god is also alluded to, in the central inscription and through the two barques in which he traverses the day and night sky, which are depicted on the shoulders.

Although Nakhtefmut's outer coffins of wood have not survived, comparable examples from other burials are quite simple in design. The most prominent and striking motif they display is the full-length figure of the goddess Nut, who was depicted on the floor of the coffin case (fig. 40). These Nut figures are often painted in frontal view, a rare phenomenon in Egyptian art, and their arms are extended on to the sides of the coffin to represent a symbolic embrace. The significance is clear: when the mummy is placed in the coffin, the deceased is located symbolically inside the womb of the great mother-goddess. Nut was not only the mother of Osiris; as the personification of the sky, she swallowed the sun each evening and gave birth to it again at dawn. The deceased, then, was equated with both Osiris and Re and was positioned at the centre of an ever-repeating cycle of rebirth.

The coffin assemblages of men and women were very similar in this period, but the distinction of gender is always apparent in the colouring of the face (red for men, yellow or pale pink for women) and in the type of headdress. While males retained the striated tripartite wig, females were now often depicted wearing the vulture headdress, a sign of divine status and perhaps an early step in the evolving tendency to identify the deceased woman with Hathor as the feminine counterpart of Osiris.

The assemblage of cartonnage case plus relatively simple anthropoid coffins seems to have spread rapidly throughout Egypt. The best-preserved examples

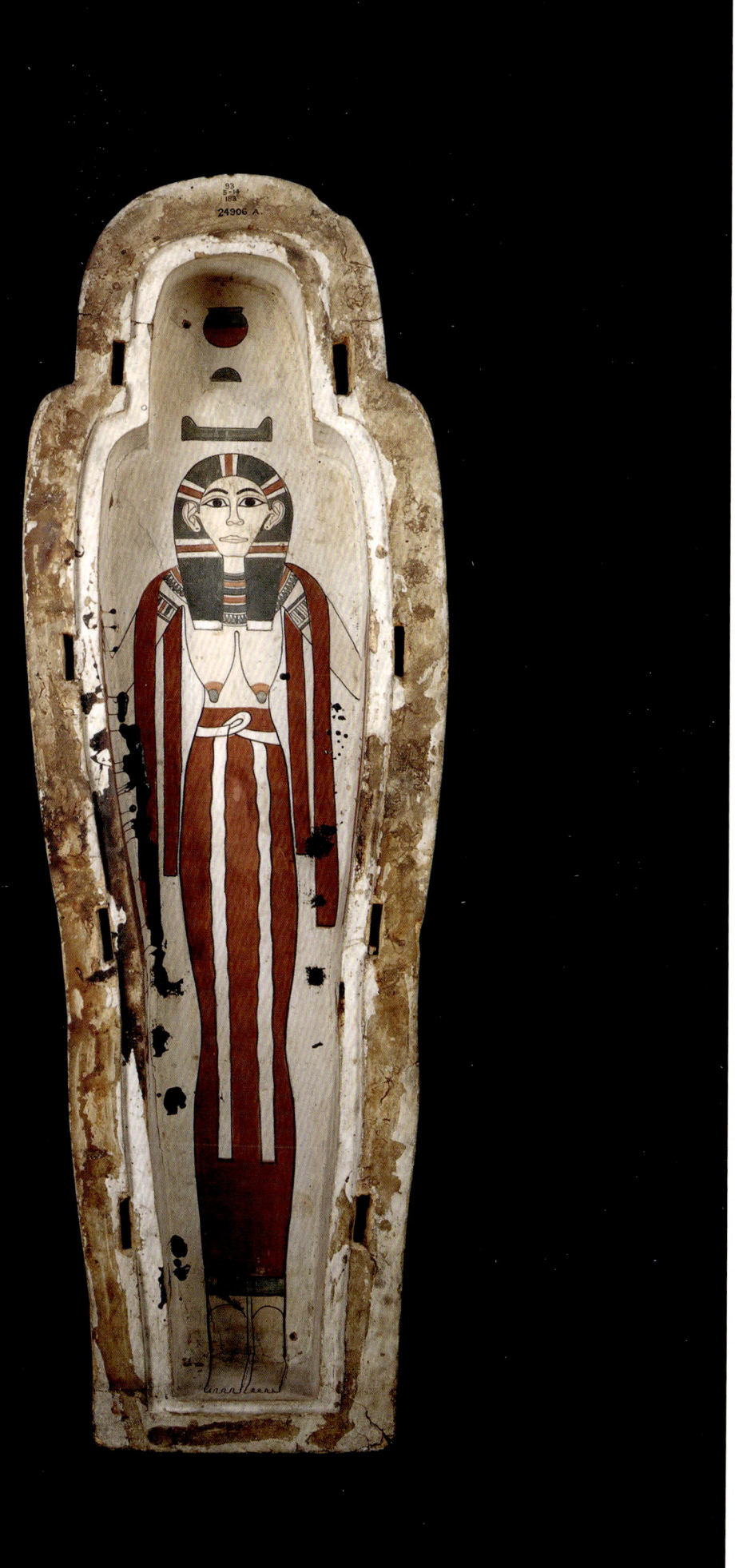

Fig. 40
Full-face figure of Nut on the interior of the coffin of Pensenhor (British Museum, EA24906)

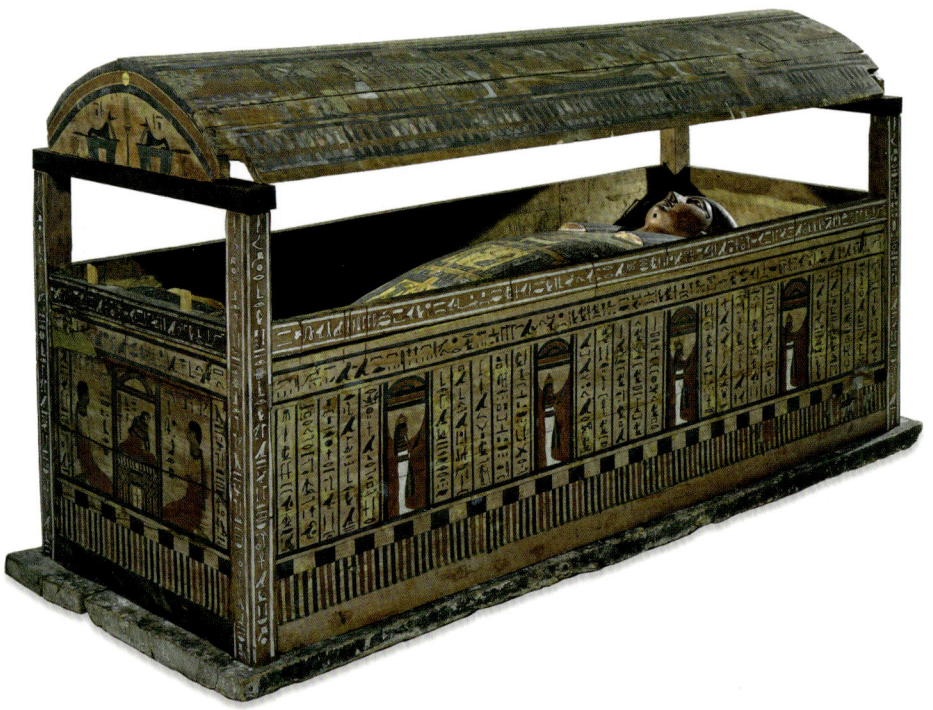

Fig. 41
Rectangular outer coffin of Hor (British Museum, EA15655), with a vaulted lid and four corner posts

have been found at Thebes, but they are attested at several sites further to the north, such as Meidum, Sedment, Lahun, Beni Hasan and Akhmim. This style of burial may in fact have had its origins in the north (perhaps even in the Nile Delta), spreading to the south in the second half of the tenth century BC, when a new line of rulers brought a more strongly unified government – one effect of which was to end the virtual independence of the southern principality based around Thebes. Nevertheless, stylistic distinctions point to the continuation of independent development in the southern and northern regions of the Nile Valley; northern coffins are recognisable by their proportions (with large wigs, small faces and a rather simple body shape), distinctive text formula, and certain iconographic traits, such as the depiction of the hands with flower motifs or patterns of beading on the surface.

The takeover of Egypt by the rulers of the Kushite kingdom (northern Sudan) in the late eighth century BC had a unifying and revitalising effect on culture. The Kushites exhibited a profound respect for traditional Egyptian beliefs (particularly the worship of Amun), and devoted special attention to Thebes and the cults of Amun and Montu, the local gods. Their interest in revivals of the past seems to have stimulated a renaissance in funerary culture, with the revival of the Book of the Dead (which had fallen into abeyance). It is in the cemeteries of Thebes that new developments in coffin styles can be traced. A new style of burial assemblage is attested for members of the high elite, in which three coffins of different forms were combined. The outer coffin was made of wood, and imitated the traditional form of the tomb of Osiris, with a vaulted top and an upright post at each corner (fig. 41); it is sometimes referred to as a *qersu* coffin. In depictions of the Osiris tomb, falcons perch on the top, and these were now represented by carved wooden figures placed on the corner posts (see fig. 100, p. 214). Within this shrine-like structure, Osiris lay confined in his shroud and surrounded by divine protectors. Here he was revived from his inert state by his son Horus, and is shown raising his head to signify his reawakening to life.

The coffin assemblages represent an adaptation of this model. The mummy was placed in an inner coffin in *sah* shape, lying on its back, and instead of the cartonnage case made in a single piece, this inner casing was of wood, made in two parts which fitted together like the halves of a shell (hence the modern term 'bivalve coffin'; fig. 42). The exterior surface was densely covered with texts and images of deities, many of them the protectors who watched over Osiris in the nocturnal vigil preceding the day of burial. Although the inner coffin was positioned horizontally, its iconography also presents a vertical aspect; it was provided with a back pillar and a plinth so that it could stand upright like a statue, conveying the notion of resurrection. It is likely that the inner coffin was placed upright during the Opening of the Mouth ceremony, but since depictions of the funeral are rare at this period, this can only be conjectured. The conceptual relationship between the different components of the assemblage is expressed more clearly than in earlier periods. Following his awakening, the reanimated Osiris leaves his tomb and ascends to the sky to enter the day and night barques of the sun god; appropriately, the two barques are depicted on the exterior of the lid of the outer coffin, while on some examples the interior surface carries a large image of Nut and the goddesses who personify the hours.

Whereas the outer and inner coffins of these assemblages were highly decorated with polychrome images and inscriptions, the design of the middle or intermediary coffin was of a contrasting simplicity. It offered a rough approximation of the human body, with head and foot depicted, but with a flat base and only sparse decoration against a surface of unpainted wood. However, on the most elaborate examples the environment of the Hall of Judgement is recreated, with the scene of the weighing of the heart and the forty-two deities who heard the deceased proclaim his innocence of wrongdoing in his lifetime. The episode (described in spells 30B and 125 of the Book of the Dead) was a crucial stage in the deceased's passage to the afterlife. It was often depicted on papyri and tomb walls in the New Kingdom and appeared on some coffin cases in the Twenty-first Dynasty, but it only became an important part of the iconography of coffins in the Twenty-fifth Dynasty (745–664 BC). The positioning of this subject between the inner coffin (representing the awakening deceased) and the outer coffin (representing the sacred space of the tomb and the ascent to the sky) probably reflects the notion that the judgement was a transitional phase in the passage to eternal life.

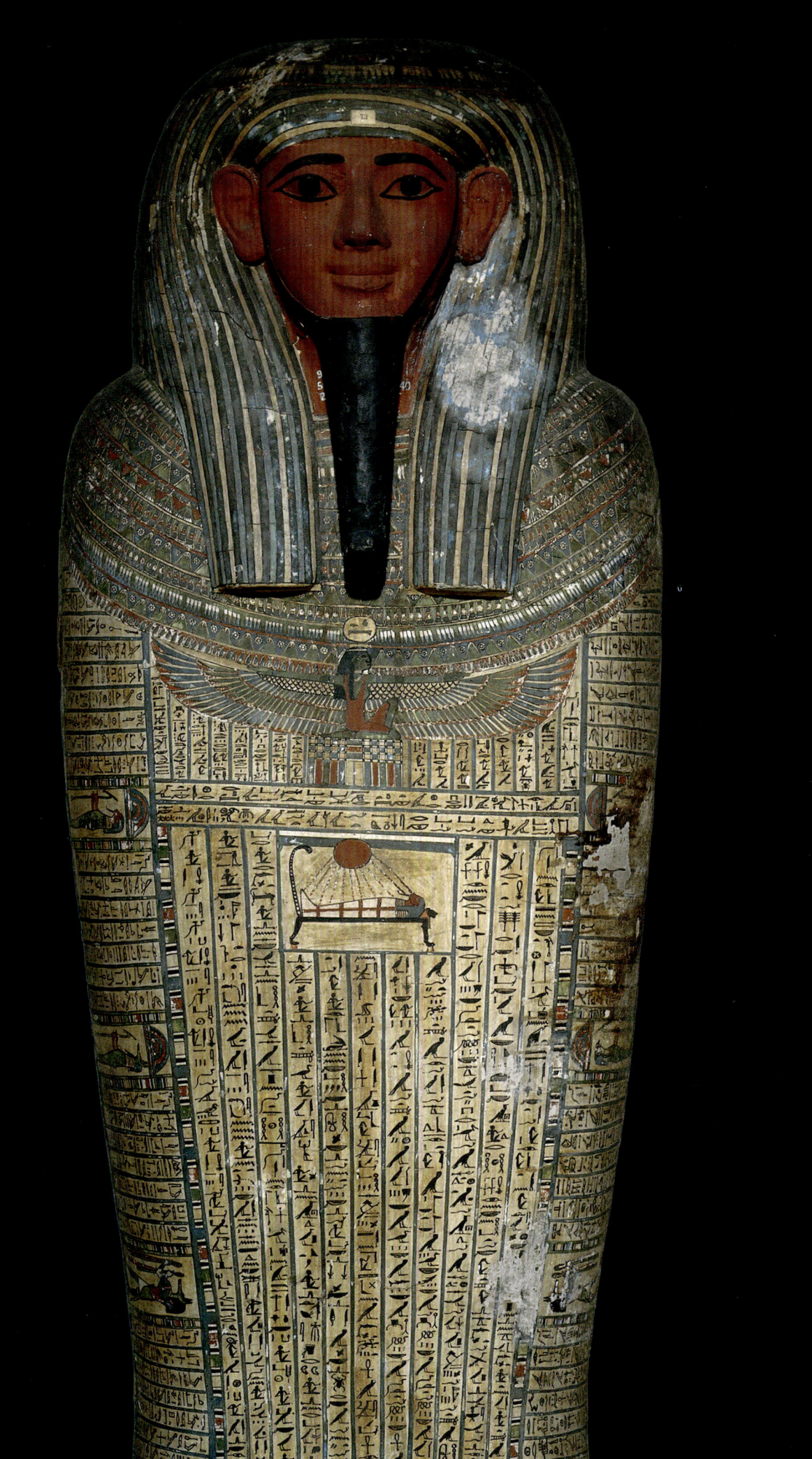

This type of coffin assemblage continued to be made for persons of high status in the Twenty-sixth Dynasty (664–525 BC). Many examples have been found which belonged to members of the higher-ranking clergy of Amun and Montu, the attendants of the God's Wife of Amun (the senior priestess at Thebes) and relatives of such influential officials as the governor Montuemhat. Although the finest examples of these coffins are from Thebes, similar sets have been discovered in other parts of Egypt, and some of these exhibit regional variations in iconography, probably pointing to the existence of local craft traditions.

There is little to differentiate between the coffins of males and females in this period, but distinctions can be recognised which correlate with the social status of the owners. At Thebes, coffins made for a 'lower elite' group, such as temple doorkeepers and slaughterers of sacrificial animals, can be identified. These assemblages usually lack the rectangular outer coffin, comprising instead three, two or sometimes only one anthropoid coffin per burial. Their iconography reflects essentially the same conceptual theme as the sets made for the 'higher elite', but the inscriptions are shorter and the repertoire of images is smaller, with more repetition in both text and image. A few particularly common scenes are painted on the lids of both inner and outer coffins: a simplified judgement (comprising just the weighing of the heart and the presentation of the deceased to a row of gods), the solar barque and the mummy lying on a bier. The two anthropoid coffins of Pakepu (cat. 43) are an example of this type of assemblage. Another common set of images recurs on the interior of the outer anthropoid coffins; here a large figure of the composite resurrection deity Ptah-Sokar-Osiris, shrouded and with the head of a falcon, occupies the floor (fig. 43), with Isis and Nephthys standing at each side as if in protection. Some features of the inner coffins appear also on those of the 'higher elite' group, such as the winged figure of Nut on the breast and a large *djed*-pillar on the back, promoting the idea of the physical resurrection of the deceased to a standing position. These bivalve inner coffins in fact closely resemble the statues of Ptah-Sokar-Osiris which at this period were among the few standard features of burial outfits.

Little is known of the role played by the coffins in the mortuary rituals at this period. At Thebes some officials were buried within the enclosures of major cult temples, such as Deir el-Bahri and Medinet Habu. These locations were probably reserved for privileged persons, and it is possible that the temple structures and the rituals performed there were believed to complement the magical force of the coffins. Other senior members of society possessed elaborate freestanding tombs, notably in the Asasif area, bordering the processional way to the temple of Deir el-Bahri. Some of these persons had stone coffins which in part copied the iconography of contemporary wooden coffins. The age-old custom of reusing older tombs also continued. Many of the New Kingdom sepulchres at Thebes have yielded coffins dating to later phases, particularly the Twenty-first,

Fig. 42
Inner bivalve coffin of Besenmut
(British Museum, EA2940)

Fig. 43
Ptah-Sokar-Osiris depicted on the base of one of the coffins of Pakepu (cat. 43)

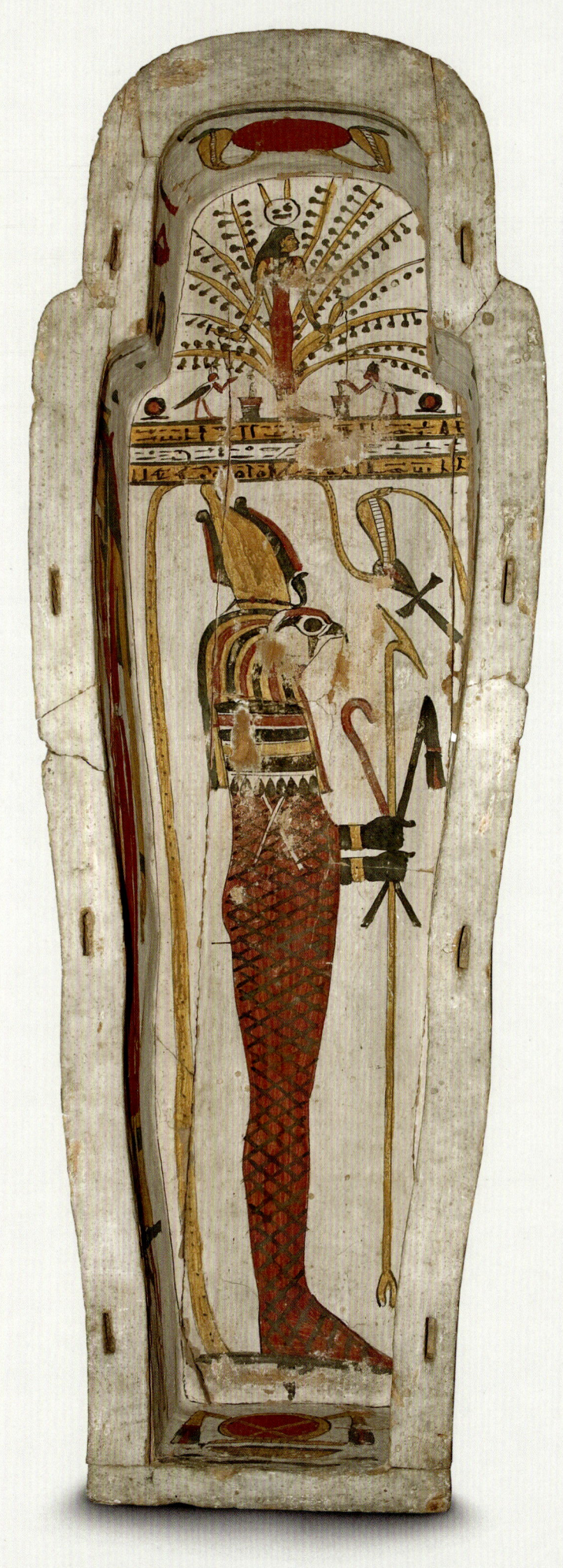

Twenty-second, and Twenty-fifth to Twenty-sixth Dynasties, and the Ptolemaic and Roman Periods. Some of these older tombs were clearly reassigned to particular families or social networks, since large family groups of coffins have been found together; Pakepu's coffins were discovered with those of some of his relatives. Although this may reflect limited availability of resources, there is little evidence for the recycling of coffins at this time. Coffins rarely show altered names or adapted features. This may indicate the renewed economic strength of Egypt or possibly a change in attitudes to burial, with the institution of a more rigorous management of cemeteries: they were now controlled by officials like Pakepu, later known as choachytes, who held responsibility for particular tombs at Thebes and looked after the cult of their occupants.

At the beginning of the period known as the First Persian Domination (525–401 BC), traditions of coffin style and decoration appear to have continued without a major interruption. Examples are traceable in tombs of elite persons in the Memphite necropolis, but a scarcity of well-dated coffins makes it difficult to follow a sequence of development through this period until the fourth century BC, when Egypt was returned to native rule. During the Thirtieth Dynasty (380–342 BC) there was a great intensity of new royal building work and a general atmosphere of the revival of cultural traditions. Something of this seems to be reflected in the styles of coffins, though it is not clear whether this represents continuity or renewal following a hiatus.

There is, however, an apparent continuity from the fourth century BC, through the brief Second Persian Domination (342–332 BC), and into the long period of rule by the Ptolemaic dynasty, the successors of Alexander the Great's general Ptolemy. The geographical distribution of the evidence for coffin styles differs from that of earlier periods, more material being preserved from sites in the northern part of Egypt – the Memphite necropolis and the Fayum area – while in the south, the city of Akhmim has yielded a large number of coffins, in contrast to the much less well-preserved material from Thebes.

Nevertheless, from the Theban necropolis come several funerary assemblages which illustrate how members of the elite were equipped for burial. That of the priest Hornedjitef, most of which is in the British Museum, is a good example (fig. 44). Dating to the middle or later years of the third century BC, Hornedjitef's assemblage included two anthropoid coffins of wood. The outer one is of massive proportions, with a large and grotesque face and a heavy, swollen body; the unrealistic proportions perhaps derived from the massive stone sarcophagi of the Late Period (715–332 BC). It also has a large plinth (now a standard feature of outer coffins). The second coffin, with gilded face, is a more accurate representation of the mummy form. It is adorned with a winged scarab and figures of the Sons of Horus, flanking an inscription containing a spell from the Book of the Dead. A frontal-view image of Nut occupies the interior of the lid, so that the deceased

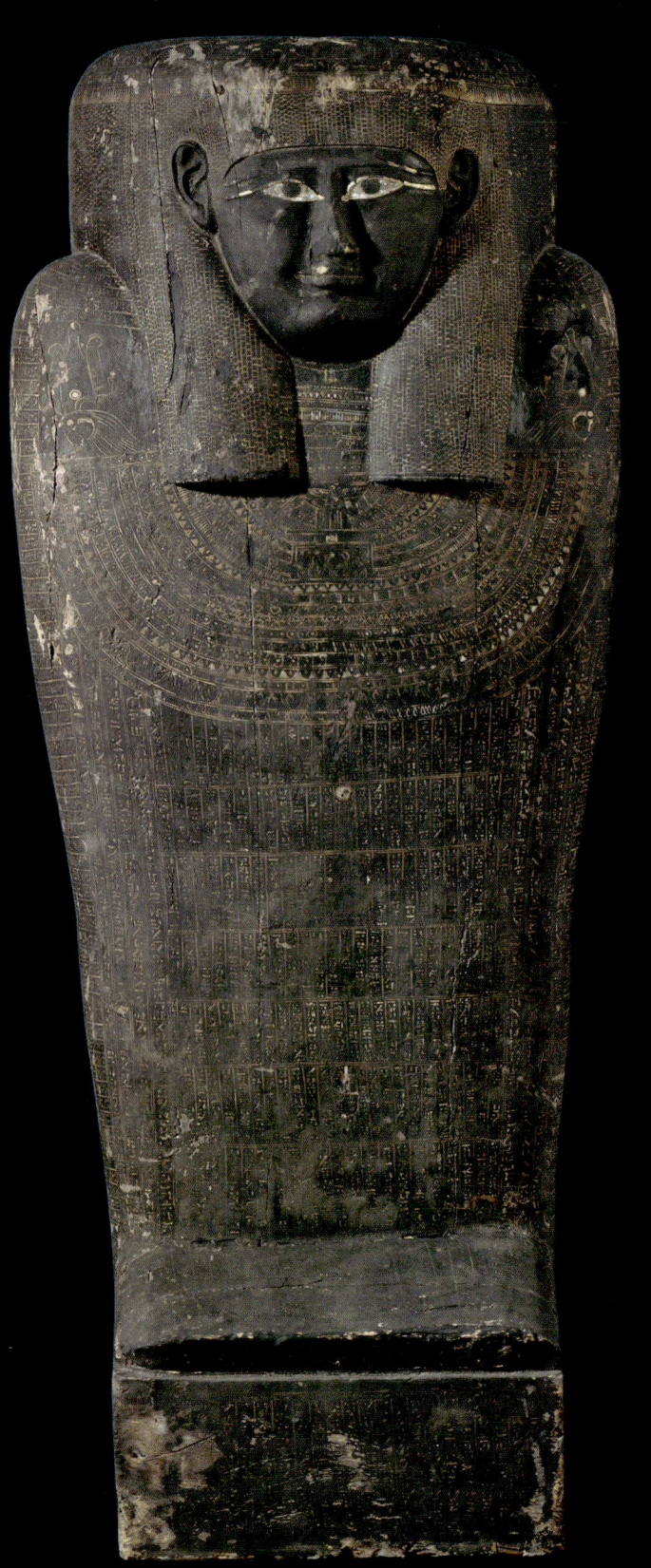
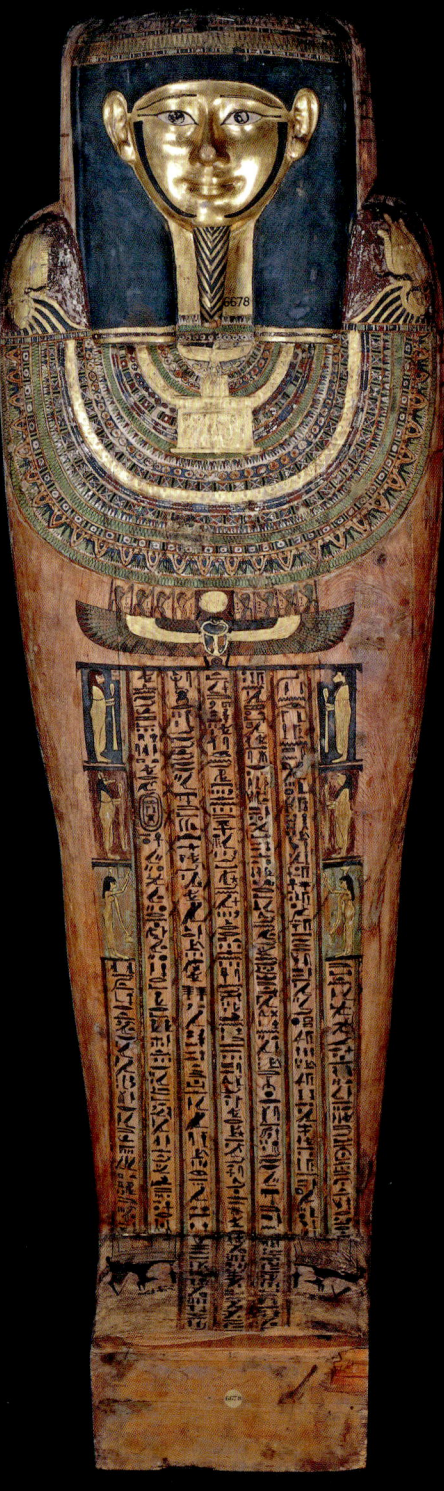

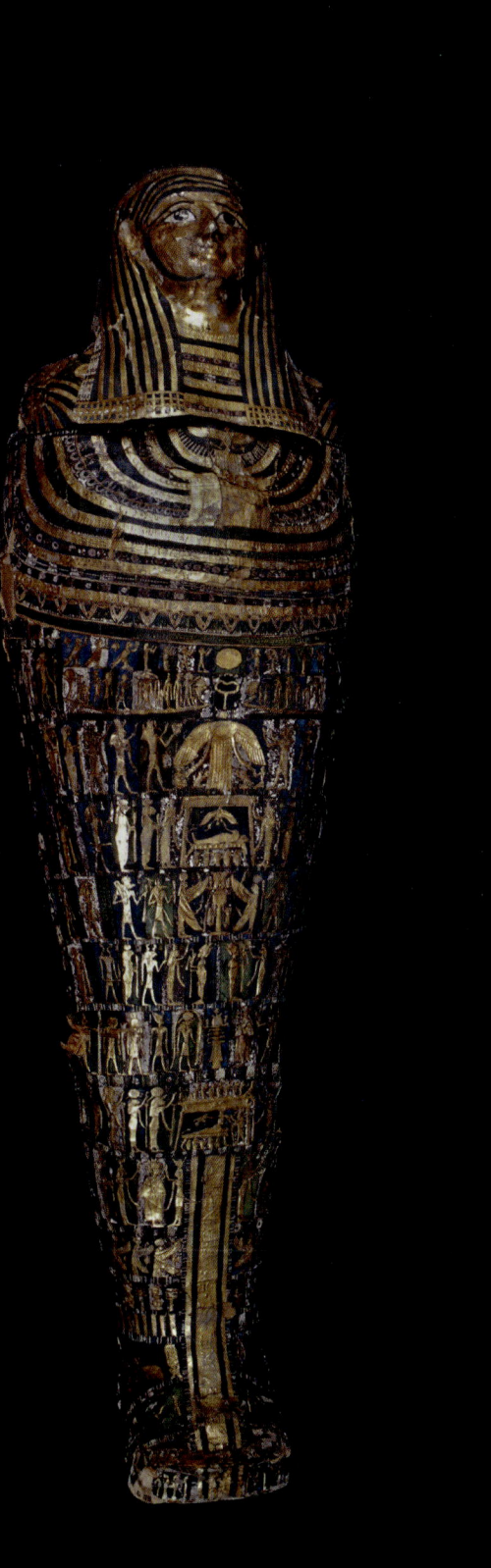

Fig. 44
Outer and inner coffins and cartonnage of Hornedjitef (British Museum, EA6677, EA6678 and EA6679)

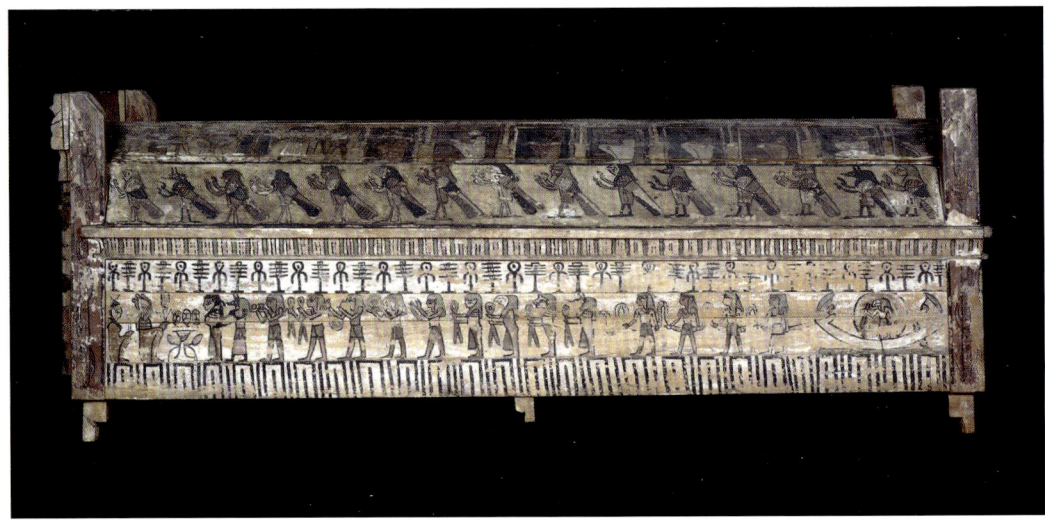

Fig. 45
Rectangular *qersu* coffin of a woman named Cleopatra, Roman Period (British Museum, EA6706)

would look into the face of the goddess, who is accompanied by astronomical images. The mummy was encased in a cartonnage cover fitting over the front, sides and feet, with a separate mask for the head. This cover is decorated with many small images drawn from the traditional funerary repertoire – the mummy on a bier, the winged scarab, Osiris and other deities – but a relatively new feature is the depiction of the *ba* (one of the aspects of the individual, approximately equivalent to the 'personality') in the form of a bird, depicted on the breast.

Contemporary coffins from Akhmim exemplify a broadly similar tradition, with an outer and inner anthropoid coffin of wood, and a mask and trappings on the mummy, usually comprising separate collar, breastplate, 'apron' and footcase of cartonnage. Coffins from many different sites can be assigned to this period on the basis of the relatively large head, the high position of the shoulders, and the very deep collar, positioned lower down the breast. There is a rather repetitive series of images, among which the mummy on the bier is notably common. The typological analysis of Late Period and Ptolemaic coffins has still to be completed, but preliminary studies indicate that there were distinct regional schools of painting and craftsmanship.

The period of Roman rule (30 BC–AD 395) witnessed the final flowering of the traditional elements of pharaonic burial practice, which now became increasingly interwoven with features of the culture of Greece and Rome. Mummification not only continued but became available to a broader spectrum of the population. Often the mummies were provided with masks or headpieces in various contrasting styles – cartonnage masks with idealised faces reflecting pharaonic tradition, plaster or gilded headpieces in Graeco-Roman style (see cat. 55.a), and the encaustic portraits on wooden panels which were entirely Roman in inspiration (see cat. 54). Such burials were often placed into the ground without coffins, but in others wooden coffins were still provided. The shrine-shaped *qersu* type with vaulted top and corner-posts was revived (fig. 45), decorated with debased versions of old motifs, such as the judgement and the solar barque. These coffins differed in construction from their earlier models, having a deep top which fitted into a baseboard on which the mummy lay. One-piece cartonnage mummy cases reappeared, although now more usually made from mud or recycled papyrus rather than textile. Some of these cases depicted the deceased as a living person wearing the fashionable dress of the day, a style of representation which also occurred on full-length painted shrouds which were wrapped around the mummy. However, with the growing dominance of the Christian church from the middle of the third century AD onwards, all such 'pagan' practices were increasingly discouraged, and the spread of an austerely simple style of burial marked the end of the rich tradition of ancient Egyptian coffins.

Further reading

Cooney, Kathlyn M. *The Cost of Death: The Social and Economic Value of Ancient Egyptian Funerary Art in the Ramesside Period*. Egyptologische Uitgaven 22. Leiden: Nederlands Instituut voor het Nabije Oosten, 2007.

Cooney, Kathlyn M. 'The Problem of Female Rebirth in New Kingdom Egypt: the Fragmentation of the Female Individual in Her Funerary Equipment.' In *Sex and Gender in Ancient Egypt*, edited by C. Graves-Brown, 1–25. Swansea: The Classical Press of Wales, 2008.

Frandsen, Paul John. 'The Letter to Ikhtay's Coffin: O. Louvre Inv. No. 698.' In *Village Voices: Proceedings of the Symposium 'Texts from Deir el-Medina and their Interpretation', Leiden, May 31–June 1, 1991*, edited by R. J. Demarée and A. Egberts, 31–49. Leiden: Centre of Non-Western Studies, Leiden University, 1992.

Miniaci, Gianluca. *Rishi Coffins and the Funerary Culture of Second Intermediate Period Egypt*. GHP Egyptology 17. London: Golden House Publications, 2011.

Niwinski, Andrzej. *21st Dynasty Coffins from Thebes: Chronological and Typological Studies*. Theben V. Mainz am Rhein: Verlag Philipp von Zabern, 1988.

Taylor, John H. 'Patterns of Colouring on Ancient Egyptian Coffins from the New Kingdom to the Twenty-sixth Dynasty: An Overview.' In *Colour and Painting in Ancient Egypt*, edited by W. V. Davies, 164–81, colour plates 50–56. London: British Museum Press, 2001.

Taylor, John H. 'Theban Coffins from the Twenty-second to the Twenty-sixth Dynasty: Dating and Synthesis of Development.' In *The Theban Necropolis: Past, Present and Future*, edited by N. Strudwick and J. H. Taylor, 95–121, plates 45–75. London: British Museum Press, 2003.

Van Walsem, Rene. *The Coffin of Djedmonthuiufankh in the National Museum of Antiquities at Leiden: Technical and Iconographic/Iconological Aspects*. Egyptologische Uitgaven 10. Leiden: Nederlands Instituut voor het Nabije Oosten, 1997.

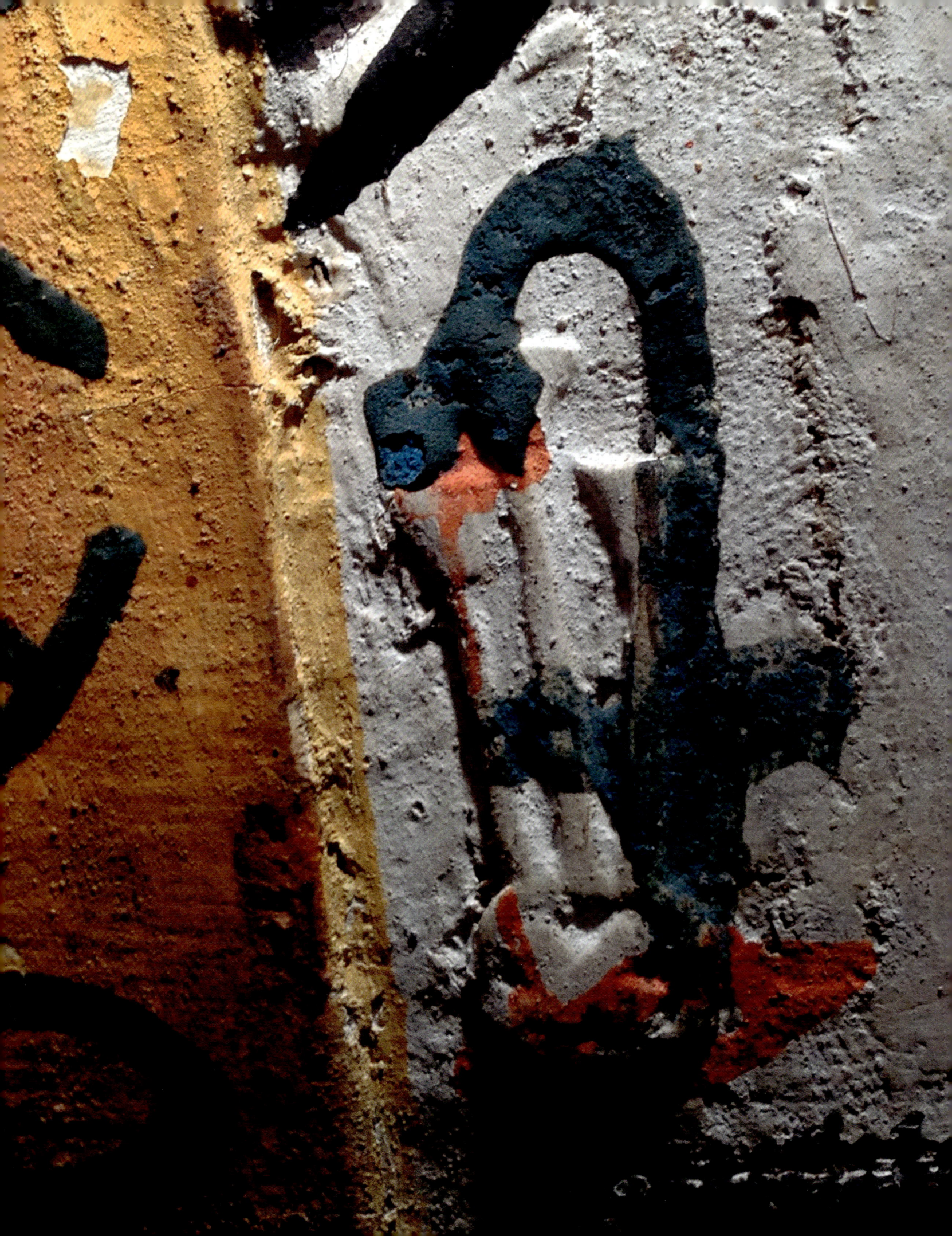

EGYPTIAN COFFINS

Materials, Construction and Decoration

Julie Dawson, Jennifer Marchant and Eleanor von Aderkas, with contributions from Caroline R. Cartwright and Rebecca Stacey

Introduction

The coffins in this exhibition present a snapshot of Egyptian craftsmen at work over a period of almost two and a half thousand years: working with assurance within a long technical tradition, dealing with the constraints and limitations of the available materials and experimenting with new ones when these came along, and responding to the economic and social circumstances of their masters and clients and the times in which they all lived. Egyptian coffins have been subjected to intensive scrutiny for many years by Egyptologists, studying their texts and iconography, but only relatively recently have systematic studies been undertaken that have employed the full range of imaging and analytical methods to investigate the materials and techniques used in coffin construction. This technical analysis, especially when viewed in the context of other craft traditions such as tomb painting, can greatly add to the story of the lives and concerns of the ancient Egyptians.

The most remarkable thing about Egyptian coffins is how many survive. However, it is important to recognise that the technical record has been skewed by accidents of preservation and by the actions of those who have come into contact with the objects since they were retrieved from burial. The materials may have deteriorated: for example, wood may have rotted due to the ingress of water into the tomb or been eaten by termites; pigments and varnishes may have changed chemically, affecting their colour. Early excavators, collectors and restorers often altered objects. The coffins of Nespawershefyt (cat. 26) are full of nineteenth-century ironmongery, and the wig of a limestone sarcophagus head (cat. 50) is overpainted with early twentieth-century restorations that cannot be removed without causing damage to the original paint. None of the Fitzwilliam

Fig. 46
Detail of relief decoration on the cartonnage coffin of Nakhtefmut (cat. 32). Raking light shows that the 'northern Egypt' hieroglyph is carved into the plaster here, but the artist who painted the inscription chose to write the hieroglyph for 'southern Egypt' over it.

Fig. 47
Head of the leopard skin depicted on the shabti box of Hornefer and Taqa (cat. 10), photographed at x30 magnification to reveal details of the painting materials and techniques.

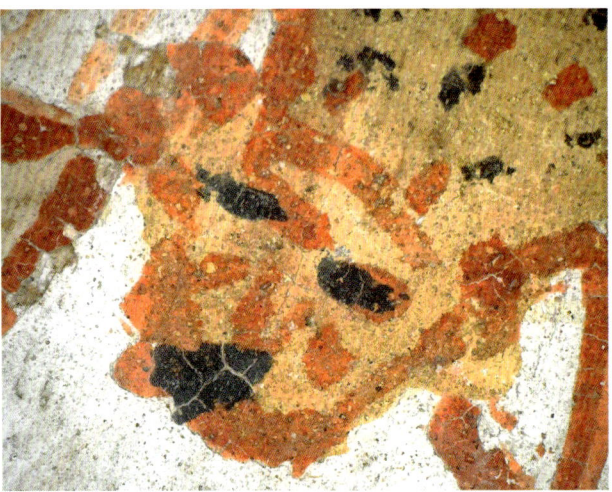

Museum's Middle Kingdom rectangular box coffins from Beni Hasan has a base; this is not because of wood deterioration but because the lids were so firmly attached that excavators in 1903 apparently removed the baseboards to access the interiors. In the past, misunderstanding of original paint and varnish layers sometimes resulted in the well-intentioned but misguided removal of these. The objects we see in museums today are rarely quite the same as those originally put into the ancient Egyptian tombs.

Examining the coffins

In this short summary, it is not possible to discuss all the types of containers that were used to hold bones and bodies over the entire history of ancient Egypt; the aim is rather to introduce the materials and techniques that feature most often and which are illustrated by objects shown in the exhibition.

Investigating the Fitzwilliam's coffins has required an array of imaging and analytical techniques and the expertise of many different specialists. The methods used will be referred to in the text and described in more detail in the Glossary. It has not been possible, or appropriate, to subject every object to all techniques.

The process began with detailed examination, with a stereomicroscope always on hand to enable scrutiny at magnifications up to about ×60 (fig. 47). A strong raking light was used to reveal information about the surface topography (fig. 48).

All features of interest were recorded photographically using a variety of lighting conditions: ultraviolet light helps characterise the organic coatings on the surface and clarify areas of restoration, while infrared is useful for finding carbon-based pigments below the surface (e.g., in underdrawings). Visible-light induced luminescence (VIL) is a photographic technique that captures the infrared fluorescence of the pigment Egyptian blue.

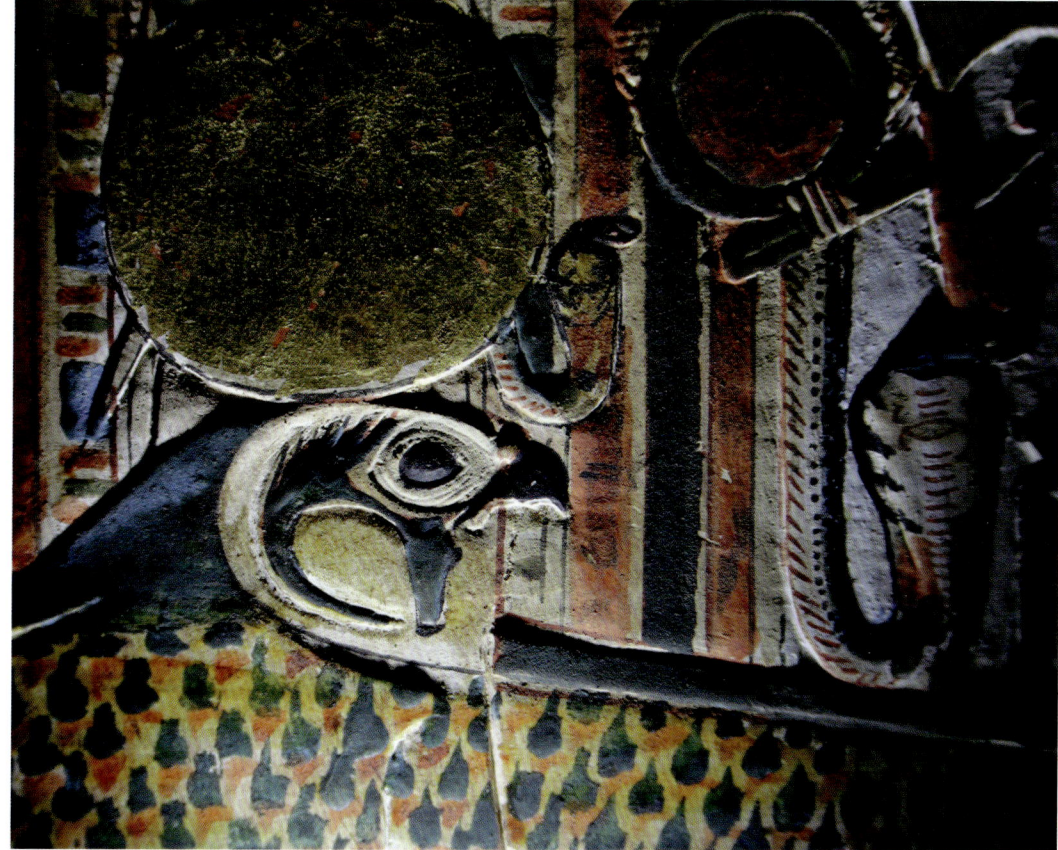

Fig. 48
Detail from the cartonnage mummy case of Nakhtefmut (cat. 32). Raking light enhances the sharp edges of the carved relief decoration and reveals fine detail cut into the paste around the eye of the falcon.

The techniques of fibre optic reflectance spectroscopy (FORS) and X-ray fluorescence spectrometry (XRF) allowed identification of pigments without the need to remove samples from decorated surfaces. Further information on decoration materials was obtained by taking tiny samples and analysing them with polarised light microscopy (PLM), X-ray powder diffraction (XRD) and Raman spectroscopy. Cross-section samples (the size of half a pinhead) helped characterise the layer structures and, where appropriate, were analysed in a scanning electron microscope with energy-dispersive X-ray spectroscopy (SEM-EDX) to locate the various inorganic pigments.

Original varnishes and resins on the coffins were identified through analysis of tiny samples using Fourier transform infrared spectroscopy (FTIR) followed by gas chromatography–mass spectrometry (GC-MS). FTIR reveals the general character of the material – for example, differentiating resins from sugary gums and fatty oils and waxes – and GC-MS enables all the individual molecular components of the material to be characterised so that their botanical origin can be determined.

Finally, X-radiography and computed tomography (CT) scanning delved beneath the surfaces of coffins to see the methods of construction, and scanning electron microscopy was used to identify all the different woods employed.

Wooden coffins

The majority of the coffins in the exhibition are essentially painted wooden boxes with two generic forms: rectangular or anthropoid. These boxes were manufactured from sawn planks or shaped wood held together by a variety of joints and other fixing methods or sometimes, in the case of anthropoid coffins, made by hollowing out large pieces of timber.

Wood in ancient Egypt: Choosing wood for coffins
— *Caroline R. Cartwright*

The skilled use of local and imported woods by carpenters and specialist woodworkers can be seen in a wide range of funerary objects. Scientific identification of the woods used has revealed that, in many instances, particular woods were intentionally selected for their properties. Reuse of good-quality timbers may not simply have been a cost-cutting stratagem; it may equally have reflected the desire to prevent good timber going to waste because its properties were well recognised and cherished. There may also have been spiritual or cultural reasons for perpetuating the use and reuse of a specific type of wood.

Much use was made of the local fig trees (*Ficus sycomorus*, sycomore fig), which grew along the banks of the Nile, particularly for large or long coffin planks: for example, in the coffins of Khety (cat. 11) and Pakepu (cat. 43). It was also popular for making the small wooden models often found in Egyptian tombs, such as granaries, bakeries and boats (e.g., cat. 12). Although fig wood is of medium quality, it is light and easy to carve. It is susceptible to insect attack, but if the worked wood is heavily painted and decorated, or protected by internal placement within a coffin when used for tenons and dowels, this drawback can be mitigated to a degree. Besides yielding edible fruits, sycomore fig trees themselves had considerable cultural and spiritual significance. Another indigenous tree, *Tamarix aphylla* (tamarisk), was used from time to time for ancient Egyptian coffin-plank segments and inserts, such as the bottom of the wig lappet on Nespawershefyt's outer coffin lid (cat. 26). Tamarisk wood, too, could be used for tenons and dowels in the internal construction of coffins. *T. aphylla* is typically found in thicket vegetation of wadis (dry river beds that contain water only at times of heavy rainfall) as well as on riverbanks. Other species of shrub-like tamarisk, typical of more arid habitats, are also indigenous to Egypt but are difficult to distinguish from one another on the basis of their wood anatomy. Tamarisk wood, like fig wood, is light, of medium to poor quality and prone to insect damage, but it is relatively easy to carve and can be serviceable if painted.

When constructing coffins, in contrast to the plank wood, carpenters often chose different types of woods for the interconnecting elements, such as the dowels and tenons. By choosing woods that are denser, such as the local acacias (including *Acacia nilotica*, Nile acacia) and sidr (*Ziziphus spina-christi*), tight joins and connections could be made between planks or between added sections. Acacia and sidr are unlikely to have been available for use as large coffin planks; their wood is often twisted or knotty. However, both are ideal where short lengths of timber are required, for precisely fitted dowels and tenons which are integral to the stability and coherence of construction, and for small objects. Good examples include the selection of *Z. spina-christi* for sections of the rim pieces of Nespawershefyt's inner coffin lid (cat. 26) and most of the dowels in the box coffin of Khety (cat. 11), and the use of *Z. spina-christi* and *A. nilotica* for dowels in the lid of the box coffin of Nakht (fig. 49). Some acacia species prefer the banks of the Nile, whilst others (with extensive taproot systems) grow in more arid locations of Egypt. Sidr, found in tree and shrub forms, inhabits riverbanks, desert wadis and scrubland thickets.

One of the most renowned timber imports to Egypt is cedar of Lebanon (*Cedrus libani*). This softwood is reputed to be easy to carve, plane and polish, although it can be rather brittle, and large knots and ingrowing bark within the timber may be problematic. Through trade in the ancient world bordering the Mediterranean Sea, cedar of Lebanon timber was often available in long lengths, well suited for use as coffin planks. The strongly aromatic and resinous wood has been regarded as a partial insect deterrent. The popularity of cedar of Lebanon wood for use in high-status coffins (e.g. cat. 15) and for other funerary objects in ancient Egypt may have been as much a measure of the expense and prestige of acquiring this imported resource as of its inherent properties. The presence of cedar of Lebanon coffin dowels and tenons seems to provide good evidence for the common practice in ancient Egypt of using offcuts of good-quality timber, as seen in the example of tenons in Nespawershefyt's outer coffin lid (cat. 26).

Fig. 49
Head end of the coffin lid of Nakht (cat. 15), with a retaining batten fixed to the underside. All structural parts of this lid are made of cedar of Lebanon. The many dowels in the lid are made of cedar, sidr and acacia.

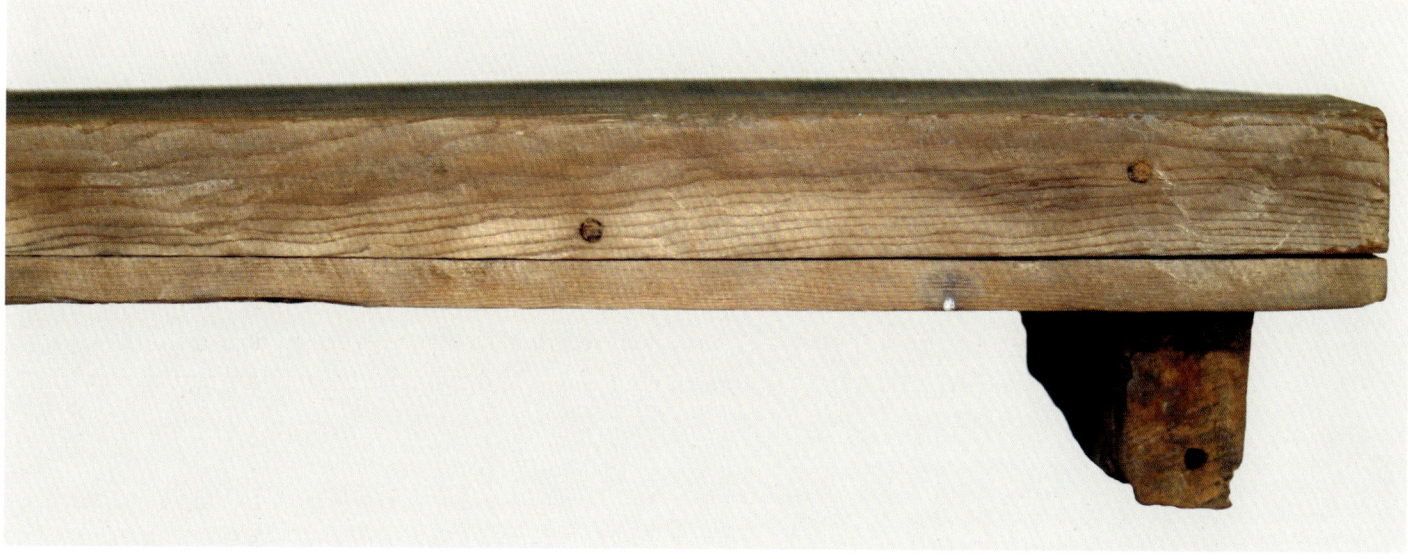

Preparation of timber

Numerous scenes in tomb paintings and a meticulously detailed model discovered in the Eleventh Dynasty burial of Meketre (fig. 50) give us clues to the way in which woodworkers approached their material. After a tree was felled and the side branches removed, the trunk was chopped into logs and taken to the carpenter's workshop. Long, solid pieces were prepared by chopping off the bark and sapwood to expose the structural wood from which coffin parts could be manufactured. Generally, wooden planks were prepared by strapping the trunk or log vertically to an upright post fixed into the workshop floor. The planks were then cut by sawing down the length of the trunk (known as through-and-through or tangential sawing; fig. 51). These planks were seasoned (allowed to dry in the open air) to remove most of their moisture content, after which they were ready for use. In addition to the saw, essential tools employed by the woodworker were adzes, chisels and wooden mallets with which to strike them, try squares, awls for making holes, small engraving tools, and bow-drills (fig. 53). Surfaces were smoothed by rubbing them down with small blocks of sandstone.

Fig. 50
Model of carpenters' workshop from the tomb of Meketre at Thebes, about 2010–2000 BC. In the centre a craftsman saws a log into planks; another cuts mortises with a chisel and mallet. To the right, three men shape a piece of wood with adzes (The Egyptian Museum, Cairo, JE46722).

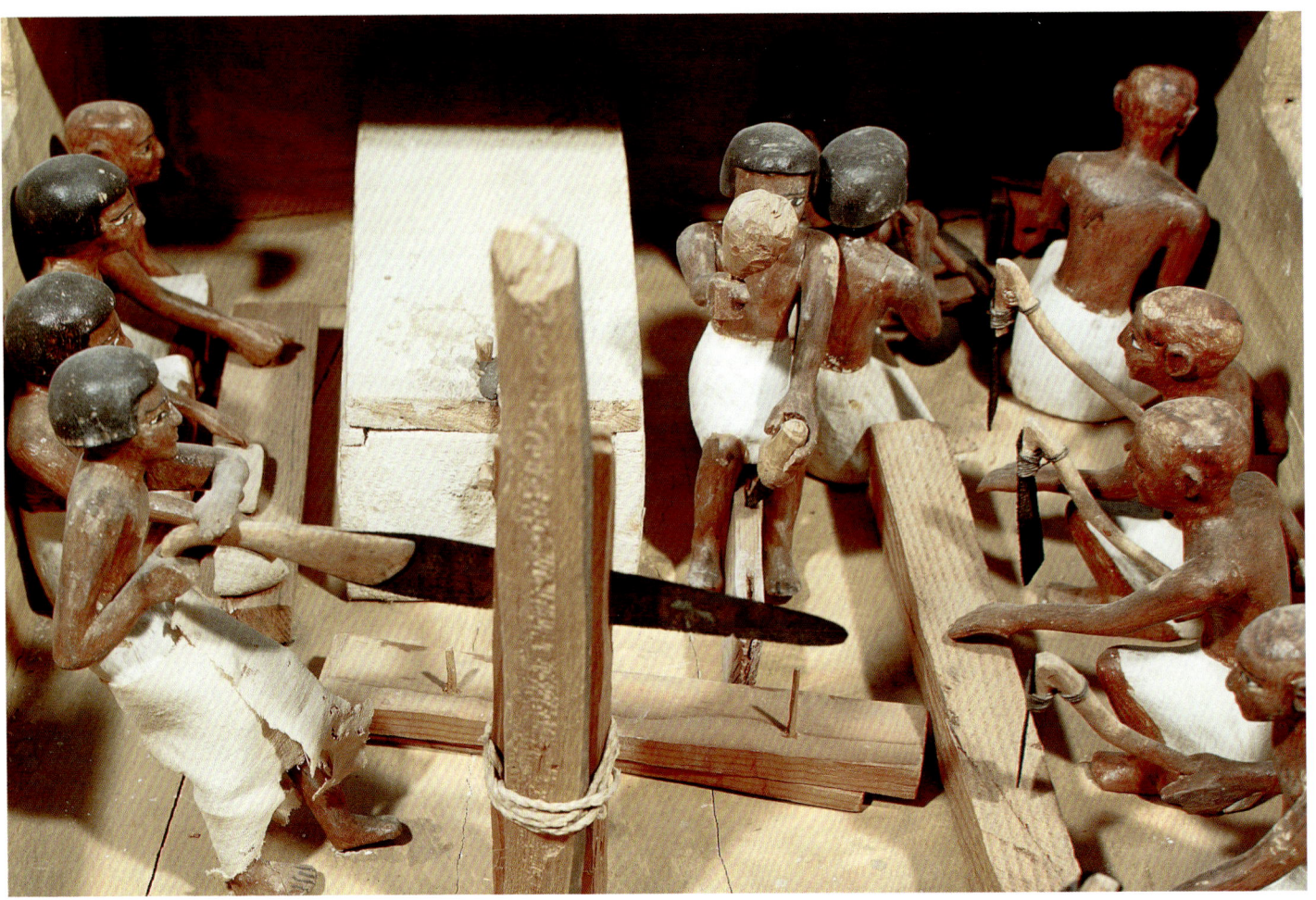

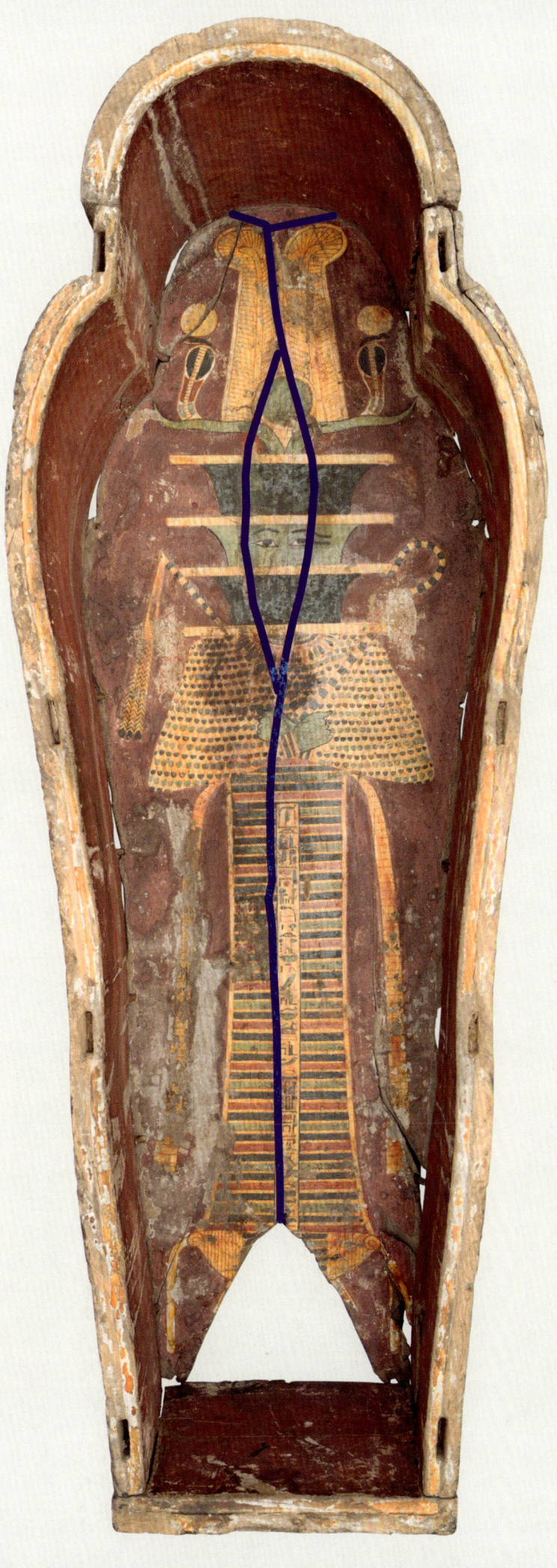

Fig. 51
The planks of sycomore fig forming the base of Nespawershefyt's outer coffin box (cat. 26) are mirror images, showing that they almost certainly come from a single piece of wood sawn along its length (tangential sawing) and then opened up and laid side by side (the edges of the individual boards are marked in blue). The fill-in board at the centre is made of tamarisk.

Fig. 54
Marks made by the slicing action of either a chisel or an adze

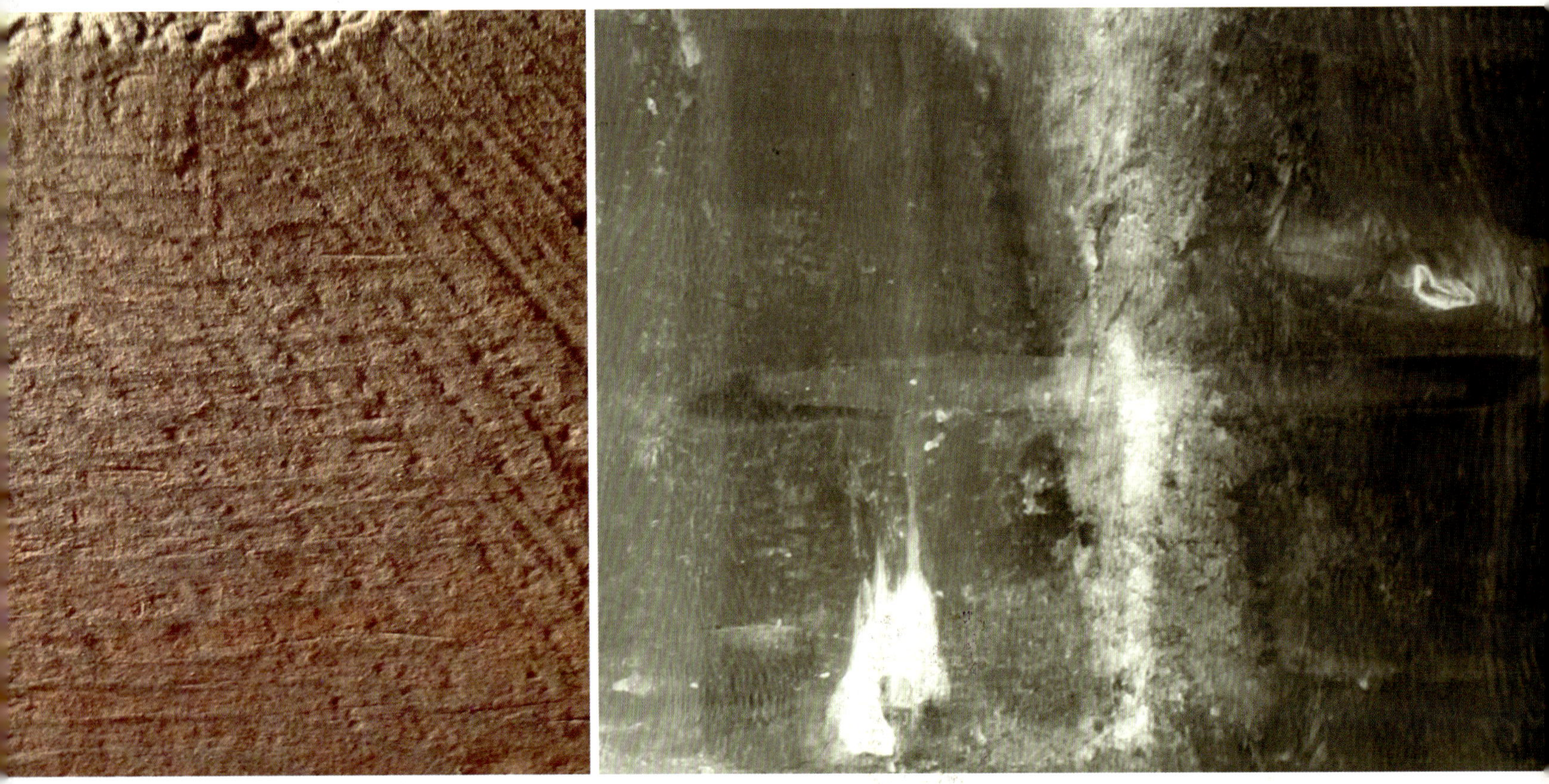

Fig. 52
Marks left by woodworking tools: saw marks on a panel from a box (Fitzwilliam Museum, E.W.98) are revealed under raking light, while the characteristic tube and cone shape created by bow drilling are shown in this radiograph of dowel holes on the intermediate coffin of Pakepu (cat. 43).

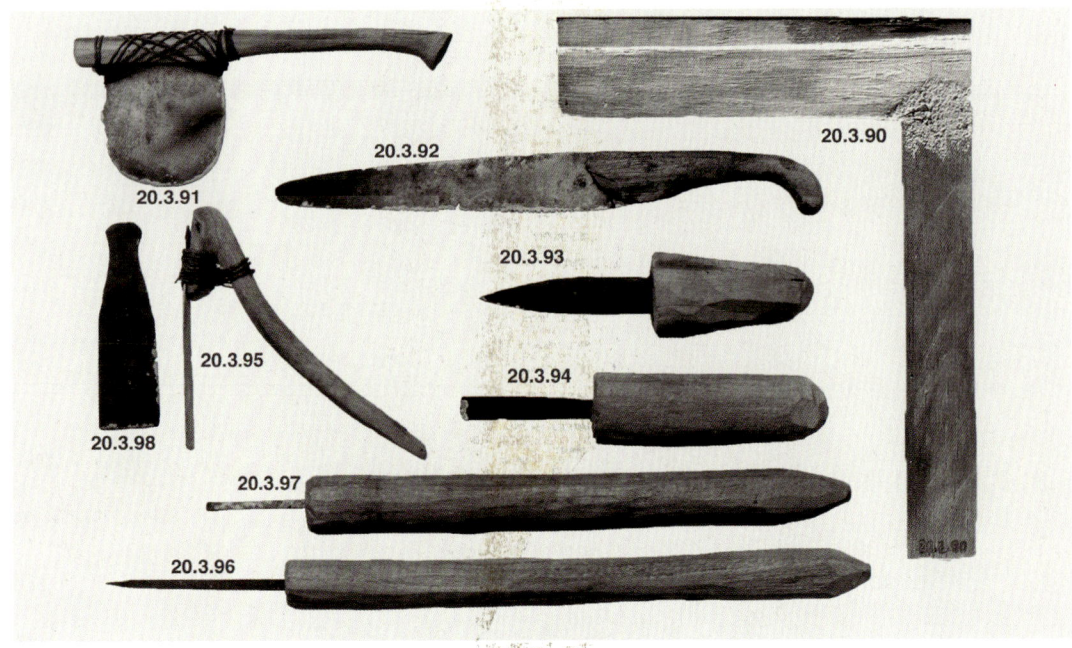

Fig. 53
Model tools from the tomb of Meketre, about 2010–2000 BC, show what full-sized examples would have looked like. From left to right, top to bottom: axe, try square, saw, adze blade, adze, two chisels and two bow-drills (Metropolitan Museum of Art, New York, 20.3.90–98).

82 Egyptian Coffins: Materials, Construction and Decoration

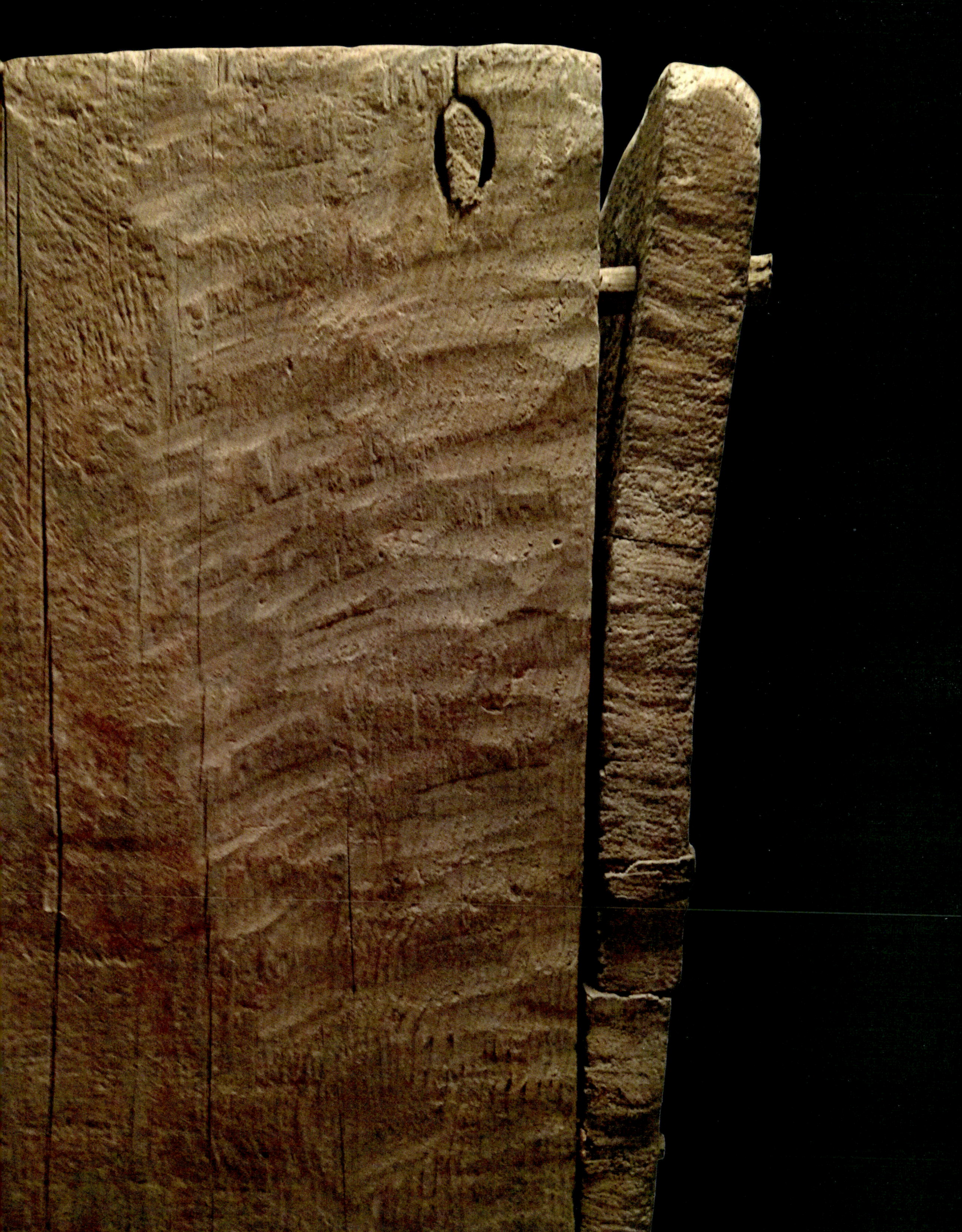

All these processes and tools leave characteristic evidence. The grain patterns visible on different components of an object indicate the direction in which the wood was cut, and remnants of the sweeping marks of the saw may show up when the surface is viewed in raking light (fig. 52). The twisting bit of a bow-drill leaves a cone shape in the bottom of a dowel hole (fig. 52), and the chop marks left by an adze or a chisel capture both the size of the blade and its direction of travel (fig. 54).

Box coffins

Ideally, a box coffin would be made from full-length, broad, straight planks. This was most easily achieved if the carpenter had the opportunity to work with the highest-quality materials, such as the imported cedar of Lebanon used to construct the coffin of Nakht (cat. 15). All other box coffins shown in the exhibition, and the greater proportion of those whose timber has been identified, are made from native wood. The coffins of Khety (cat. 11) and the mourning women (cat. 21) are both examples of sycomore fig constructions in which – although there are significant knots and other flaws present – a good box has been made from relatively few components. The curved edge boards of the coffin of Henenu (cat. 3) show how the natural shape of trunk and branch could be accommodated to get planks of sufficient length to make the side of a coffin. But numerous box coffins were necessarily constructed partly or completely as complex jigsaw puzzles from small, irregularly shaped, often reused pieces, such as the fragment from the coffin of an unknown woman (cat. 14).

A wide variety of fixing methods has been documented across the range of ancient Egyptian woodwork. Dowelling seems to have been the most common means of holding edge-jointed planks together on early box coffins, although mortise and tenon joints are also found. The corners are often butt joints or variants of simple mitre joints, usually with a small butt joint or half dovetail at the top. These are sometimes made more secure by supplementing the dowels with ties at the top and bottom of the corners. Examples with copper ribbon staples have been excavated, but the coffin of Khety shows a more typical method. Two drilled holes were connected by a channel on the face of the panel. A wet rawhide or sinew tie was lashed through these holes and wedged firmly in

Fig. 55
A corner of the coffin of Khety (cat. 11), showing a tied joint

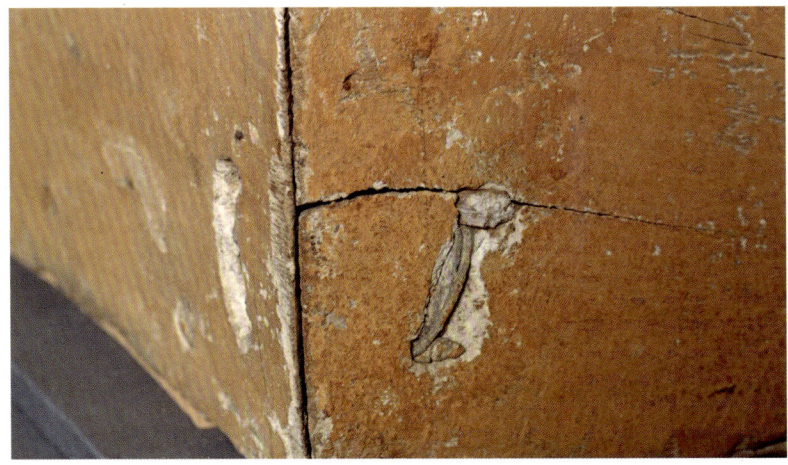

place by dowels. As the tie dried it would have shrunk, pulling the edges of the joint together (fig. 55). This type of connection, thought to be derived from ship building, was used also to lash supporting battens to the underside of coffins, or to tie thin panels of wood together. In the Middle Kingdom anthropoid coffin of Userhet, the technique was used to effect a repair on a manufacturing fault (see cat. 20.2).

Box coffin lids are often composed of flat planks, as can be seen on the coffins of Henenu and Khety, but the coffin of Nakht has a more elaborate lid. This complex construction gives an external appearance of depth and solidity but is made of rather thin planks and is in fact concave underneath. To position both types of lid, a retaining batten drops down inside the coffin from each end of the lid (see fig. 49). Two dowels pushed through holes in the end panel and this internal batten ensure a secure closure.

A quite different method of box construction is illustrated by the much later *qersu* coffin (see cat. 44). Here the side panels were fixed with integral tenons into four stout corner posts, and the vaulted lid was probably composed of planks pinned to semicircular end pieces.

Anthropoid coffins

The box and lid of some of the earliest wooden anthropoid coffins were each hollowed out from a tree trunk or other large logs. This method of manufacture does not, however, reflect an inability to make complex shapes in wood; examples of sophisticated furniture manufacture are known from the Archaic Period (3030–2700 BC), and many coffins from later periods were made partially or completely in this way. Where the depth of available timber allowed, such as in the coffins of Userhet (cat. 20) and Madja (cat. 22), the face, wig and feet would be carved as integral features rather than made separately and attached. The axe, adze and chisel were the principal tools used for shaping the exterior and interior of these coffins. The working of the wood was hidden on the exterior by thick layers of surface preparation, but is revealed in an X-radiograph of Userhet's coffin that shows where paste has pooled into marks created by the blows of the tools (see cat. 20).

From the early New Kingdom, the majority of anthropoid coffins were built from an assemblage of planks and carved pieces – in some cases, very many. The intermediate coffin of Pakepu (cat. 43), for example, has a lid made from 27 separate sections, held together with at least 55 dowels; the box is constructed from 47 different pieces, with at least 88 dowels (fig. 56). There are, of course, changes in construction over the course of more than 1500 years that reflect the different styles of anthropoid coffins, regional circumstances and the habits and traditions of particular workshops. The growing corpus of coffin-wood

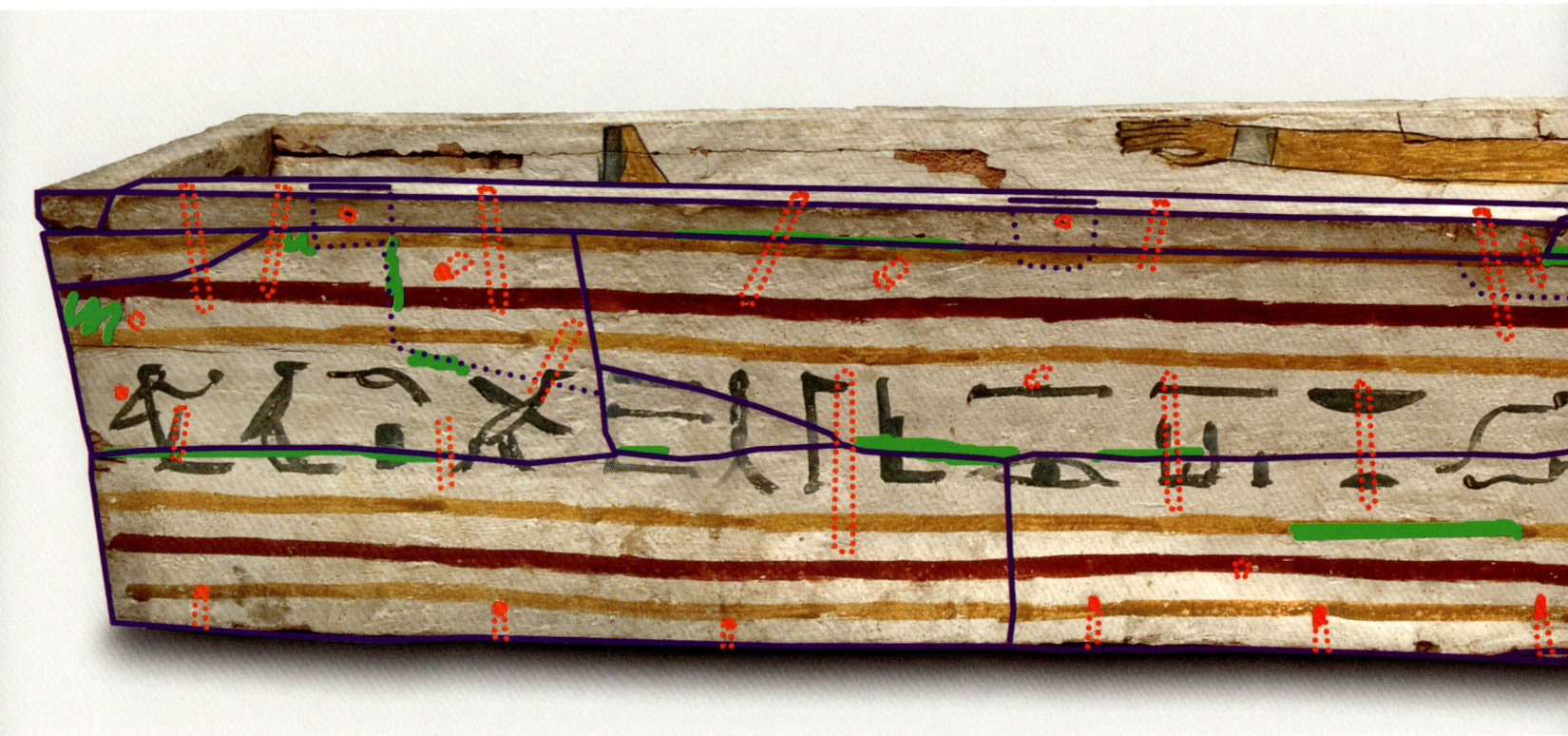

identifications and published technical examinations show that these coffins are mostly made from native timber, and that a great variety of woods might be found in any one coffin set. Gathering and synthesising all the manufacturing evidence is, however, still a work in progress, and attempts to establish patterns of practice are inevitably skewed somewhat by the adaptations carpenters had to make in order to cope with the materials in front of them. This factor is reflected to some extent in the variable quality of the finished products; it is a testament to the skill and ingenuity of the carpenters that they were able to produce complex objects from what sometimes must have been unpromising starting materials.

An anthropoid coffin lid consists of long boards to make the main structure; the sides were added as a rim around this. At the foot is a vertical board, in front of which angled panels are positioned to create the feet. Additional layers build up the head and wig, with other sculptural features such as faces, hands and ears generally added separately. The box consists of a baseboard attached to long, curving planks which shape the sides; a separate rounded headboard; and a flat footboard closing the box. The box and lid are usually locked together with pegged mortise and tenon joints. To make the coffin, the carpenter attached the roughly faceted pieces to each other and then carved them to the final shape. Marks to help with the order of construction or positioning of cuts sometimes survive on the finished coffin (fig. 57).

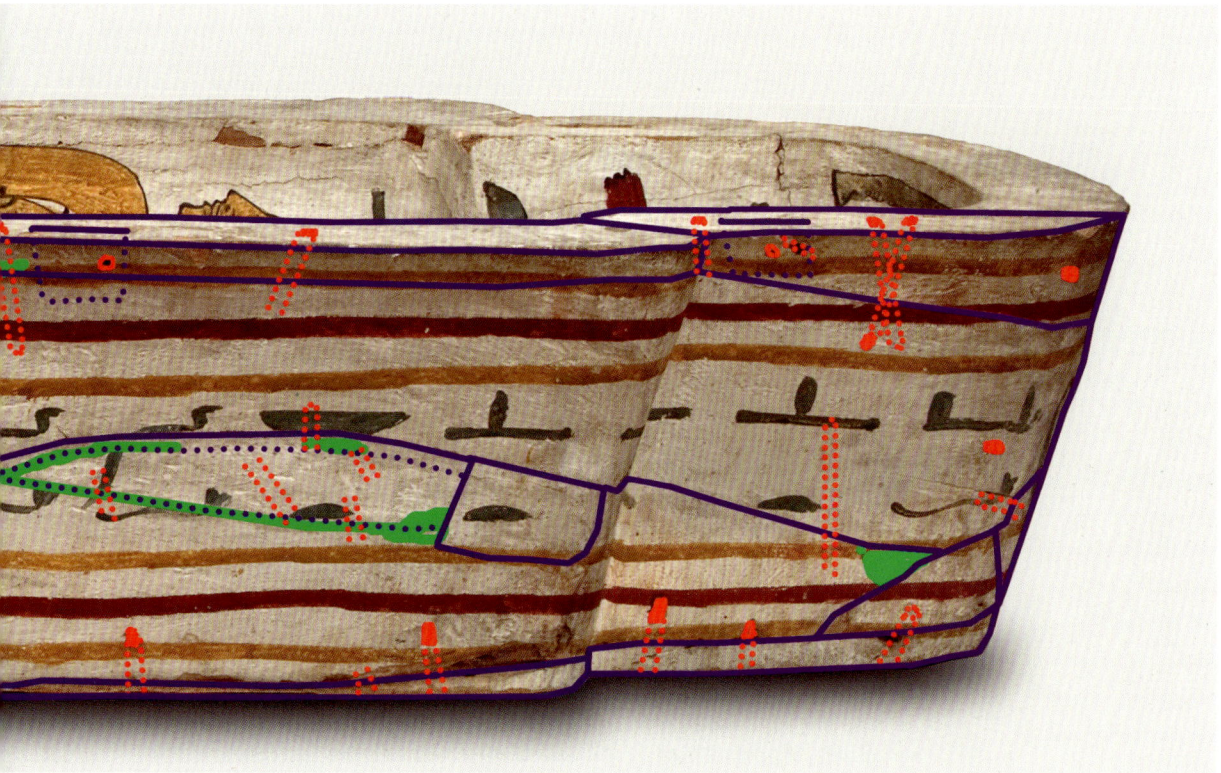

Fig. 56
The side of Pakepu's intermediate coffin box (cat. 43), marked up to show the edges of separate pieces of wood (blue), the many dowels (red) and area of thick paste (green).

Mortise and tenon joints and dowels are the most common methods of fixing abutting timber elements together in anthropoid coffins, often supplemented by a coat of animal glue between the pieces, but a variety of other joints was used for specific purposes. For example, when two or more pieces of timber were needed to construct the long sides of coffin lids some variety of scarf joint might be used, with the pieces pinned together with dowels or butterfly cramps. The footboards of Nespawershefyt's coffin boxes (cat. 26) offer examples of neatly cut dovetails, and that of Pakepu's intermediate coffin (cat. 43) is a collection of butt joints.

The curved head ends of coffin boxes might be carved from a single tree trunk or other large piece of wood – see the outer coffin box of Nespawershefyt and the head end from a yellow coffin (cat. 31) – or might be constructed from a number of pieces. The joint structure employed in Nespawersehfyt's inner coffin, for example, is a refined example of coopering: three individual blocks of wood, each cut with a gentle curve, are held together by internal tenons across slightly angled joining edges to create the semicircle shape. The fitting is accurate and secure (fig. 59).

In terms of complexity of construction, the feet of anthropoid coffin lids presented a particular challenge. They often required a number of pieces of wood, small fill sections and dowels in several different directions to make a secure structure (fig. 58).

Fig. 57
Marks for positioning a mortise on the rim of Pakepu's intermediate coffin box (cat. 43)

Fig. 58
Left side of the foot end of Pakepu's intermediate coffin lid (cat. 43) marked up to show the separate pieces of wood (blue), the dowels (red) and areas of thick paste (green) on the left

Fig. 59
The head end of Nespawershefyt's inner coffin box (cat. 26), showing the coopered joints

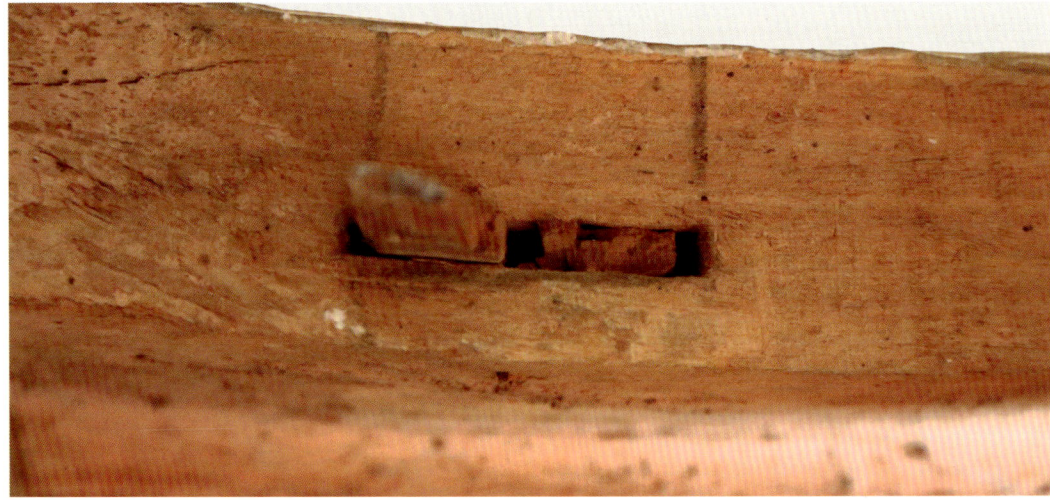

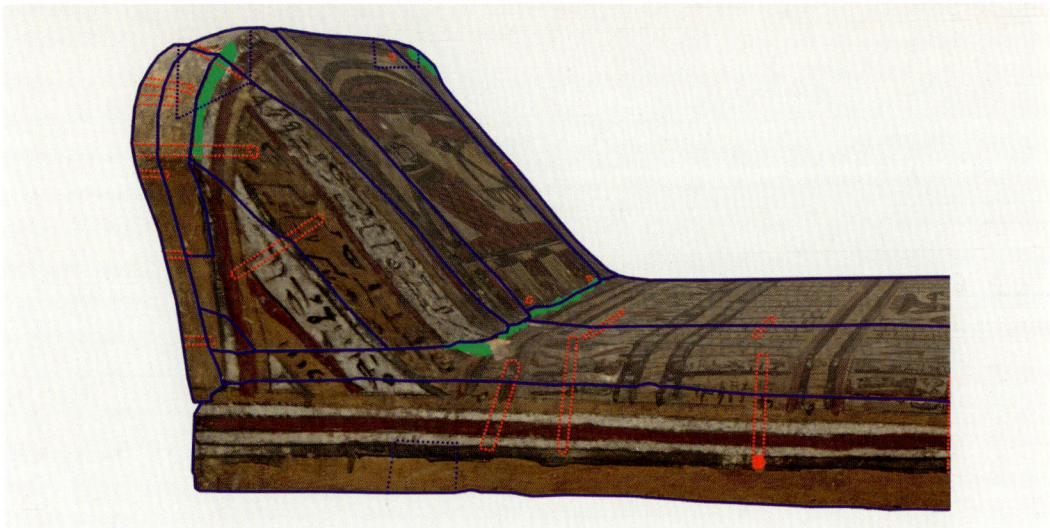

Reuse, repairs and preparing the surface for decoration

The value of wood and, in times of economic stress, its relative scarcity, is reflected not only in ingenious coffin construction methods and the incorporation of many fragments of timber, but also in the presence of numerous pieces that show clear evidence of reuse from earlier objects. For example, some parts of the coffin of Nakht (cat. 15) are riddled with redundant dowel holes, and the planks of Nespawershefyt's inner coffin box (cat. 26) are full of old mortises. Numerous methods of repair and making good were used to cope with these features and other structural issues, such as diseased or damaged timber that had to be removed, areas of potential weakness, such as knots, and the many gaps between ill-fitting sections of wood.

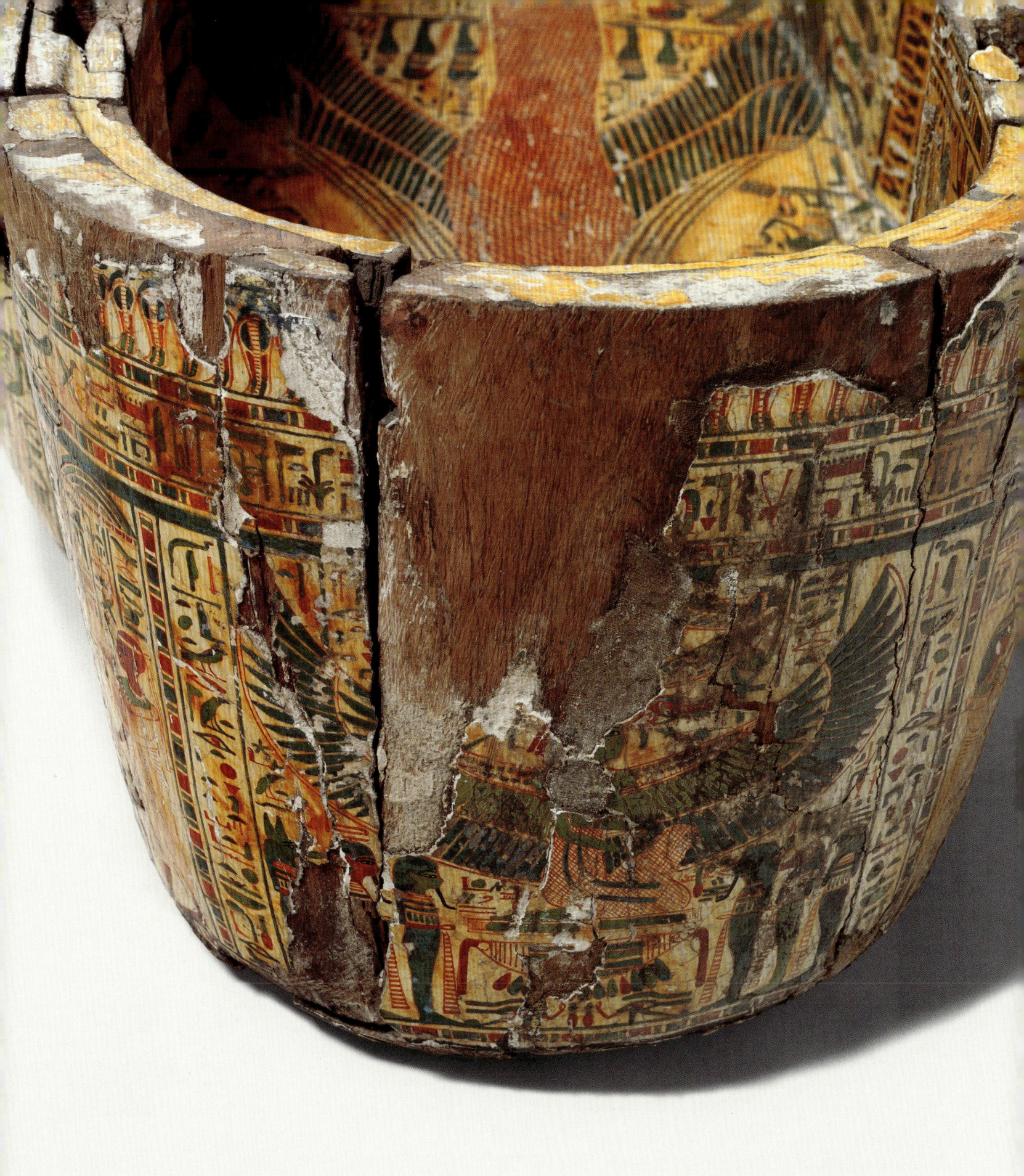

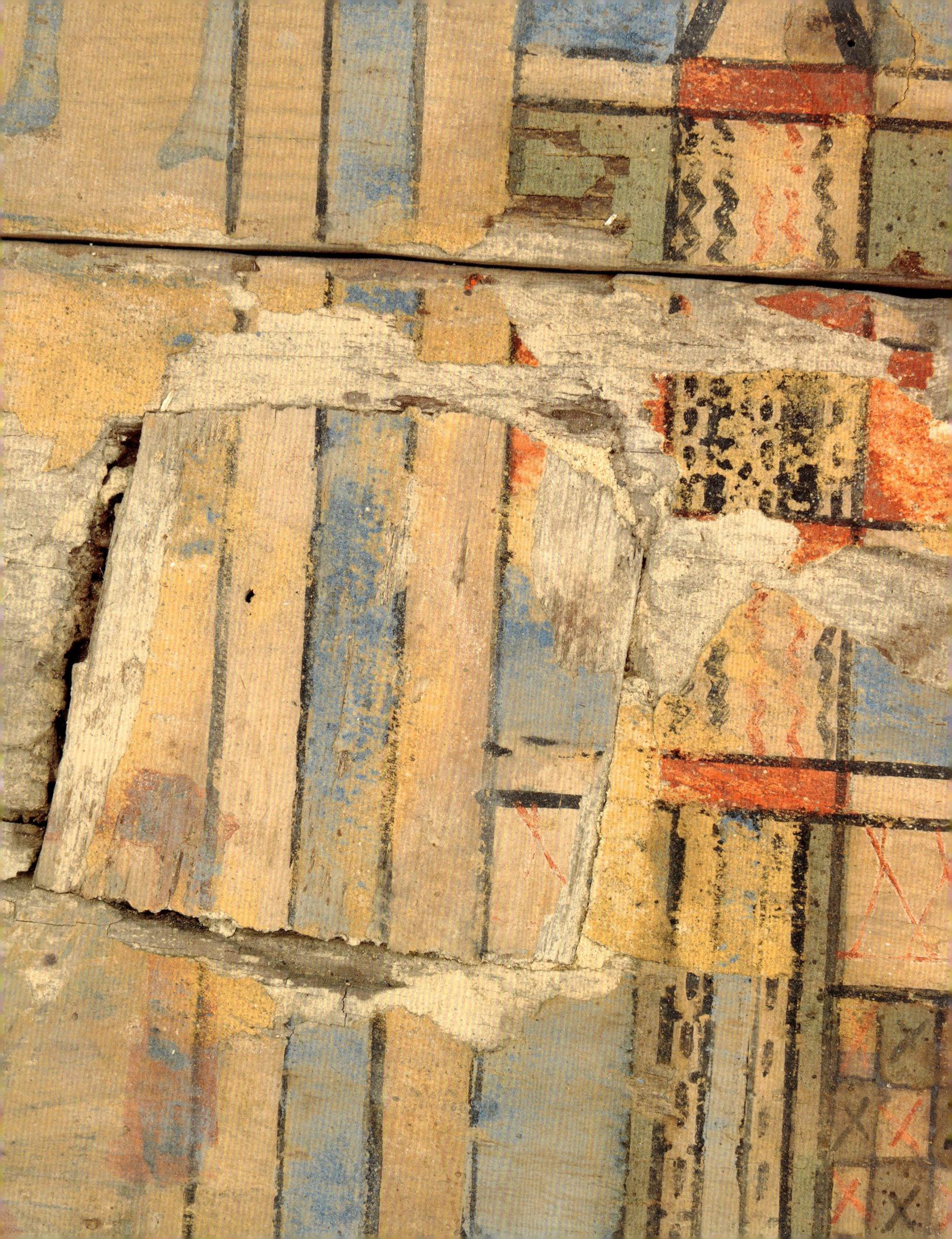

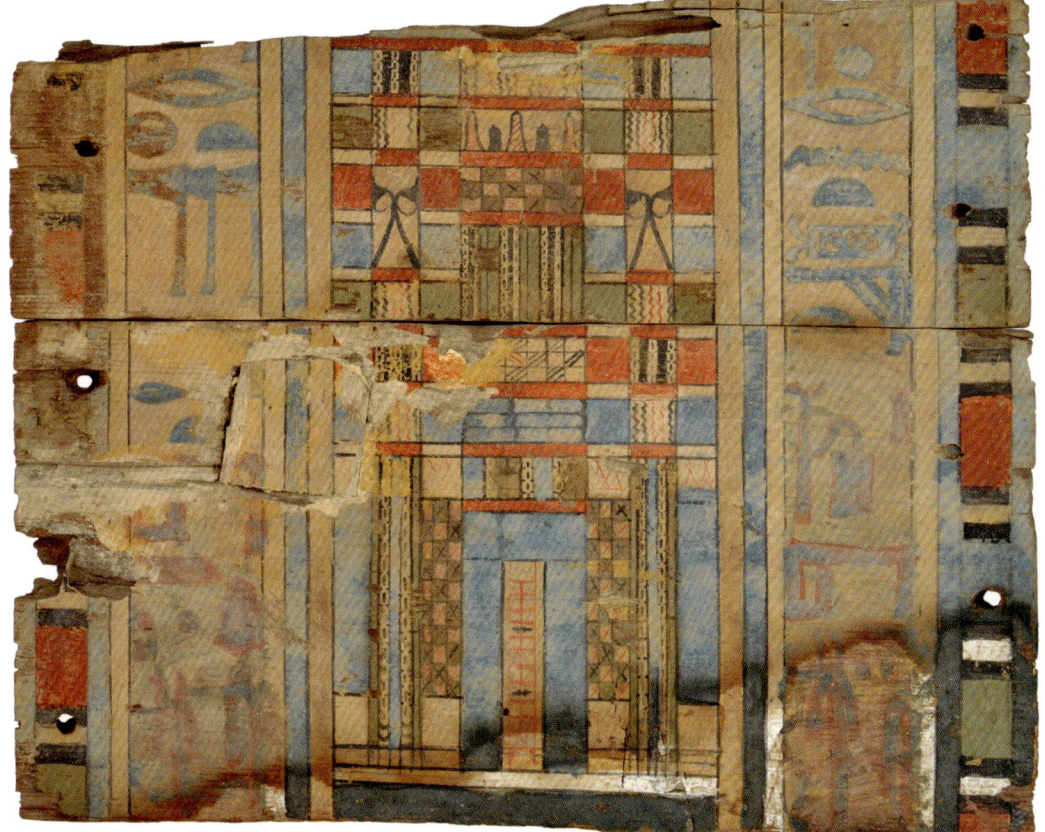

Fig. 60
Patching by means of a square piece of wood is clearly visible on this end panel from the Middle Kingdom box coffin of a person called Userheta (Fitzwilliam Museum, E.67.1903)

Patching with another piece of wood was one option (fig. 60) and knot holes were sometimes drilled out and filled with plugs, as in Khety's coffin (cat. 11). Twists of linen might be packed into spaces between planks, as in the white coffin footboard (see cat. 23.1). The intermediate coffin of Pakepu (cat. 43) is a good illustration of the use of pastes. For example, paste was used to build up the toes, fill knot holes in the wig lappets, and seal joints on the undecorated underside of the lid. X-radiographs reveal the sheer quantity of coarse paste used to make good the sides of the box (see cat. 43.2). The surface texture suggests that a wide-toothed comb may have been used to apply the coarse paste.

Mud, clay and calcite pastes have all been identified being used in this way on coffins. These materials are likely to be mixed with a binding medium rather than being true plasters (materials that react with water to harden). Examples from the Fitzwilliam's coffins are mostly calcite pastes with varying amounts of earths present, which alter the colour from white to yellow, pink and brown; they tend to be coarse and often contain small stones and vegetable matter. On the anthropoid coffins in particular, patches of woven linen were also used to cover repairs, bridge wide joins and improve structural stability. In some cases, most of the surface might be covered with fabric to help key the paste to the wood.

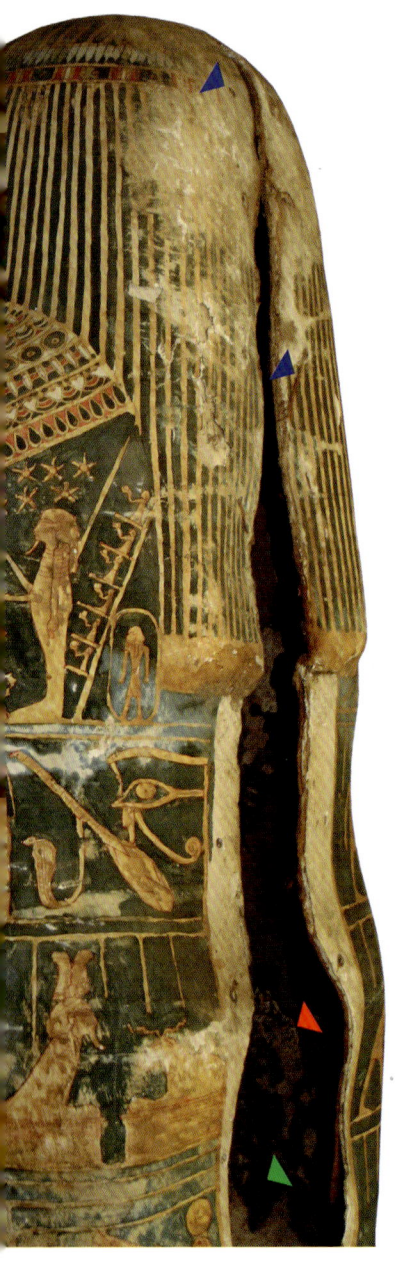

Fig. 61
The cartonnage coffin of Hor (Fitzwilliam Museum, E.8.1896), seen from the side. The mummy was removed by tomb robbers long before the case was excavated in 1896. Inside the empty shell, the first layer of linen can be seen. Fragments of the coarse white paste layer cling to the linen (red arrow), and on top of these are remains of the mud and straw core material (green arrow). Pairs of lacing holes and remnants of the lacing (blue arrows) are visible along the open rear slit.

Many coffins have a final, fine white preparation layer across the surface, usually made from calcite and/or chalk and generally combined with a binder. Within the Fitzwilliam's collection, the paste on the coffin of the mourning women (cat. 21) is unusual because it contains small amounts of gypsum and bassanite, but this may represent mixed source materials. This final layer was generally used to create a smooth, neutral surface and colour for painting but could also be used to sculpt fine details on an anthropoid coffin: for example, on the wigs of the inner coffin and mummy board of Nespawershefyt, a tool has been pressed into the paste layer to create the three-dimensional locks of hair (see cat. 26.5). At this stage, features that had been modelled in paste, such as ears, would also be incorporated.

If the natural colour and texture of the wood could provide the finish required, it was left without a ground or only lightly covered. On the *qersu* coffin (cat. 44), the red acacia wood was merely enhanced by rubbing red earth pigment into the surface. Exotic cedar coffins such as Nakht's (cat. 15), which seem to have been valued for their rich colour and fine grain, were often left uncovered, or with only a thin ground.

Cartonnage coffins

After wood, cartonnage is probably the most important material for elite coffin manufacture in ancient Egypt. Cartonnage is a laminated composite made of layers of linen stiffened with glue and plastered on the external and, usually, the internal surface. This cheap and versatile material was used to different extents from the First Intermediate Period (beginning about 2170 BC) onwards.

The Eleventh Dynasty mask of Tjay (cat. 18) is an early example. The negative impression of the facial features on the interior paste layer and lack of other materials or tool marks support the theory that masks like these were made over a wooden template. The construction methods of the full-body cartonnage cases of the Twenty-second Dynasty are less readily discerned, and have been the subject of considerable investigation in recent years. From examination of the technical evidence and several replication experiments, the basic process of manufacture outlined below has been proposed, but there are still many questions to be answered. The cartonnage case of Nakhtefmut (cat. 32) was cut open by the excavators in 1896 and sealed shut by an early restoration, so most of the manufacturing evidence is hidden or lost, but some of the features described can be seen in the CT scans (see fig. 99) and the cartonnage of Hor (fig. 61).

The craftsmen started out with a mummy-shaped core made of mud and straw, which they covered with a layer of coarse gypsum paste; this was quick-drying, so would rapidly create a hard shell. The core stayed moist inside this shell, which meant that it could be scraped out at a later stage. A patchwork of

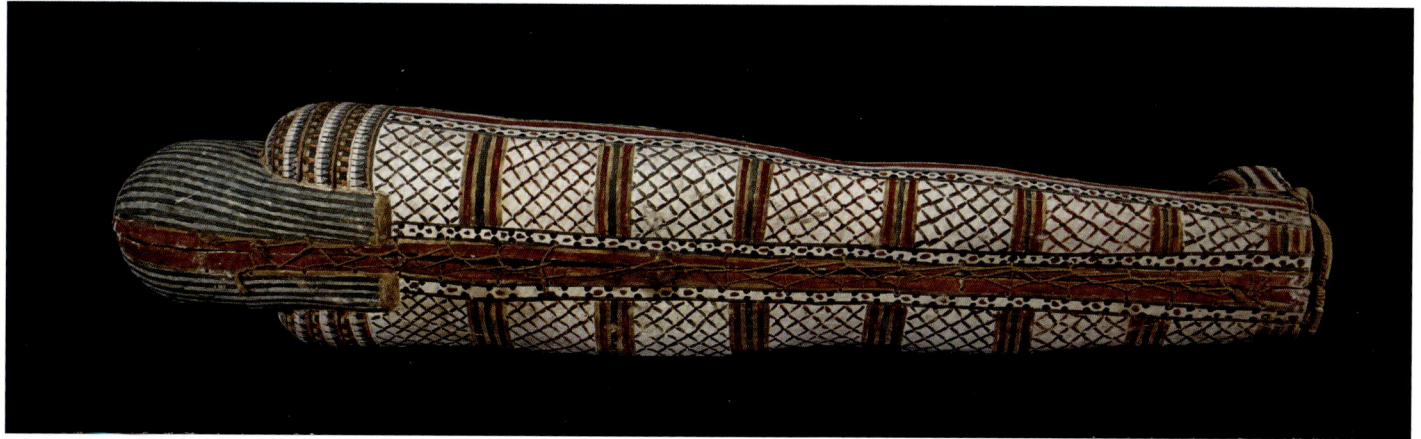

Fig. 62
The back of the cartonnage coffin of Djedameniufankh (British Museum, EA29577), showing how the slit was laced together. The footboard is also visible.

linen cloth pieces soaked in glue was then built up in layers over the gypsum shell, leaving only the section at the base of the feet uncovered. The density and orientation of weave varied; some layers were placed on the bias so that the fabric would conform more easily to the shape of the core. Since the faces of these cases have regular, well-proportioned features, it has been proposed that a wooden face template may have been placed over the core to allow moulding of the face and then removed when the core was scraped out. Alternatively, the face could have been produced separately and then stuck into position before any surface decoration was added. A slit was cut down the length of the back of the completed case and, in some instances, across the shoulders and at the feet, and regularly spaced holes were punched through from the external surface along the length of the slit. The core was then removed. After this, a coat of fine calcite paste was applied over the surface. The wrapped mummy was placed inside the case and the slit was closed by lacing through the punched holes (fig. 62); the lacings were covered with a strip of linen, and subsequently covered with more paste. A wooden board was dowelled or laced into the open foot end of the case.

The decoration of most cartonnage cases was simply painted onto the surface, but a richer effect could be created with plastically modelled relief, as seen on the cartonnage of Nakhtefmut (see fig. 48). The design was drawn on the paste surface, the outlines delineated with a sharp tool, and the surrounding paste then scraped away to leave the decorative elements proud of the surface. In places on the background, so much paste has been removed that the final layer of linen is partially revealed. Most of the cut edges are very crisp, but some shapes have a softer outline and may have been lightly modelled in paste rather than simply cut out. Fine details were cut into the surface with a pointed tool. This relief modelling echoes the technique of openwork cartonnage, created by cutting the background away completely (see cat. 49).

Although wooden inner coffins became more common again in the Late Period, from about 715 BC, cartonnage cases left a legacy in the form and decoration of the coffins, and also in the technology used to create them. The approach to plastering is very different between the inner and intermediate coffins of Pakepu (cat. 43). On the intermediate coffin, there is simply a layer of thin paste over the wood. On the inner coffin, the multiple layers of plaster, linen fabric and glue resemble the structure and composition of cartonnage and extend across the join between box and lid, sealing the mummy into the coffin as it would have been sealed in a cartonnage case (cat. 43.1).

In later periods the cartonnage from which mummy trappings and masks were made is generally similar structurally to that already described, except that from the Ptolemaic Period (332–50 BC) papyrus scraps were often used in place of linen. However, the more sculptural Greek- and Roman-style masks required increasingly creative use of both paste and cartonnage to make the features, clothes and adornments of the person represented. Very few technical studies of such masks have been published; however, structures similar to that of the Fitzwilliam's gilded mask (cat. 55.a) have been reported. The mask is made of a single piece of linen, moulded over a template and bulked out with a layer of chopped flax, probably a by-product of linen manufacture. This structure is encased in an internal and an external layer of calcite paste. The left arm and hand are made of a separate piece of cartonnage, attached to the main structure. A final surface layer and details of the right hand, garland, lips, nose and hair are all executed in a fine, ivory-coloured calcite paste.

A different manufacturing technique is represented by the mask of a Roman man (cat. 53). This is made of true gypsum plaster (a material which sets by reaction with water and which we know today as plaster of Paris), a slurry of which was cast into a mould. Mass-produced faces of this type were given individual features with additional plaster paste moulded freehand and in some cases, for the hairstyle, extruded (rather like squeezing cake icing through a piping bag and nozzle). This mask was then set down onto a surround of cartonnage made of layers of plaster and linen shaped to fit over the head and shoulders of the mummy. Part of this structure survives attached to the mask.

Decorating coffins

Pigments and paint

Paint is made up of pigment particles held in suspension in a binding medium, the most common of which in ancient Egypt were plant gums and animal glue. The identity of the major pigments making up the palette of the Egyptian artist has been known since the late nineteenth century, but detailed examination and analysis, especially over the last twenty-five to thirty years (and mostly on tomb paintings rather than coffins), have lengthened the list.

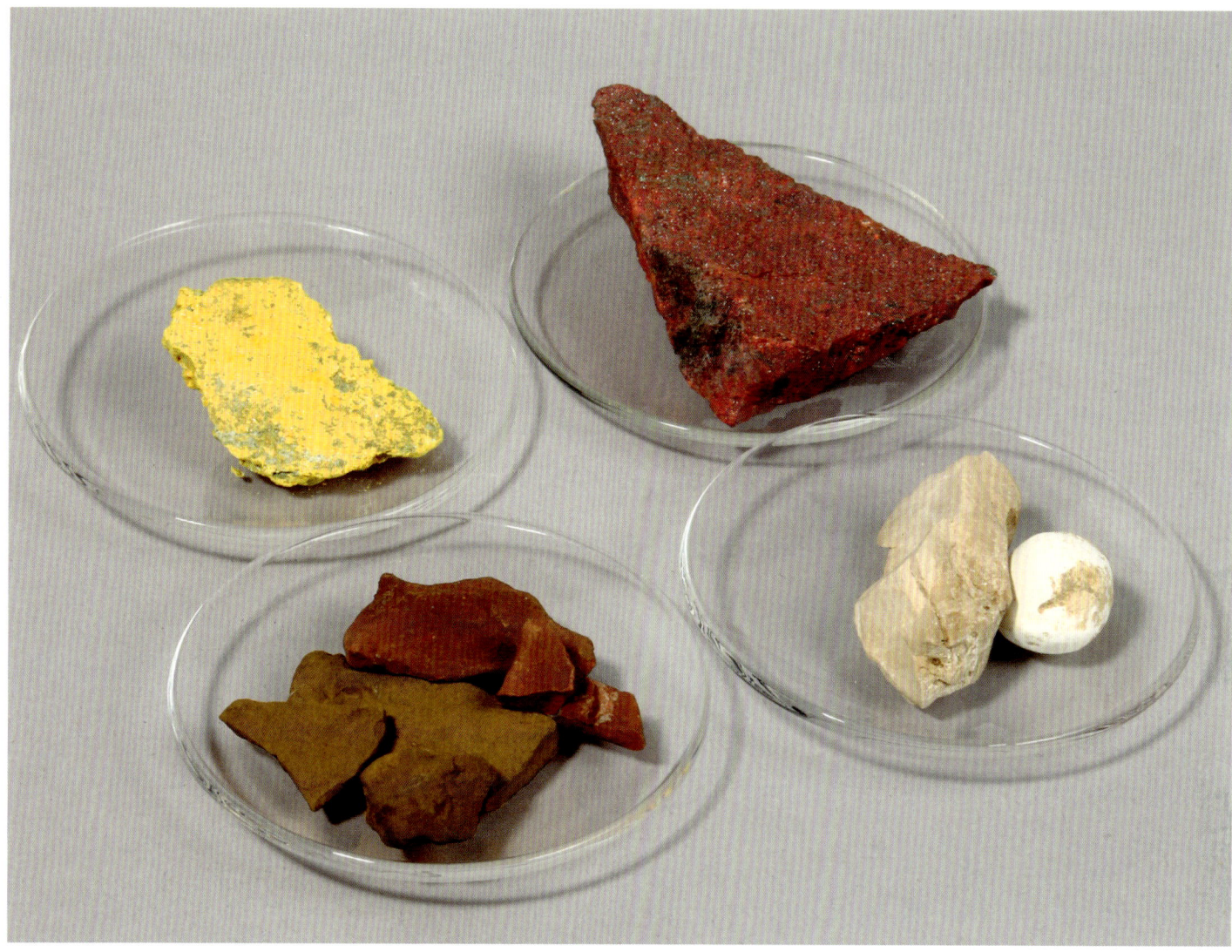

Fig. 63
Examples of mineral pigments; from top left clockwise: orpiment, cinnabar, limestone, red and yellow ochre.

Before the Ptolemaic Period, most pigments were ground-up native or imported minerals (fig. 63). Exceptions are the manufactured glassy frits, Egyptian blue and Egyptian green (fig. 64), and the carbon-based blacks, such as soot and charcoal. Reds were painted principally using red earths, derived from widely available deposits rich in iron oxide minerals, such as haematite and ilmenite. There are isolated instances of cinnabar (mercury sulphide) on New Kingdom and Third Intermediate Period objects (about 1550–715 BC), but it is found more extensively from the Late Period onwards. Additionally, realgar (arsenic sulphide) has been identified from the New Kingdom onwards, but rarely so far on coffins.

There were several ways to make yellow, but the most abundant pigments were yellow earths, which include iron oxides (such as goethite) and iron sulphates (jarosite and natrojarosite). These different materials provide subtle variations in

Fig. 64
Examples of Egyptian blue and red ochre (British Museum, EA 5563, EA 5568, EA5568.b, EA5569)

Fig. 65
A paint pot containing traces of natrojarosite, Roman Period, excavated at Hawara (Fitzwilliam Museum, E.85.1911)

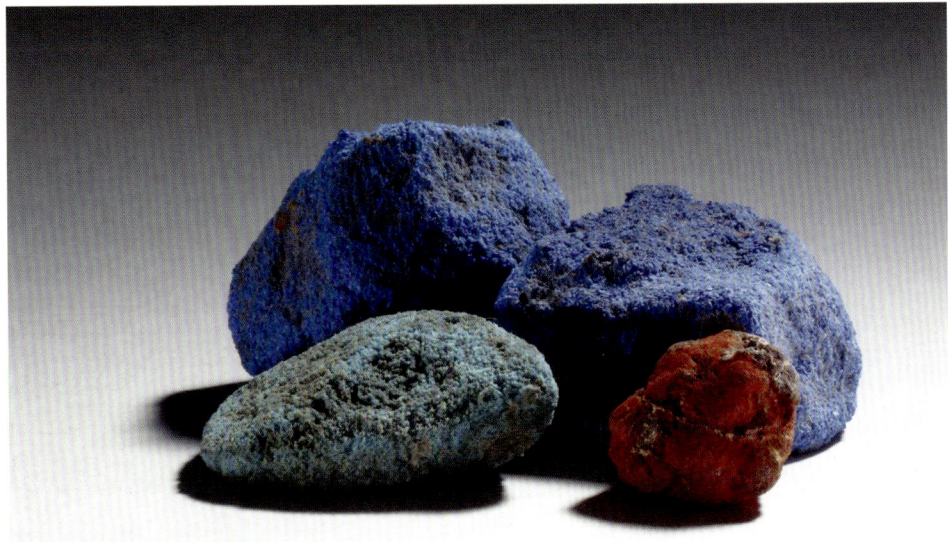

the colour palette. Iron oxides are found throughout the ancient Egyptian period, and provide a range of shades of yellow depending on their overall composition. Iron sulphates (fig. 65) have been identified on objects from about 2700 BC to the end of the Roman Period (about AD 395), contributing in particular to the pale, soft yellow hue that is often seen on coffin backgrounds in the Middle Kingdom (about 2010–1790 BC). It can be challenging to differentiate between the various yellow, orange and red earths due to their chemical similarities and the tendency for these materials to be found closely associated with each other in nature.

The bright lemon-hued pigment orpiment (arsenic sulphide) was widely used. The crystal structure catches the light, conferring a sparkle to the surface, and the pigment was probably used as a substitute for gold. It is found extensively on the Fitzwilliam coffin collection and has been noted as early as the Middle Kingdom. However, orpiment may oxidise to a colourless pigment, resulting in the whitening of yellow areas of decoration over time.

The ancient Egyptians are generally credited with creating the earliest manufactured pigments: Egyptian blue and Egyptian green. Egyptian blue was common from the Fourth Dynasty (about 2640–2505 BC) and is the only blue pigment found so far on coffins of the Pharaonic Period. Egyptian green is known from the Eleventh Dynasty (from about 2120 BC) and is thought to disappear after the Twenty-first Dynasty (about 945 BC). Both pigments were made by heating copper minerals (or scrap metal from copper and bronze working) with limestone and quartz sand. An alkali (in the form of plant ash, natron or salts from Nile river water) was added to reduce the melting temperature. The process produced a glassy 'frit'. Whether this material was blue or green depended on the relative proportions of the mixture and the temperature reached during firing, different combinations creating physically different frits.

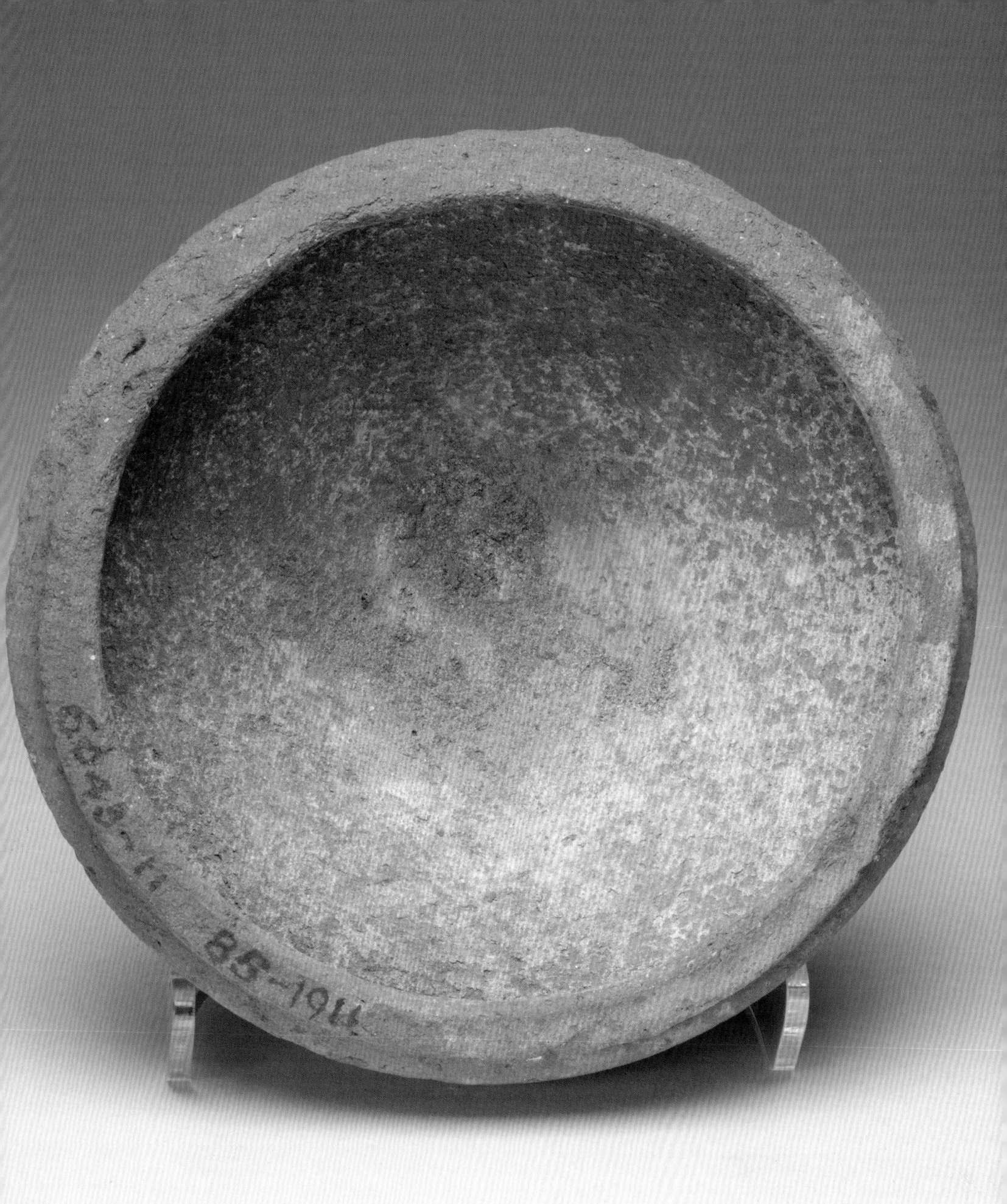

Other green pigments used by the Egyptians are almost all copper based, the exception being green earth (iron oxide based), which came into use from the Twenty-second Dynasty and continued through to the Roman period (up to AD 395). As further analytical work is carried out, the copper-based greens are proving to be more and more complicated. Pigments include malachite, chrysocolla, copper-wax, copper-proteinate, copper carbohydrate and verdigris (copper acetate). Many of these materials are susceptible to deterioration, forming copper chlorides such as atacamite and chlorite, and some can themselves form as deterioration products of other copper pigments. The mineral malachite is the earliest known green. It was gradually replaced by Egyptian green, but returned to the palette in the steady diversification of green pigments.

Identification of white pigments on a coffin is not entirely straightforward, as areas of white may be achieved either by leaving the preparation layer uncovered or by application of a separate white paint layer to the decoration. The two are not always obviously different, especially as both preparation layer and paint are generally calcium based. The most common white pigment is calcium carbonate, chipped from the extensive ranges of limestone hills. This is found in different forms: sparitic calcite, which is more crystalline and coarse, and micritic chalk, which is made up of microfossils. Microfossils can help to identify the origins of the chalk. For example, the chalk of the paste used to make the Roman cartonnage mask (cat. 55.a) was found to be local to the findspot of the object at Hawara, south of Cairo. Within the Fitzwilliam collection, the calcium sulphates (gypsum, bassanite and anhydrite) have been found only in pastes and preparation layers, a trend which seems to agree with research carried out in other institutions. Huntite, a bright white magnesium calcium carbonate, has been identified on a number of Egyptian coffins in other collections. Particularly bright whites have been noted on several objects in the Fitzwilliam, but so far huntite has been positively identified only on the cartonnage mummy case of Nakhtefmut (cat. 32).

As more technical examination and analyses are carried out, it is becoming clear that some materials were introduced earlier and were used more widely than previously thought. Orpiment and huntite, for example, were described thirty years ago as exotic materials with restricted use, but their use is now seen to be widespread.

Major changes to the range of pigments available came as Egypt was drawn under the influence and then rule of first the Greeks and then the Romans (from 332 BC). As noted above, the range of greens increased and other new pigments were introduced, including lead white, red lead, indigo (blue) and madder (pink). These materials invigorated the traditional palette with new shades of pink and orange, delicate mauves and deep purple. The vibrancy and range of colours are seen on the gilded mask and footcase (fig. 66) and the red mummy shroud (cat. 54). Analysis carried out at the Getty Conservation Institute on

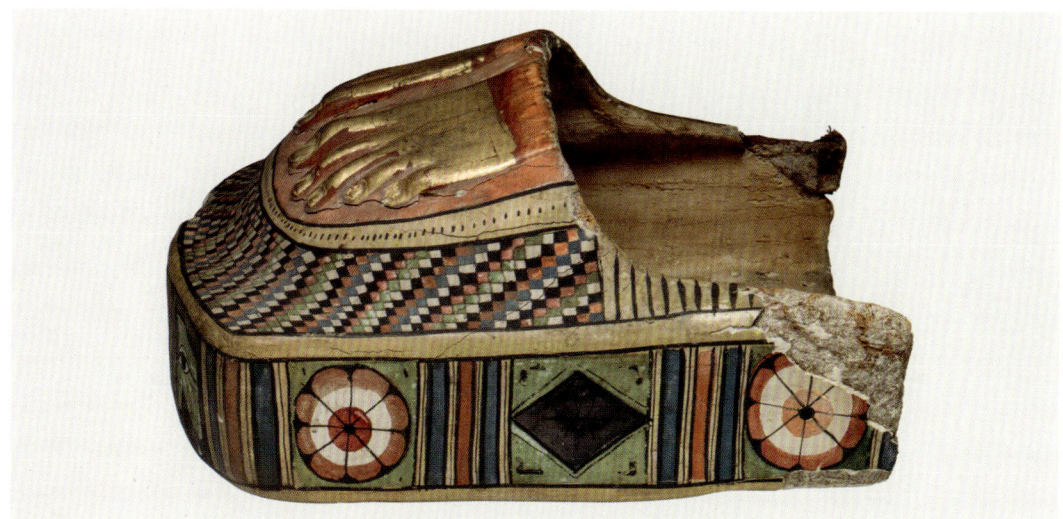

Fig. 66
Sideview of the Roman footcase (cat. 55.b)

red lead pigment from these three objects, as well as from seven other Roman Egyptian red mummy shrouds, has shown that the pigment on all three of the Fitzwilliam's objects was sourced from the Roman silver mines at Rio Tinto in Spain, where it was a by-product of silver refining.

Resins and varnishes used on coffins
— *Rebecca Stacey*

Resins are sticky, water-resistant exudates from plants and have been exploited for millennia for use as general-purpose adhesives and coatings. Their fragrant and antibacterial properties make them useful in medicines, for incense and in embalming. They are usually the main ingredients of the varnishes applied to ancient Egyptian coffin surfaces, and were used as adhesives for applied decoration and inlays. They sometimes appear on coffin interiors as deposits of embalming treatments transferred by contact with the mummies they once held.

Interpretation of the composition of varnishes and resins can be complicated by the mixing of materials and the effects of ageing, which change the chemical composition. The translucent yellow varnishes – for example, on the coffins of Nespawershefyt (cat. 26) – invariably comprise *Pistacia spp.* resin (also known as mastic; fig. 67), sometimes mixed with oil, as on Nakhtefmut's cartonnage (cat. 32) or other resins. Conifer resins are sometimes seen in these mixtures, and conifer tars, manufactured from resin or wood by heating, may be found in the darker or black varnishes and deposits. The dark varnishes – seen, for example, on the head end from a yellow coffin (cat. 31) and Nakhtefmut's Sons of Horus figures (cat. 34) – show considerable variability in composition and can be particularly challenging to identify. Some contain bitumen, a petroleum

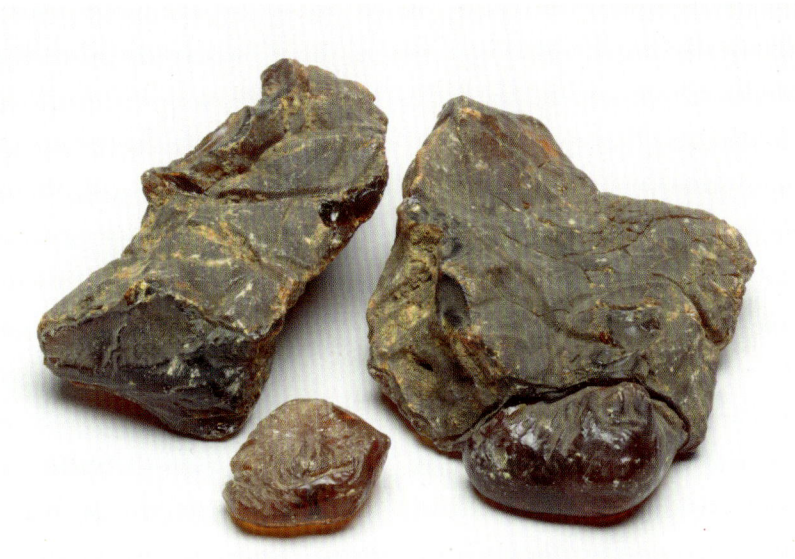

Fig. 67
Pistacia spp. resin found at Abydos (Fitzwilliam Museum, E.114.1903)

Fig. 68
Brushes made of plant fibres and sticks, probably from Thebes, about 14th century BC (British Museum, EA36893 and EA36889)

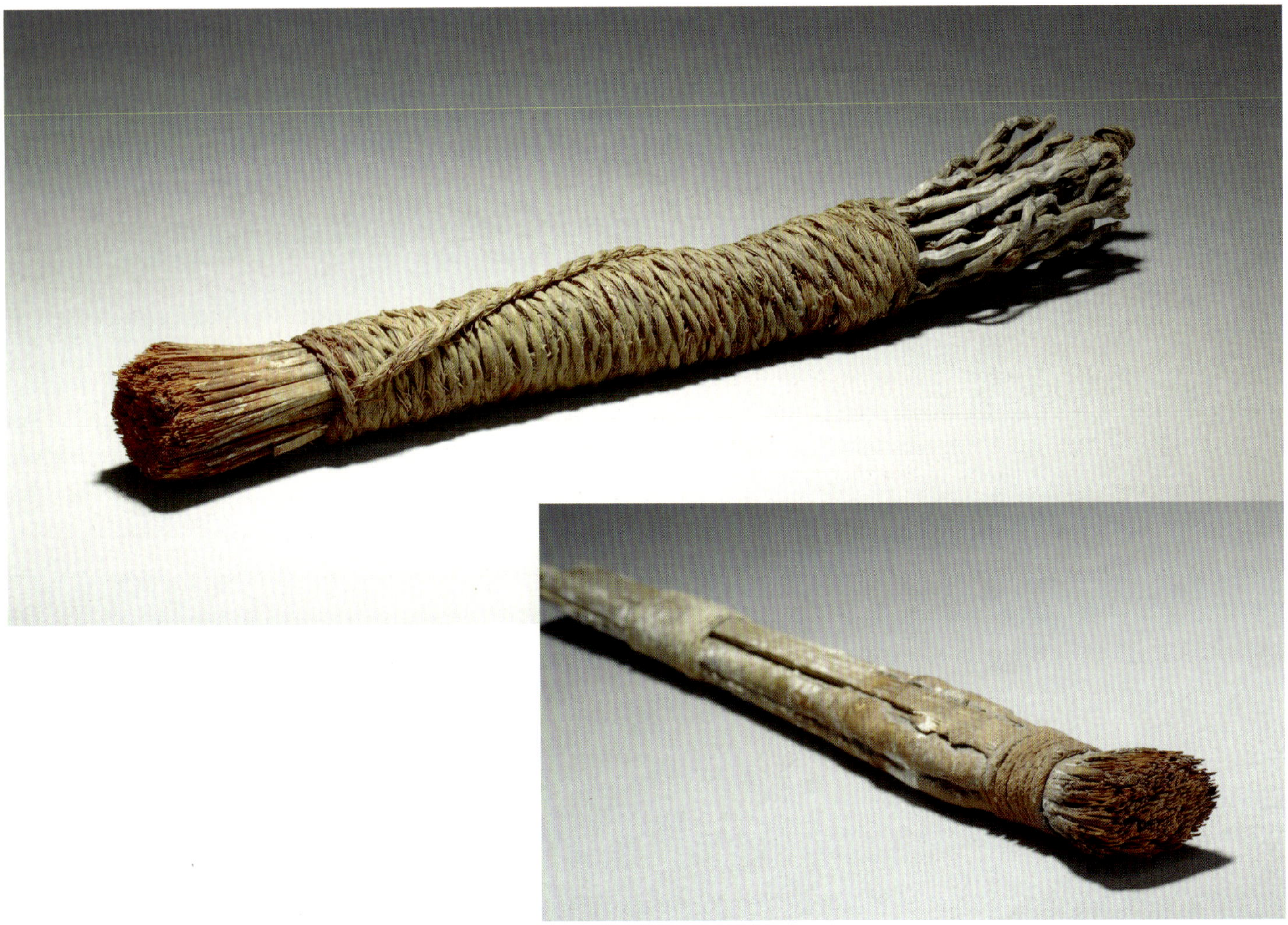

100   Egyptian Coffins: Materials, Construction and Decoration

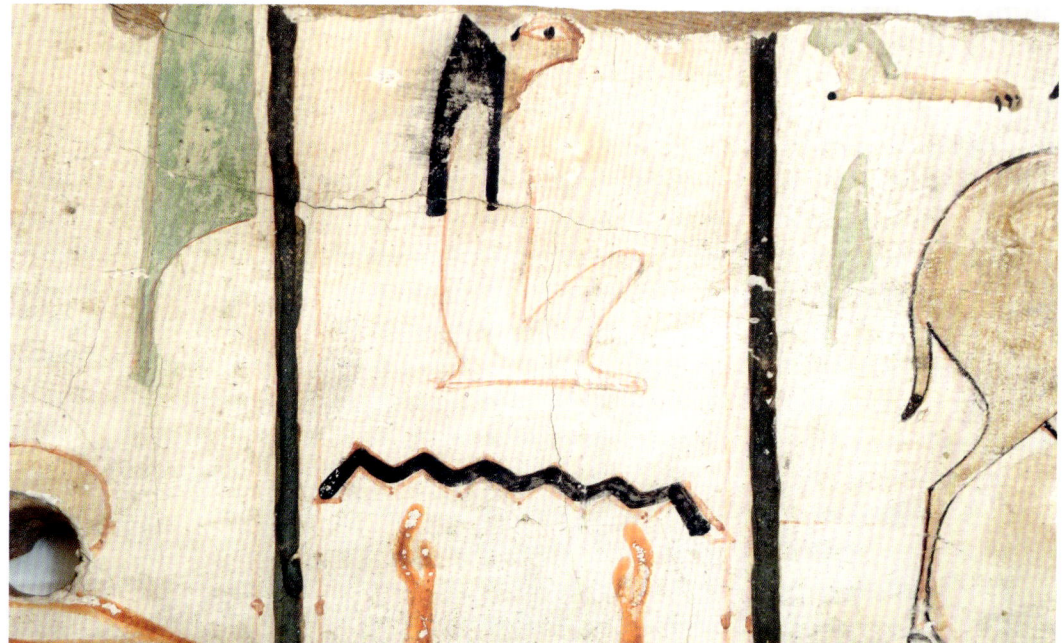

Fig. 69
Blobs of red paint indicate where text dividers should be placed on the coffin of Wepwawetemhat (cat. 13)

product with widespread sources in the Near East. Others are compositionally indistinguishable from the yellow varnishes and may be varnished black paints. Some of the blue paints appear dark or black due to the optical effect produced by the darkening of either overlying varnish or gum binding medium, due to ageing.

Methods and techniques of decoration

A painter's toolkit included a variety of pens and brushes made from single reeds, bundles of plant fibres or sticks of fibrous wood (date palm) frayed at the end. A number of these brushes have been found at archaeological sites in Egypt (fig. 68), often still caked with pigment, and detached brush fibres are often seen caught in the paint on coffins. Short hairs found in several varnish layers on coffins in the Fitzwilliam's collection may suggest that Egyptian painters also used brushes made from hair. Pigments were prepared by grinding on hard stone blocks and mixing the powder with medium, and the paint dispensed from a variety of vessels used as paint pots (see fig. 65).

At the start of the decorating process, setting-out lines were usually applied to position the basic elements of the design and text. Small blobs of paint indicate where these should be placed; there are examples on the red text dividers of the coffin fragment of Wepwawetemhat (fig. 69) and for the spacing of stripes on the inner coffin of Pakepu (fig. 70). When applied to the preparation layer, the lines were often covered over as the painting progressed (see fig. 93 on pp. 170–1). Where they are visible on the surface, the characteristic strokes of a

Fig. 70
Inner coffin of Pakepu (cat. 43). At the foot end, black marks (marked) were applied along the edge of the plinth to indicate the positioning of the coloured bands.

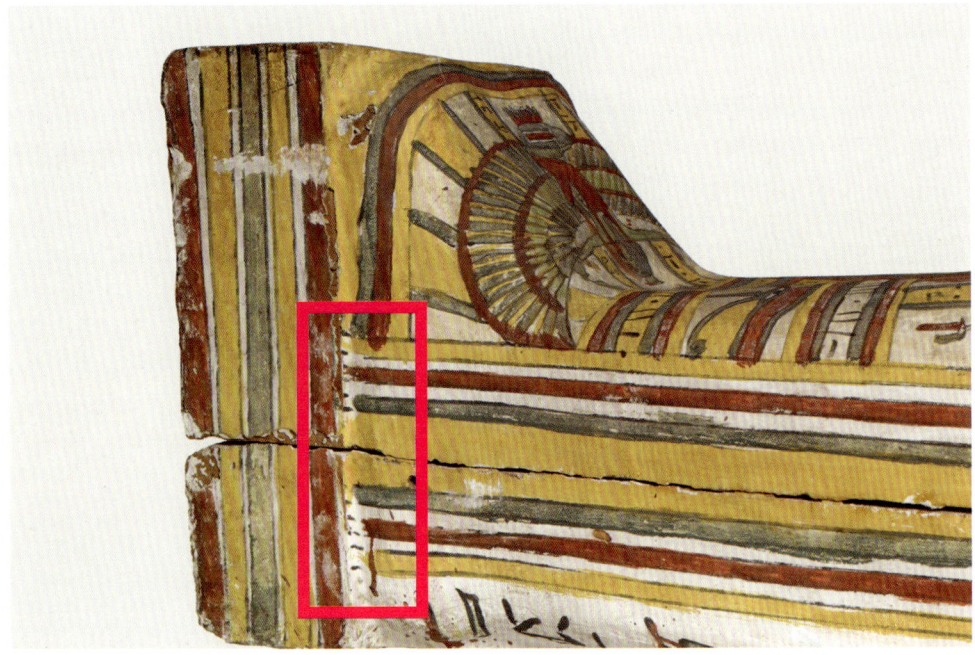

pen against a straight edge are clear: the small blot where the initial pressure was applied, the trailing off of the line as the charge of paint on the pen ran out (see cat. 11.1). Sometimes, there is a slight feathering along the line where the straight-edged guide was removed from the line of wet paint.

Although there are many examples of freehand painting on Egyptian coffins, such as the exterior surface of Pakepu's intermediate coffin box (cat. 43), preliminary drawings of the scenes and text were usually executed in red or black and can sometimes be seen where the painted areas deviate from the drawing (fig. 71). A damaged fragment of cartonnage (fig. 73) shows that these sketches were also sometimes carried out ahead of the application of the preparation layer, perhaps as practice for the actual decoration. The preliminary drawings are often re-emphasised as black or red outlines on completion of the rest of the painting. Though drawings were carried out freehand and with the use of straight edges (fig. 72), the regularity and repeatability of many curved shapes, such as the sweep of broad collars and wings, show that templates and scribers were also used (fig. 74).

Colour was applied in blocks within the drawing outlines. At first sight, each colour appears to be composed of a single pigment. However, complexity in the use and combination of materials is documented increasingly as the paintings on more coffins are examined and analysed. In the red-yellow pigment range, variation in hue was effected by exploiting the natural colour diversity in the ochres, but combinations of realgar and red ochre, as well as yellow earth and orpiment, have also been identified. It is not uncommon for more than one type of red or yellow pigment to be used on a single object, creating subtle tonality and striking combinations of colours.

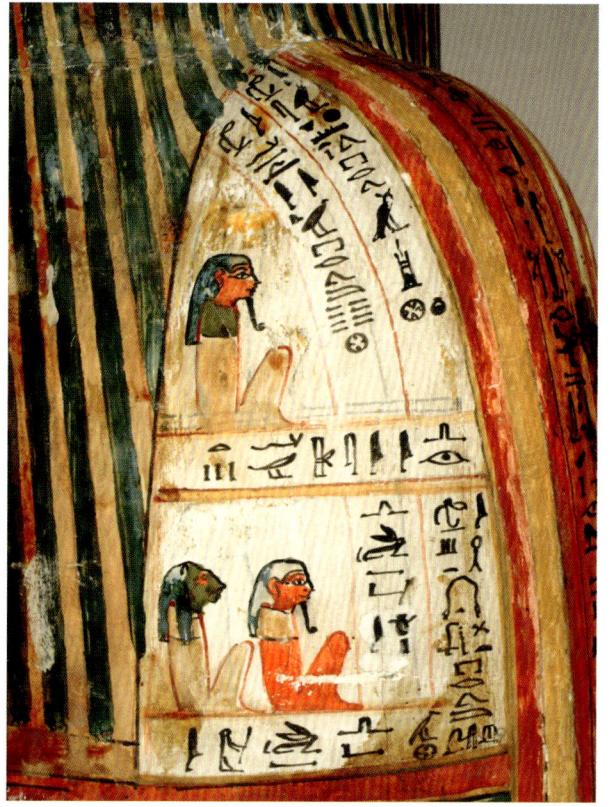

Fig. 71
Text and figures on the back of Nakhtefmut's cartonnage mummy case (cat. 32). The initial black drawing is visible underneath the final painting: the positioning of the text dividers and the single seated god has changed slightly.

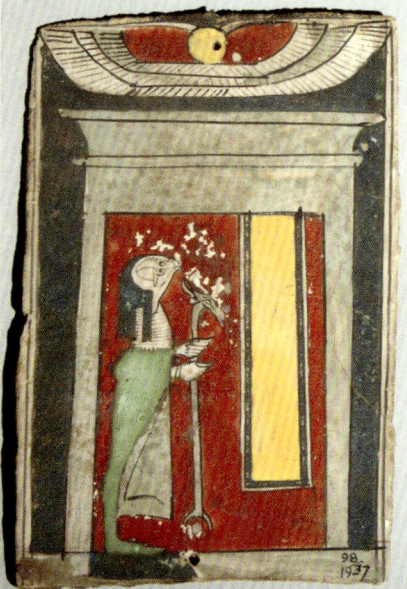

Fig. 72
A cartonnage fragment, probably Roman Period (Fitzwilliam Museum, E.98.1937), showing a falcon-headed god within a shrine, surmounted by a winged sun disk. A combination of the use of a straight edge and freehand drawing on the sun's wings has resulted in awkward curves.

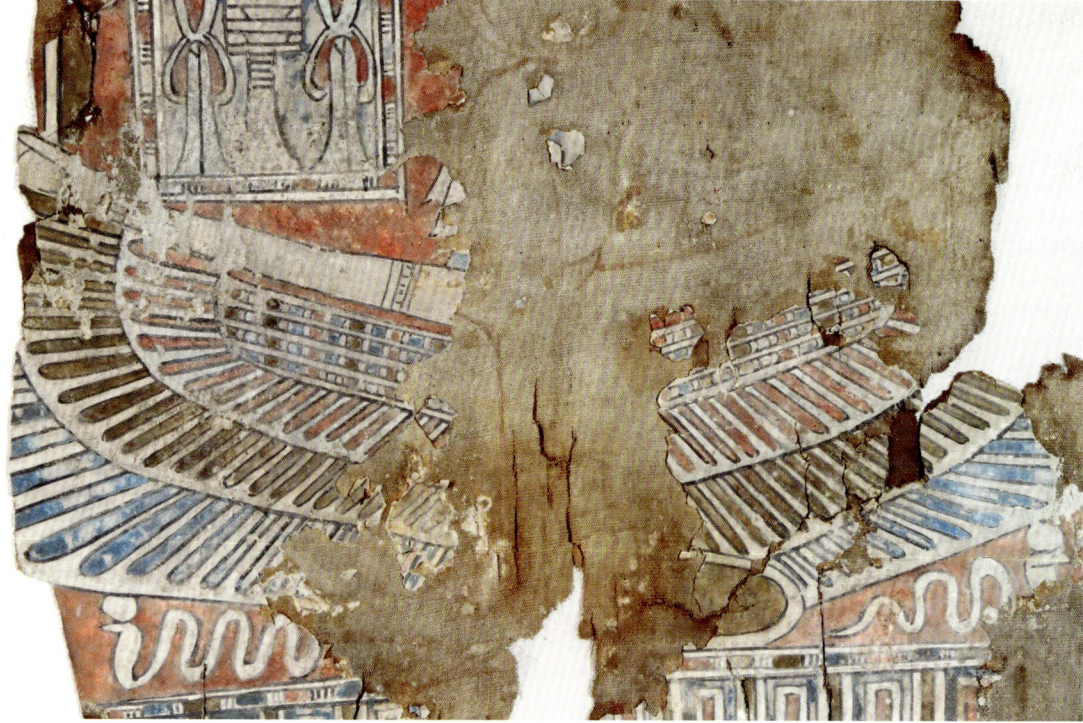

Fig. 73
A cartonnage fragment, probably from a Roman coffin (Fitzwilliam Museum, E.1.1869), showing a red drawing of the goddess Nut underneath the preparation layer

Julie Dawson, Jennifer Marchant and Eleanor von Aderkas

Fig. 74
Footboard of Djeher's coffin (cat. 47), decorated with a *shen*-hieroglyph (meaning 'eternity'). At the centre of the perfect circles is a hole where perhaps a point was held and the circles drawn using a pen attached to a string. Alternatively, some sort of beam compass may have been used.

Fig. 75
Green area, built up with overlapping layers of different colours of paint on Nakht's coffin (cat. 15)

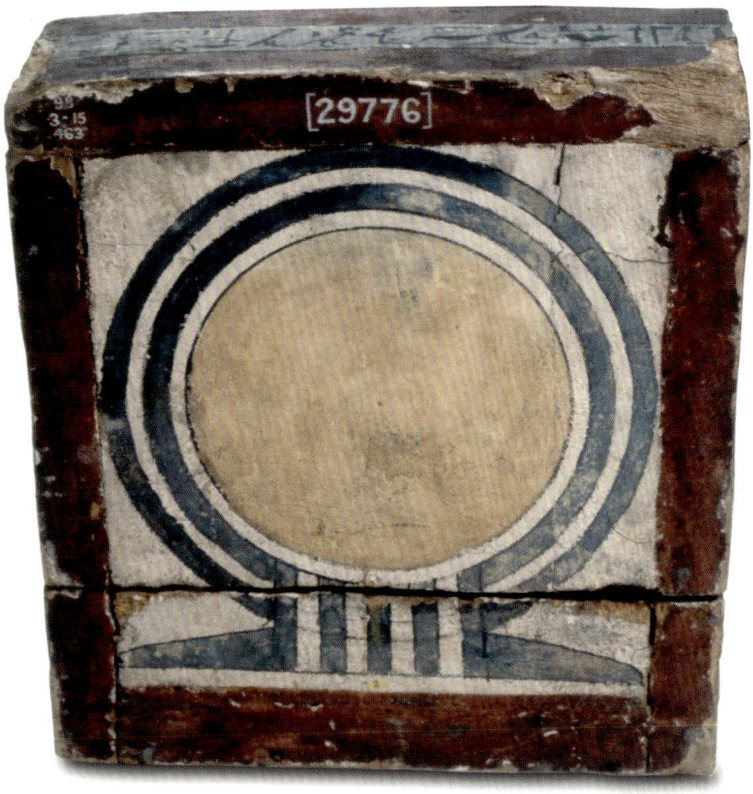

A range of colours could be achieved by grinding certain pigments to different levels of fineness, as with orpiment and Egyptian blue; Egyptian blue could also be thinly applied to achieve a washed-out pale tone (see fig. 72). Colour could be lightened through mixing with white. For example, Egyptian blue combined with lead white was identified on the Ptolemaic Period cartonnage fragment showing Nut (cat. 16), and there are several instances from earlier periods of mixtures of other colours and calcite. Reds and blues were mixed with carbon-based black to darken them; for example, the red on the interior of the outer coffin of Nespawershefyt (cat. 26). Greens have been produced from various combinations of blue and yellow or blue and green pigments. These may be mixtures or overlapping layers of different coloured paint, as on Nakht's coffin (fig. 75). The Roman Period saw more options for colour mixtures, as demonstrated by the gilded cartonnage mask (cat. 55.a).

The order in which paint colours were applied varies across objects, but generally each colour was applied in turn, suggesting that a single batch of paint was produced and used across the coffin, or even a whole batch of coffins, in the workshop before mixing the next colour. The gums and glue used as media in paints would have had a tendency to congeal, dry or need reheating, making this a practical working method. Egyptian green and Egyptian blue were often the last colours to be added. This possibly reflects the different texture and thickness

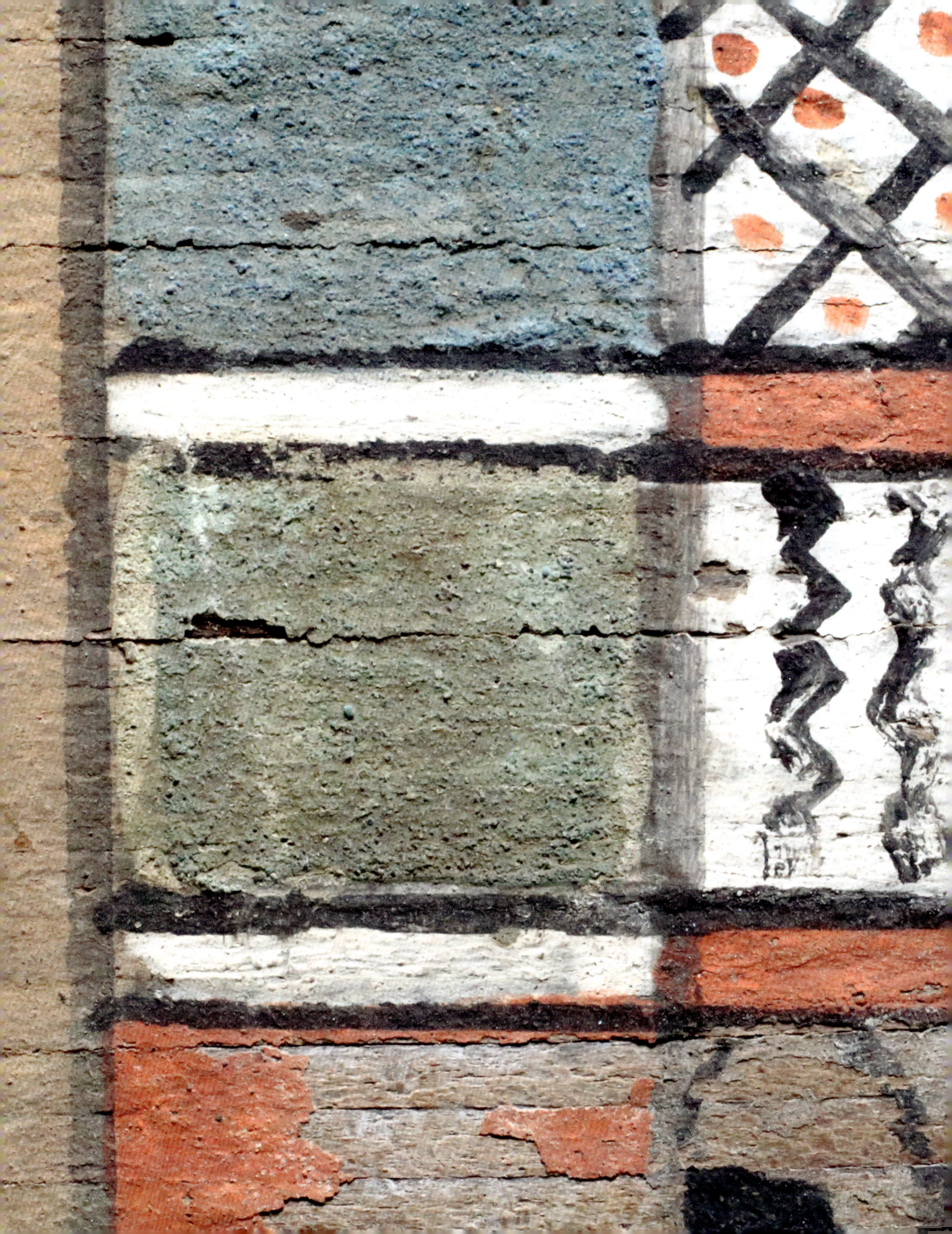

Fig. 76
Detail of the side panel of Nakht's coffin (cat. 15), showing how the Egyptian blue has pooled towards the bottom of the stripe

of application of these paints, qualities which also give some further clues to the working methods of the painters: Egyptian blue in particular is an excellent indicator of the orientation of a coffin part during painting. Often applied thickly as a viscous paint, it tended to gather in incipient drips as it dried (fig. 76 and cat. 11.1, pp. 140–1).

Figures and decoration were generally drawn and painted directly onto the white preparation layer, possibly utilising the underlying white to produce a brighter colour. Coloured backgrounds tended to be painted up to the edges of decorative elements. Yellow coffins are an exception to this (cat. 26). On examples of these coffins, a thin layer of yellow has been found, applied all over the preparation layer to underlie the decorative elements, as well as creating the background. The yellow, together with the final thick varnish coating, gives an overall golden effect.

The surface finish on a coffin depends on the granularity of the pigment and how much binder was used. Coffins such as Nakht's (cat. 15) were painted with thin granular paint, causing the light to scatter on the surface, resulting in a matte finish. The red paint on a cartonnage fragment (see fig. 72) is glossy, the paint well ground, thickly applied and containing more binder. Varnish layers also produce a glossy surface and saturate colours. It is not clear what colour they were originally, but varnishes which now appear yellow can alter the appearance of underlying pigments.

Gold leaf was used for emphasis and might be applied before or after painting (fig. 77). Inlay was also used to enrich the decoration and emphasise particular features: carved relief could be filled with caked pigment, such as calcite (e.g., on the *qersu* coffin, cat. 44), or with glass, stone, frit or metal set in adhesive (e.g., eyebrows, eye outlines and eyes).

A striking range of painting techniques can be observed on the coffins. Some reflect the changing character of the decoration in response to stylistic variation; others may illustrate the wishes of the purchaser, the cost of the commission, the availability of time and materials or the practices of particular workshops. The drawing on the coffin fragment of Wepwawetemhat (cat. 13) is extremely delicate, with blocks of colour applied in thin layers and examples of subtle shading and detail: brown patches on the coat of the bull were created with stippling from a small brush and the body of the gazelle was apparently textured by playing the fingertips lightly over the wet paint (fig. 78). The decoration on the coffins of Nespawershefyt (cat. 26) is realised in a few bold colours; it is intricate, dense and full of sculptural effects created mostly by painting and modelling in Egyptian blue and green (fig. 79), enhanced further by fine detailing in black. In contrast to these intricate painting styles, much of the painting on Pakepu's coffin was rapidly executed and accomplished without any preliminary drawing; a considerable amount of the paint was watery and was allowed to run across surfaces (see cat. 43).

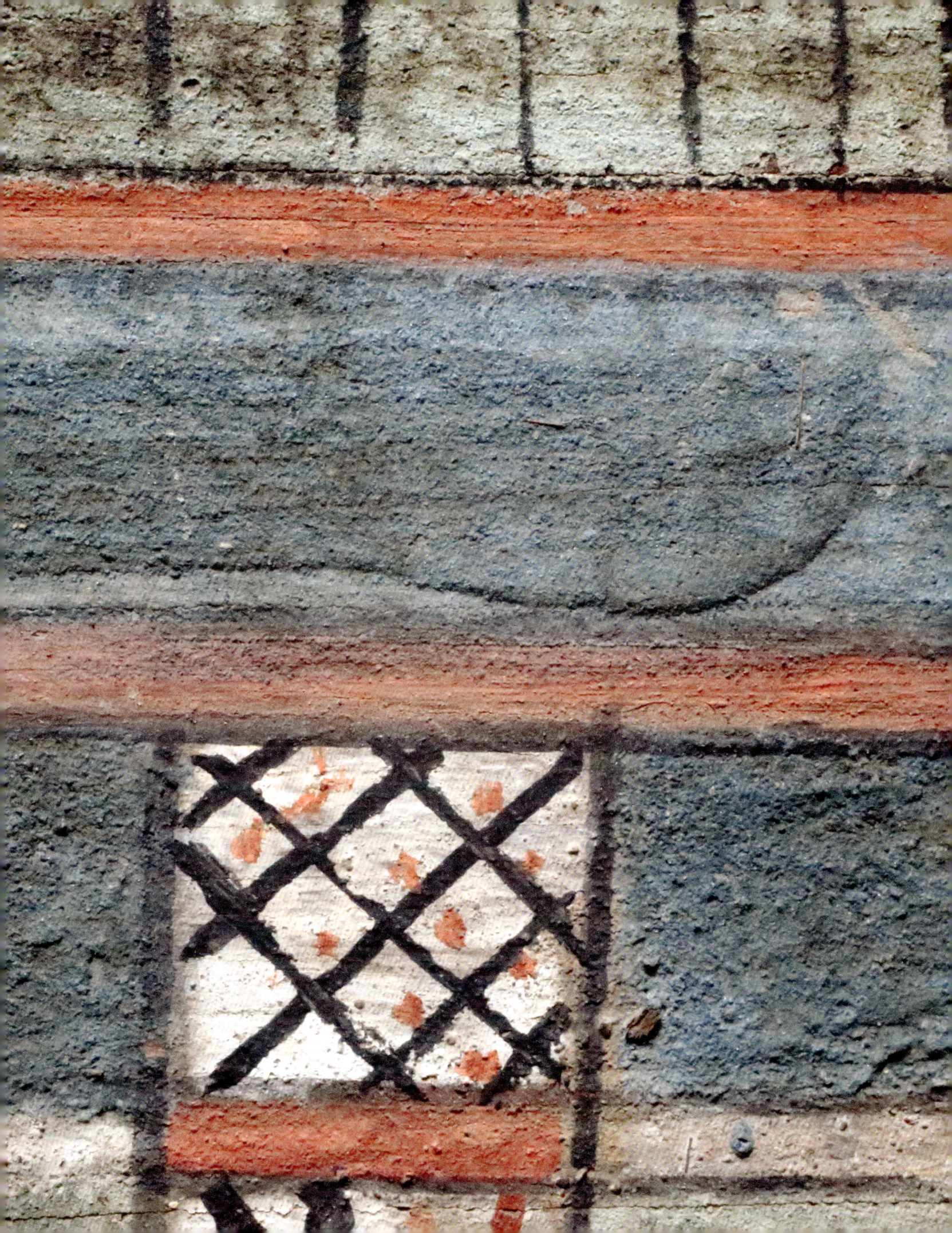

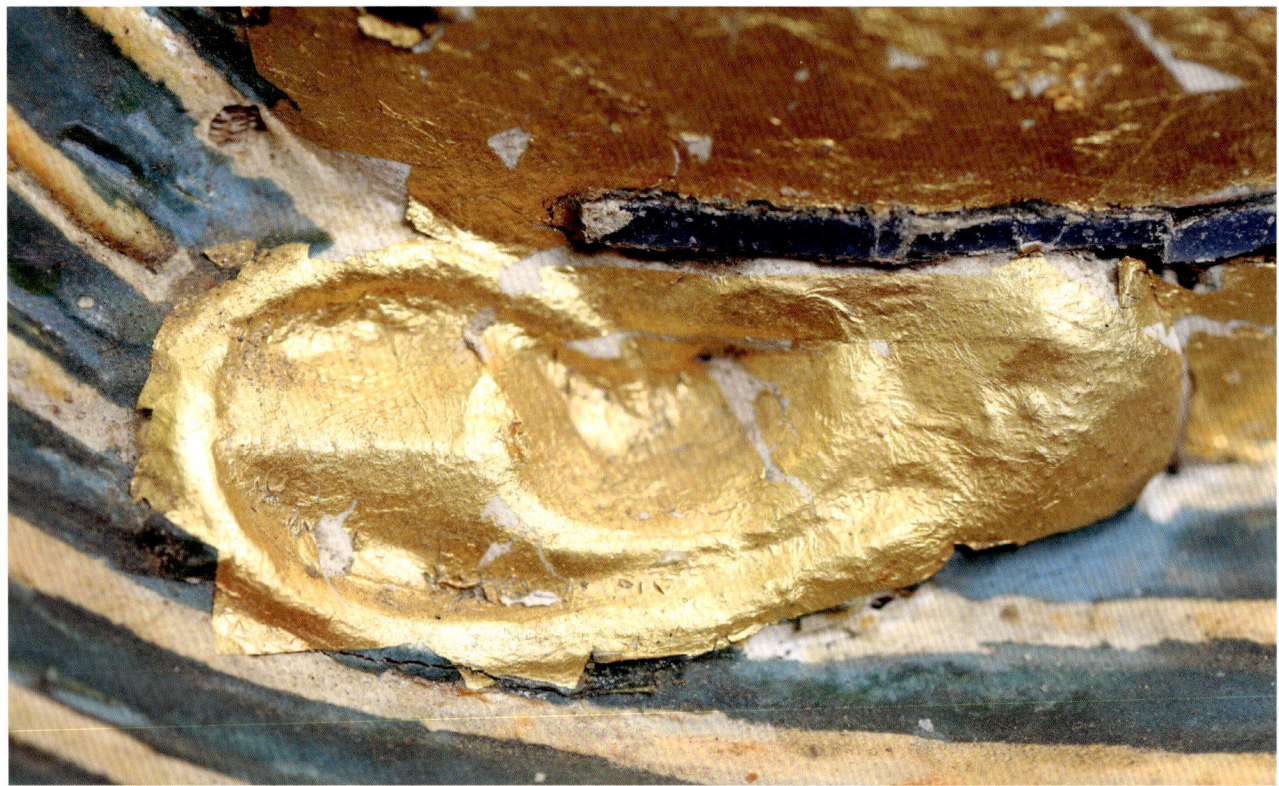

Fig. 77
Gilded ear on the cartonnage mummy case of Nakhtefmut (cat. 32), showing the cut edges of the gold leaf squares that overlie the painted blue stripes of the wig

Connecting with the craftsmen

Studying craft technique can be a powerful way to experience a connection with apparently remote and alien cultures. Whilst we do not have evidence that lets us track all the choices made by a client or a craftsman for a particular coffin in this exhibition, technical study can reveal in detail the sequence of working, any evidence of struggle with recalcitrant materials or the need to stretch resources, and how the success of one stage of the process impacted on the next. For example, symmetry in the design of the decoration is a key feature of most anthropoid coffin lids. Basic equality between the left and right sides was dependent, in the first place, on the accuracy of the carpenters. If this was not achieved, the decorative scheme was already compromised. If the coffin was symmetrical but the draughtsman lost the centre line at an early stage of the drawing process, this would force compromises onto the painter filling in the vignettes. Nothing has gone seriously awry on any of the coffins in the exhibition, but many minor issues have been recorded in this essay and in the catalogue entries. For the team examining the coffins in this project, there was a particular thrill in discovering these very human stumbles and touches within the work: the numerous mistakes covered up or corrected, the doodled eyes on the underside of the Nespawershefyt's inner coffin box (fig. 80), the handprints

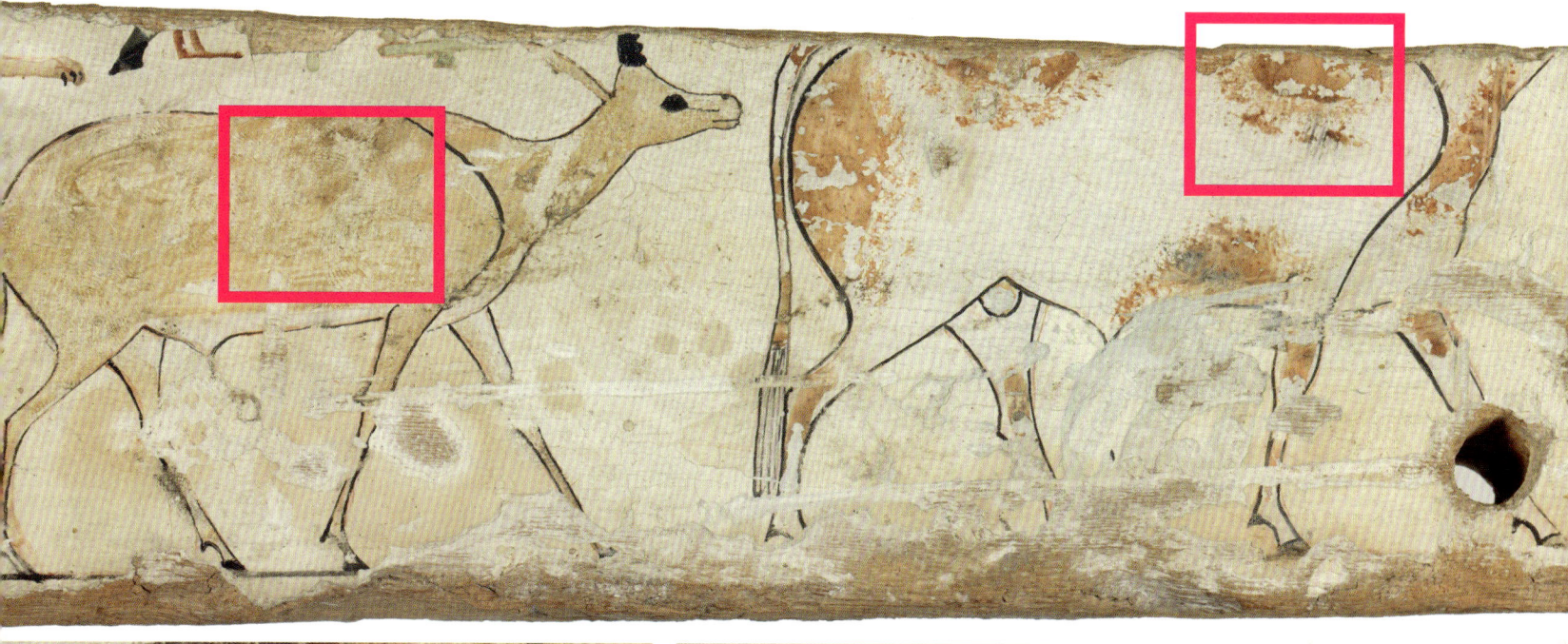

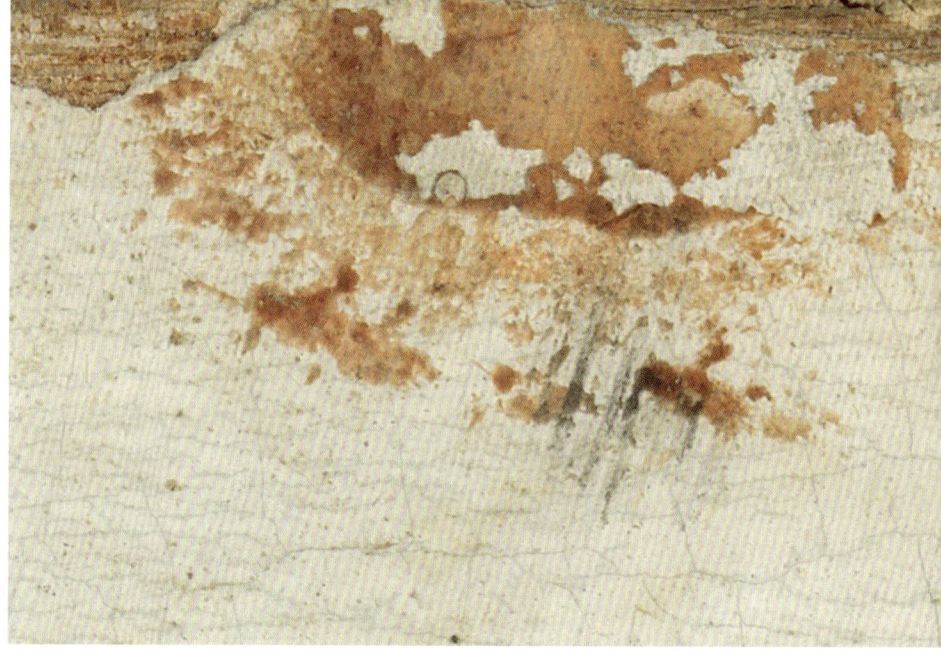

Fig. 78
Detail of a fragment of the coffin of Wepwawetemhat (cat. 13) under raking light, showing texture created with a fingertip on the figure of the gazelle (left) and stippling with a fine brush on the brown patches of the bull's coat (right)

Julie Dawson, Jennifer Marchant and Eleanor von Aderkas

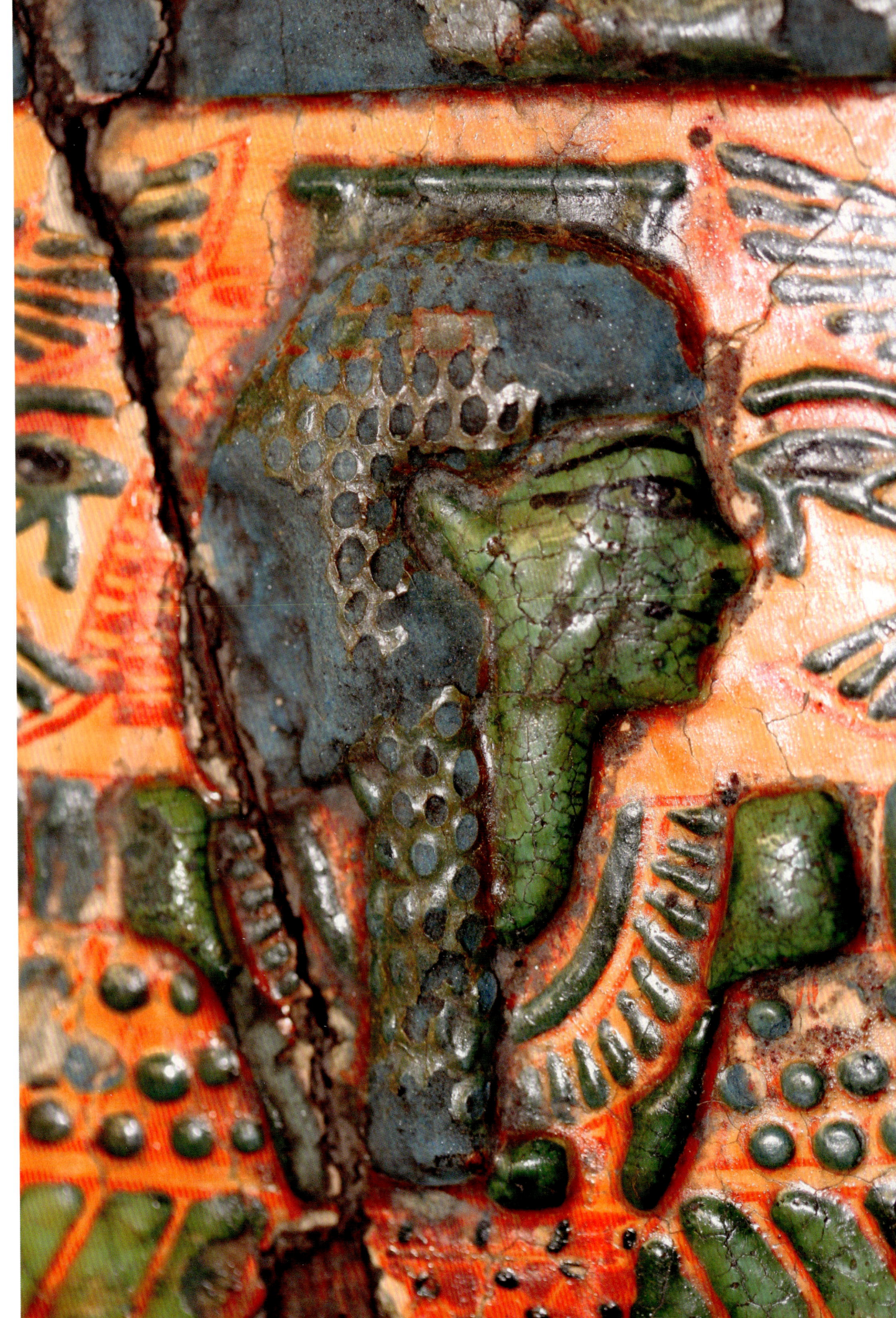

Fig. 79
The goddess Nut at the centre of Nespawershefyt's inner coffin lid (cat. 26). Losses in the overlying varnish layer emphasise the fine detail of the wig modelled in Egyptian blue.

in varnish along the underside of the rim of his inner coffin lid, where it was picked up and moved whilst still wet to the touch (fig. 81).

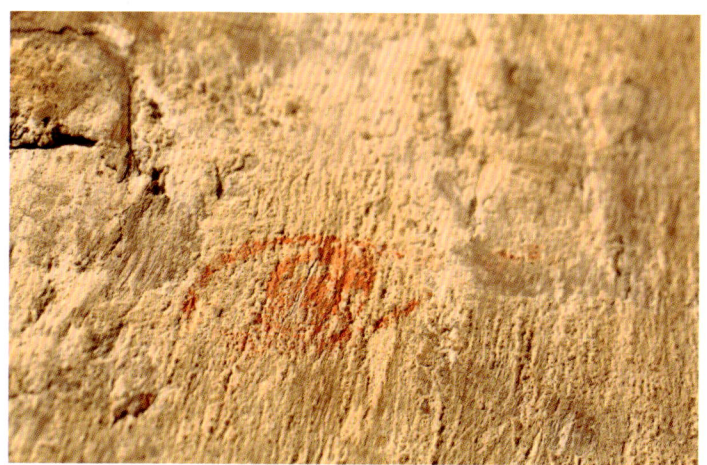
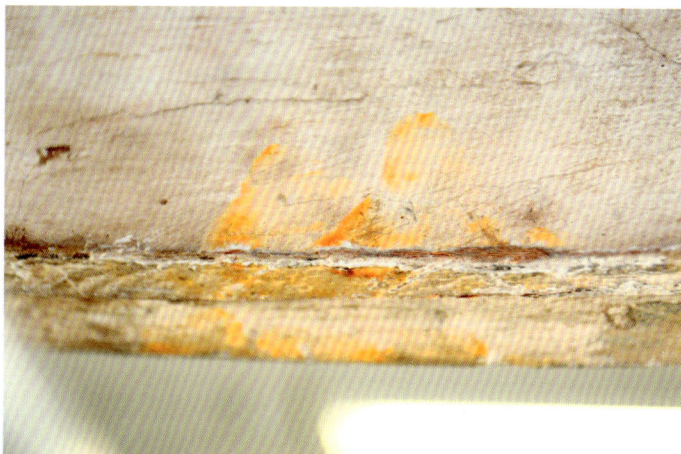

Fig. 80
A doodled eye on the underside of the inner coffin box of Nespawershefyt (cat. 26)

Fig. 81
A handprint in varnish on the underside of the rim of the inner coffin lid of Nespawershefyt (cat. 26)

Further reading

Amenta, Alessia. 'The Vatican Coffin Project. In *Thebes in the First Millennium BC*, edited by Elena Pischikova, Julia Budka and Kenneth Griffin, 483–99. Newcastle upon Tyne: Cambridge Scholars Publishing, 2014.

Gale, Rowena, Peter Gasson, Nigel Hepper and Geoffrey Killen. 'Wood'. In *Ancient Egyptian Materials and Technology*, edited by Paul T. Nicholson and Ian Shaw, 334–71. Cambridge: Cambridge University Press, 2000.

Killen, Geoffrey. *Egyptian Woodworking and Furniture*. Princes Risborough: Shire, 1994.

Krekeler, Anna. 'Zur Herstellungstechnik einteiliger ägyptischer Kartonagesärge aus der Zeit um 800 – 750 v. Chr.' *Zeitschrift für Kunsttechnologie und Konservierung* 21 (2007): 13–32.

Lee, Lorna, and Stephen Quirke. 'Painting Materials.' In *Ancient Egyptian Materials and Technology*, edited by Paul T. Nicholson and Ian Shaw, 104–20. Cambridge: Cambridge University Press, 2000.

Newman, Richard, and Susana M. Halpine. 'The Binding Media of Ancient Egyptian Paintings.' In *Colour and Painting in Ancient Egypt*, edited by W. V. Davies, 22–32. London: British Museum Press, 2001.

Pages-Camagna, Sandrine, and Helene Guichard. 'Egyptian Colours and Pigments in French Collections: 30 Years of Physicochemical Analyses on 300 Objects.' In *Decorated Surfaces on Ancient Egyptian Objects: Technology, Deterioration and Conservation*, edited by J. Dawson, C. Rozeik and M. M. Wright, 25–31. London: Archetype, 2010.

Rowe, Sophie, Ruth Siddall and Rebecca Stacey. 'Roman Egyptian Gilded Cartonnage: Technical Study and Conservation of a Mummy Mask from Hawara.' In *Decorated Surfaces on Ancient Egyptian Objects: Technology, Deterioration and Conservation*, edited by J. Dawson, C. Rozeik and M. M. Wright, 106–21. London: Archetype, 2010.

Scott, David A. 'Greener Shades of Pale: A Review of Advances in the Characterisation of Ancient Egyptian Green Pigments.' In *Decorated Surfaces on Ancient Egyptian Objects: Technology, Deterioration and Conservation*, edited by J. Dawson, C. Rozeik and M. M. Wright, 32–45. London: Archetype, 2010.

Serpico, M., and R. White. 'The Use and Identification of Varnish on New Kingdom Funerary Equipment.' In *Colour and Painting in Ancient Egypt*, edited by W. V. Davies, 33–42, plate 8. London: British Museum Press, 2001.

Singleton, D. 'An Investigation of Two Twenty-first Dynasty Painted Coffin Lids (EA24792 and EA35287) for Evidence of Materials and Workshop Practices.' In *The Theban Necropolis: Past, Present and Future*, edited by Nigel Strudwick and John H. Taylor, 83–87, plates 28–42. London: British Museum Press, 2003.

Taylor, J. H. 'The Development of Cartonnage Cases.' In *Mummies and Magic: The Funerary Arts of Ancient Egypt*, edited by Sue D'Auria, Peter Lacovara and Catharine H. Roehrig, 166–67. Dallas: Dallas Museum of Art, 1992.

Walton, M. S. and Trentelman, K. 'Romano-Egyptian Red Lead Pigment: A Subsidiary Commodity of Spanish Silver Mining and Refinement.' *Archaeometry* 51, no. 5 (2009): 845–60.

Julie Dawson, Jennifer Marchant and Eleanor von Aderkas

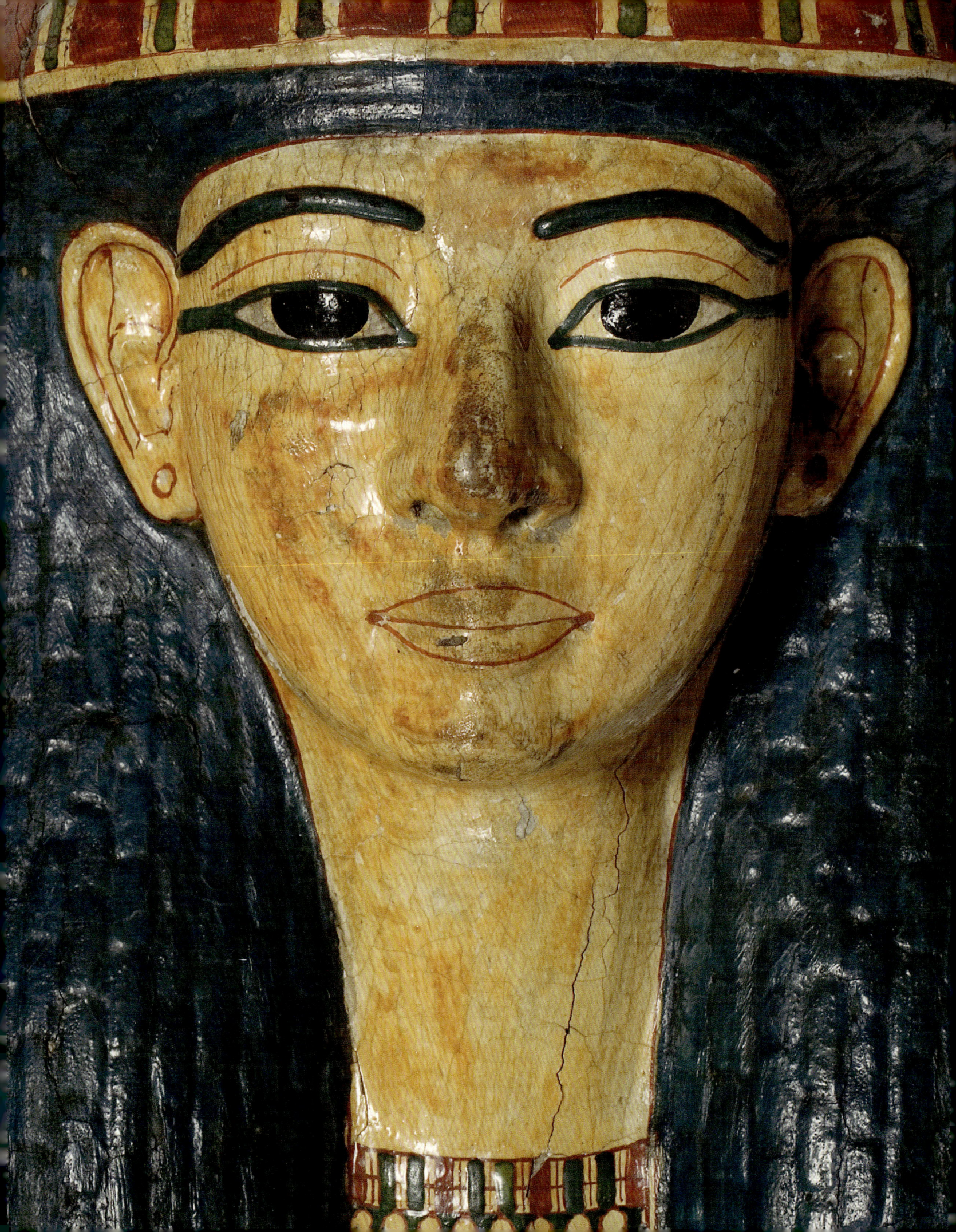

CATALOGUE

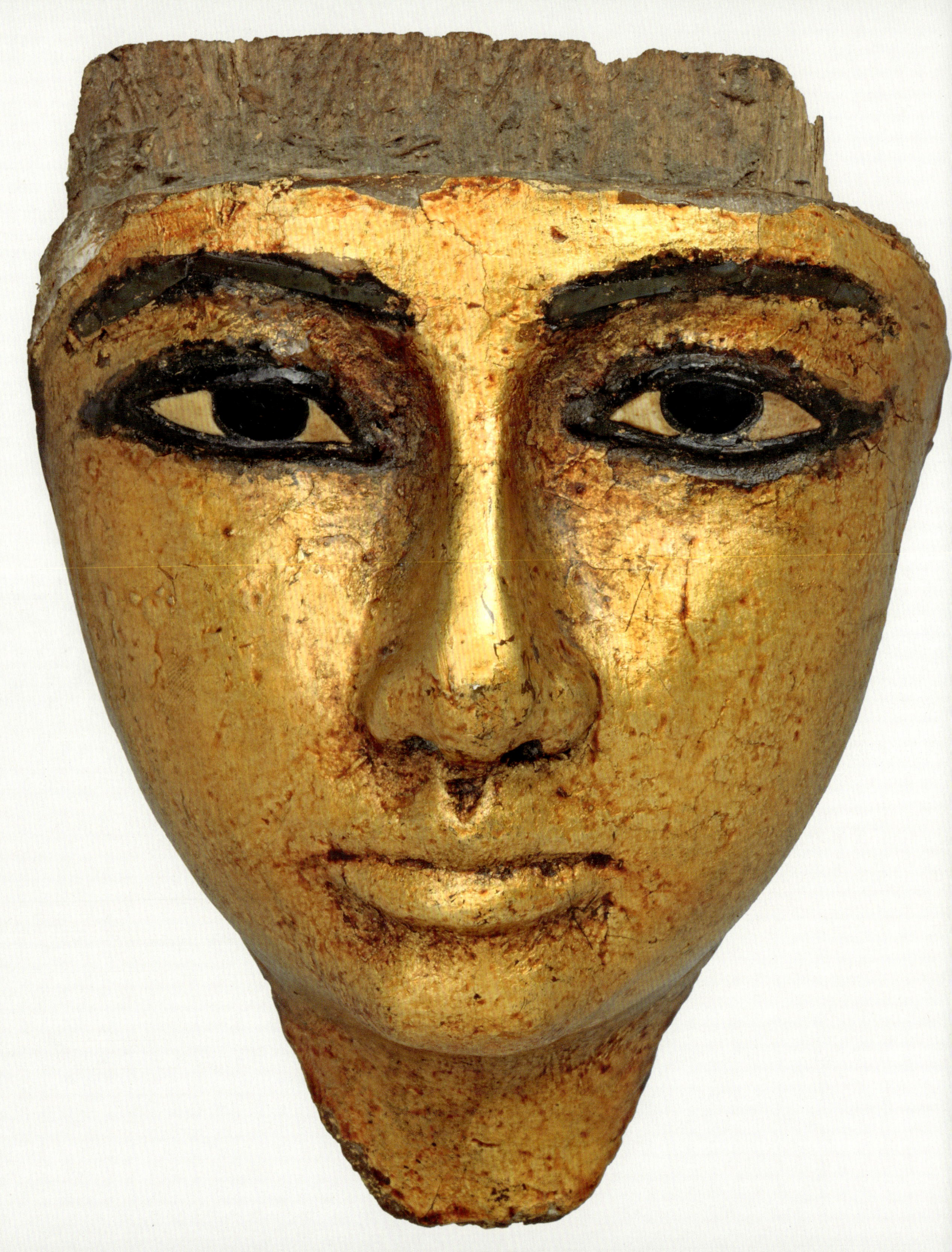

Previous page
Detail of the coffin of Nespawershefyt
(cat. 26)

Introduction

Many museums around the world have in their collections one or more faces from ancient Egyptian coffins. These faces were fixed to the front of anthropoid (human-shaped) coffins from about 1500 BC onwards (fig. 83). They could be painted or gilded (fig. 82), often with a separate beard attached (fig. 84) and sometimes with inlaid eyes and eyebrows.

As they survive now, separated from their coffins, these faces present us with beautifully crafted images of the people they represent. Using modern imaging and analytical techniques, we are able to examine the way they were created, decorated and fixed to the coffins. This tells us about the techniques – and skill – of the craftsmen who made them. The people whose faces they are meant to represent, however, are now completely anonymous. Any connection with the individuals who lived, died and were buried inside the coffins to which the faces were originally attached has been lost. By studying the more complete coffins in our collection, supplementing analytical work carried out at the Fitzwilliam with the results of studies currently being undertaken around the world, and by studying the texts and decoration of these coffins, we are able to place these objects into the context in which the people lived. We can know something of the burial customs, as well as economic factors, that affected the choices available to an individual when it came to selecting a type of coffin and how it would be decorated. And this, too, helps us to understand the choices available to the craftsmen responsible for creating these striking objects.

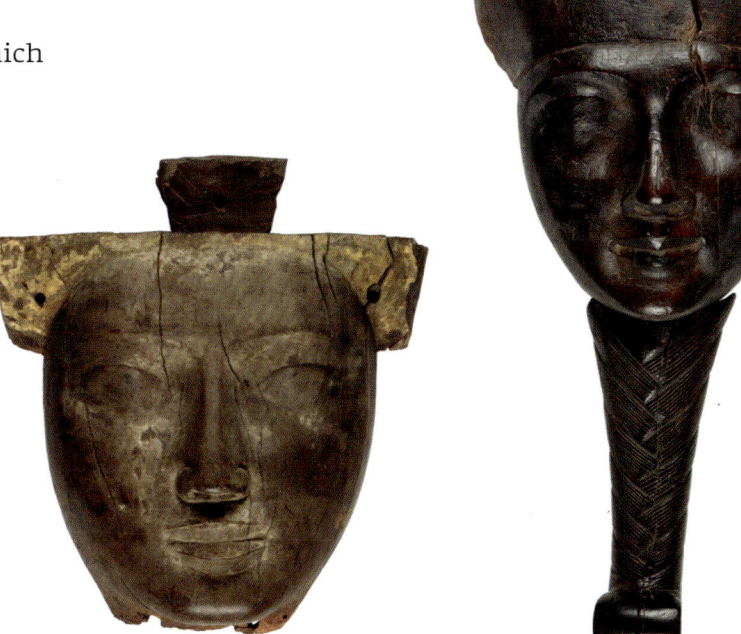

Fig. 82 opposite: Gilded face from a coffin (Fitzwilliam Museum, E.GA.505.1947; given by R. G. Gayer-Anderson)
Fig. 83 left: Face from a coffin (Fitzwilliam Museum, E.49.1926; given by the British School of Archaeology in Egypt)
Fig. 84 right: Face with a beard from a coffin (Fitzwilliam Museum, E.GA.111.1949; given by R. G. Gayer-Anderson)

Catalogue

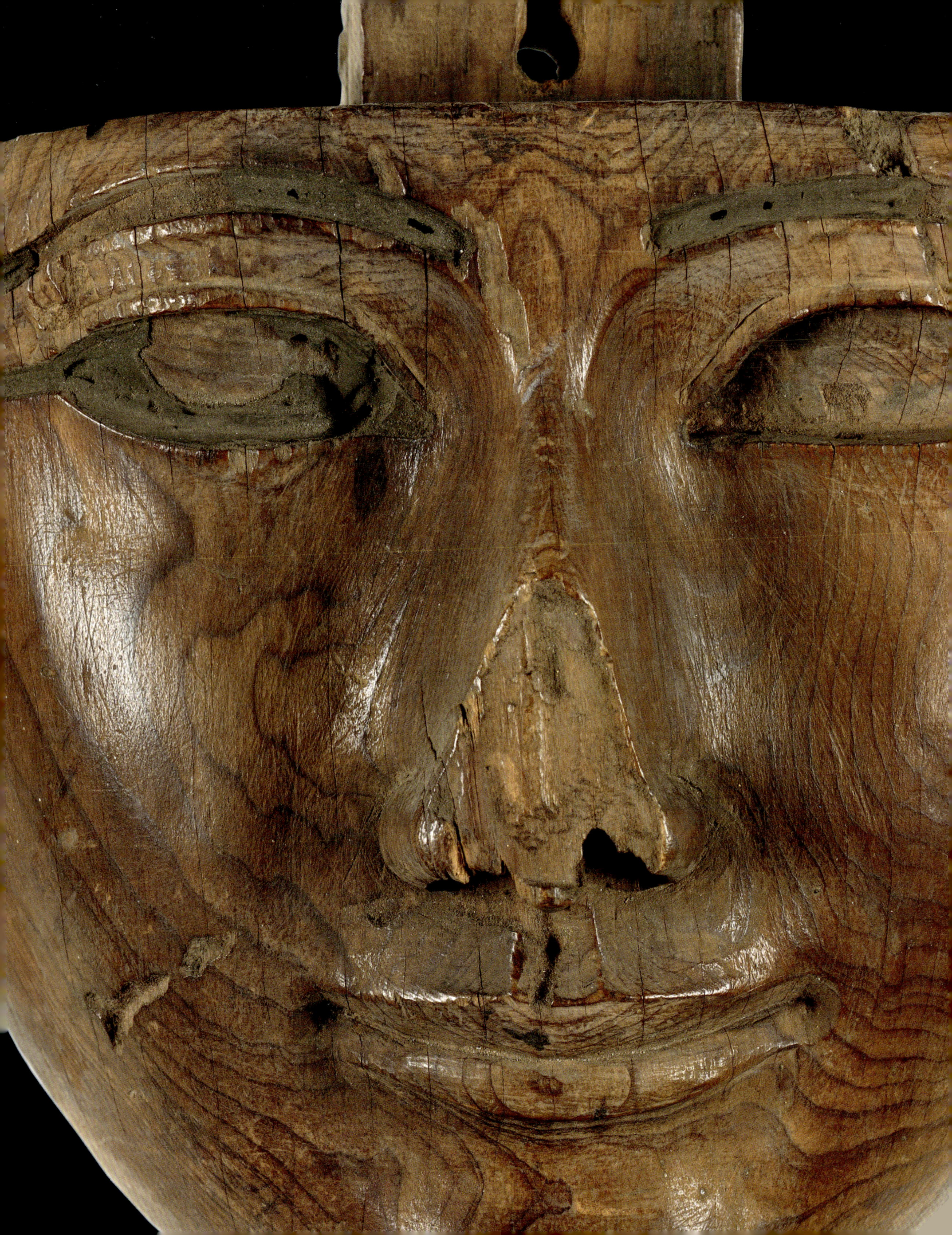

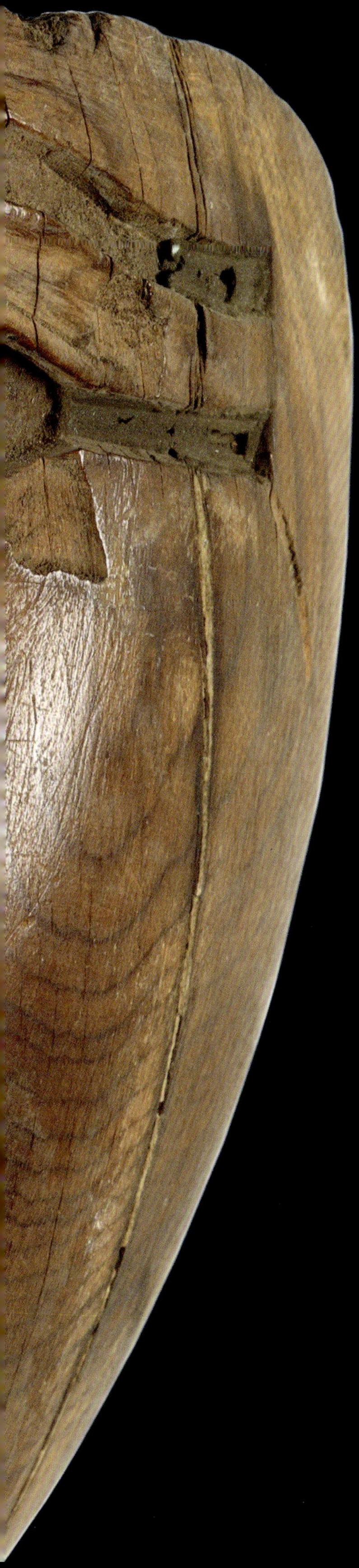

Cat. 1

1

Face from a New Kingdom coffin

This coffin face is carved from sidr, with recesses for inlaid eyes and eyebrows. The inlays are lost, but impressions of them survive in the remains of the adhesive, which is made of Egyptian blue and gum.

About 1550–1070 BC
Fitzwilliam Museum, E.GA.501.1947
(given by R. G. Gayer-Anderson)
15.1 × 15 × 7.7 cm

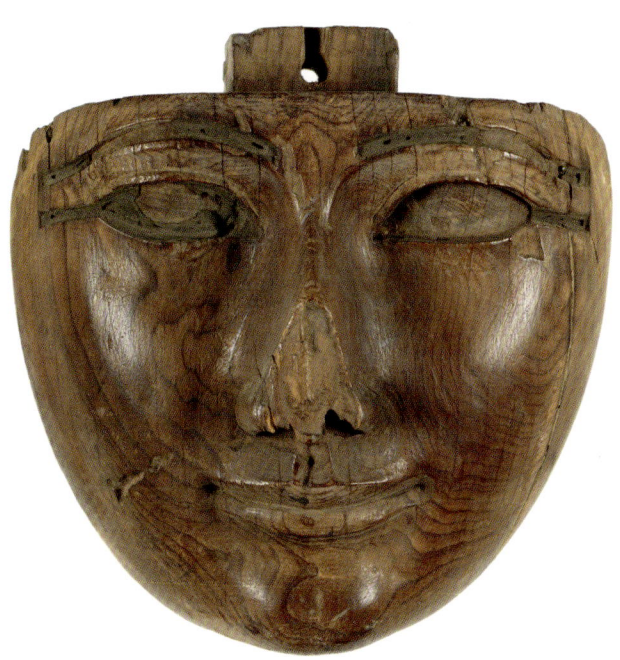

Cat. 1.1

Early burial practices

Earliest burials include food and drink, provided in bowls and beakers, indicating that the Egyptians believed in some form of continuing existence after death for which nourishment was required. Without any textual material, we are unable to say what exactly the form of these beliefs was. The remains of many of these interments have survived until modern times, and the ancient Egyptians themselves would naturally have come across the remains of earlier burials and seen the way that bodies were preserved when buried in the hot desert sand. Perhaps it was this that made them decide to place their dead into containers to provide better protection from the danger of being disturbed by passers-by or roving dogs, jackals and other scavengers.

The earliest containers for bodies included reed baskets, wooden coffins, pots and simple depressions in sand or rock lined with bricks and then plastered. Bodies were usually placed in a contracted foetal position, lying on their sides. Evidence from recent discoveries shows that this position continued to be used in ancient Egyptian burials of all periods, although at later dates it was restricted to people who could not afford an elaborate burial.

During the Old Kingdom (about 2700–2170 BC), the era in which the pyramids at Giza were constructed, members of the royal family were buried in an elongated position. This period saw the beginning of the development of an elaborate bureaucratic system for running the country under a single ruler, and officials proudly proclaimed their job titles in their tomb chapels, displaying their high status for all eternity, while their bodies rested in stone-cut burial chambers. As a result, these corpses no longer dried out naturally in the hot sand and it was necessary to mummify them. The royal, elongated position for mummies was soon more widely adopted (fig. 85) and this required the development of longer, rectangular burial containers. At the same time, there was a move away from organic materials towards stone sarcophagi, again initially for the royal family and later used more widely. Inscriptions invoking gods, such as Anubis, and giving the names and titles of the deceased appear on coffins from the Fourth Dynasty (about 2640–2505 BC) onwards.

Fig. 85
A cedar wood coffin, dating to about 2575–2465 BC, found at Giza with a mummy still inside (Museum of Fine Arts, Boston, 33.1016)

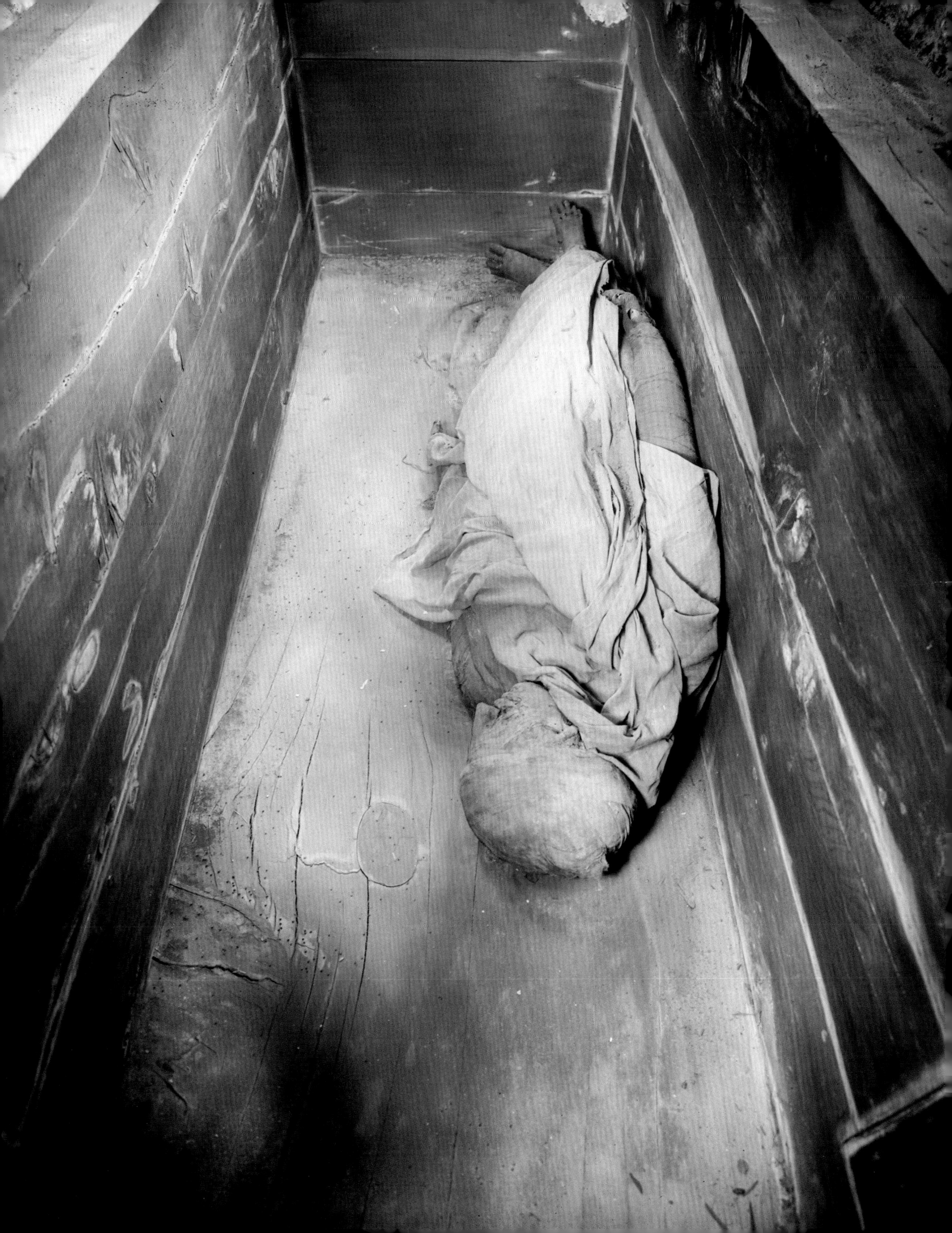

2

Large pots, made of Nile silt, used for burial

The upper pot was used as a lid, and the body would have been placed in a crouched position inside the lower one.

About 2700–2170 BC
Fitzwilliam Museum, E.P.550 and E.P.549 (unknown provenance)
43.3 × 63.3 cm (diameter);
67.5 × 70.5 cm (diameter)

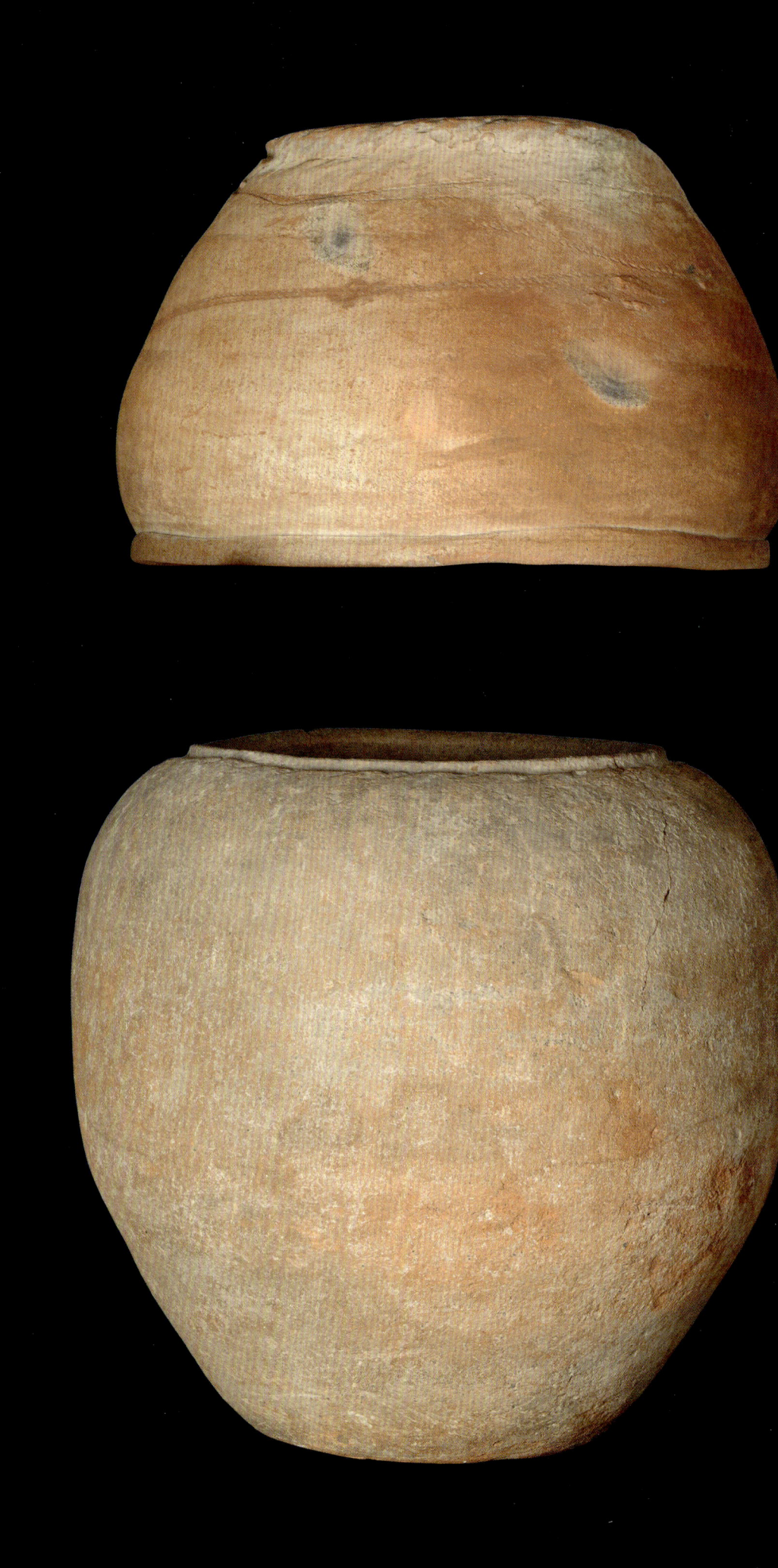

3

Rectangular wooden coffin of Henenu

The coffin is made of irregularly shaped, edge-jointed planks of sycomore fig. The mitred corners have a small butt joint at the top. The floor fits within the walls and is fixed in with dowels. The coffin has a flat lid, with retaining battens on the underside to keep it in place.

The wood appears to be full of flaws, which have been covered by the white paste ground, over which there is a coat of pale yellow paint. The blue text is laid out within a framework of black ruled lines. The interior is coated with white paste.

The inscriptions on the coffin tell us that it was made for a man called Henenu. His body was probably stretched out on its side, lying with his face close to the eye-panel on the outside (cat. 3.2). The coffin was found at Asyut, an important provincial settlement at the time. Henenu's titles indicate that he was probably an important administrator in that region, although he did not hold the high status of a local governor.

About 2345–2150 BC
British Museum, EA46633
(excavated by D. G. Hogarth)
150.5 × 47.5 (including lid) × 50 cm

Cat. 3

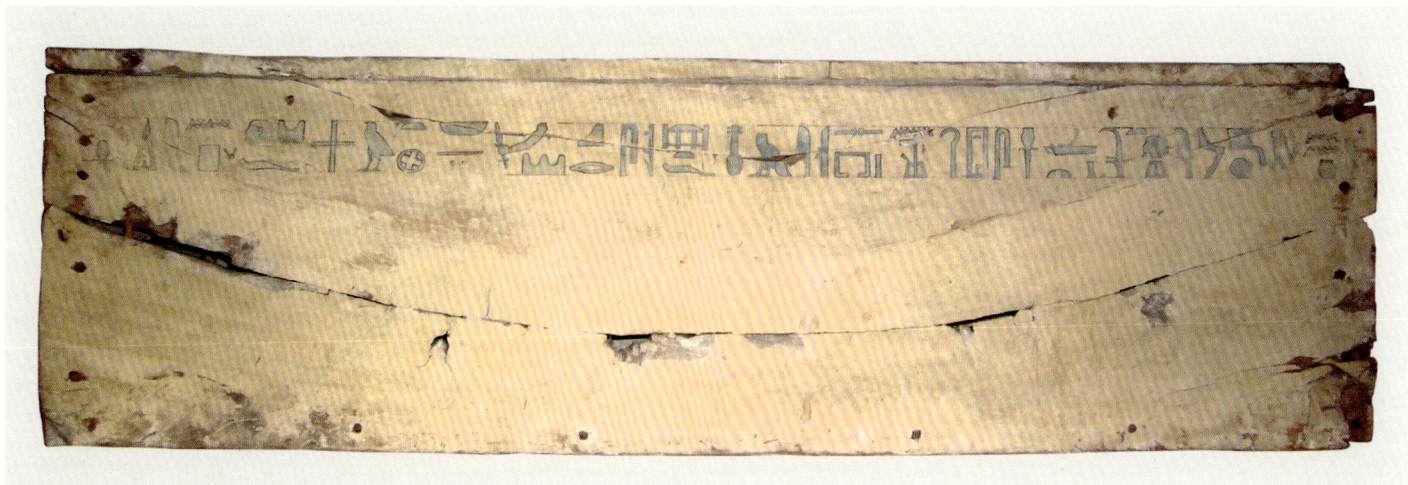

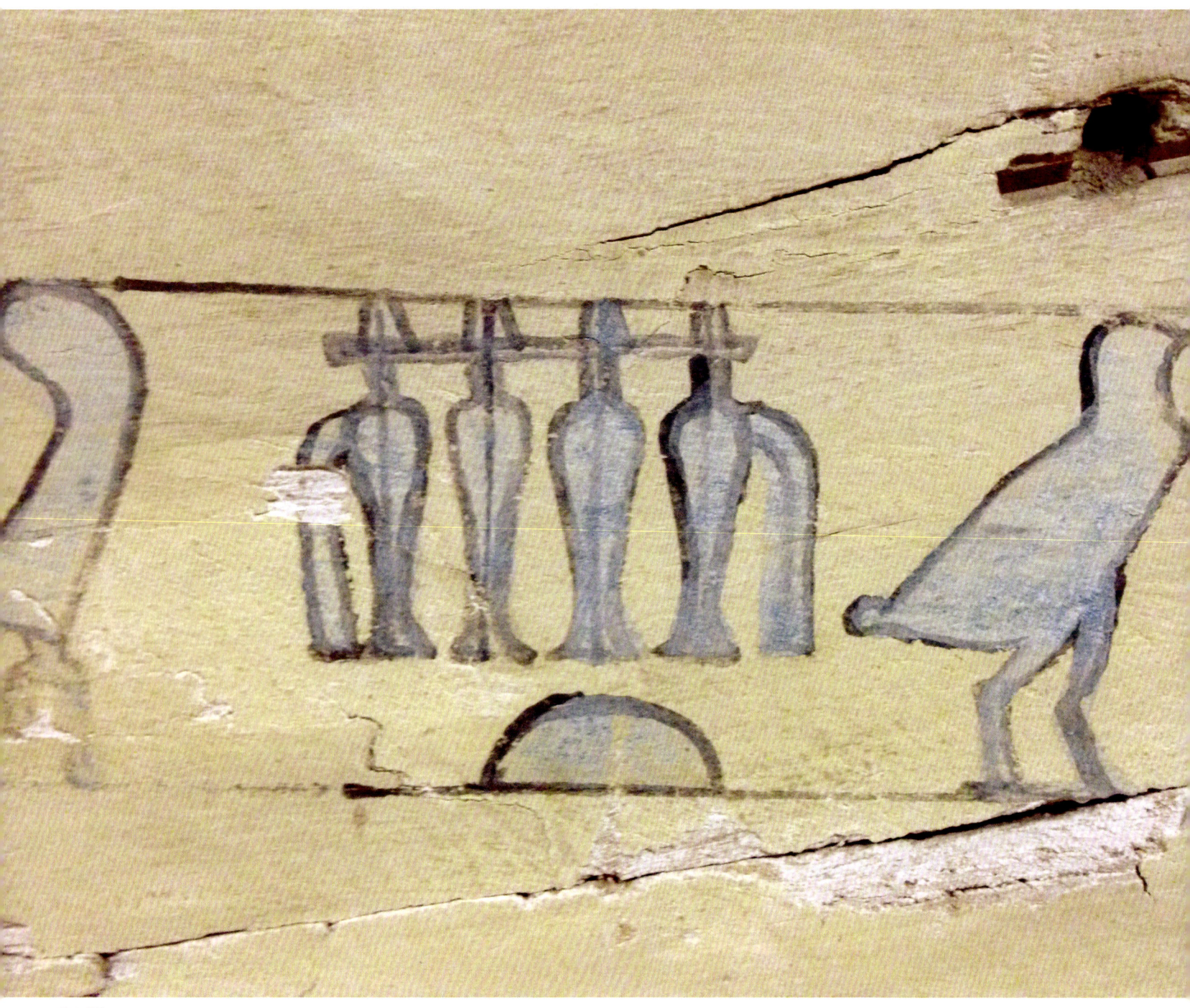

Cat. 3.1

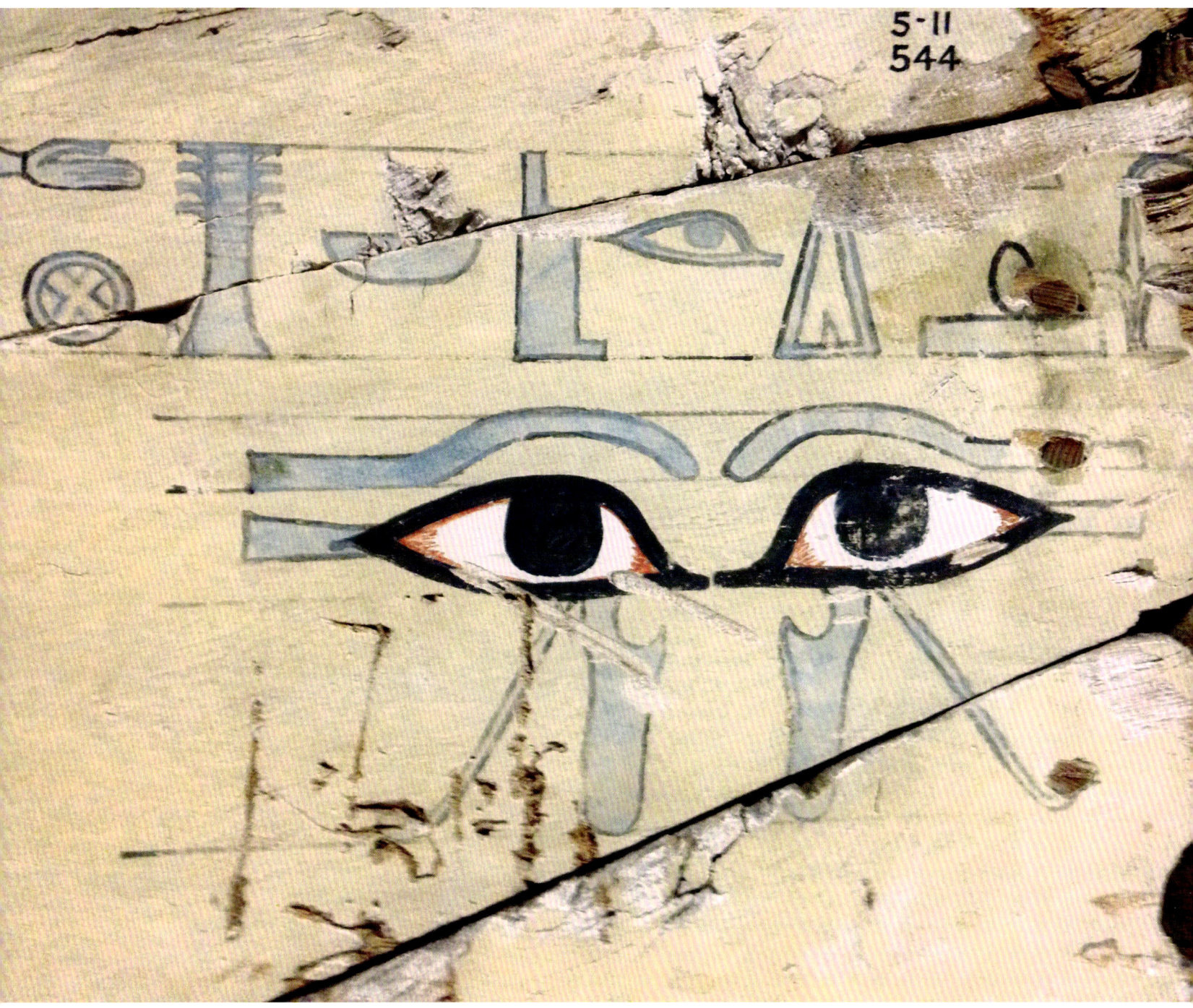

Cat. 3.2

Funerary gods and beliefs

From earliest times, the Egyptians believed that each person had a number of spirits, which embodied essential aspects of them and which continued to exist after that person had died; the best known of these are the *ka* and the *ba* (fig. 86). Texts were inscribed on coffins so that their owners could be identified and a deceased person's spirits would know where the body was located. Statues could be provided in a person's tomb as substitutes for the body, particularly as a physical resting place for the *ka*, so that it could receive offerings.

Early texts mention various gods associated with the afterlife. Chief among these is Osiris (cat. 5), believed to have been the original king of Egypt and from very early times thought of as the king of the underworld, who was murdered by his evil brother Seth. Osiris is usually shown with royal regalia, often seated on a throne and wearing the white crown of Upper Egypt, together with his wife, Isis (cat. 6), and her sister Nephthys (cat. 7). The two sisters protected the body of Osiris and were instrumental in bringing him back to life. In a reflection of this, they were often depicted on the head and foot of a coffin, sometimes shown as female figures with wings, harking back to a myth in which they turned themselves into birds and cried over the body of Osiris.

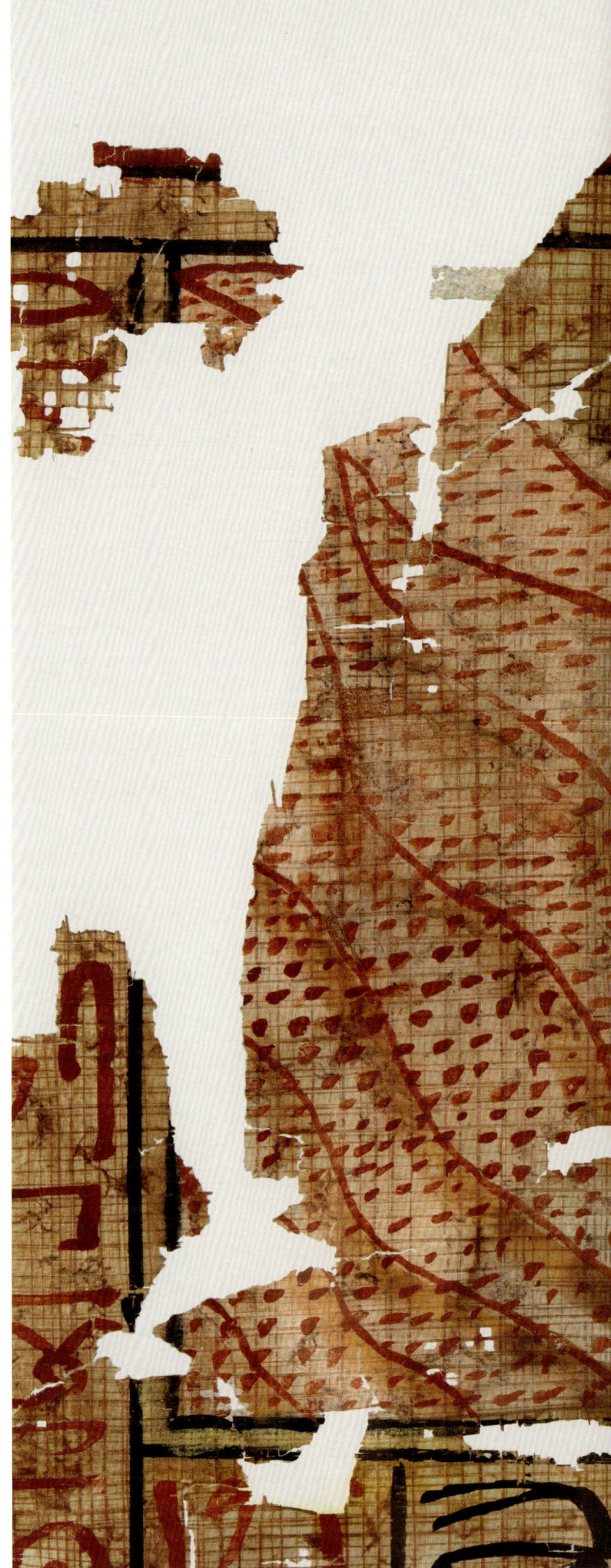

Fig. 86
Detail of the Papyrus of Ramose (Fitzwilliam Museum, E.2.1922), showing a *ba*-spirit, in the form of a bird with a human head, flying out of a tomb

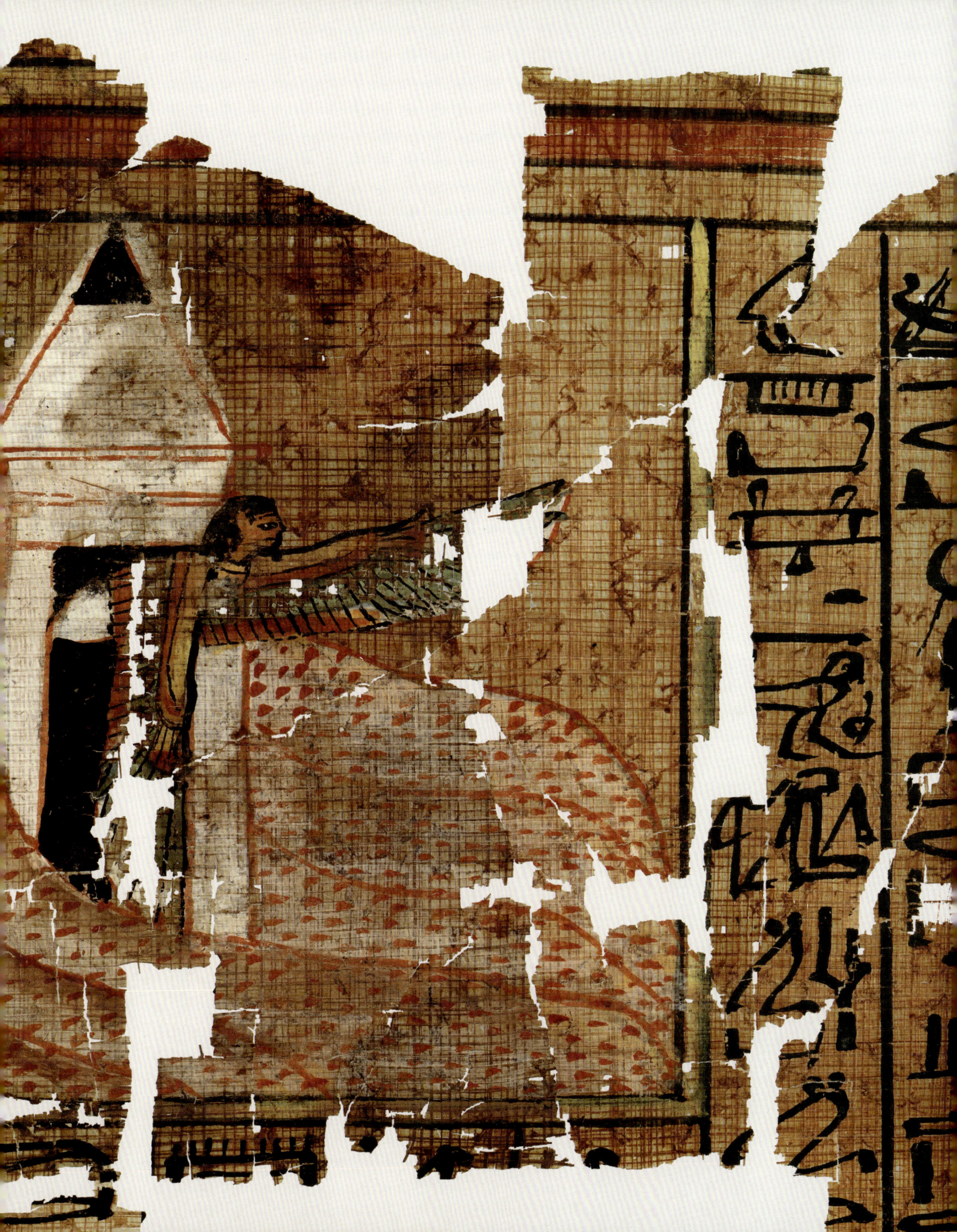

4

Painted limestone statue of a man called Ankhwedjes

The statue probably originated in a tomb, where it would have served as a replacement for the body in case this suffered damage. The statue could then provide a home for its owner's *ka* and receive offerings.

About 2505–2215 BC
Fitzwilliam Museum, E.35.1907
57.8 × 21.3 × 32.5 cm

5

Limestone stela of man and woman before Osiris

This stela (stone slab) shows a man named Meh and his wife, Nebty, standing in front of the god Osiris, king of the underworld, who can be recognised by the white linen wrapped around his body and his green skin. Here we see him wearing the white crown of Upper Egypt on his head, flanked by feathers, and holding a crook and flail, all emblems of a king.

The lower scene shows a man and woman making offerings to a seated couple. The stela almost certainly came from a tomb; the seated couple may be understood to be receiving offerings in the afterlife.

About 1290–1185 BC
Fitzwilliam Museum, E.GA.4700.1943
(given by R. G. Gayer-Anderson)
43.5 × 27.5 × 7.5 cm

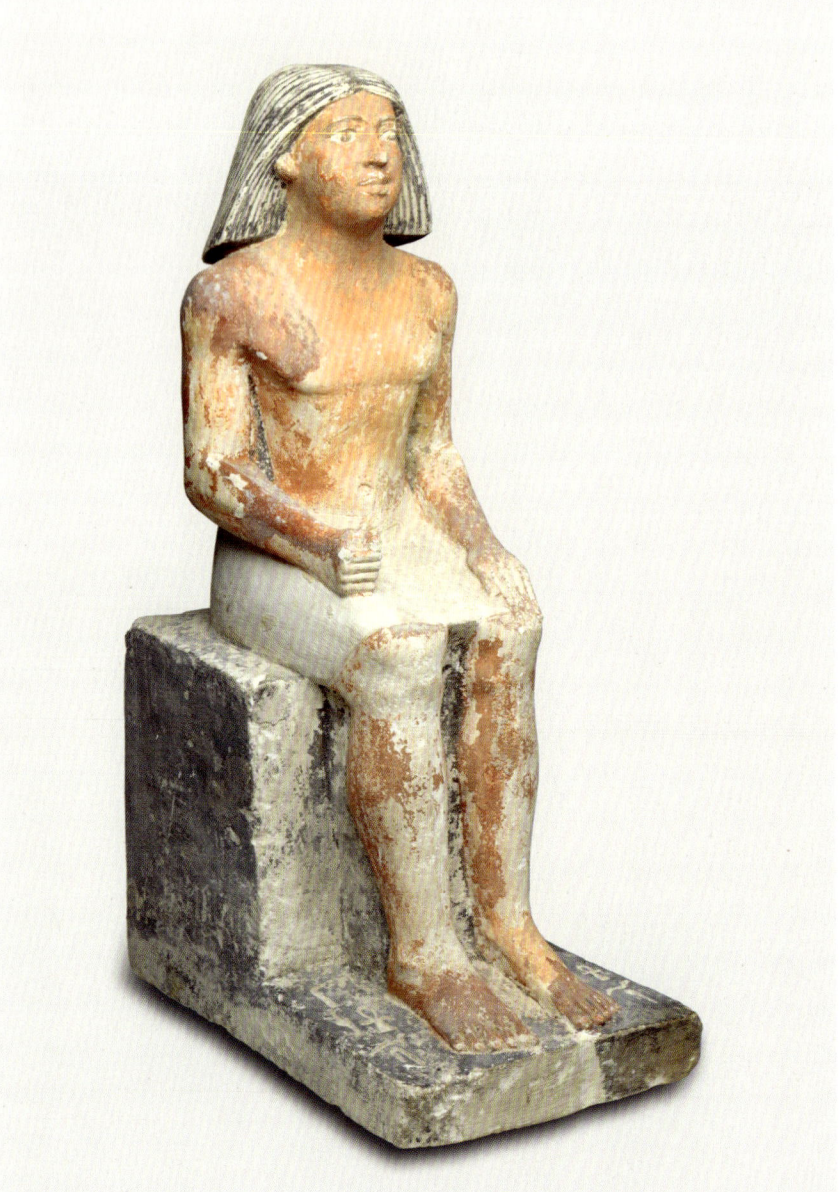

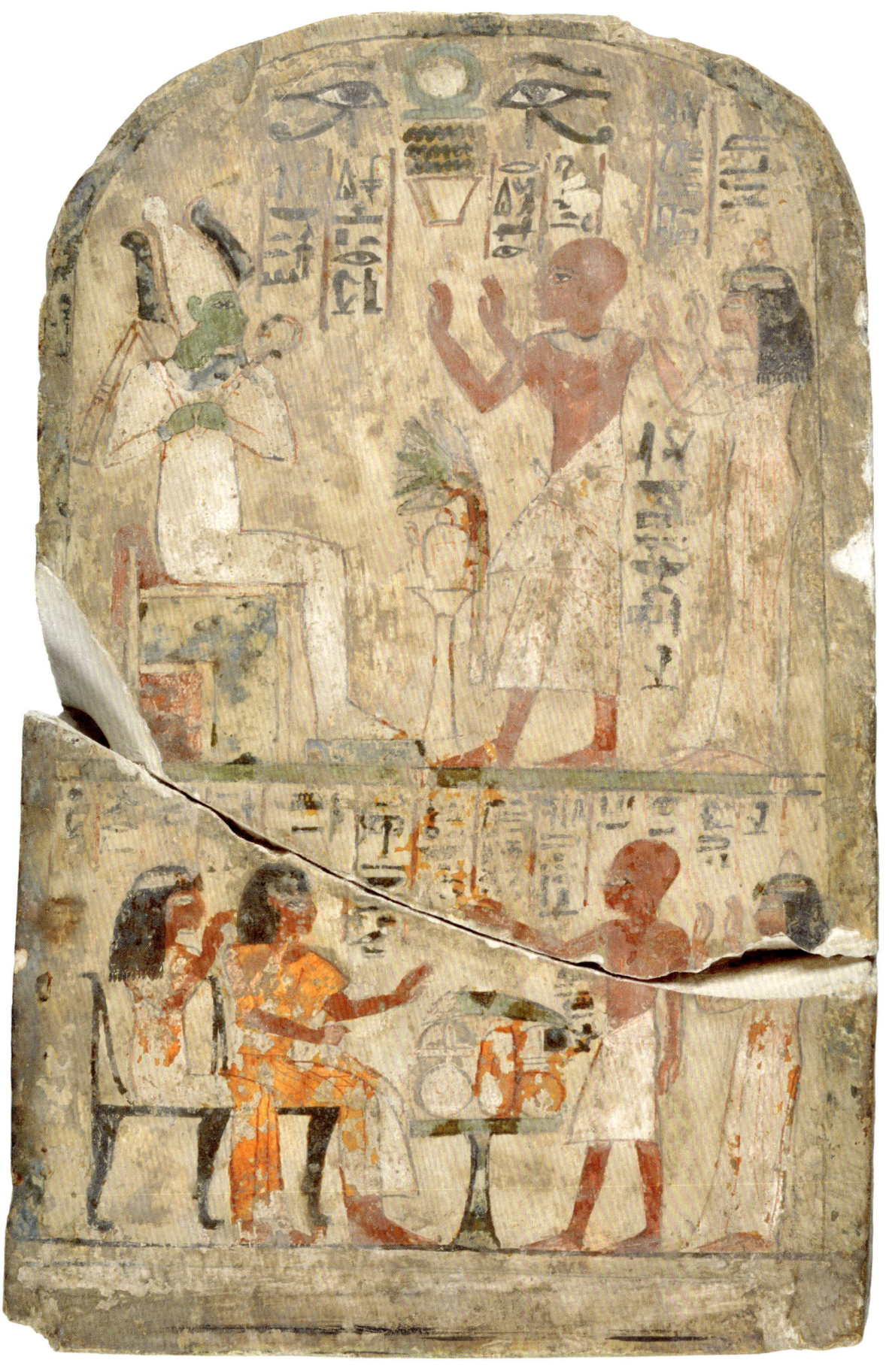

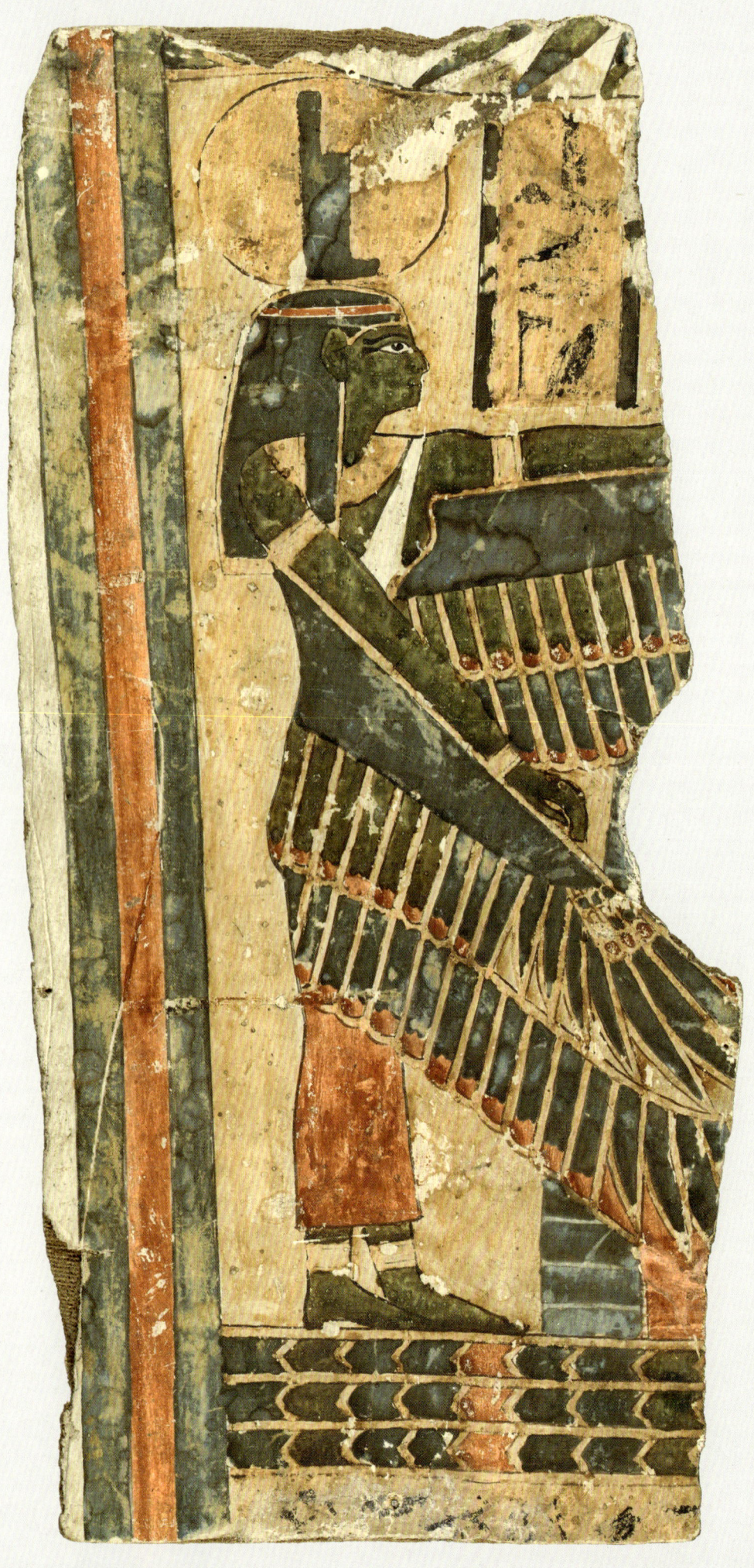

6

Cartonnage coffin fragment showing the goddess Isis

The goddess Isis, identified by the hieroglyph on her head, is depicted here as a woman with wings extending from her arms. With these she protected the body of her husband, Osiris, after he was murdered. Her sister Nephthys is also sometimes depicted in this way, and the pair were often shown on the head and foot of a coffin.

About 945–735 BC
Fitzwilliam Museum, E.GA.2887.1943
(given by R. G. Gayer-Anderson)
37.3 × 14.4 × 0.5 cm

7

Wooden panel showing the goddess Nephthys

Nephthys is shown with the hieroglyphs that spell her name on her head. Depictions of her and her sister Isis were included on coffins to provide protection to the body inside, in the same way that these goddesses protected Osiris's body.

About 664–200 BC
Fitzwilliam Museum, E.GA.4331.1943
(given by R. G. Gayer-Anderson)
33 × 18 × 3 cm

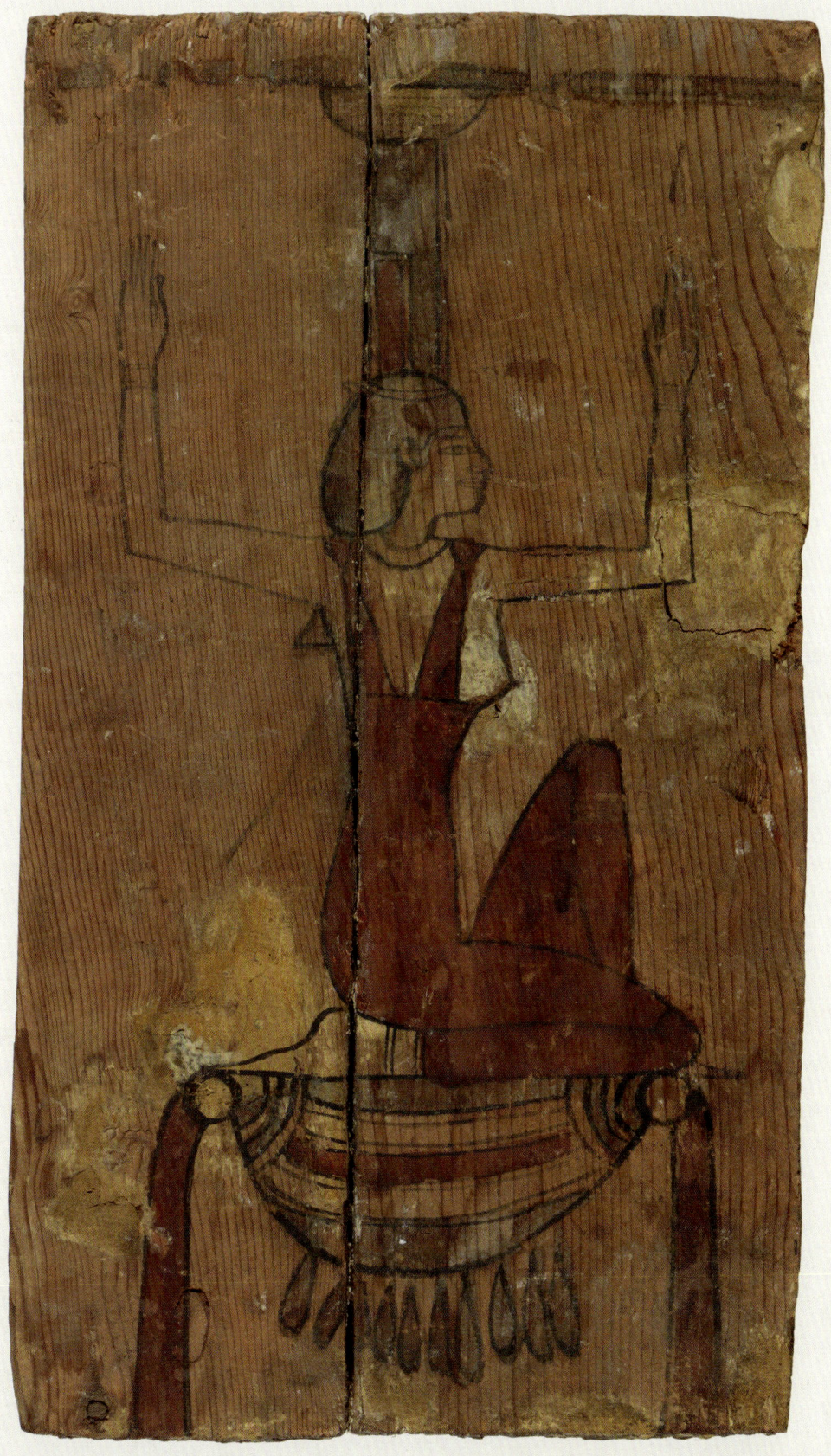

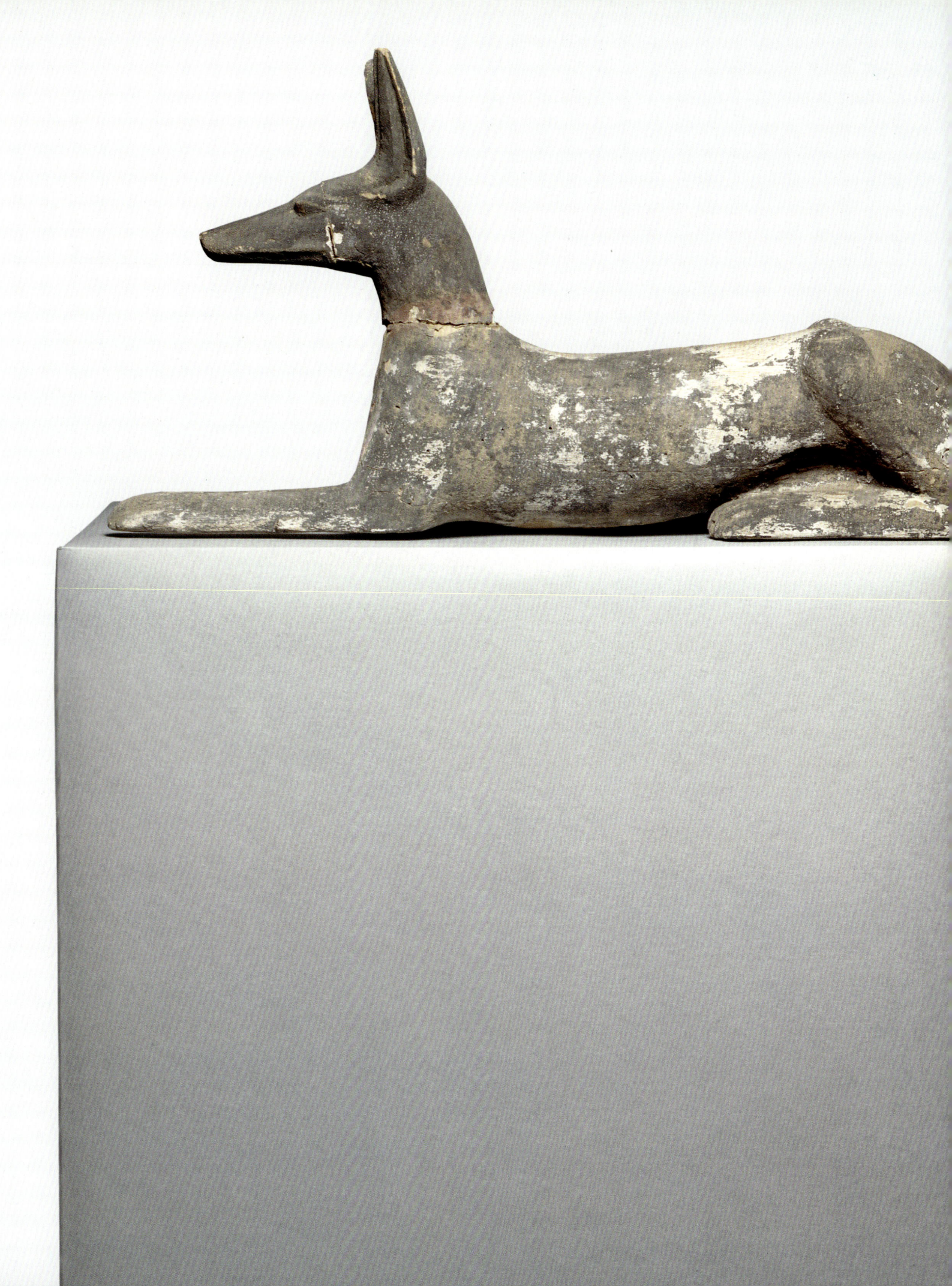

Cat. 8

8

Wooden figure of Anubis

This figure of the god Anubis – shown here as a jackal, although he can also be depicted as a human with a jackal's head – is probably from a Twenty-fifth Dynasty (745–664 BC) outer coffin (fig. 87). Anubis received the dead into the afterlife and presented them to Osiris.

About 1070–715 BC
Fitzwilliam Museum, E.GA.4315.1943
(given by R. G. Gayer-Anderson)
56 × 58.1 × 9.1 cm

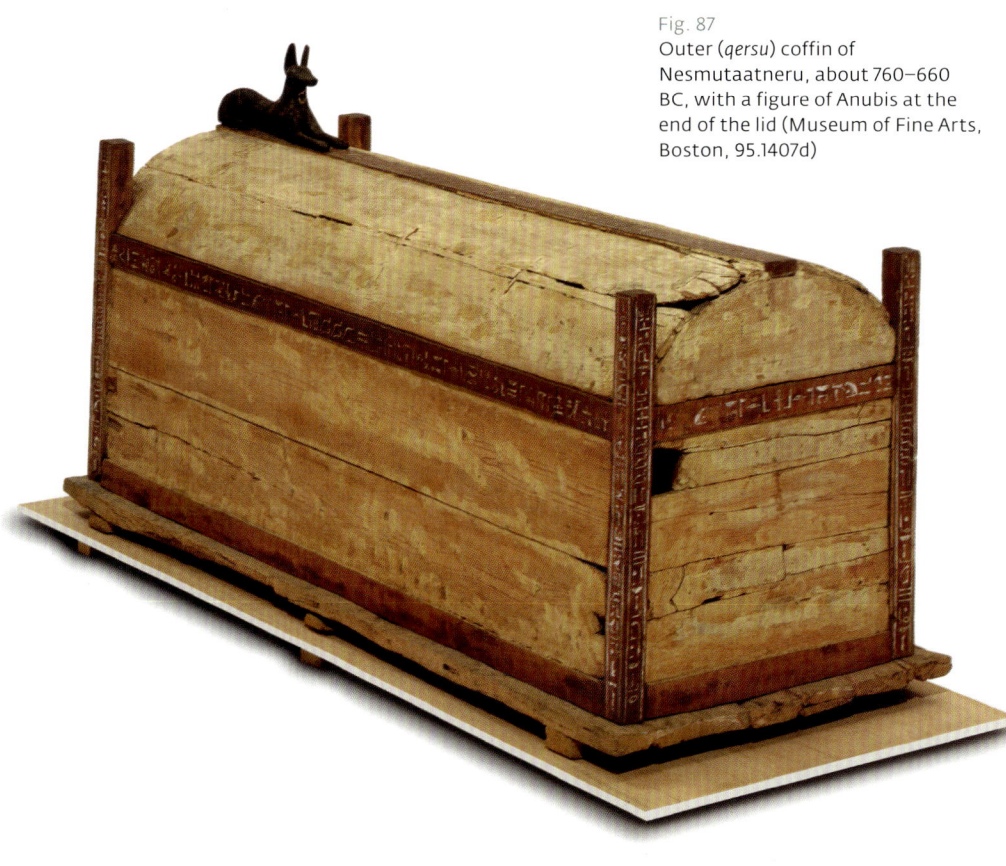

Fig. 87
Outer (*qersu*) coffin of Nesmutaatneru, about 760–660 BC, with a figure of Anubis at the end of the lid (Museum of Fine Arts, Boston, 95.1407d)

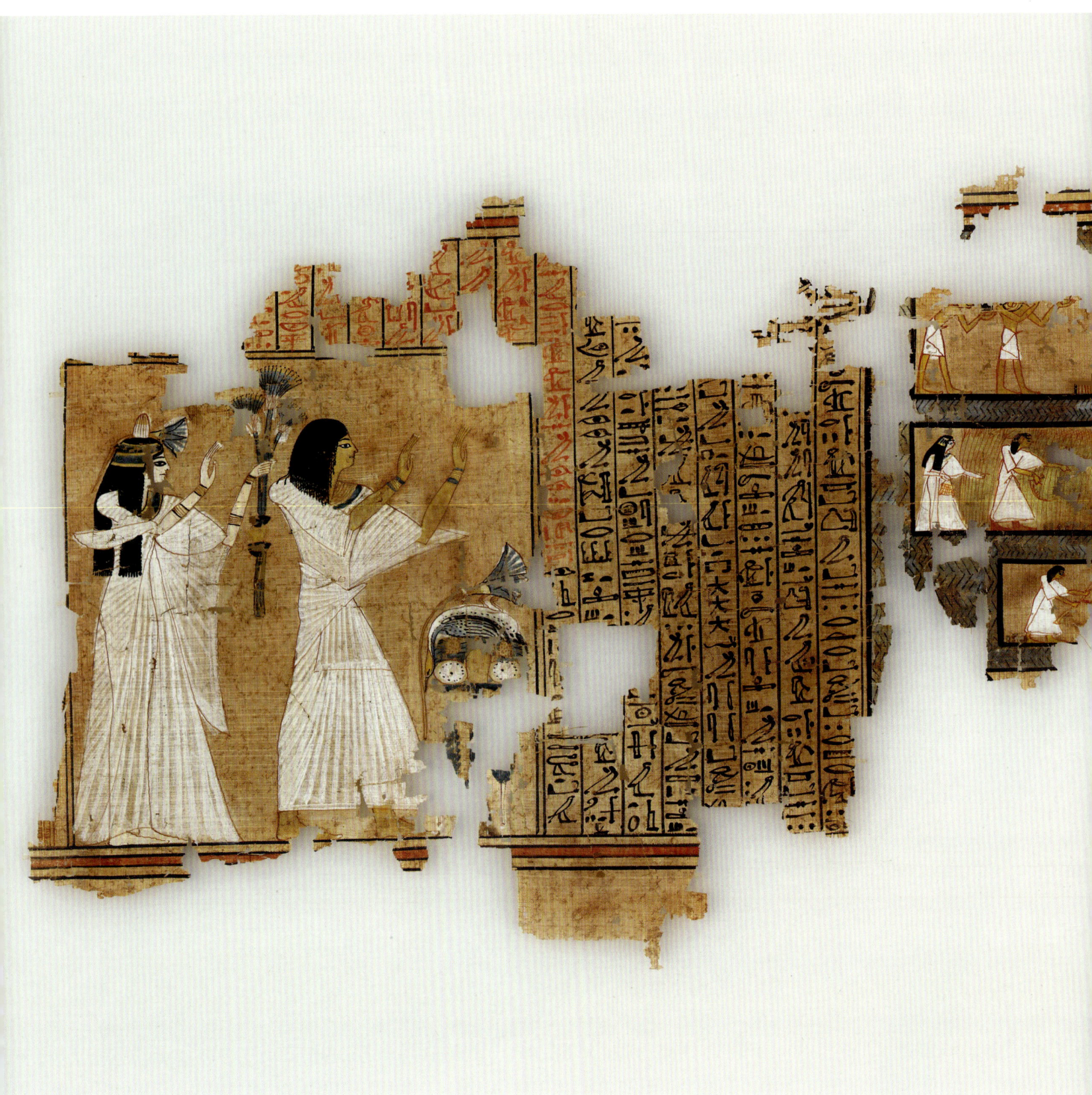

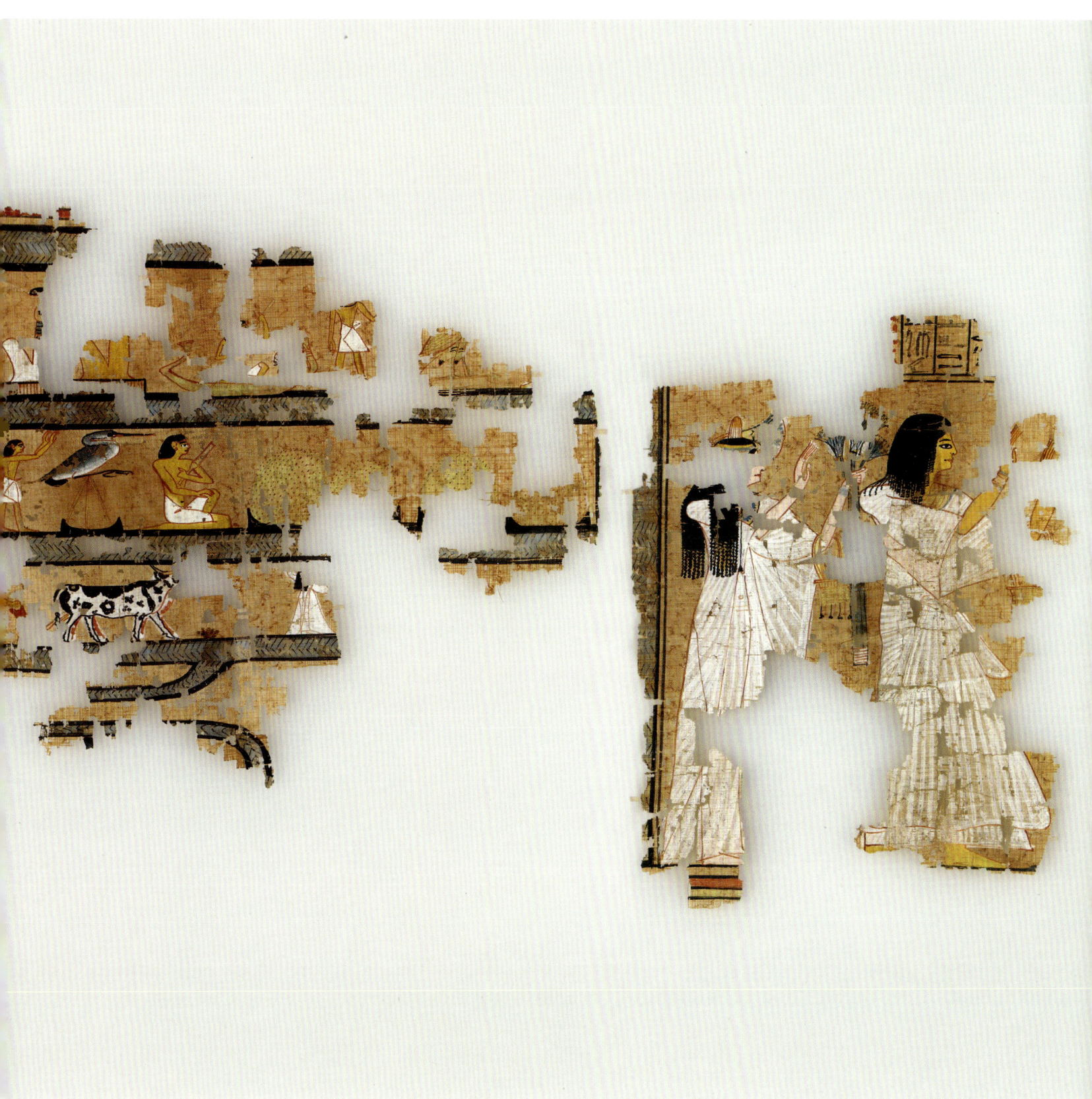

9
The Fields of Iaru in the Papyrus of Ramose

This papyrus belonged to a man named Ramose, shown at the left with his wife as they prepare to enter the Fields of Iaru in the underworld. Depicted as an area of fertile land surrounded by water courses, the Fields of Iaru are reached by the dead after they successfully pass through the Hall of Judgement, where their deeds during their lifetimes were assessed before Osiris and a tribunal of gods. In the centre of the papyrus, the couple are shown carrying out agricultural work in the fields. Ramose is depicted using a hoe and, slightly to the right, there are cattle pulling a plough. Above and to the left, we see Ramose and his wife harvesting. At the right-hand end of the papyrus, the couple appear again.

A papyrus of this kind, nowadays called a Book of the Dead, was included in a person's burial equipment to ensure safe passage through the difficulties of the underworld and the judgement itself by means of the magical spells it contained.

About 1290–1275 BC
Fitzwilliam Museum, E.2.1922
(given by the Friends of the Fitzwilliam Museum)
51 × 111 × 0.4 cm

10
Container for *shabti* figures

From about 2000 BC onwards, figures known as *shabti*s were specially made to be included in burials. These were most commonly in the form of mummified people, often holding hoes and baskets of seeds. As we know from the scenes on Ramose's papyrus, the dead were expected to carry out agricultural work in the Fields of Iaru. *Shabti*s were provided to carry out this work on behalf of the person whose name was included in the inscriptions on them.

This box has two sections and is inscribed with the names of two people: a priest called Hornefer and a chantress of Amun called Taqa, probably Hornefer's wife. It was made to contain the couple's *shabti*s and would have been buried with them.

About 1290–1185 BC
Fitzwilliam Museum, E.205.1932
(bequeathed by Edward Towry Whyte)
34.5 × 26 × 16 cm

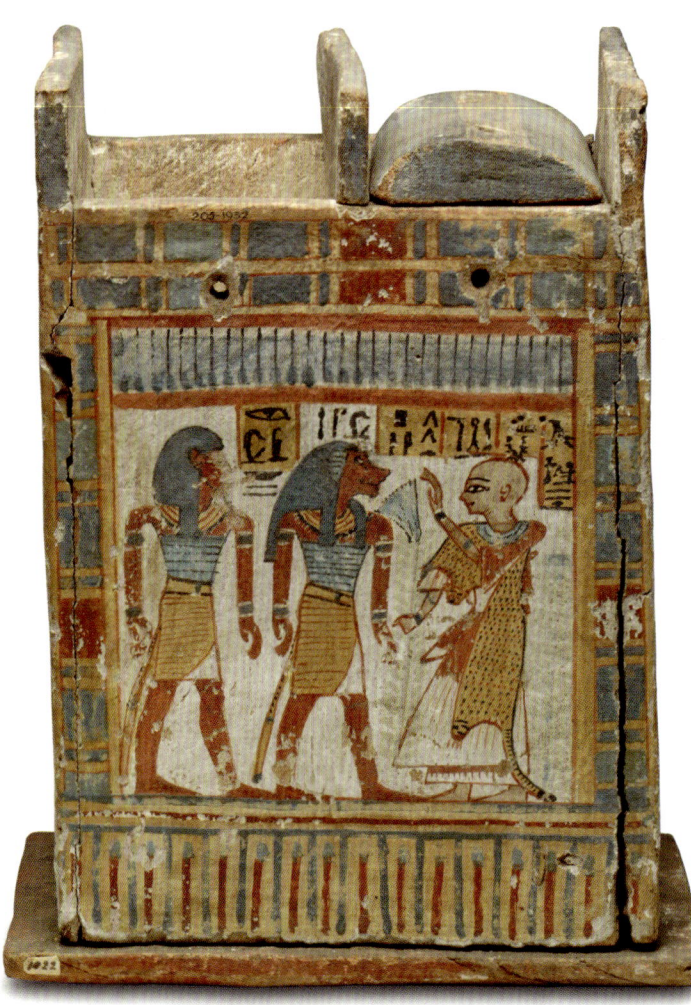

Cat. 10.1
Hornefer is shown before two gods, identified as Hapy and Osiris. He wears a leopard skin (see fig. 47).

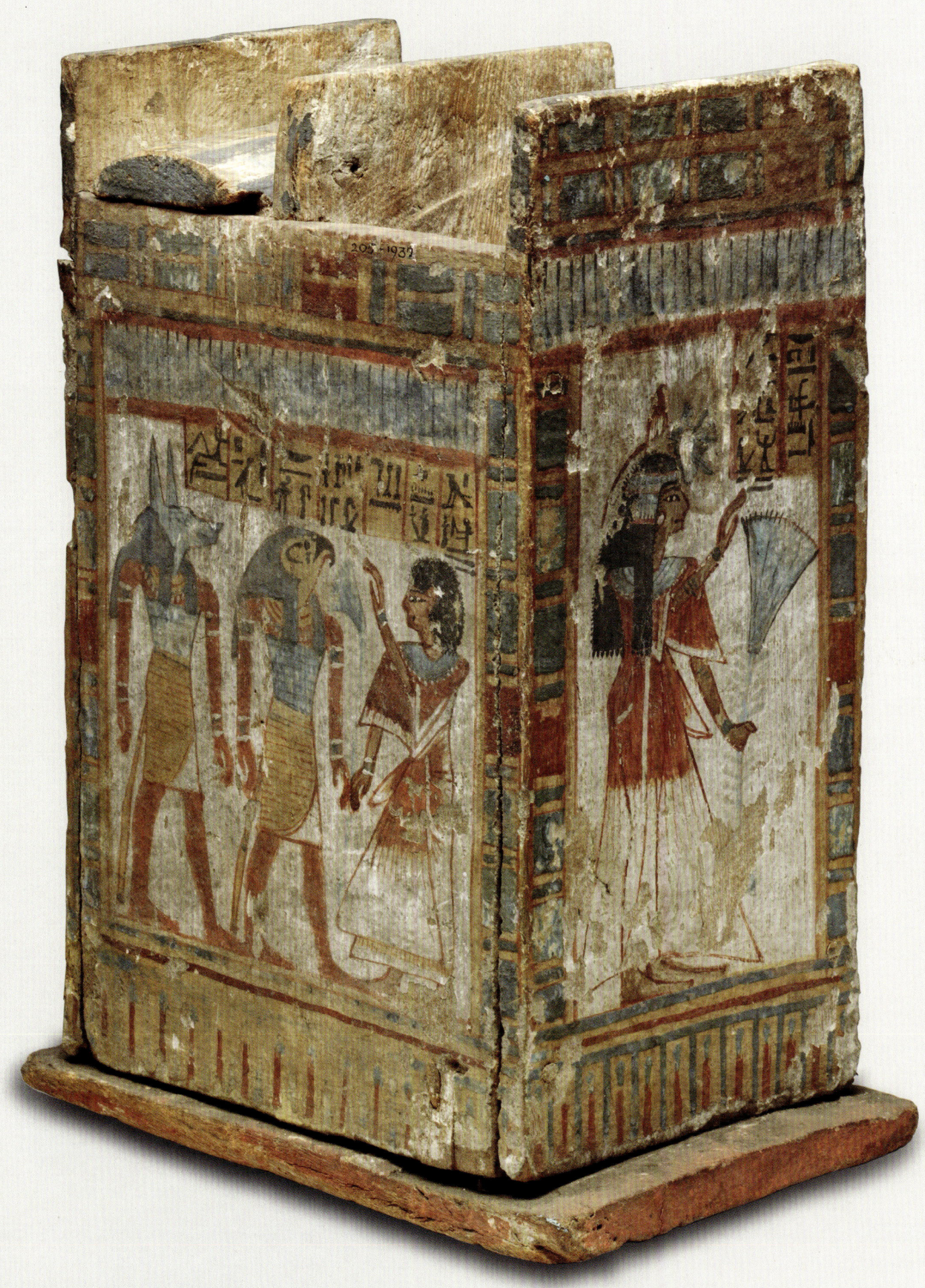

Late Old Kingdom to early Middle Kingdom

Rectangular wooden coffins became the standard burial container from the late Old Kingdom onwards. At the end of this period, Egypt's centralised authority was disrupted, possibly as a result of environmental changes affecting agricultural production. Local rulers throughout the length of the Nile Valley became increasingly powerful, taking charge of the administration of food production in their areas and acquiring the trappings of the wealthy elite. This period of disunity, known as the First Intermediate Period (about 2170–2010 BC), was brought to an end when Egypt came back under the control of a single king.

During the following period, the Middle Kingdom (about 2010–1790 BC), local rulers continued to have a degree of administrative control, and their burials show their status: their offering chapels were highly decorated and they were well provided with funerary offerings, and painted and inscribed coffins. Models showing groups of people preparing food were included to ensure that the dead received nourishment and demonstrated that these people had servants to work for them – even in the afterlife. The interiors of coffins, which had begun to include painted scenes and offering lists during the Old Kingdom, were now regularly decorated with friezes of objects, showing equipment used during funeral rituals and items of daily use that would have been included in tombs.

Over time, coffin decoration came to include a panel with two *wedjat* eyes, a special form which included the eyebrow above each eye and also decoration below the eyes taken from the markings of raptors associated with the god Horus (fig. 88). The word *wedjat* means 'wholeness, well-being' and was also a symbol of protection; the association with Horus derives from a myth in which one of his eyes was damaged and then restored to a healthy state. The coffin would have been placed in the tomb so that the eye-panel faced to the east. The body inside would have lain on its side facing the eye-panel, magically allowing the person inside to see the early morning sun, which was reborn each day after travelling through the underworld during the night. These were to become standard features of rectangular coffins of the First Intermediate Period and the Middle Kingdom.

Fig. 88
A gold amulet in the form of a wedjat eye (Fitzwilliam Museum, E.45.1955). On coffins, wedjat eyes gave the deceased the power of sight, as well as serving a protective function.

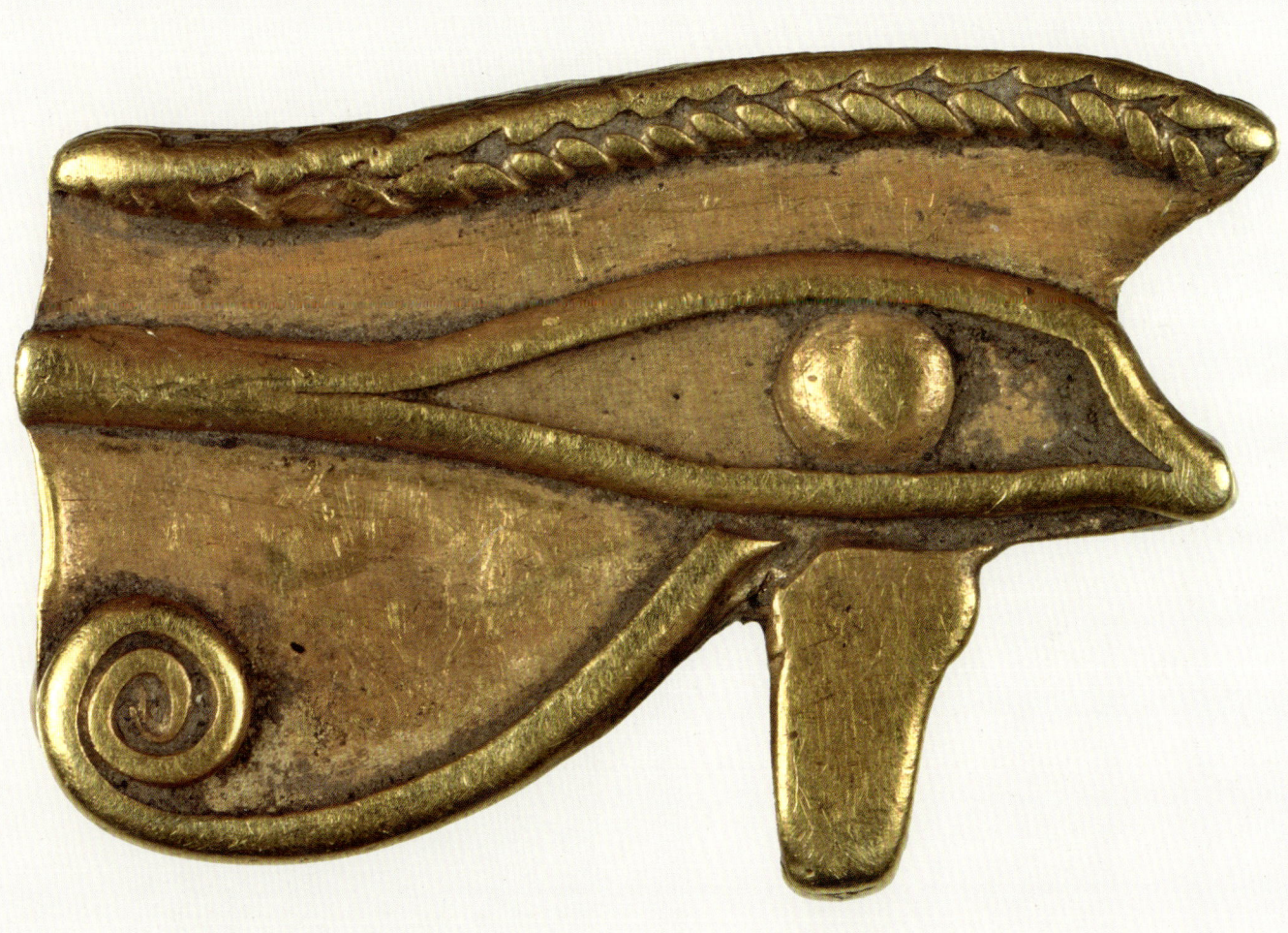

11

Coffin of Khety

This rectangular box coffin belongs to a man named Khety, whose tomb was found, still intact, at Beni Hasan. The coffin inscriptions contain standard formulae calling for Osiris and Anubis to provide offerings for Khety's use in the afterlife. Khety's job titles are not specified, but it is likely that he was a fairly wealthy person since his burial included models (cat. 12) of people working on his behalf, presumably reflecting his earthly standard of living as well as his intentions for his status in the afterlife. An eye-panel is painted on one side of the coffin to allow Khety to see out.

The coffin is made of sycamore fig. The joints are secured with dowels, most of which are made of sidr. Each side of the box is constructed from two edge-jointed planks, tangentially sawn and only roughly finished. The corners are mitred with a small butt joint at the top. In addition to the dowels along each corner, there is a tied joint at top and bottom (see fig. 55, p. 84). Dowel holes along the bottom of the panels indicate how the base fitted within the walls. The lid is made of two full-length planks. On the underside are three roughly shaped retaining battens pegged into the planks across the centre and one at each end. The carpenters cut two marks into the top of the foot-end panel of the box to match up with marks on one of these battens, presumably to give an indication of which way round the lid fitted (cat. 11.2). The interior is bare wood, except for a thin white paste sealing the joints. On the exterior, a very thin discontinuous layer of calcite acts as a ground for the earth pigment paint. Flaws in the wood were filled with a rough paste and painted with a slightly darker paint. The placing of the text and the eyes is guided by drafting lines drawn against a straight edge using a reed pen (cat. 11.1). The lines continue from the coffin box to the lid, suggesting that the final decoration was applied after the coffin was complete and closed. The text was sketched in black then coloured with a thin layer of Egyptian blue. A small trail of blue droplets shows where the scribe let his brush drip onto the surface of the lid.

About 2010–1950 BC
Fitzwilliam Museum, E.71.1903
(given by the Beni Hasan Excavation Committee)
50 × 186 × 44.4 cm

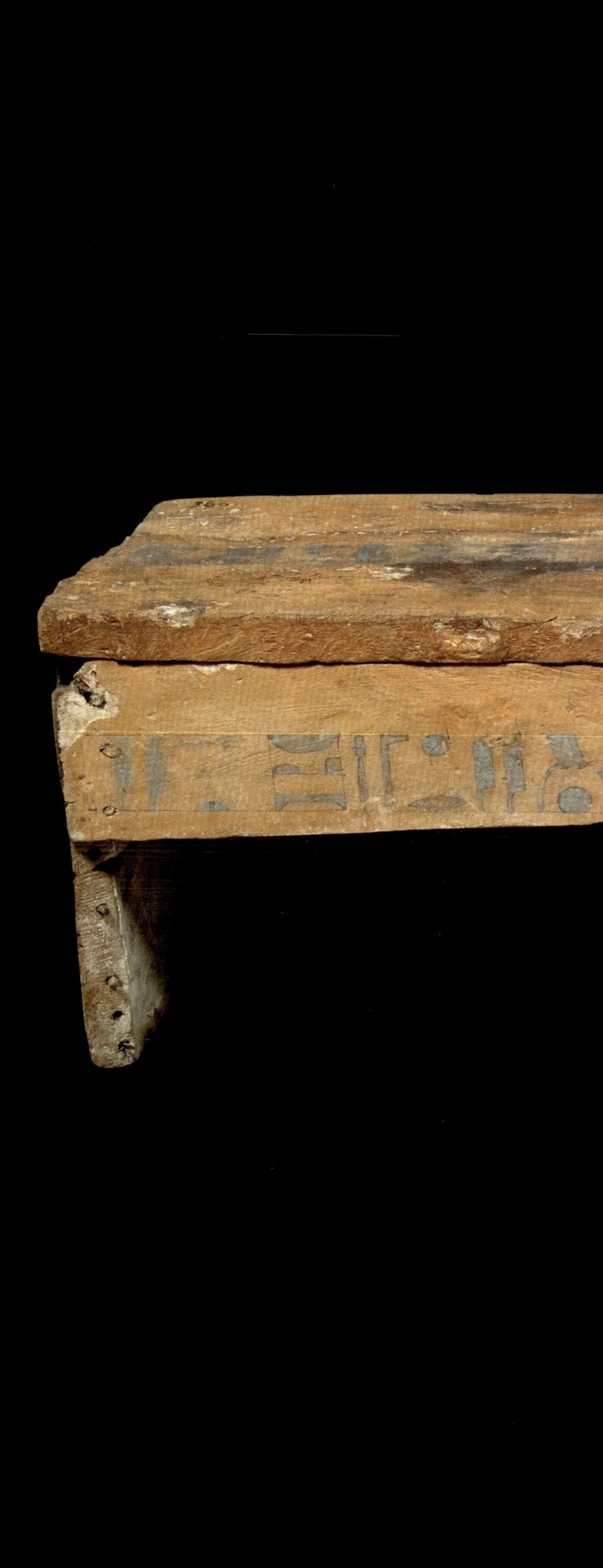

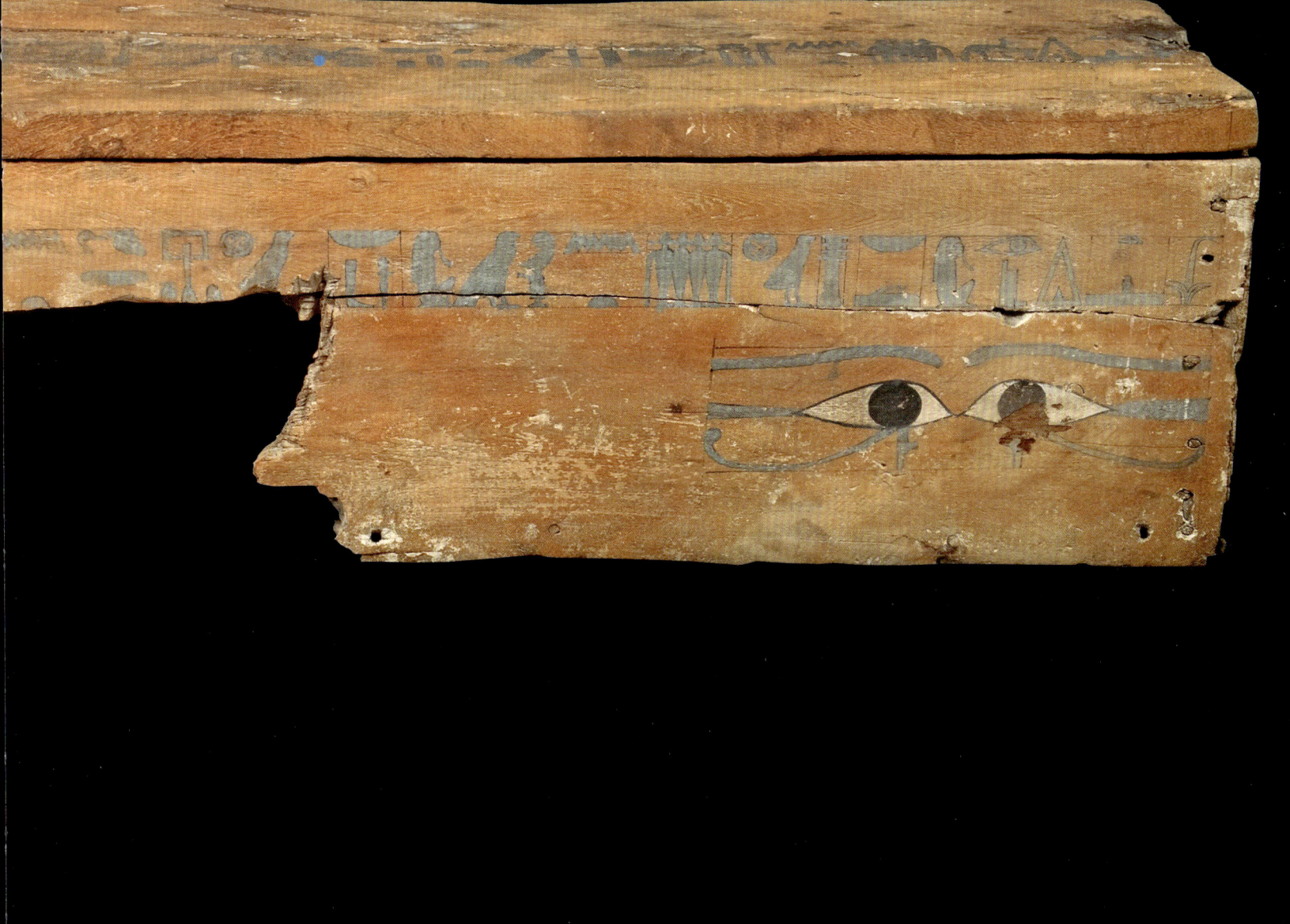

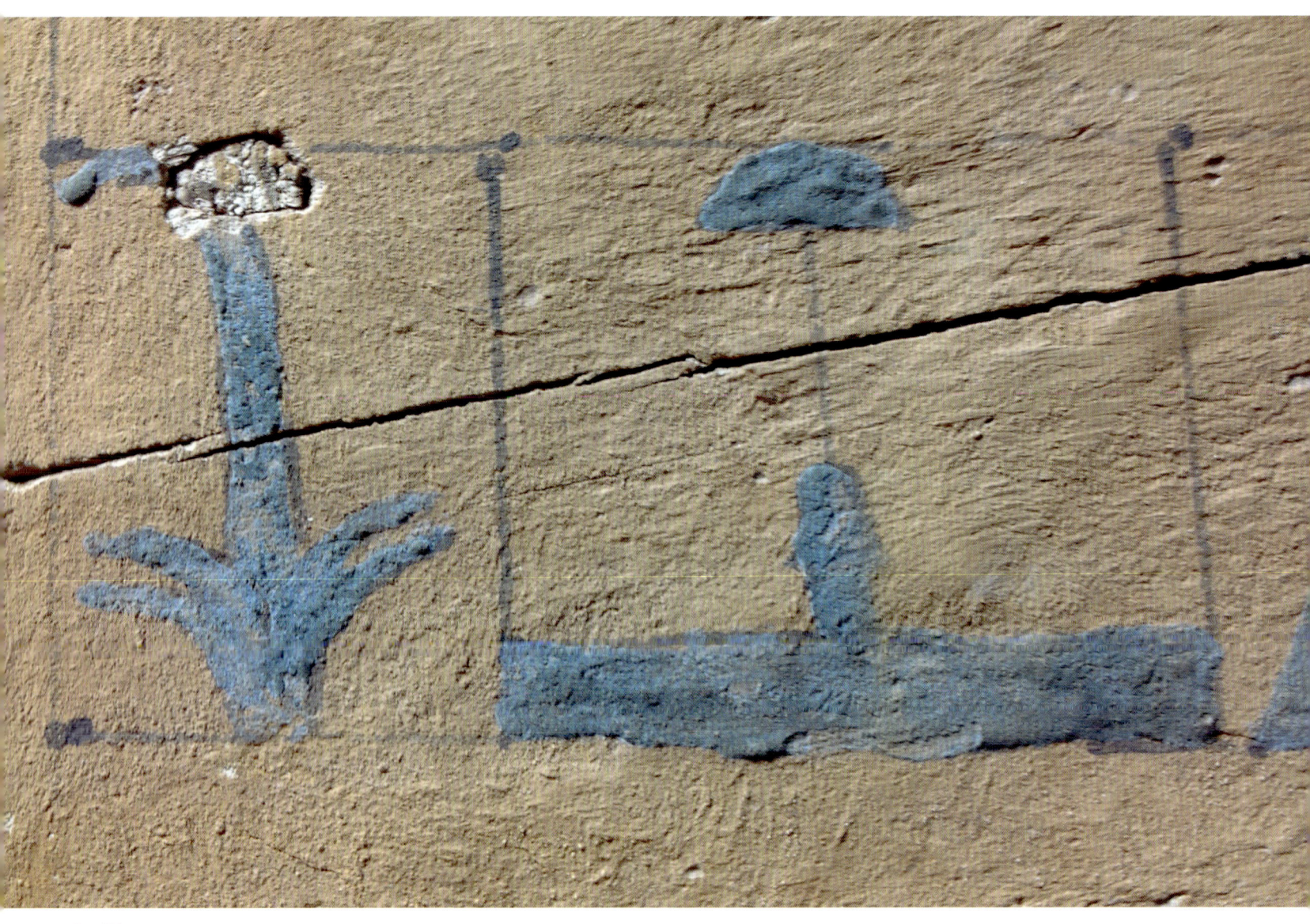

Cat. 11.1
Detail of the text on Khety's coffin showing the text neatly positioned between black lines drawn against a straight edge, with areas blocked out into rectangles before the hieroglyphs were written. The vertical dividers have slightly missed the guide marks and have a pronounced left-leaning slope. The text was sketched in black before being painted using a thin layer of Egyptian blue.

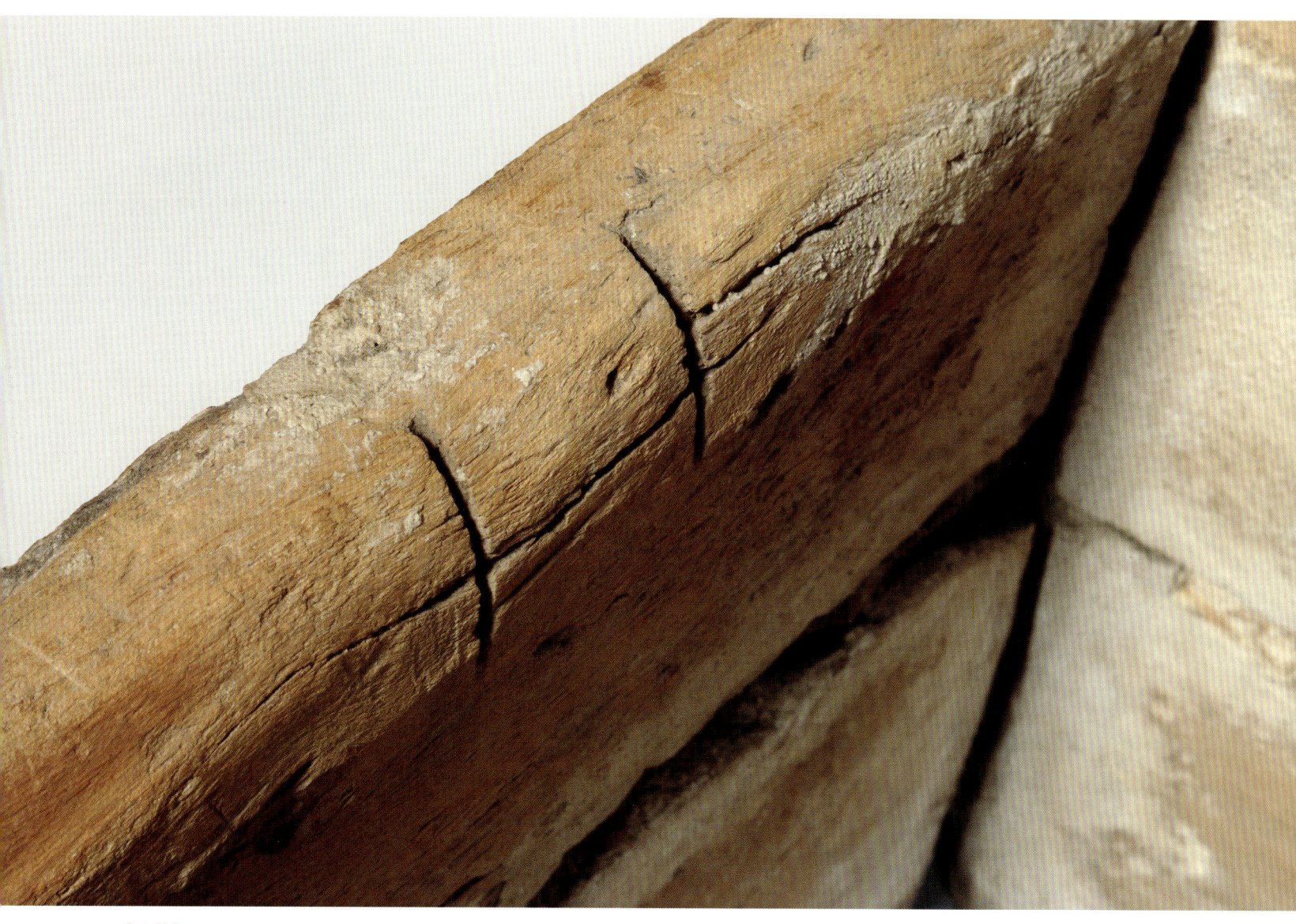

Cat. 11.2
Locating marks cut into the upper edge of the foot end panel of Khety's coffin

12

Models from the tomb of Khety

These models, made of painted sycomore fig wood and linen, came from the tomb of Khety. The boats allowed Khety to travel south, sailing with the prevailing north wind, or north, rowing with the current of the river Nile; in particular, he could go to and from Abydos, the main centre for the worship of Osiris. The other models show the preparation of bread and beer (staples of the Egyptian diet), the slaughtering of an ox and a granary being filled with grain, supervised by a scribe.

About 2010–1950 BC
Fitzwilliam Museum, E.71.a.1903, E.71b.1903, E.71c.1903, E.71d.1903 and E.71e.1903 (given by the Beni Hasan Excavation Committee)
40.5 × 62 × 12.4 cm;
25 × 59 × 12 cm;
16.3 × 29.0 × 23.0 cm;
18.5 × 41.4 × 29.7 cm;
25.0 × 29.0 × 23.6 cm

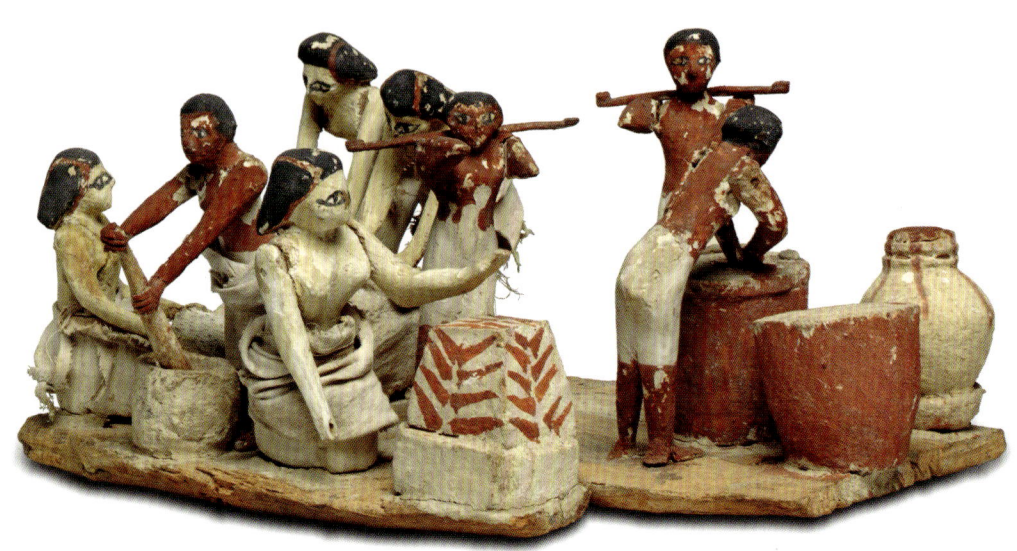

Cat. 12.1

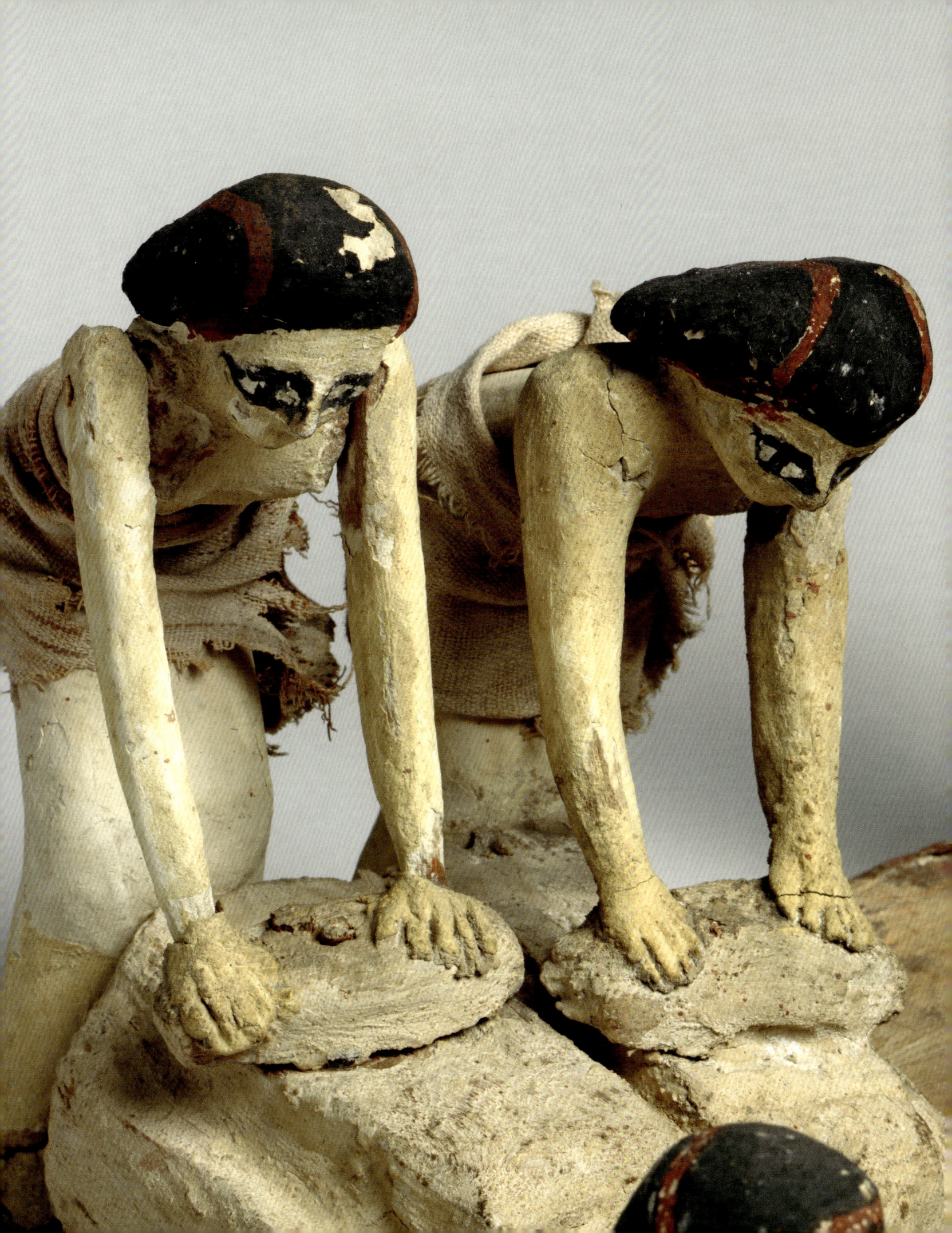

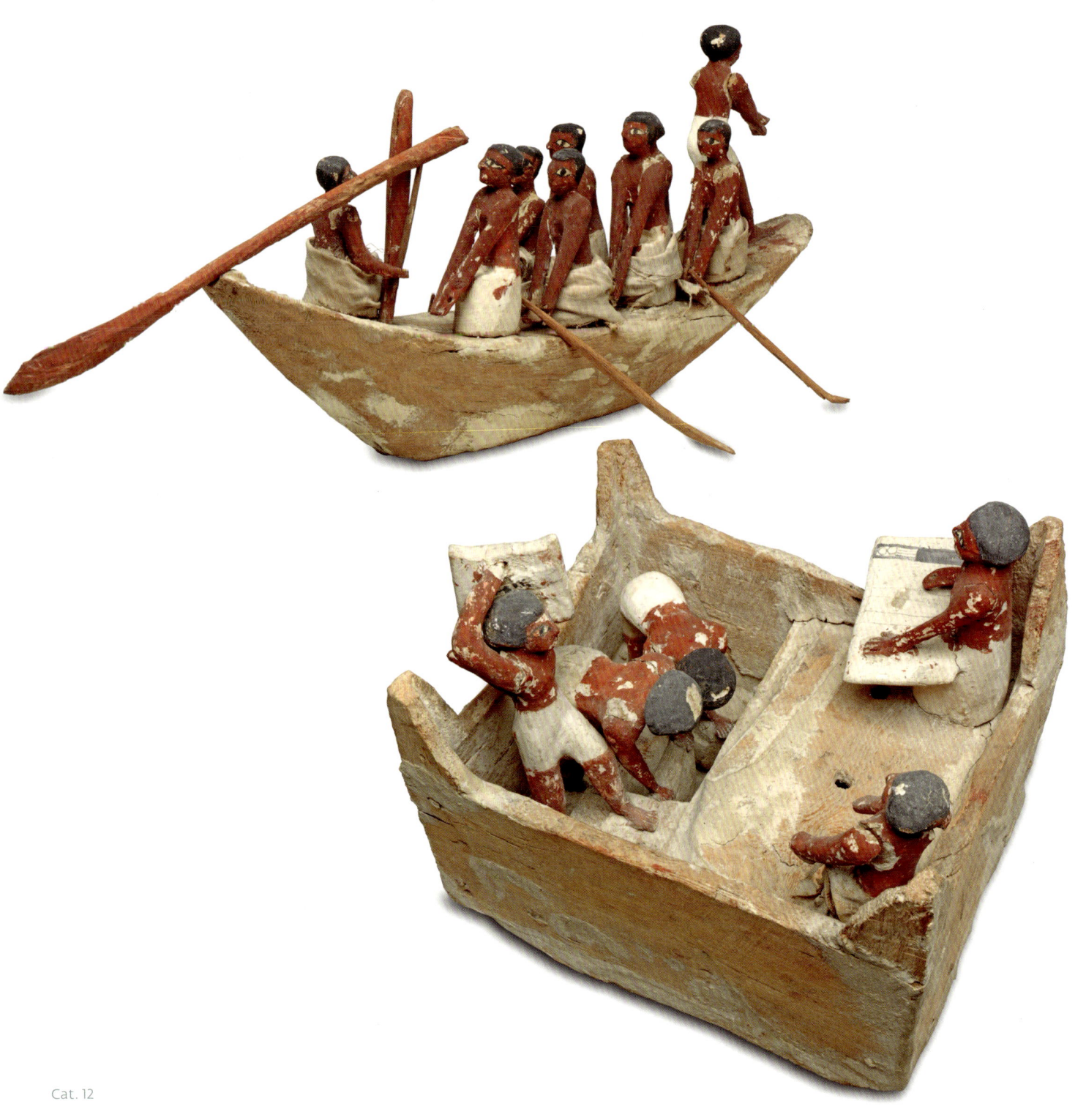

Cat. 12

Catalogue

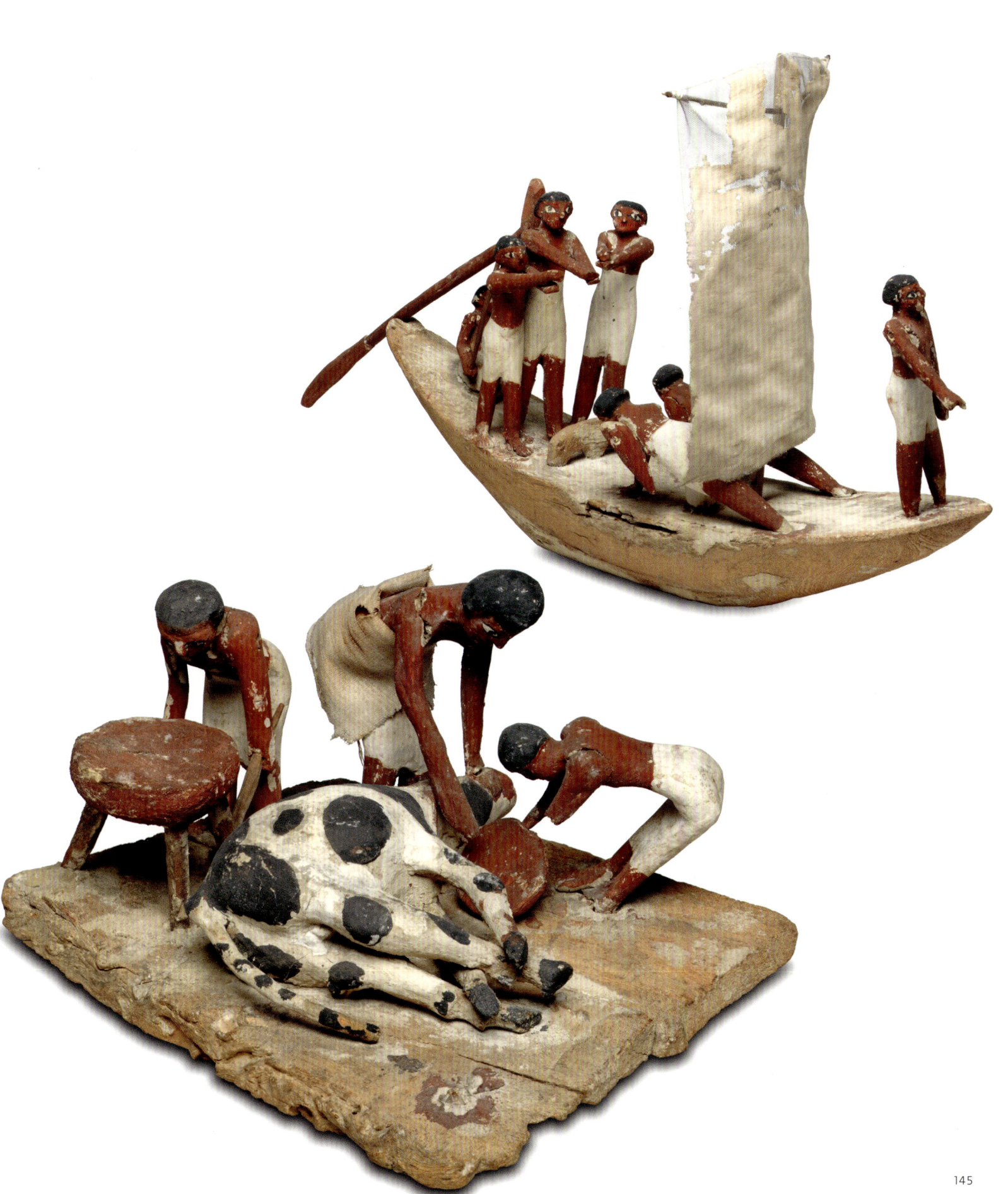

13

Fragments from the coffin of the master physician, Wepwawetemhat

Master physicians were often members of the royal entourage, but very few doctors' names are known from ancient Egypt. The fragments, which come from the bottom edge of the long side of the coffin box, are made of sycomore fig. The decoration is very delicately executed in red earth, Egyptian blue and Egyptian green, yellow (orpiment), brown, carbon-based black and additional white on a calcite preparation layer (see fig. 78, p. 109).

About 1975–1790 BC
Fitzwilliam Museum, E.W.66a,b
(unknown provenance, but probably from Asyut, Egypt)
8.9 × 147.7 × 3.4 cm

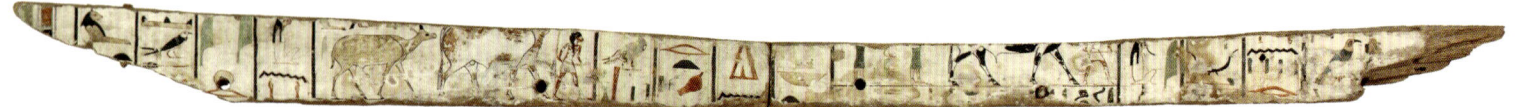

Cat. 13

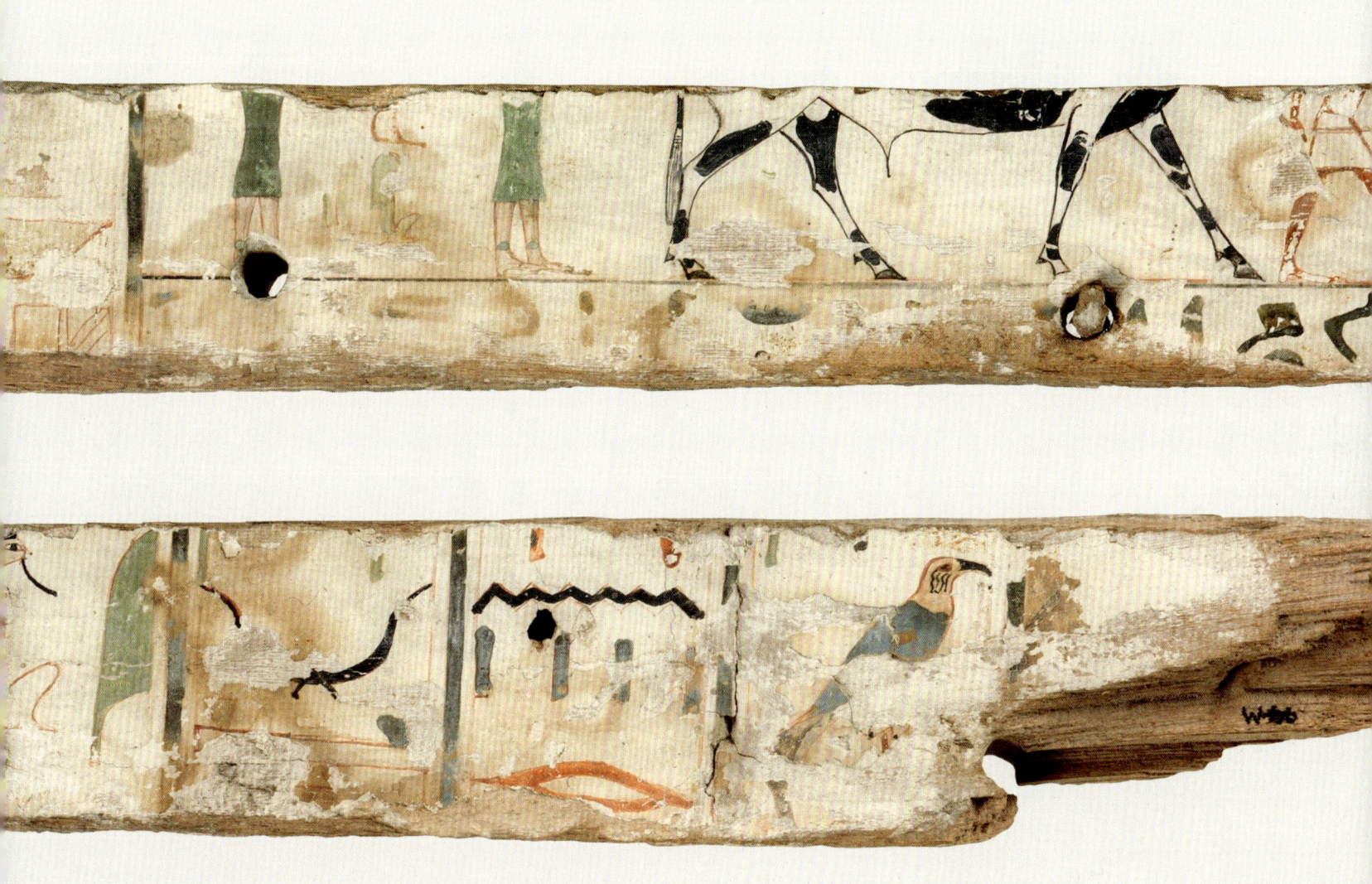

Cat. 14.2
Detail of patching with two pieces of wood dowelled through from the yellow side of the fragment.

14

Fragment from the coffin of an unknown woman

The interior is inscribed with Coffin Texts (see p. 37). The exterior is painted with yellow earth, the text applied in Egyptian blue and outlined in carbon-based black. The interior bears delicate bands of red and blue hieroglyphs, with black dividing lines.

The fragment is made of sycomore fig. Small patches of the same wood are pinned in place with sidr and acacia dowels (cat. 14.2).

———

About 2055–1985 BC
Fitzwilliam Museum, E.W.82
(unknown provenance, but probably from Asyut, Egypt)
7.7 × 72.7 × 2.8 cm

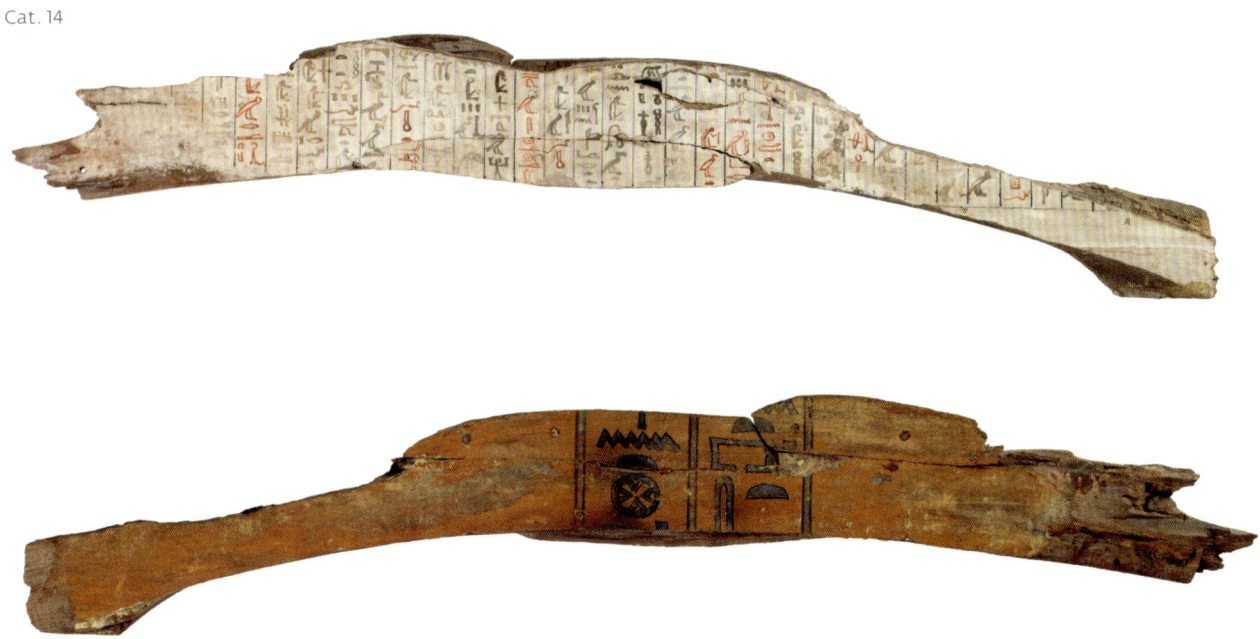

Cat. 14

Cat. 14.1
The outside of the coffin with columns of texts. Although only a tiny portion survives, the texts can be recognised as standard phrases, describing the owner as being 'honoured of the whole town' and 'the revered one of Renenutet of her house'.

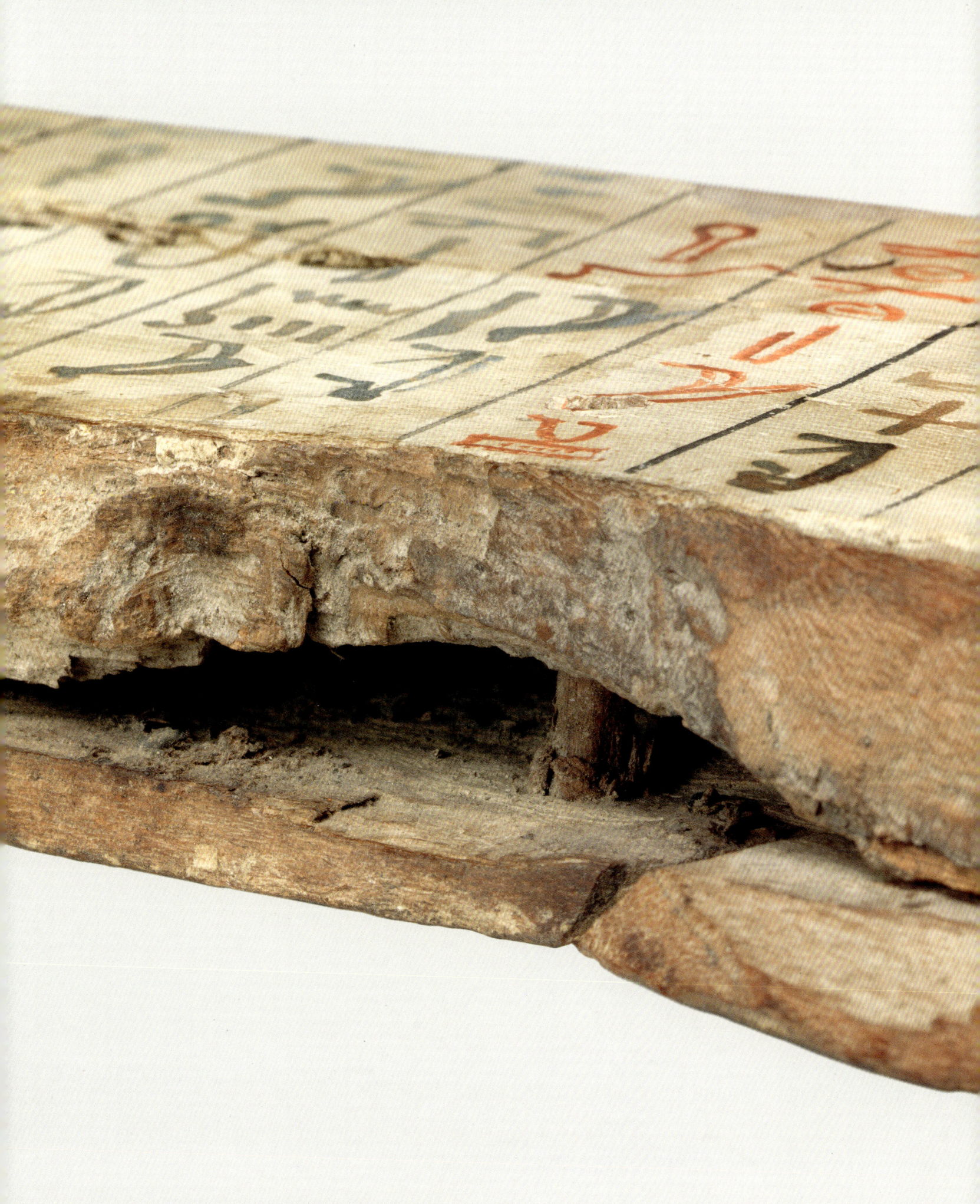

The dead become Osiris

Coffins of the Old Kingdom, especially stone sarcophagi, might be decorated with a panel-like motif. Known as 'palace façade' decoration, this is thought to represent the exterior of early palaces, made of mud-brick and draped with brightly coloured hangings. This motif continued to be used on wooden coffins, such as the cedar coffin of Nakht (cat. 15).

A major innovation on Nakht's coffin is the text on the lid which calls her 'Osiris'; in other words, Nakht was not going to join Osiris in the afterlife, but was going there *as the god Osiris*. This feature becomes a regular feature on coffins during the Twelfth Dynasty (about 1975–1790 BC). The same text also calls upon the sky-goddess, Nut, to stretch herself over the deceased. Nut-texts appear on the lids of coffins and the ceilings of tombs from this period onwards. Another innovation is the inclusion of appeals to four protective deities known as the Sons of Horus in the inscriptions on the outside of the boxes of contemporary coffins. Over time, these gods became associated with protection of the internal organs removed from a body during the process of mummification.

The distinguishing feature of mummification during the Middle Kingdom was the quantity of linen used to wrap the deceased's body and the burial mask that was placed on the face or over the head of the mummy (fig. 89). The combination of white linen and a mask came to be identifiers of the dead prepared for entry into the afterlife in a form the Egyptians called *sah*. During the Middle Kingdom, from around 1900 BC, coffins in the shape of a body (anthropoid) began to be used, decorated to represent a body wrapped in white linen and with a mask over the face, as can be seen in the coffin of Userhet (cat. 20). Such coffins were placed inside a rectangular coffin, preserving the traditional outer appearance of a burial container.

Fig. 89
The mummy of a man called Wah (Metropolitan Museum of Art, New York, 20.3.203) was discovered wrapped in 375 square metres of linen with a funerary mask covering his face

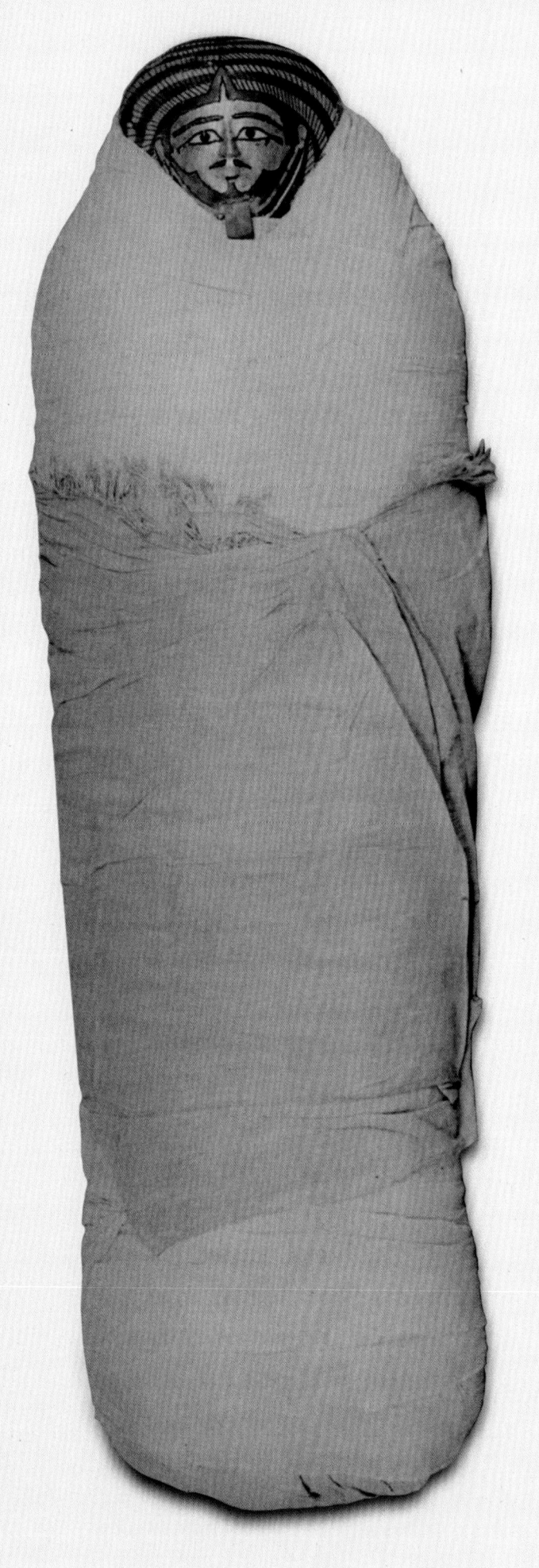

15

Wooden box coffin belonging to a woman named Nakht

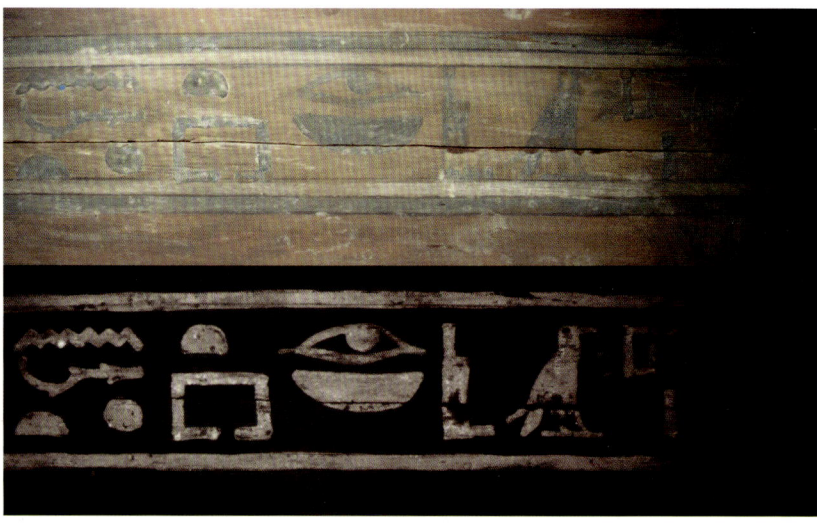

Cat. 15.2
Foot end of the coffin of Nakht

The wood is good-quality cedar with few knots. Cedar is not native to Egypt and had to be imported, which meant it was expensive. The coffin was made for a woman called Nakht, described as a 'lady of the house'. The inscriptions tell us that she was the daughter of a person named Warti-hetep; the tomb in which her coffin was found contained three other burials, perhaps of family members. All four sides of the coffin are decorated with the palace façade motif and with inscriptions appealing to gods, including Osiris and Anubis, for offerings to be provided for Nakht in the afterlife. The inscription on the side decorated with eyes uses the phrase 'for the *ka* of', indicating explicitly that the offerings were for the benefit of Nakht's *ka* spirit. A major change from these standard texts, however, is to be found in the first line of inscription on the lid of the coffin (cat. 15.1): here Nakht herself is addressed as Osiris. It also appeals to the goddess Nut to spread herself over Nakht, causing her to be a 'god without enemies'. The vertical texts on the sides of the coffins mention other gods, including the Sons of Horus, who provided protection for the dead person within the coffin.

Parts of the coffin, in particular the side decorated with eyes, have suffered water damage, probably from moisture seepage into the tomb. The wood here is fibrous and fragile. The loss and deterioration of the pigments in these areas have reduced the pattern and texts to ghostly black-brown silhouettes.

Each panel of the box is made from two planks of similar width, joined with dowels. The corners are dowelled through mitred edges, with a butt joint at the top (cat. 15.2). There are a number of redundant dowel holes, which do not line up with each other. This is especially the case on the back panel of the box and on parts of the lid and suggests that some of the wood of this coffin has been recycled. The lid is a complex piece of carpentry, using multiple pieces of wood to build a hollow structure, but one which gives an impression of depth. The dowels in the box are cedar, those in the lid mostly sidr and acacia.

The wood is carefully smoothed on the exterior. The interior preserves many tool marks – those of a saw along the face of the planks and a chisel on the retaining battens that are attached to the underside of the lid. The interior joints were sealed with paste. Parts of the exterior surface were coated with a base layer of white calcite and gypsum, but in many places the paint was applied directly to the wood. A central vertical setting-out line (only visible with infrared reflectography) was placed on both end panels and black lines ruled along a straight edge were used to lay out the palace façade design. This was painted with red and yellow earth, Egyptian blue and calcite. The green areas are complex - made from yellow earth, calcite, Egyptian blue and a copper-based green pigment.

About 1915–1870 BC
Fitzwilliam Museum, E.68.1903
(given by the Beni Hasan Excavation Committee)
54.5 × 185 × 43.8 cm

Cat. 15.1
Detail from the lid of the coffin, photographed in visible light (top) with a VIL image showing areas of Egyptian blue (below). The hieroglyphic inscription begins 'Words spoken: O Osiris, lady of the house, Nakht'

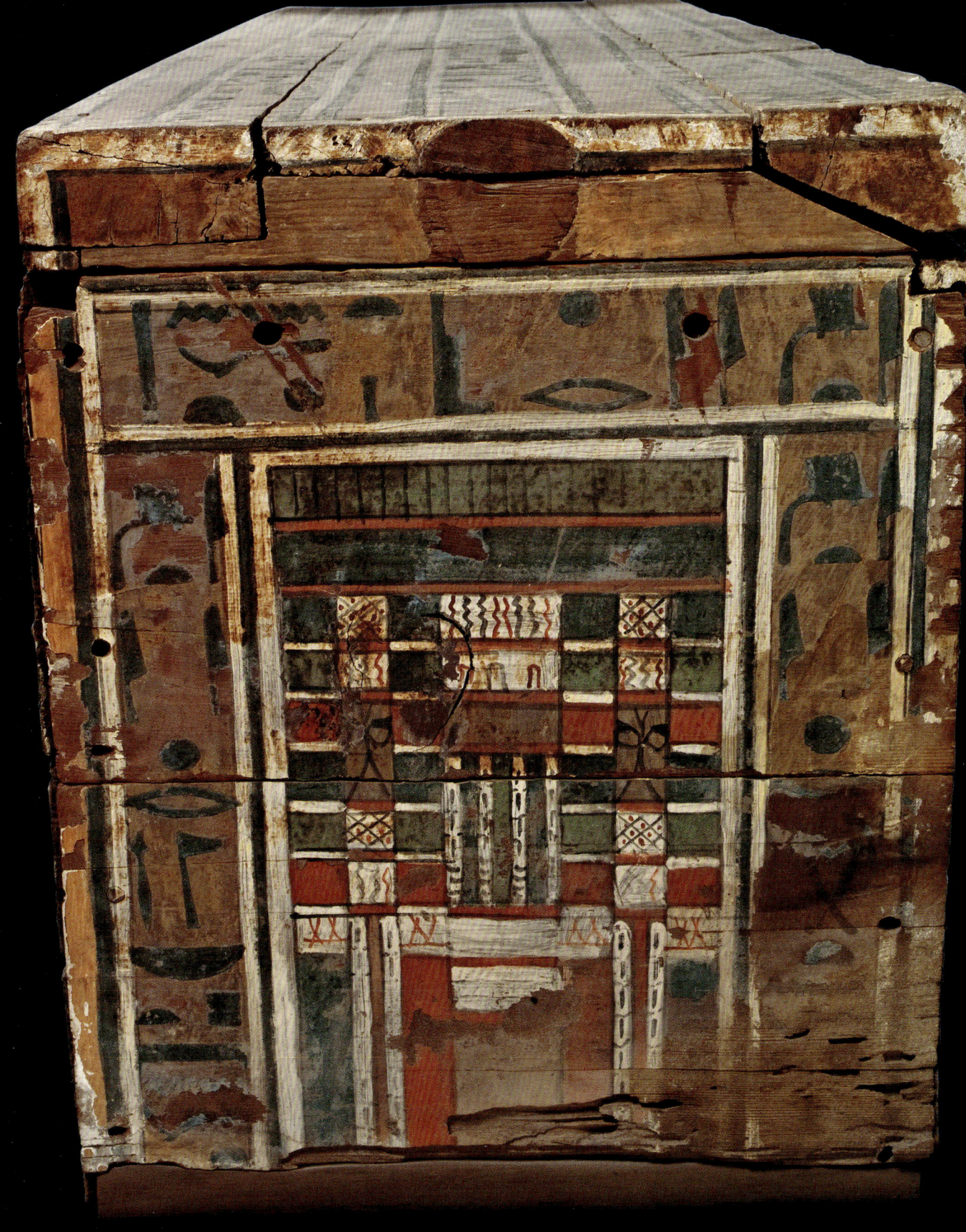

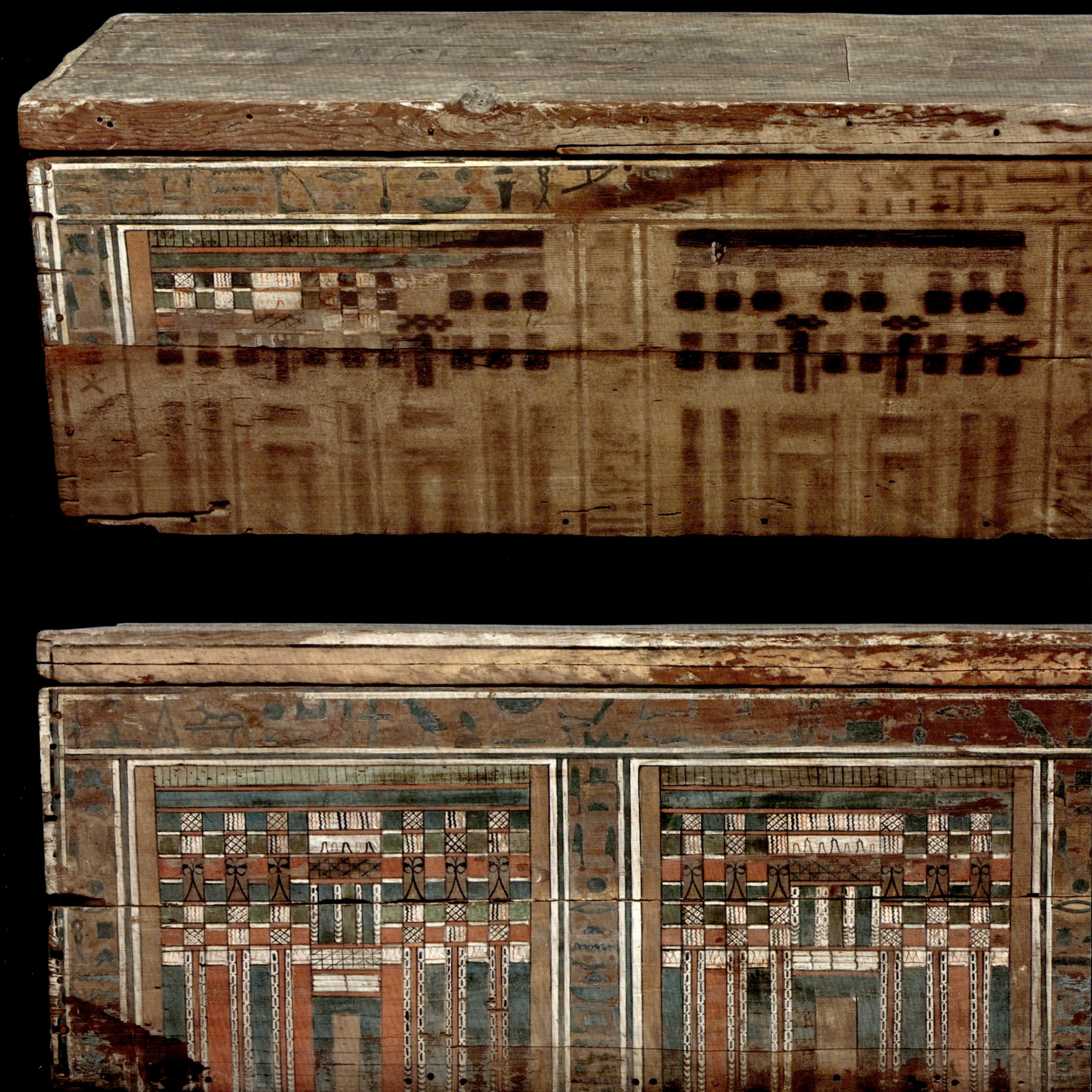

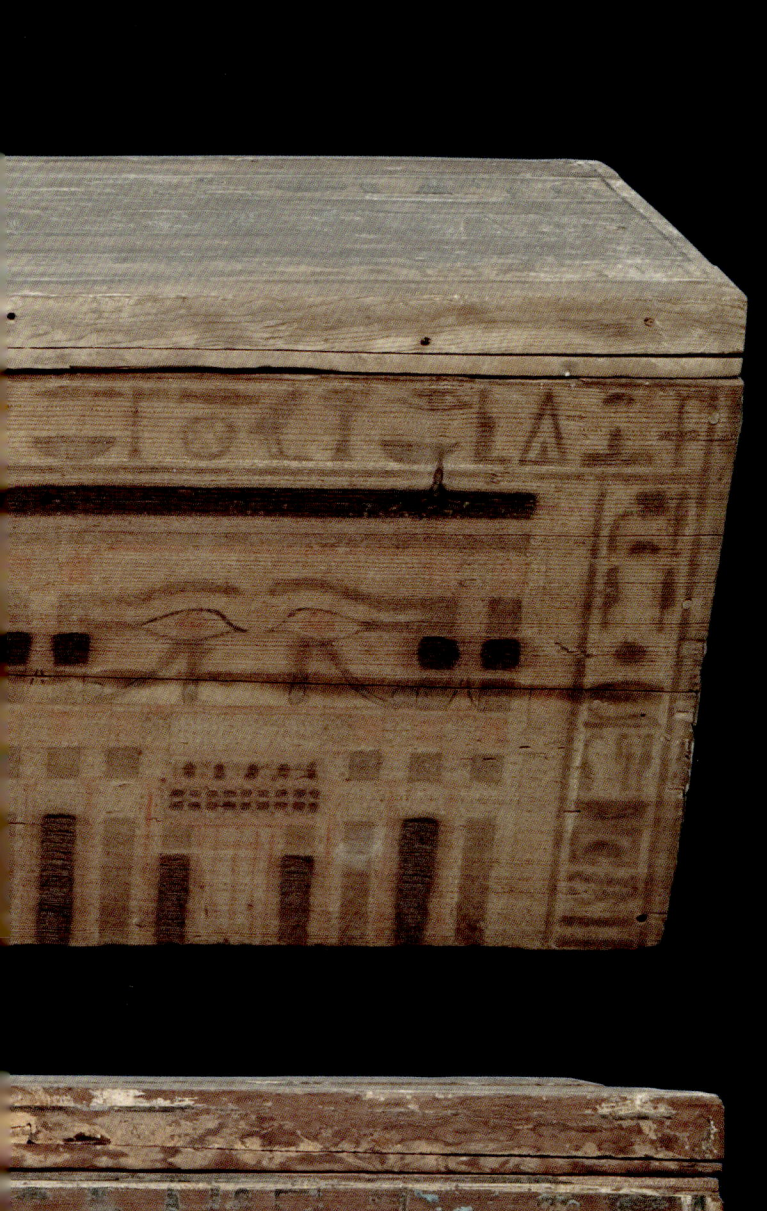

Cat. 15
The side of the coffin decorated with an eye-panel would have faced east. The wood and paint were damaged by water ingress into the tomb.

Cat. 15.3

16

Cartonnage fragment showing Nut

The sky goddess Nut is depicted here in the form of a winged female figure, holding feathers in her hands and with a sun disc on her head. Although this is a much later piece that would have overlain a mummy in the Ptolemaic Period (332–30 BC), many coffins from about 2000 BC onwards have inscriptions calling upon Nut to stretch herself over the person inside the coffin to provide protection.

332–30 BC
Fitzwilliam Museum, E.GA.291.1949
(given by R. G. Gayer-Anderson)
14 × 45.5 × 0.1 cm

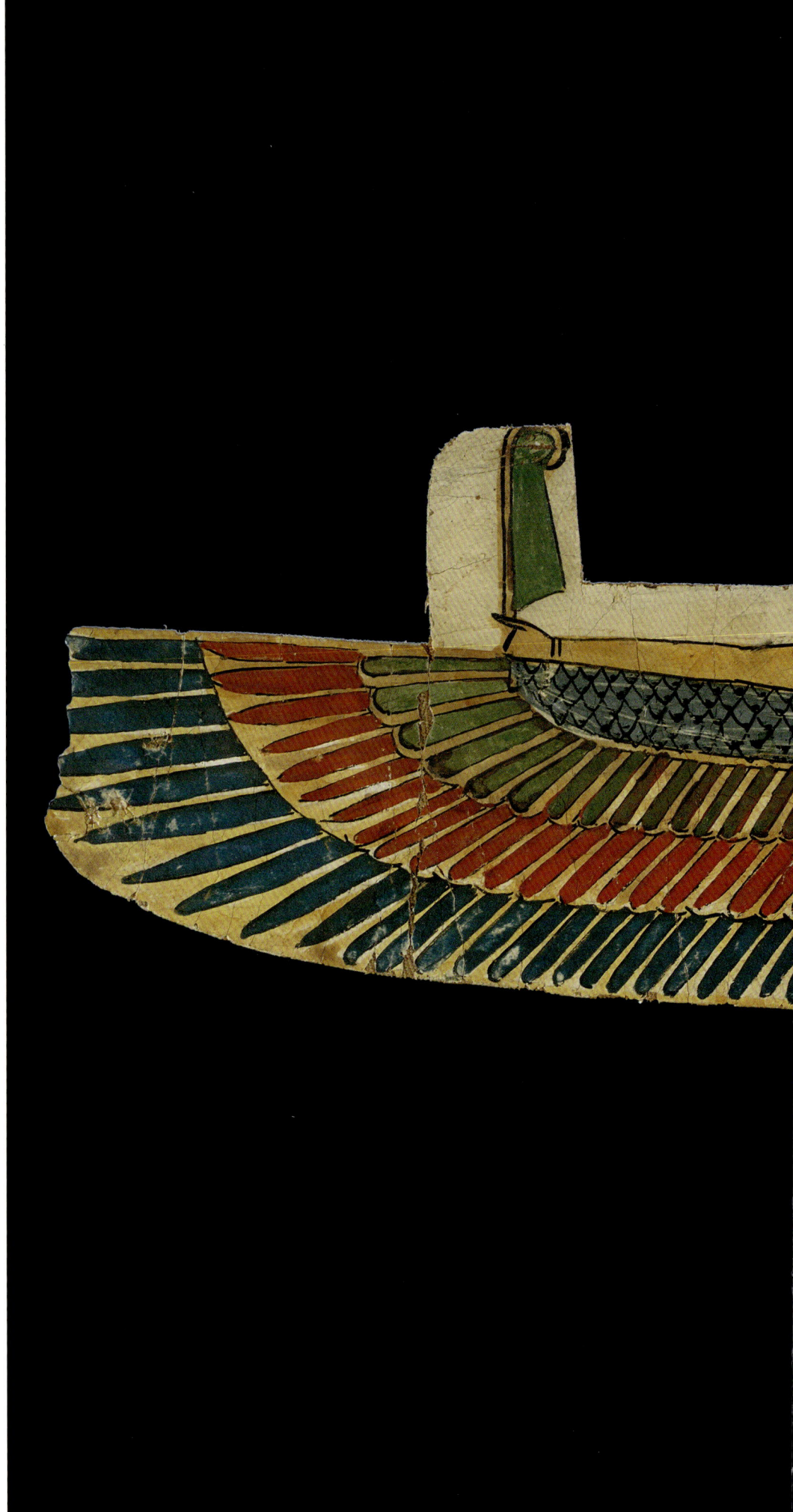

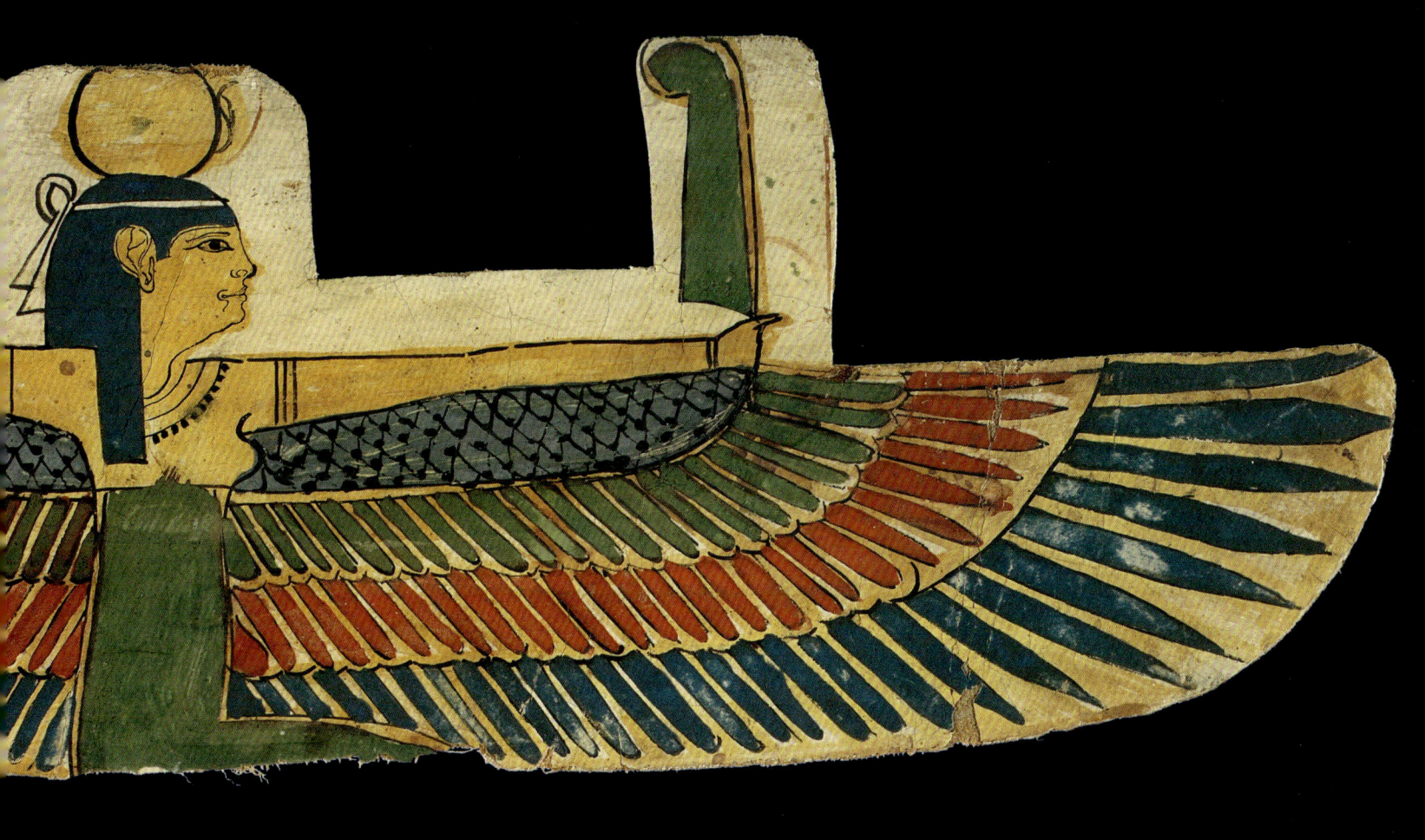

17

Faience amulets of the Four Sons of Horus

The Sons of Horus appear in early religious texts as protectors of Osiris. As the dead became more closely associated with that god, these figures began to appear on their coffins or, in the case of later amulets like these, wrapped in the bandages around their bodies.

Probably 664–525 BC
Fitzwilliam Museum, E.33a.1955, E.33b.1955, E.33c.1955 and E.33d.1955 (given by Sir William Elderton)
6.3 × 2 × 0.8 cm;
6.2 × 2 × 1 cm;
6.2 × 1.8 × 0.8 cm;
6.4 × 1.8 × 0.8 cm

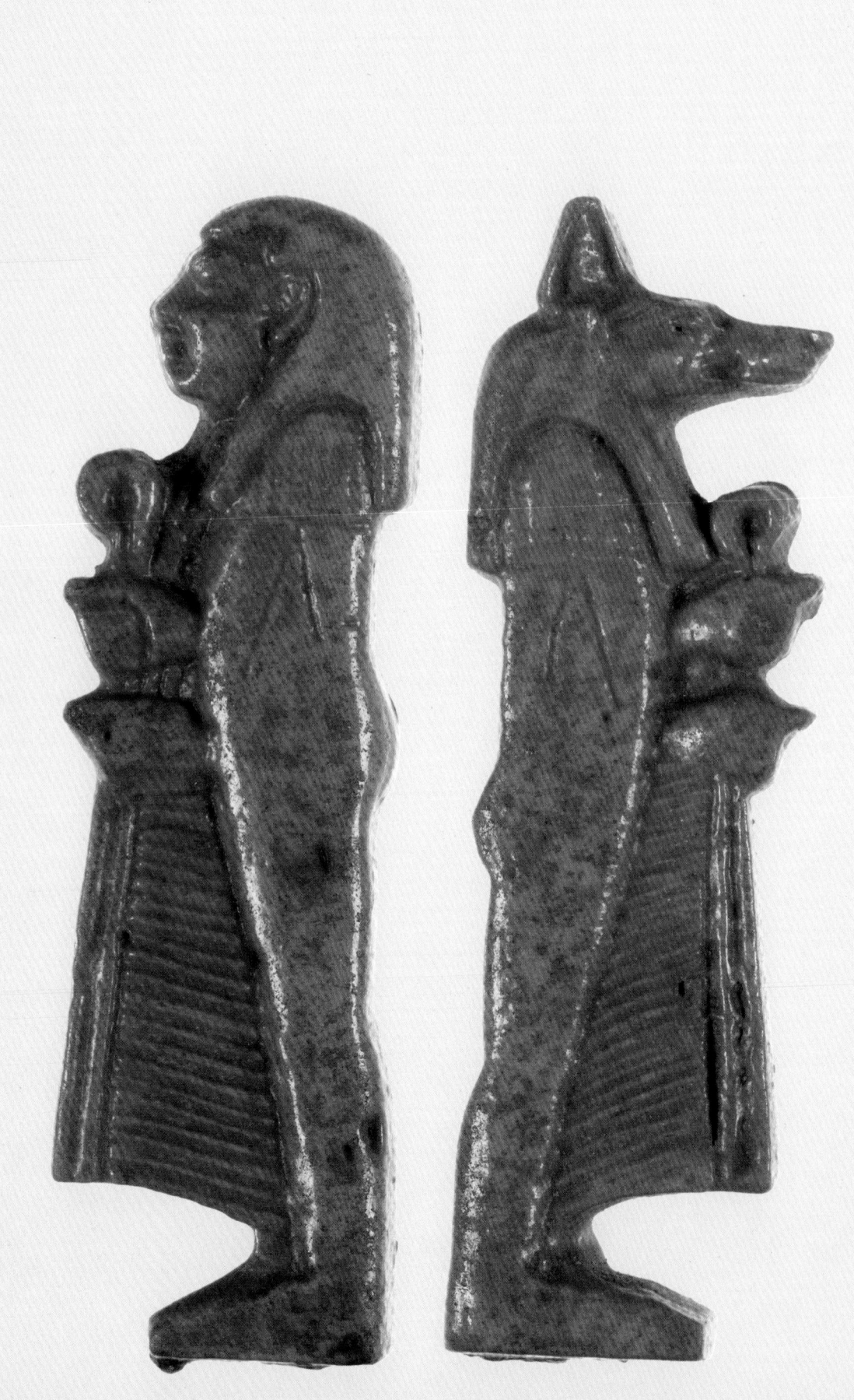

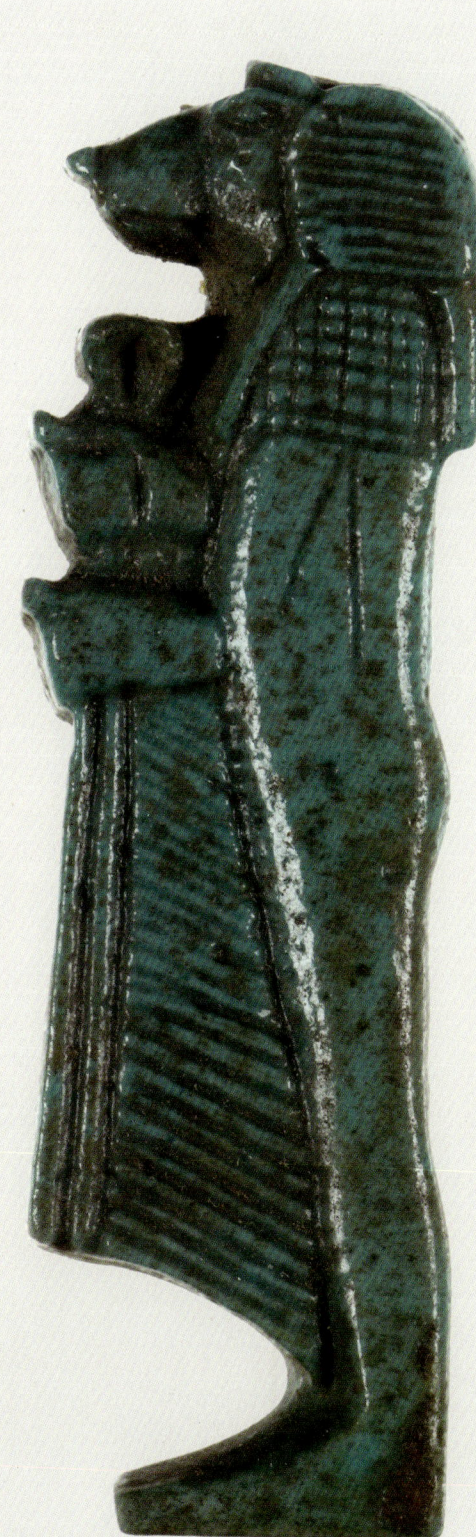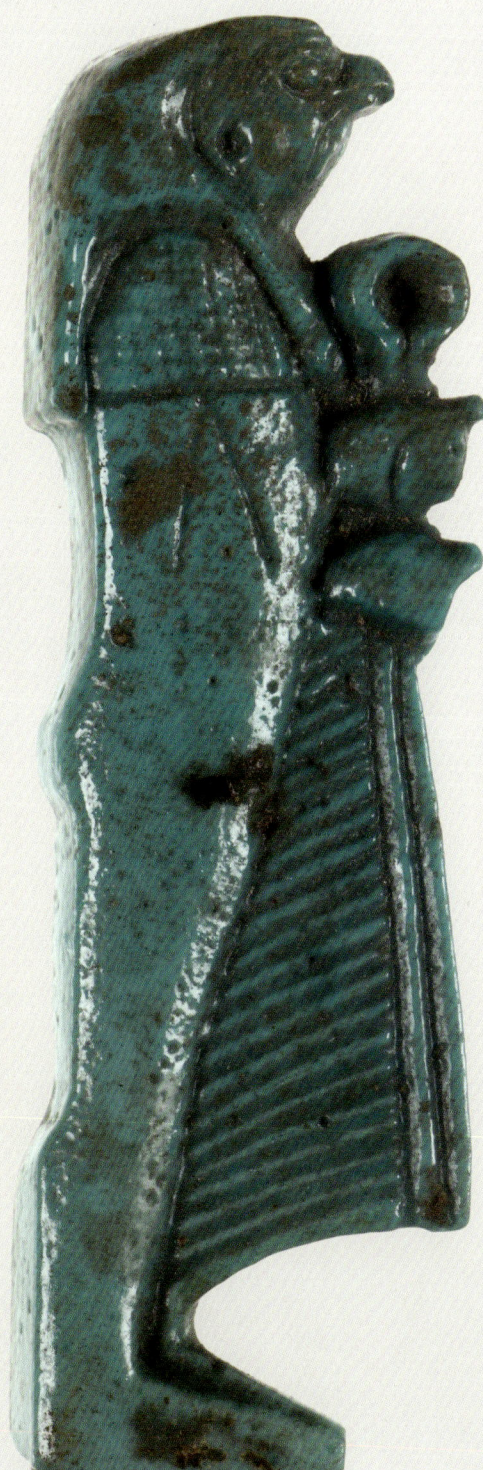

18

Cartonnage mask of a man called Tjay

This mask was lying over the face of Tjay's mummy, found undisturbed in his coffin in tomb 275 at Beni Hasan. By the end of the First Intermediate Period (about 2010 BC), the ideal form of the dead, known as *sah* in ancient Egyptian, was a mummy wrapped in white linen with a mask covering its face.

The mask is made a layer of white calcite paste covered with scraps of linen impregnated with plant gum. A final paste layer was applied over this, and the ears were modelled in paste. The yellow flesh is painted with an arsenic pigment, probably orpiment. The corners of the eyes are painted with red earth and the cosmetic lines with Egyptian blue.

About 2055–1985 BC
Fitzwilliam Museum, E.198.1903
(given by the Beni Hasan Excavation Committee)
27.5 × 19 × 9 cm

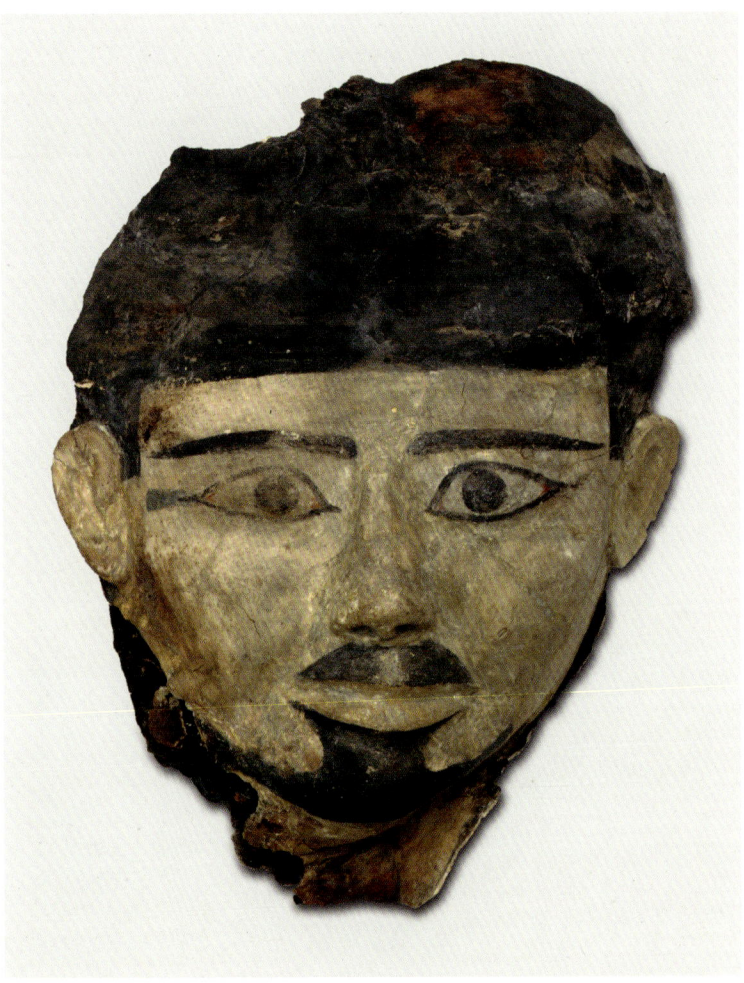

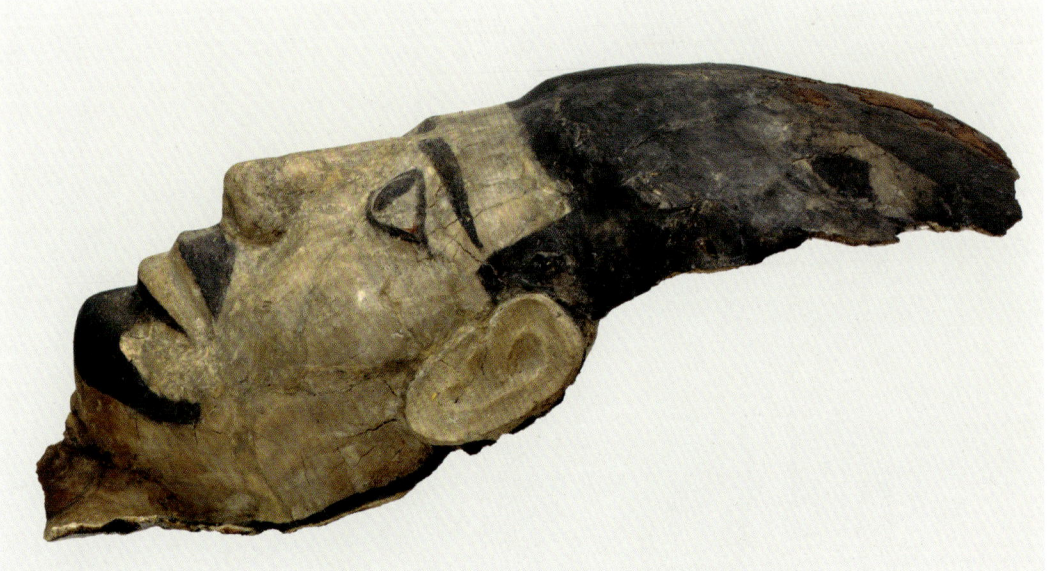

Cat. 18.1

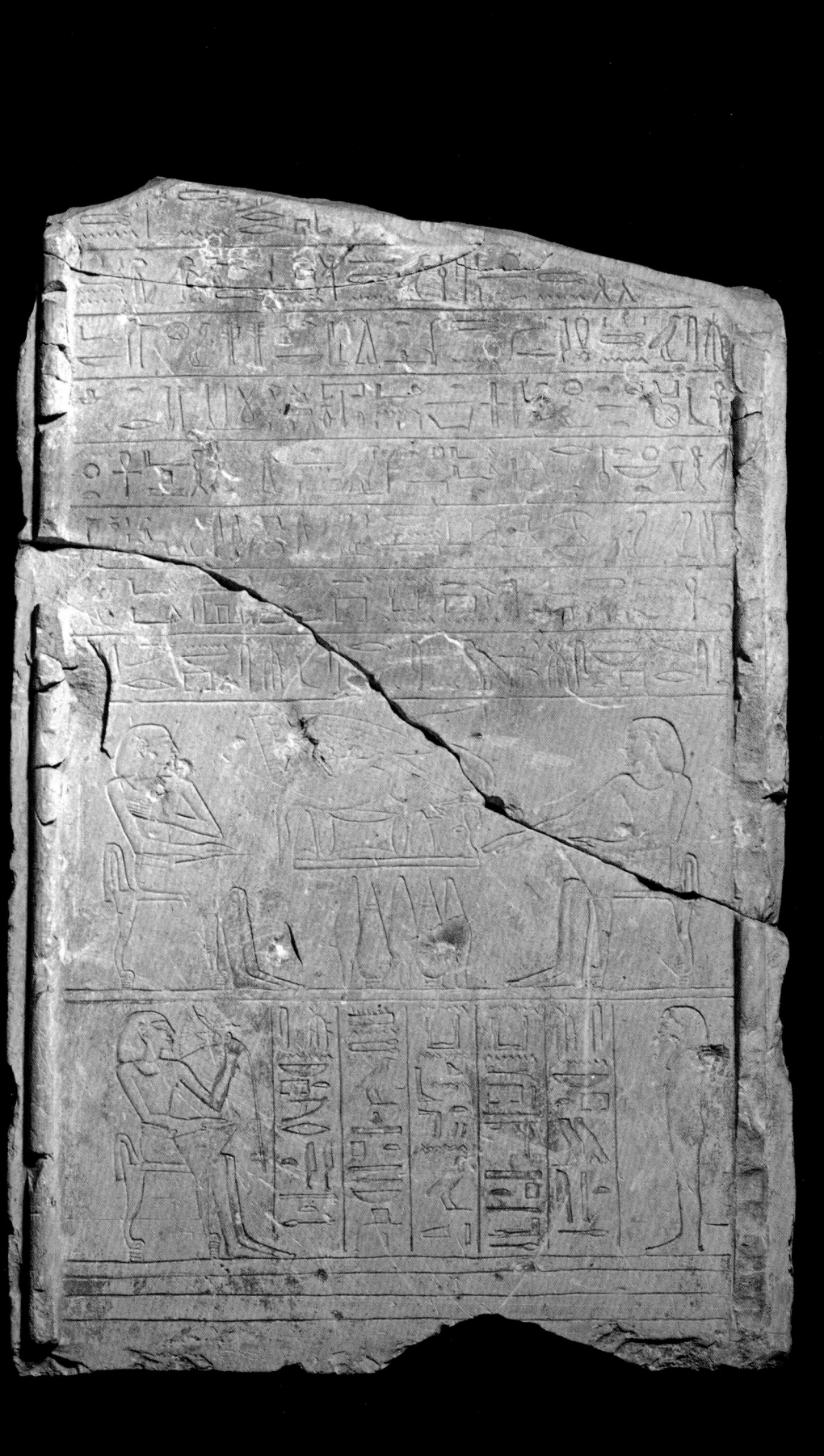

19

Limestone stela of three brothers

This inscribed stone slab (known as a stela) shows three seated figures together with a fourth figure which is wrapped in linen with a mask covering the face, clearly prepared for burial. The stela was found at Abydos and probably came from an offering chapel associated with a tomb.

About 1975–1790 BC
Fitzwilliam Museum, E.51.1901 (given by the Egyptian Research Account)
87 × 53 × 11 cm

20

Anthropoid coffin of Userhet

This anthropoid (human-shaped) coffin was found at Beni Hasan, in tomb 132, inside a rectangular coffin very like Nakht's (cat. 15). Pottery from the same tomb, together with the form of the outer coffin (now at the University of Liverpool), suggests a date late in the Twelfth Dynasty (about 1855–1790 BC). The coffin decoration shows Userhet prepared for burial, as if the coffin itself is meant to perform the function of the white linen wrappings around his body and the mask over his face. Like earlier mummies, this coffin lay on its side, so that the eyes were close to the eyes painted on the outside of the rectangular coffin (fig. 91).

Userhet's face is painted black, a colour associated with Osiris, and the line of inscription down his front identifies him with that god, beginning, 'O Osiris, warrior Userhet'. The title 'warrior' is not common at this period and was not used for others buried in this cemetery; it may signify Userhet's status locally rather than being a military title. The rest of the text, like that on the coffin of Nakht, calls on Nut to spread herself over him. The decoration on Userhet's chest represents a broad collar of coloured beads, a feature that occurs on many later coffins.

The box and lid (including the face and ears) were each carved from a single piece of sycomore fig; the beard is a separate piece of wood. A long strip of sycomore fig dowelled in along the left-hand side was needed to make good the rim of the box, giving a secure anchor for the pegged tenons that hold the coffin halves together. Strips of open-weave linen were glued to the surface to help the thick calcite preparation layer stick to the wood. The decoration was painted with red earth, Egyptian green, Egyptian blue and carbon-based black.

Completely invisible from the exterior is evidence of a major problem encountered by the makers of Userhet's coffin: at some point during manufacture, the hollowed-out box split from top to bottom. The damage was repaired with the same technique used to strengthen the corner joints of the coffin of Khety (cat. 11): the slit was sewn together with rawhide or sinew stitches (cat. 20.2). These were partially sealed on the interior surface with patches of paste. The X-radiograph shows details of the repair (fig. 90).

There are also early twentieth-century repairs and restorations to much of the surface of the coffin.

About 1855–1790 BC
Fitzwilliam Museum, E.88.1903 (given by the Beni Hasan Excavation Committee)
33.2 × 182.4 × 41.2 cm

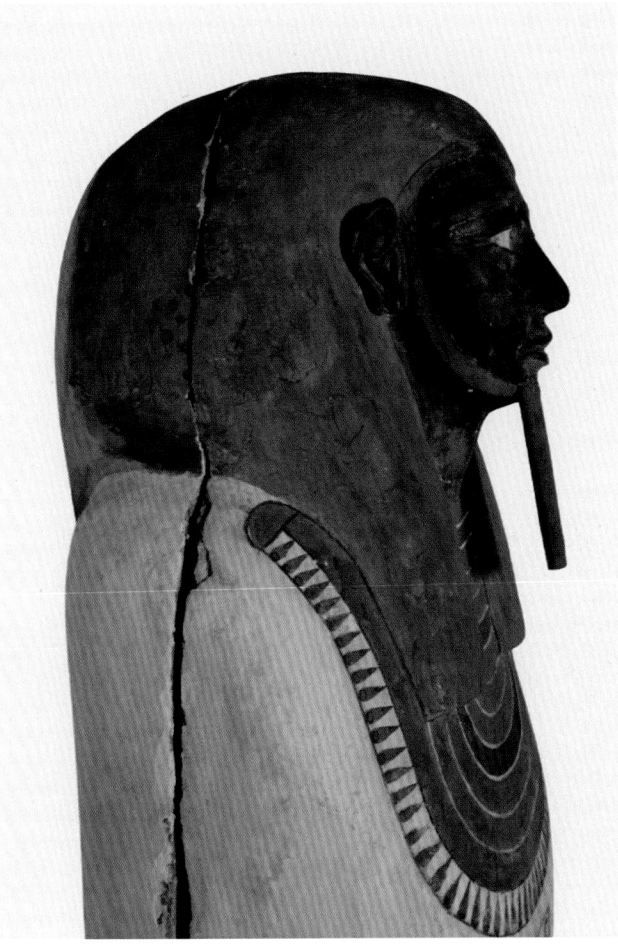

Cat. 20.1

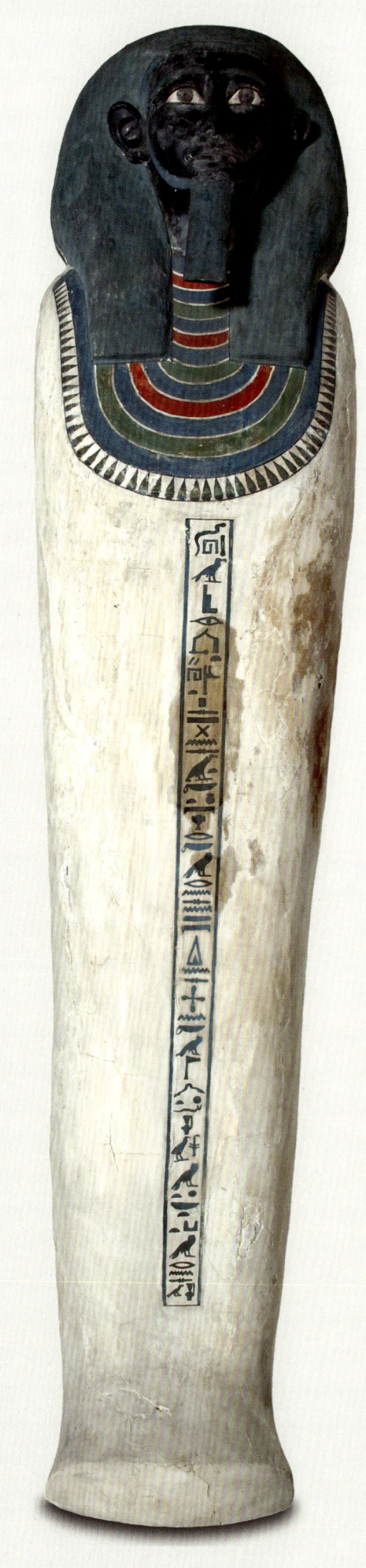

Cat. 20.2
Interior of the coffin box. The split, which runs down the left hand side, was repaired with four stitches (marked on the drawing) and covered with a coarse paste, which was used also to repair damage at the head end of the box. The marked square indicates the area shown in the X-radiograph (right).

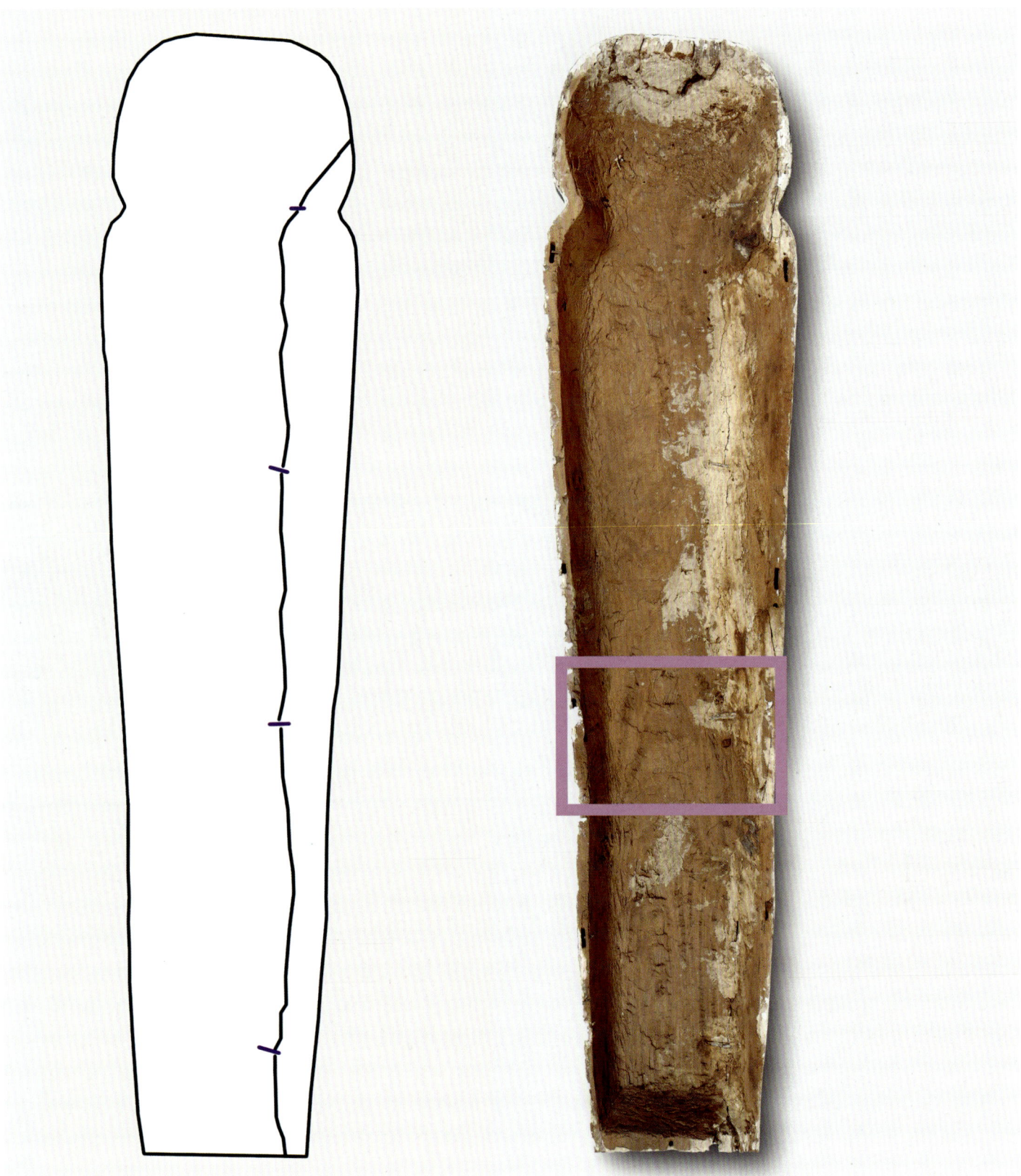

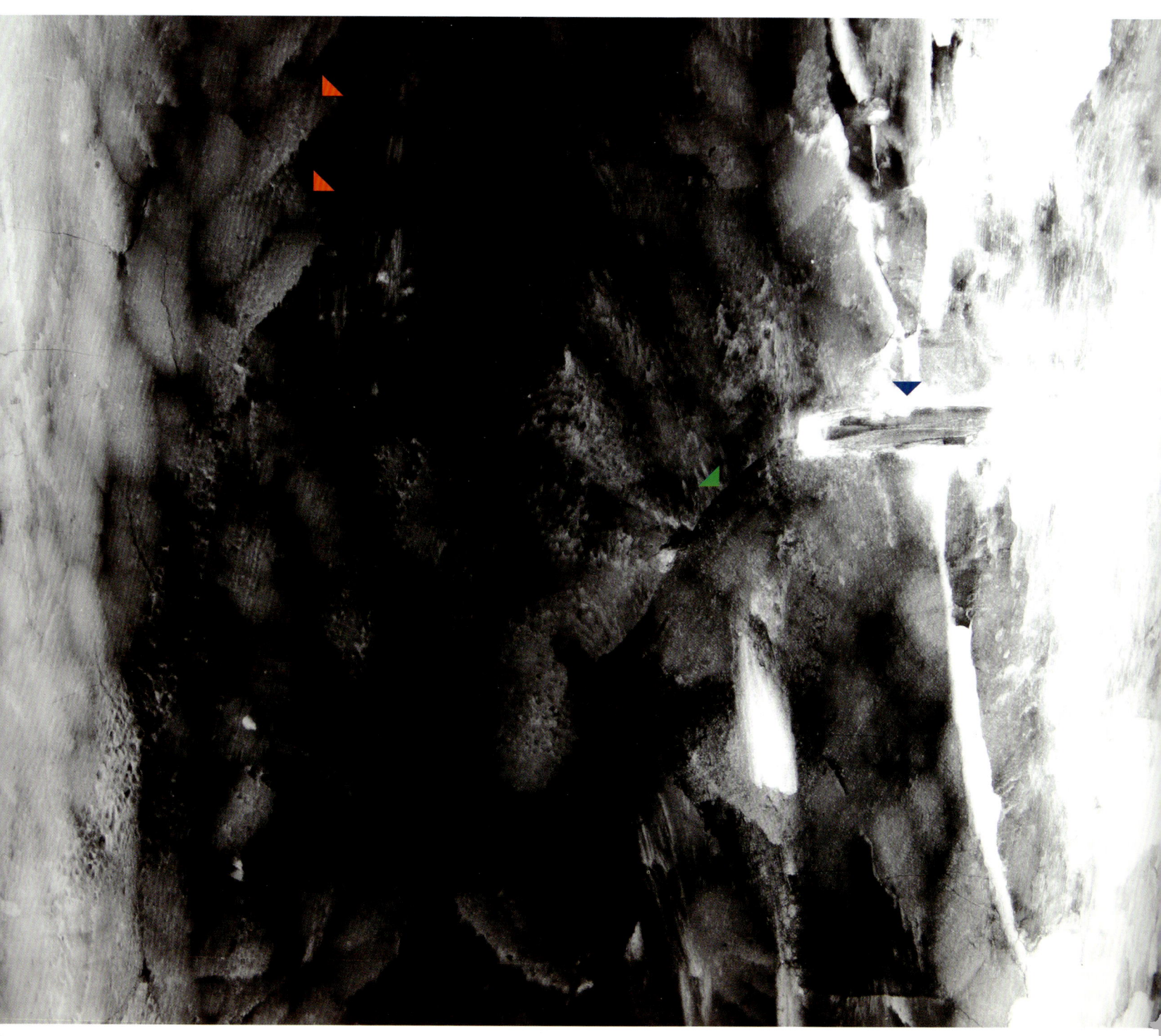

Fig. 90
X-radiograph of part of the coffin box showing the split, one of the stiches (blue arrow) and the patch of linen (green arrow) which covers it on the exterior under the layer of paste. Tool marks (red arrows) all over the exterior, now filled and hidden by the white surface layers, also show up on the radiograph.

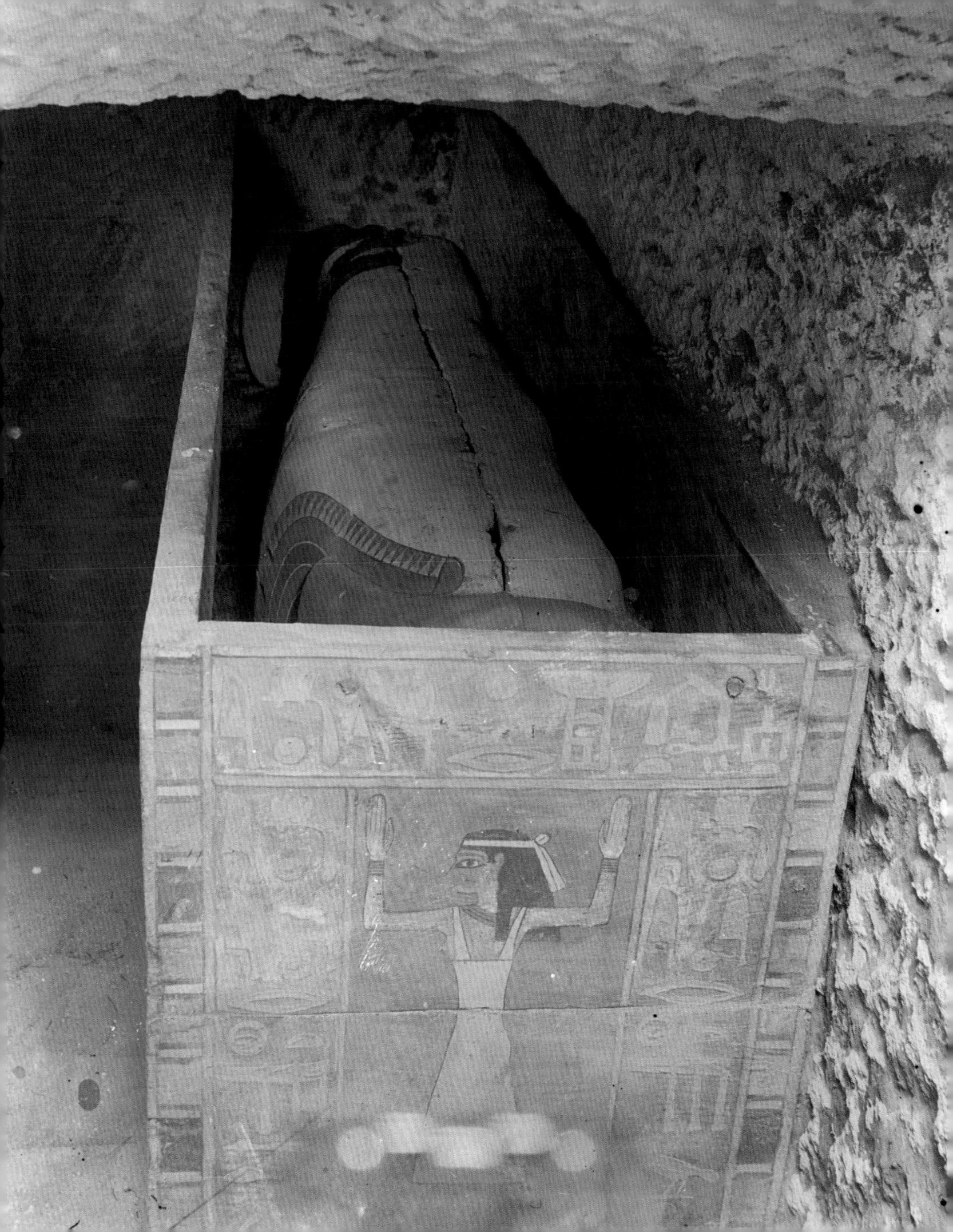

Fig. 91
Excavation photograph showing the anthropoid coffin of Userhet lying on its side within the outer, rectangular coffin (now in the University of Liverpool)

Decorated anthropoid coffins

The period following the end of the Middle Kingdom is known as the Second Intermediate Period (about 1790–1550 BC) and was another time when Egypt was not under the rule of a single king. The ruling elite at Thebes (present-day Luxor) chose to be buried within a type of coffin known today as *rishi*, a term derived from the Arabic for 'feather', because of the characteristic pattern of feathers on the lid (fig. 92). Although they have an anthropoid shape, the overall appearance of these coffins is rectangular, usually with a narrow face and a large wig. It is almost as if the craftsmen involved usually made box coffins and had now been asked to make anthropoid coffins with only the most rudimentary idea of how to do this. It is not clear how widespread the use of *rishi* coffins became; for example, at Abydos during the same period rectangular coffins continued to be used, but now with a depiction of the burial procession of the deceased (cat. 21).

Early coffins of the New Kingdom (from about 1525 BC) are a modified form of white anthropoid coffins like Userhet's (cat. 20), but with the addition of text bands, previously seen on rectangular coffins, transferred to the lid and sides of the coffin. This created a series of panels, which came to be filled with decoration. Initially, these coffins had a white background colour, sometimes decorated with colourful funerary scenes (cat. 22); later, from around 1450 BC, they had a black background colour (cat. 24).

From this time onwards, bodies were always placed on their backs inside coffins, looking up at the sky. Archaeological evidence suggests that this became regular practice during the late Middle Kingdom, but it may have started earlier: an ancient Egyptian story dating back to the early Middle Kingdom relates that a man living in exile is asked by the king to come back to Egypt in his old age so that he can receive an elaborate burial, in which he will lie in his coffin looking up at the sky. From this time onwards, a vulture with outspread wings became a regular feature in the decoration over the chest of the deceased.

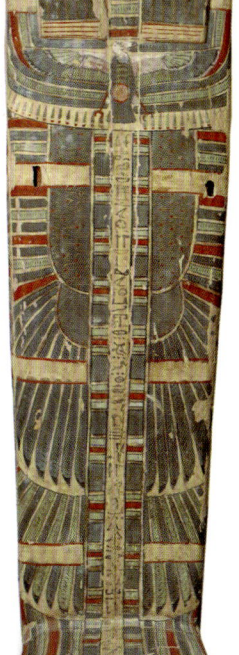

Fig. 92
Rishi coffin (British Museum, EA54350), with a typical feathered pattern, made for a woman named Taiuy

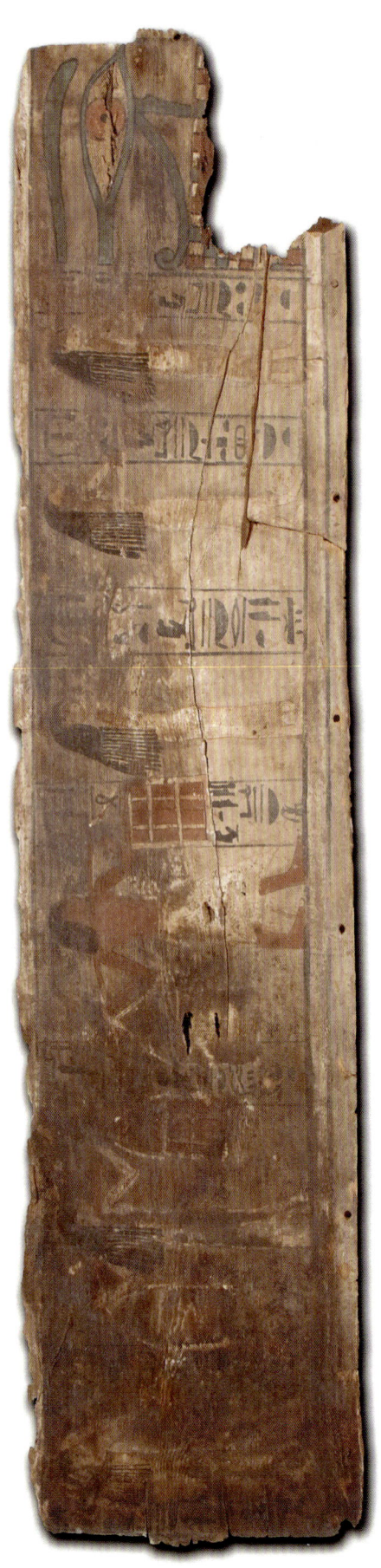
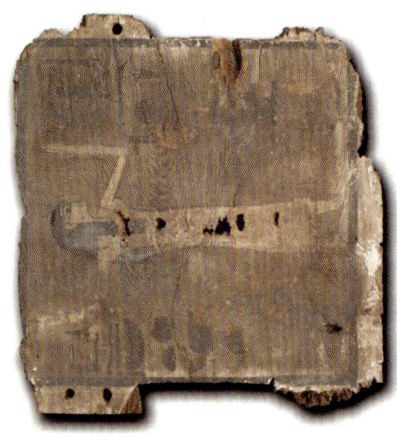
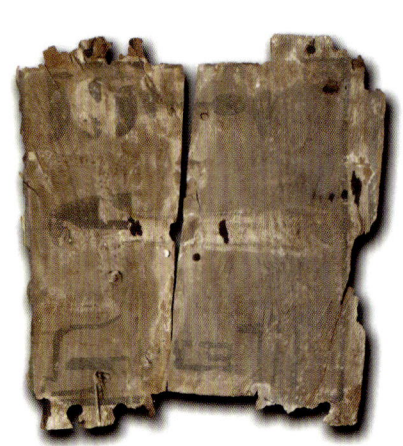
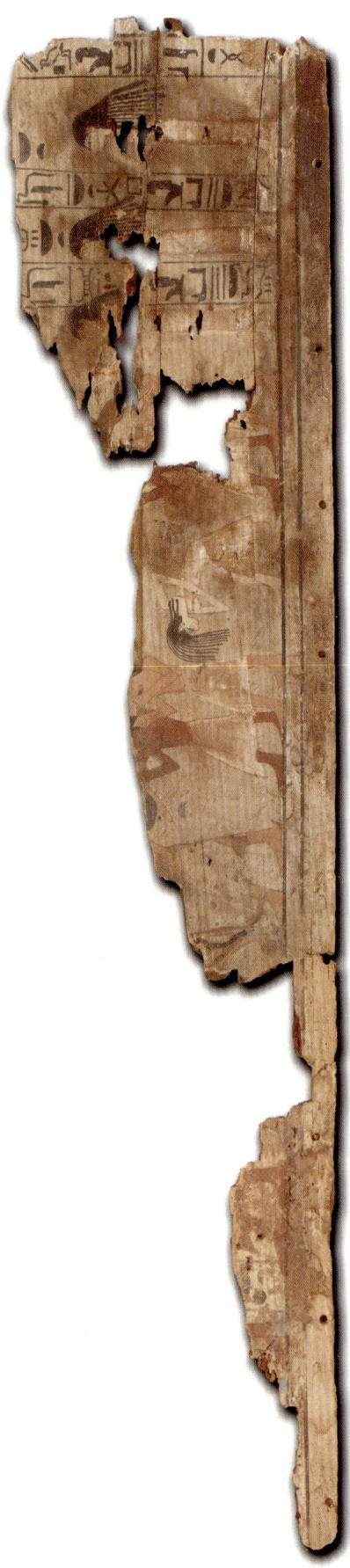

21
Coffin of the mourning women

These water- and termite-damaged wooden planks were found by John Garstang at Abydos in 1900. Based on their shape, he believed that they came from a Middle Kingdom coffin. They form a rectangular box typical of that period, but the decoration is rather different. On the outside of the coffin are scenes relating to the funeral of the deceased: the funeral procession itself, offering bearers carrying items into the tomb and also the coffin (now lost), and women mourning. These features are not found on Middle Kingdom coffins but were first used towards the end of the Second Intermediate Period, a time when the centralised government system had broken down and, for the first time, foreigners ruled parts of the country. It is probable that the coffin dates to that period or to the beginning of the New Kingdom, when Egypt was once again under the rule of a single king.

A lone eye appears on one long side, and there are traces indicating that there was one on the other side too. This is most likely because the body lay on its back inside the coffin, rather than on its side and close to the eye-panel, as in older coffins.

The coffin is made mostly of sycomore fig, with dowels of sidr. The long sides were probably constructed from single, full-depth planks, as was the foot panel. The head panel was constructed from two planks (the upper of sidr) of approximately equal depth roughly fitted together with two pegged mortise and tenon joints (from which the tenons are now lost).

The coffin parts were joined at the corners with wide dovetails, secured with dowels. Regularly spaced, horizontal dowel holes along the bottom of the long panels show where the coffin base was attached. Vertical dowel holes in the undersides of the end panels suggest that these panels (which are not as tall as the side panels) were fixed onto the top of the base board.

A thin white calcite, gypsum and bassanite preparation layer coats the exterior of the coffin. On the end panels a black underdrawing and central setting-out line can be seen with infrared reflectography (fig. 93).

The painted surface is heavily discoloured and abraded, making it difficult to assess the original colour scheme. The background appears to have been yellow, painted with yellow earth/jarosite on the long panels and orpiment on the head end panel. However, there is evidence of a mixture of earth and orpiment in some locations. This variation in pigment use continues in the flesh of the figures. On the long panel, jarosite/yellow earth and different shades of red earth have been identified, sometimes mixed with white to produce a lighter colour. Orpiment was again identified on the flesh on the head end panel.

Pigments were mixed to create subtle variations, and carefully positioned adjacent colours give a dramatic effect.

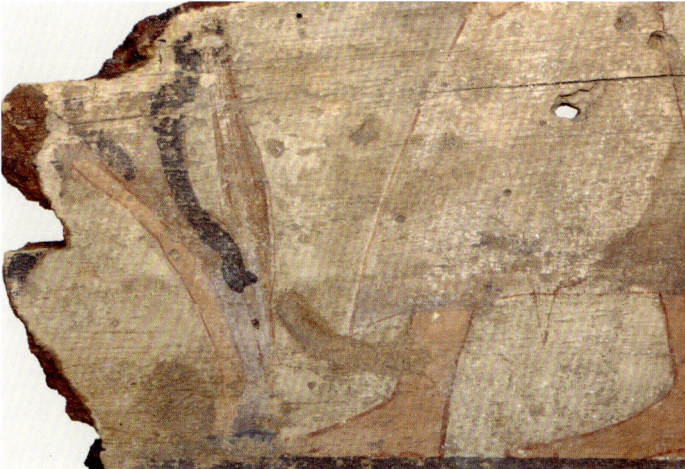

Cat. 21.1

The pale-skinned women and the orange-skinned men are outlined in red, and the deep red figures in black. The pale flesh on some figures is also haloed in white, an effective means of making them stand out from the background. The pale robes of the figures may have a red wash of ochre over them.

Little remains of the cow or ox on the right-hand long panel except the hooves, but it is worth noting the careful tonality and subtly variegated painting of this area (cat. 21.1).

About 1680–1510 BC
Fitzwilliam Museum, E.283.1900 (given by the Egyptian Research Account)
Sides: 42 × 187 × 1.7 cm; 33 × 161 × 1.7 cm
Ends: 38 × 36 × 1.7 cm

Next page

Fig. 93
Infrared reflectography photographs of the end panels, showing the setting-out lines down the centre of the figures. The initial black drawing of the figures is also visible.

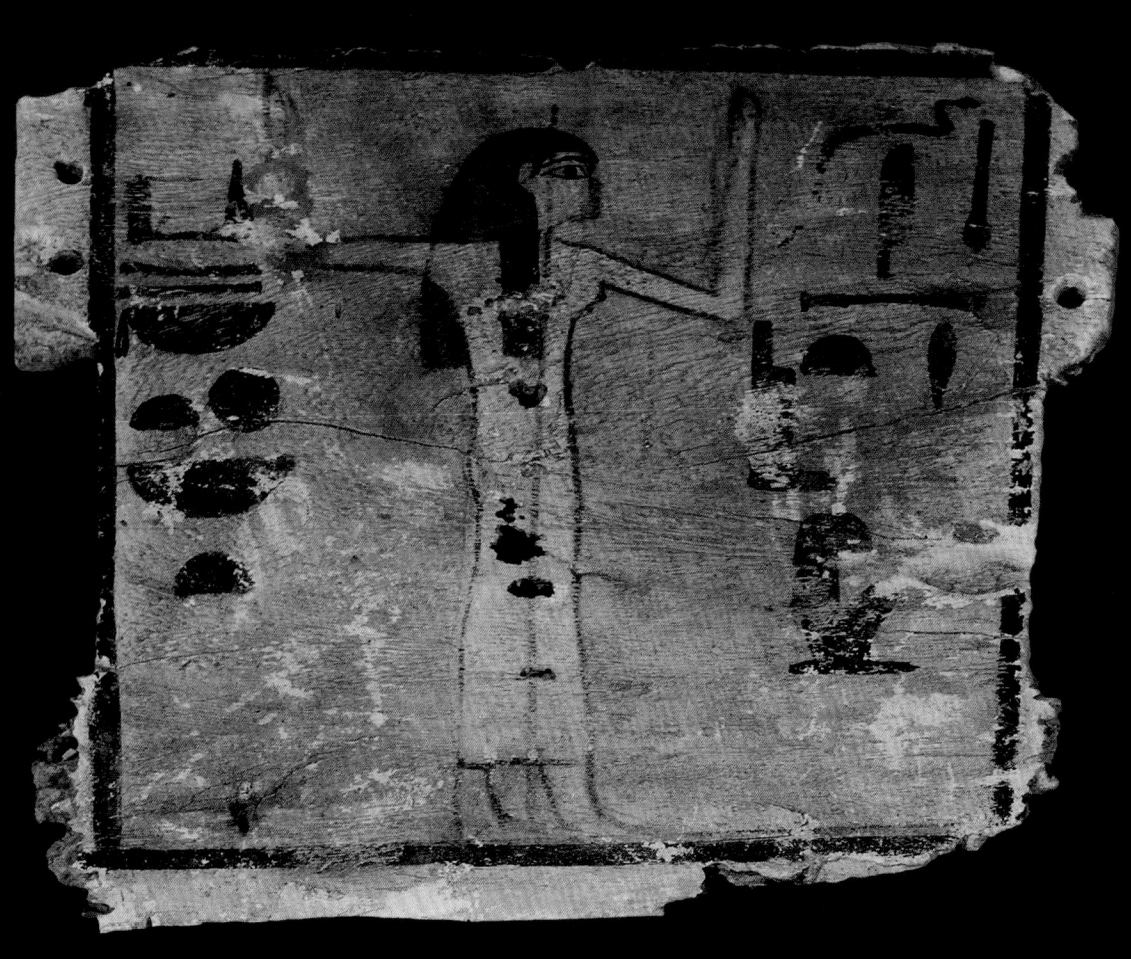

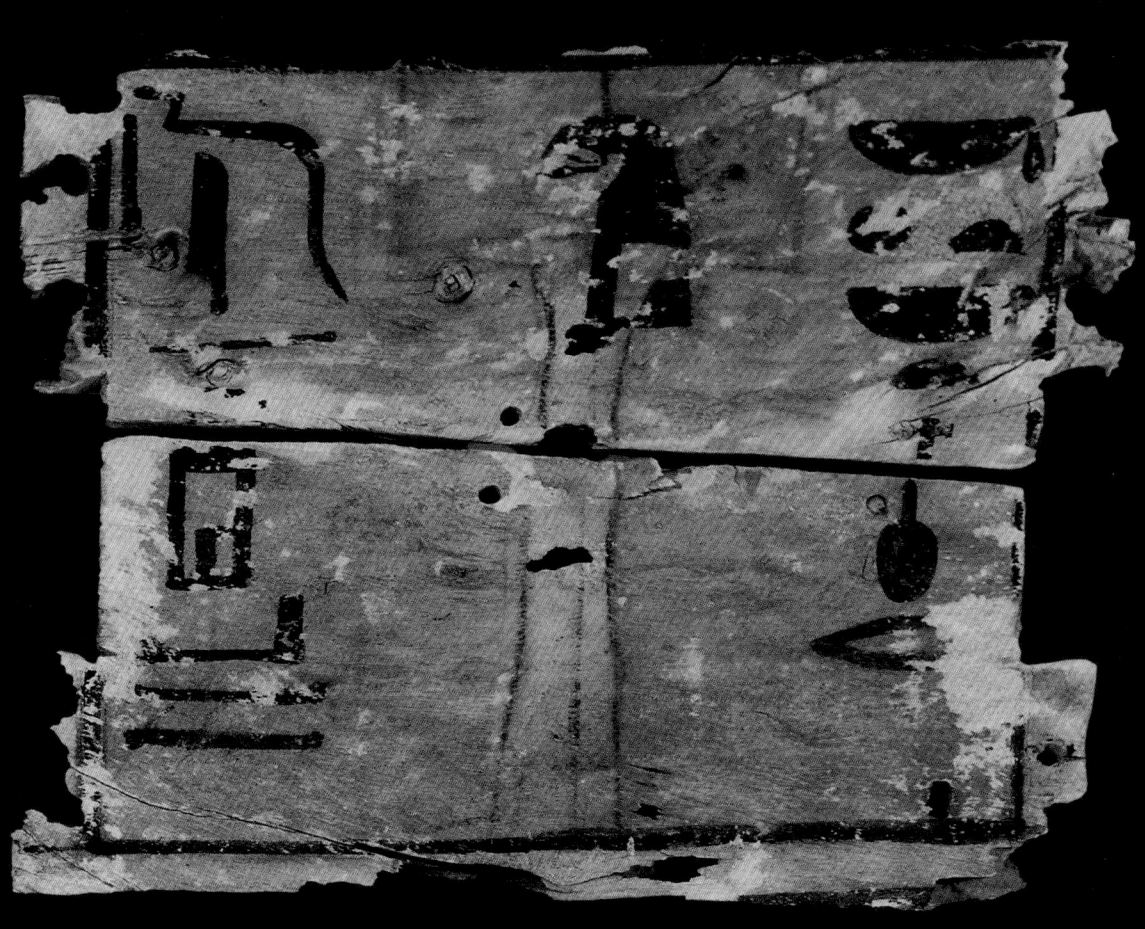

22

Coffin of Madja

The shape of this coffin, made for a woman called Madja, is reminiscent of Userhet's coffin (cat. 20), with its face, wig and rounded shape. Here, too, the owner is shown wrapped in white linen with a mask covering her face. But the face is not black, and the white linen wrappings have bands of inscription dividing up the space, rather like the inscription bands on earlier box coffins. On one side, in the gaps between the bands, are funeral scenes, with the coffin being dragged by two men, watched by mourners, reminiscent of the decoration of the coffin of the mourning women (cat. 21). On the other side is a depiction of Osiris and a seated couple (cat. 22.1), who are receiving offerings. The lid is painted with four images of Anubis.

The coffin was found in an undisturbed tomb at Deir el-Medina, with the body of Madja still inside. In the same tomb there was also the coffin of a man, probably her husband. He was almost certainly one of the workers who created the tombs in the Valley of the Kings and who lived in Deir el-Medina in houses provided for them by the government.

The box and lid, including the face and the foot of the coffin (which is not hollowed out), are each cut from a single piece of sycomore fig. The lid has two tenons that fit into mortises in the box, fixed in place by dowels. The box and the lid are both roughly hewn on the inside and painted white. The plastered exterior of the coffin is painted in black, yellow and red, blue and green on a white background.

About 1510–1400 BC
Musée du Louvre, E14543 (from excavations in 1934–5 at Deir el-Medina)
62 × 184 × 46 cm

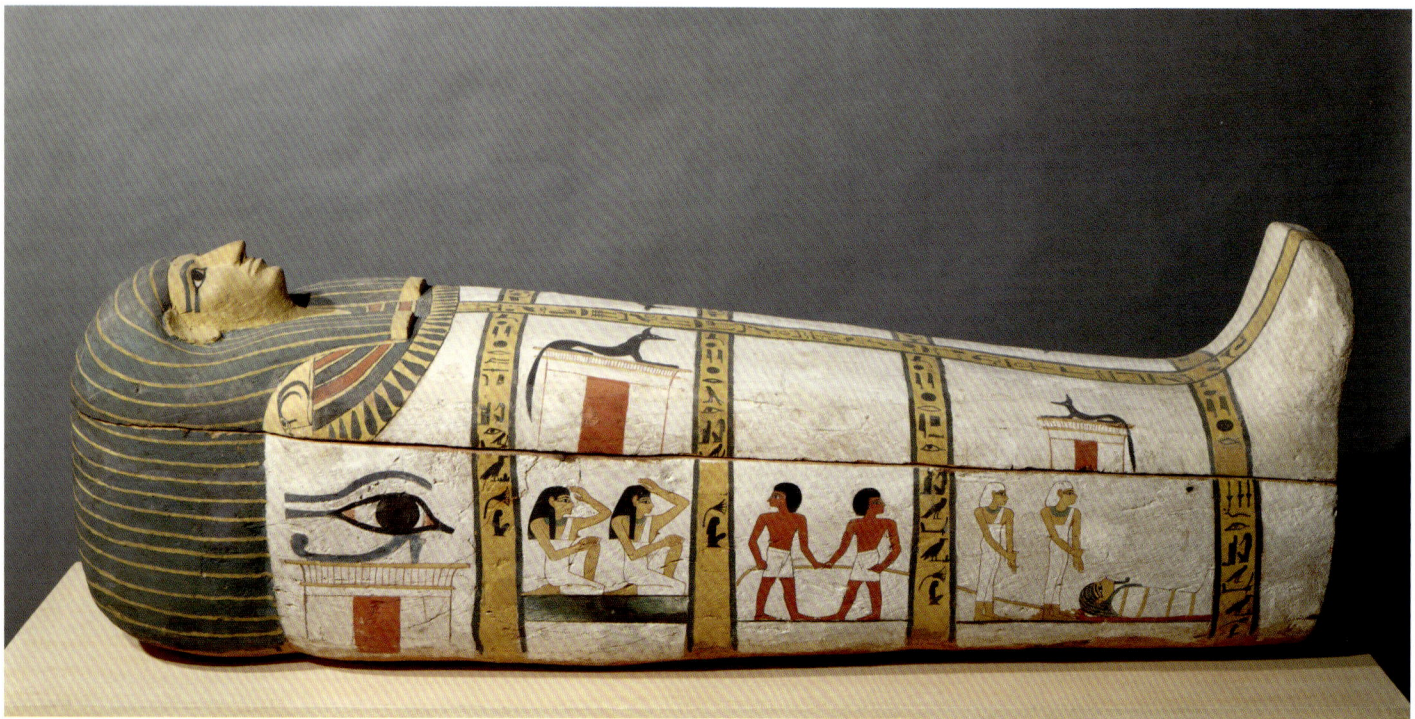

Cat. 22

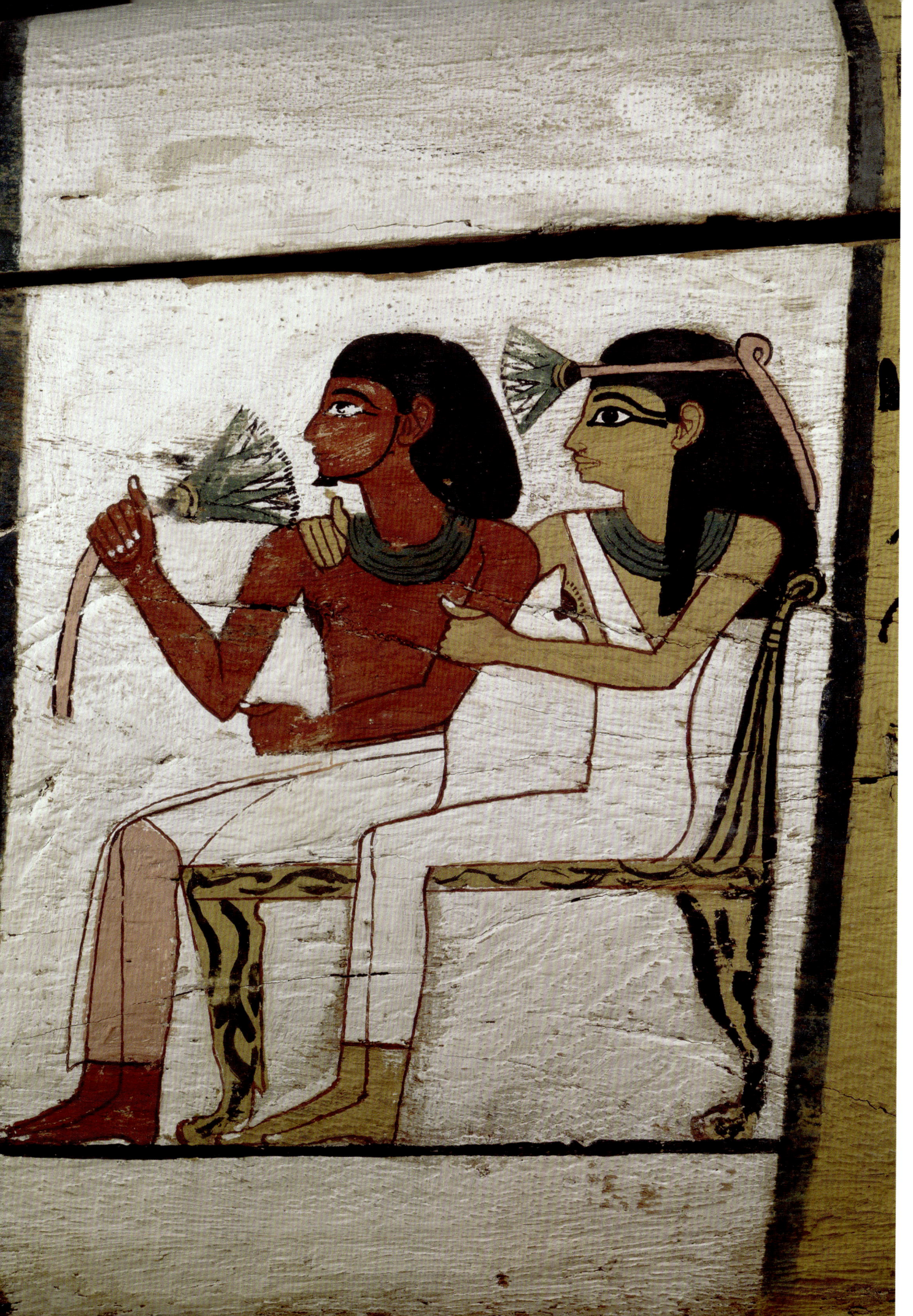

23

Early Eighteenth Dynasty footboard

This is part of the footboard from a white anthropoid coffin (see cat. 22), made of several pieces of sycomore fig joined using animal glue, acacia and sidr dowels and loose tenons. Poorly fitting joints have been packed out with wedges of wood, a gritty paste/mud or fabric scraps (cat. 23.1). It is decorated with a figure of Isis, whose name is written above her left arm and (in abbreviated form) on her head.

The surface is partially covered with a coarse yellow preparation layer (made of calcite, gypsum and bassanite) overlaid with a white coat (containing natural chalk). There is a pink underdrawing of Isis, who is painted with yellow earth, red earth, carbon-based black and Egyptian green.

About 1500–1400 BC
Fitzwilliam Museum, E.GA.2910.1943
(given by R. G. Gayer-Anderson)
17.3 × 38 × 1.8 cm

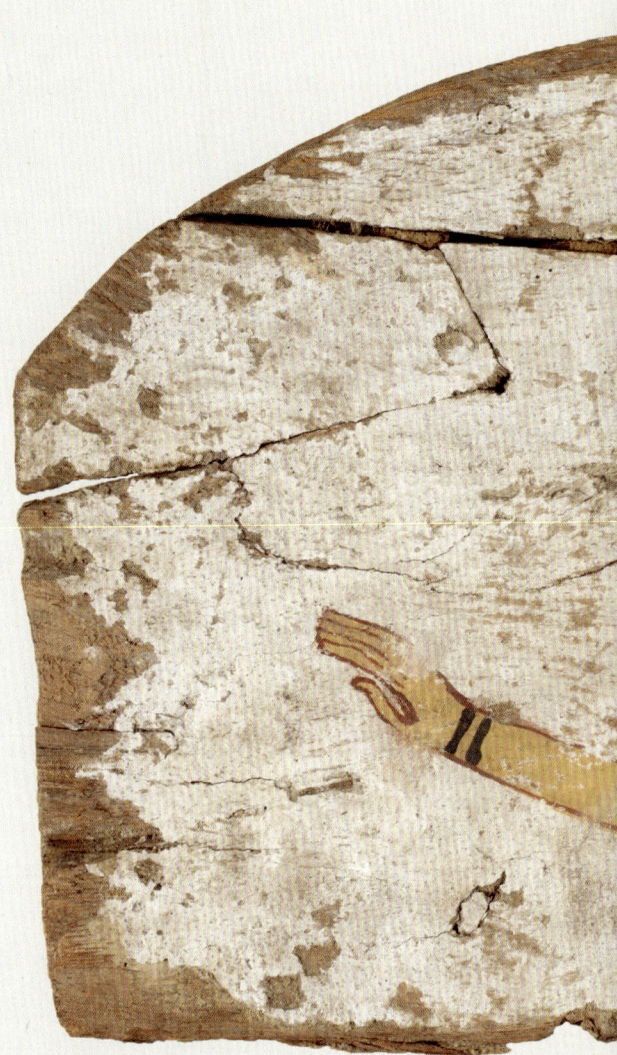

Cat. 23

Cat. 23.1
The bottom edge of the footboard was once connected to another piece of wood with a pegged tenon (now lost from the mortise). Scraps of linen were used to pack out the joint.

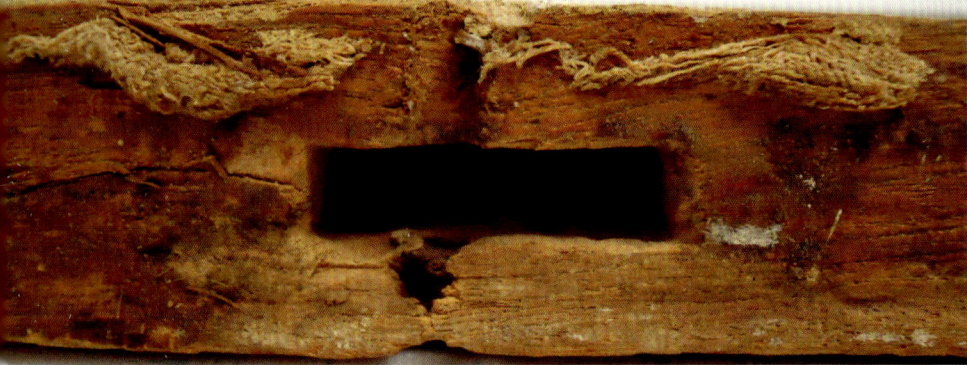

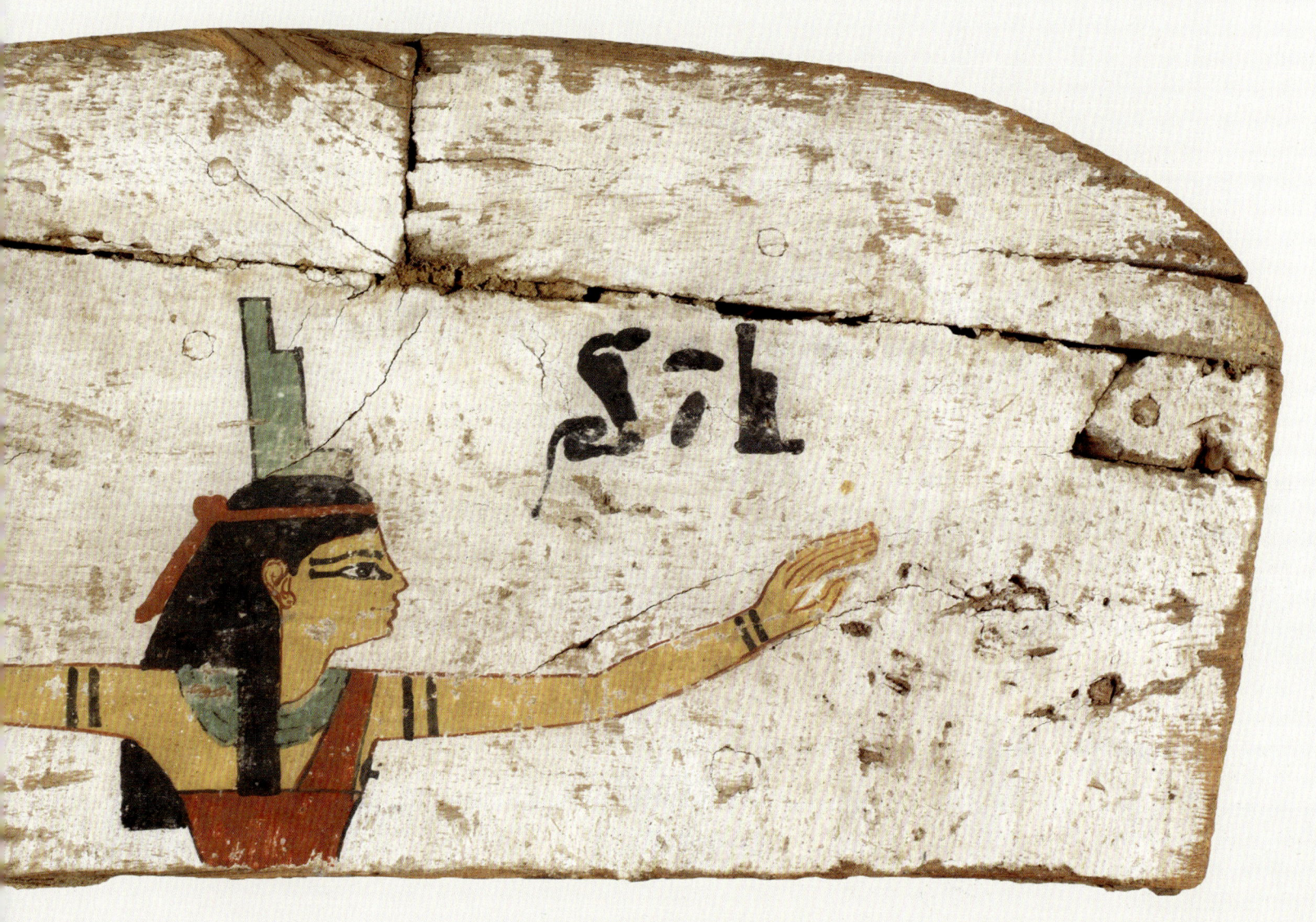

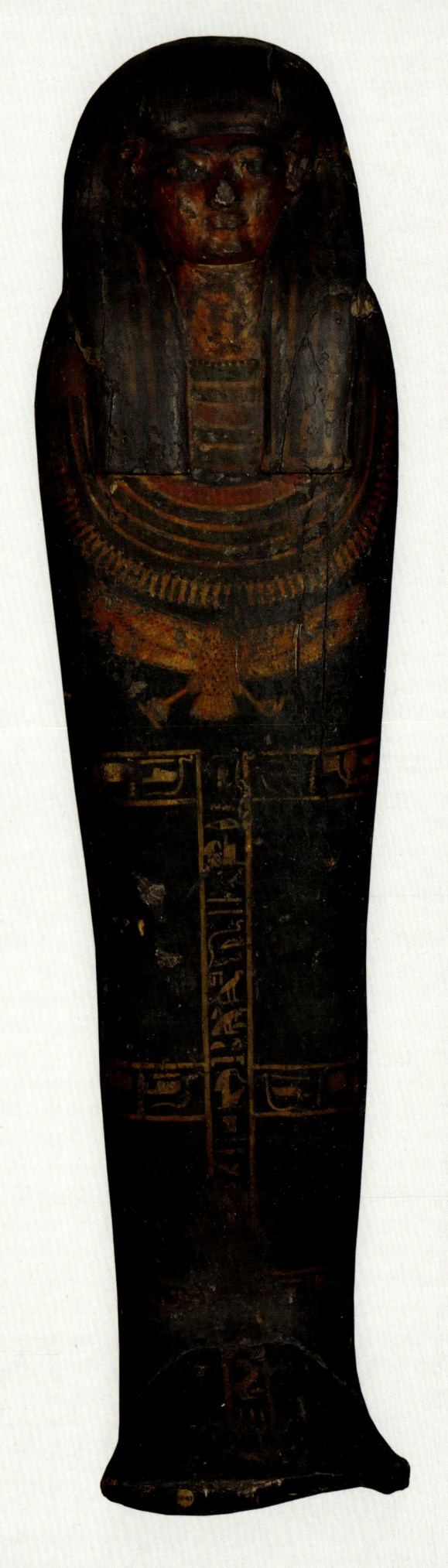

Cat. 24

24

Wooden anthropoid coffin of Tamyt

Like the white coffin of Madja (cat. 22), Tamyt's coffin has bands of text on a plain background, but here the coffin background is a black bitumen, probably meant to represent the fertile mud of the river Nile; black is also sometimes used for the flesh of Osiris. The vulture on the front represents Nut, summoned by the now familiar inscription to spread herself over the coffin owner. Other texts appeal to Anubis and the Sons of Horus. The colours of the painting are difficult to discern through the thick, dark layer of pistacia resin varnish over the surface. The text and figures are yellow, and details of the decoration in red, green and possibly blue are visible (cat. 24.1).

The coffin appears to have been bought 'off the shelf' rather than made especially for Tamyt, because her name is written in a lighter paint and had to be squeezed into the gaps left in otherwise standard inscriptions.

The coffin box is notable as it partly hollowed out from a single large piece of wood, built up with side, end and rim pieces.

About 1480–1350 BC
British Museum, EA6661
(provenance unknown)
64 × 198 × 50 cm

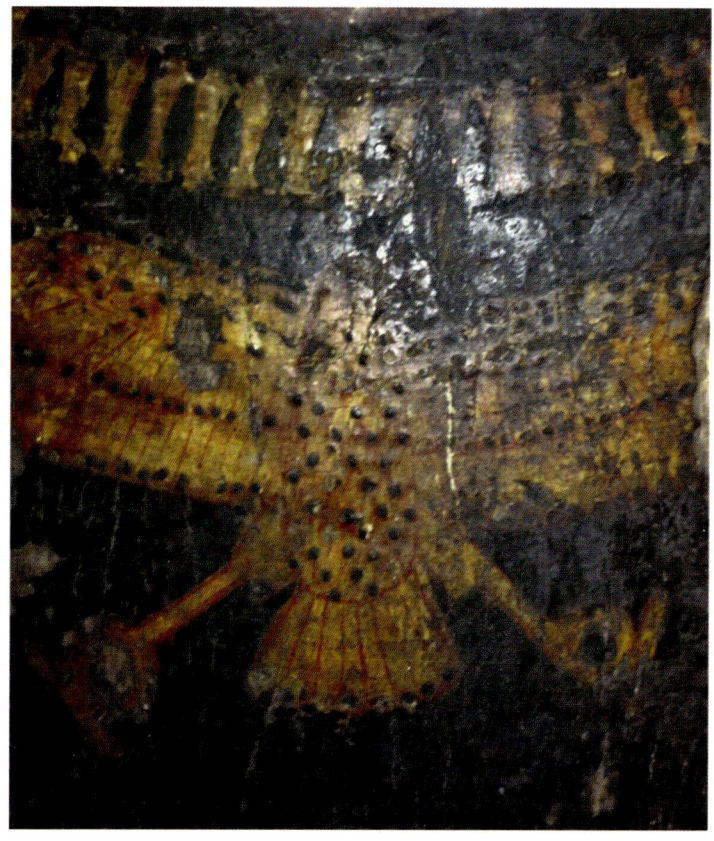

Cat. 24.1
Although the coffin seems to be black and deep yellow at first sight, many coloured details are present. For example, the beads on the collar and raised relief spots on the vulture appear to be green or blue.

Economic and political influences

Many of the coffins described so far include reused materials, particularly the coffin of Nakht (cat. 15). It is unclear whether these were pieces of wood from unused coffins or other objects, or used coffins that were being reworked into new ones. However, from the late New Kingdom (about 1170 BC) onwards, it is certain that complete coffins from older burials were being given a 'makeover' (cat. 25). Around this time, a number of tomb robberies were being reported and investigated, and this continued into the Third Intermediate Period (about 1070–715 BC), when there was again a breakdown of central control in Egypt. Indeed, robbery seems to have been so prevalent that very few coffins of the Nineteenth and Twentieth Dynasties (around 1290–1070 BC) have survived unaltered by later reuse.

Towards the end of the New Kingdom, the temple of Amun-Re at Karnak (at present-day Luxor) became increasingly powerful, with its high priests finally proclaiming themselves kings. During the Twenty-first Dynasty (about 1070–945 BC) this became even more noticeable, and an association with the temple conferred great status. This is probably why Karnak officials like Nespawershefyt had their names and titles repeatedly inscribed on their coffins (cat. 26). In contrast, in the Twenty-second Dynasty (about 945–735 BC) there is clear evidence that people working at that temple were given only restricted access to various items of burial equipment, in particular wooden coffins and Books of the Dead. The burial of Nakhtefmut, for example, included a set of *shabtis* (or *ushabtis*, as they came to be known later), made of low-fired mud rather than stone, wood or faience, in a crude wooden box (cat. 35), and his body was contained in a cartonnage case rather than a wooden coffin (cat. 32). Whilst Nakhtefmut's inscriptions tell us that he worked at Karnak, this is not emphasised and the main focus is on his family line.

Changes to Nespawershefyt's job titles clearly demonstrate that his coffin was made in advance of his burial, whereas a cartonnage case had to be made after the body was already mummified, so that the body could be inserted into the case while the material was still flexible. Cartonnage had been used for funerary masks from about 2100 BC, so was a known material, but the move to using cartonnage, in preference to wood, for the innermost coffin protecting a person's body was a radical change.

During the Third Intermediate Period there was also a change in the practice of mummification: the internal organs, after preparation for burial, were not placed in canopic jars (fig. 94) but wrapped up and placed inside the body. It is thought that this was due to concerns about tomb robbery and the wish to ensure that the internal organs were protected within the coffin, together with the body it contained. The coffins themselves were lavishly decorated and inscribed; both Nespawershefyt's coffins and Nakhtefmut's cartonnage case are masterpieces of the coffin-makers' art.

Fig. 94
Canopic jars were containers for the inner organs of a mummy. These examples, with lids representing the Sons of Horus, are from tomb E11 at Abydos, about 664–525 BC (Fitzwilliam Museum, E.217a.1900, E.217b.1900, E.217c.1900 and E.217d.1900).

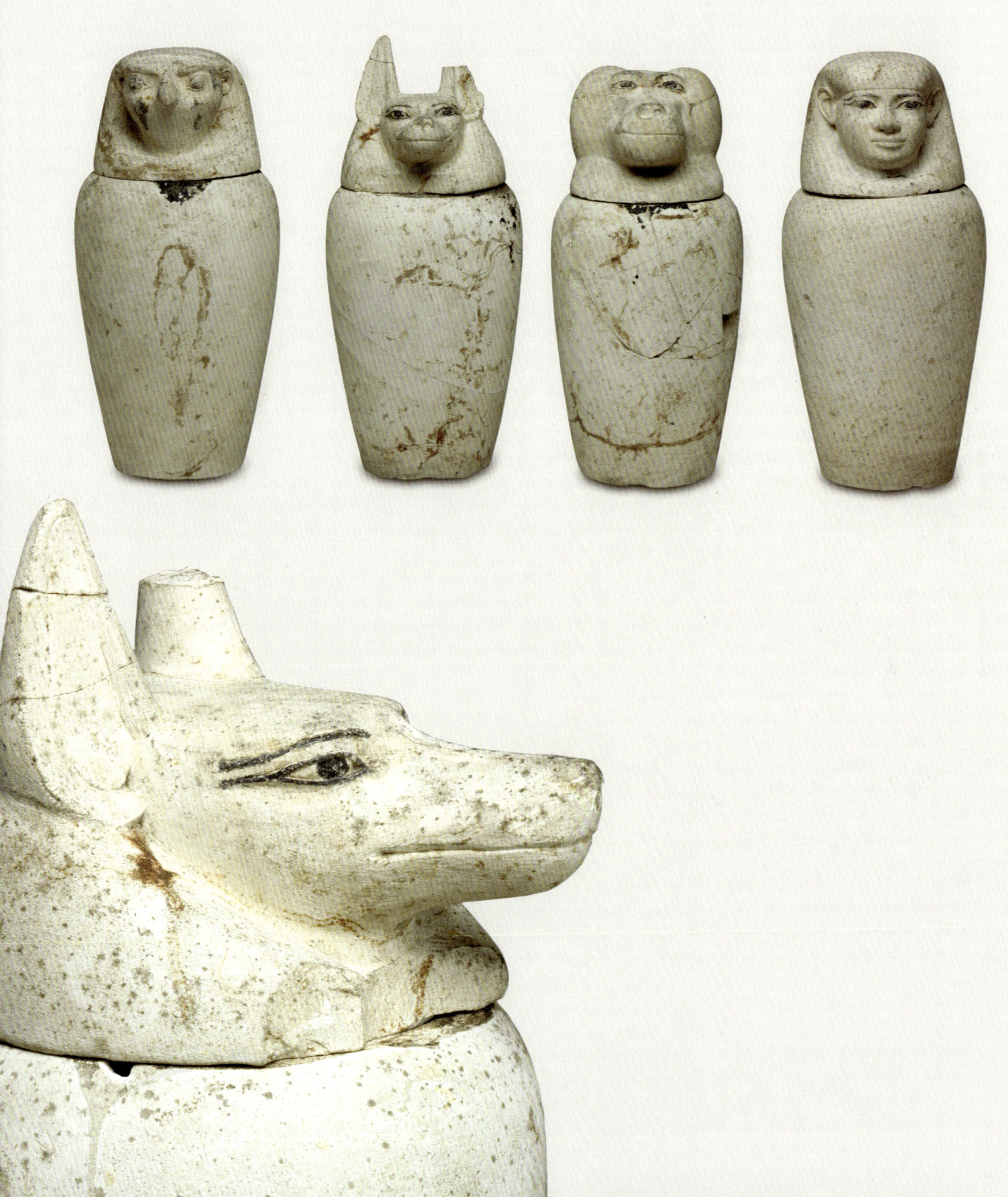

25

Reused lid from the coffin of Muthotep

On the sides of the lid, the remains of older decoration and inscriptions are visible below the current finished surface (cat. 25.1), which was created by covering it with linen, before applying a new layer of paste. The most recent inscriptions indicate that the coffin belonged to a chantress of Amun called Muthotep, who lived around 1185–1070 BC.

Originally made about 1250–1185 BC
British Museum, EA29579
(unknown provenance)
181 × 53.8 × 23.5 cm (at foot)

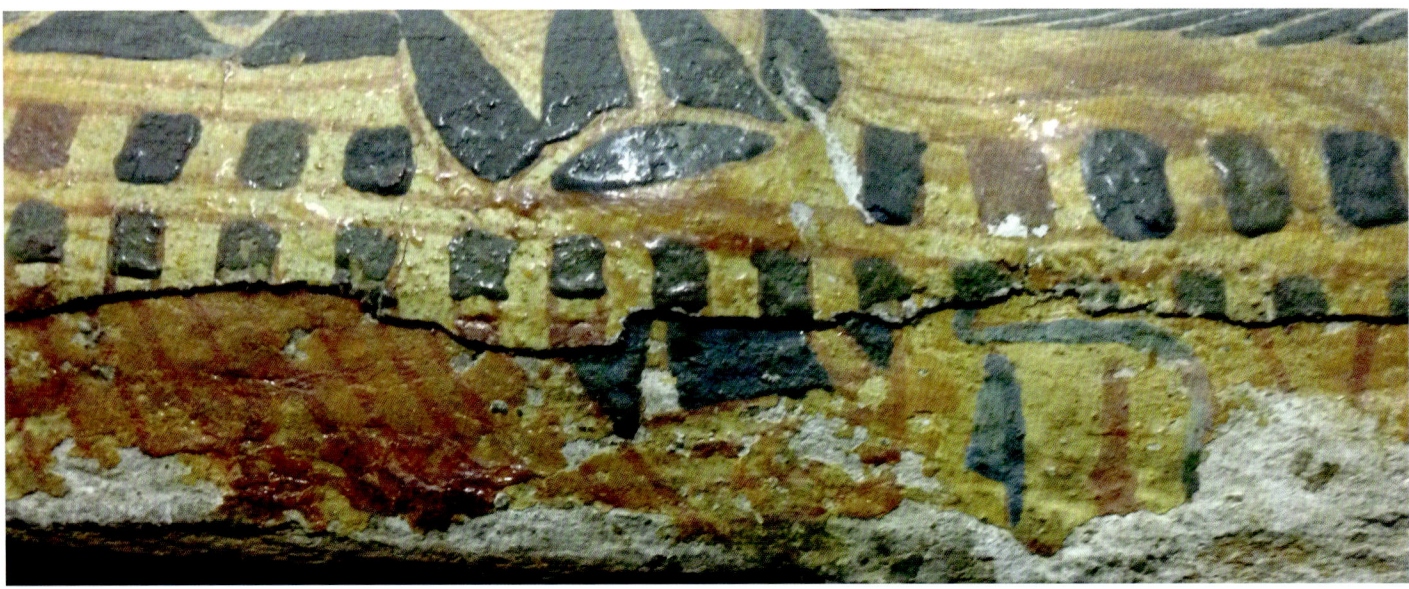

Cat. 25.1
Detail from the side of Muthotep's coffin lid, by the right elbow, showing old decoration under a new layer

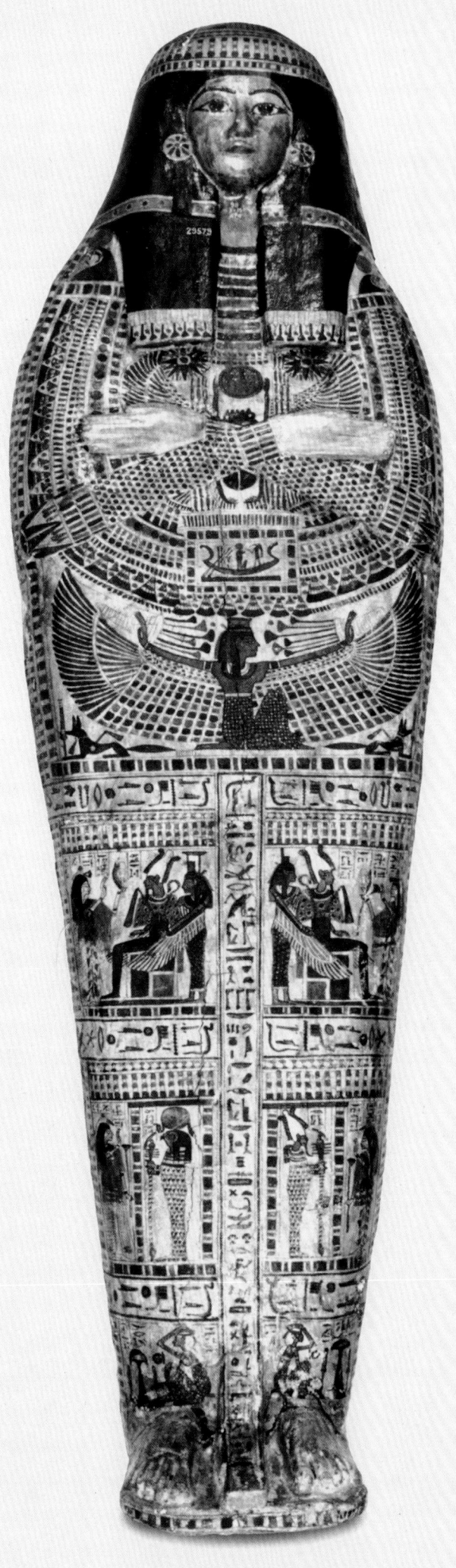

26

Coffin set of Nespawershefyt

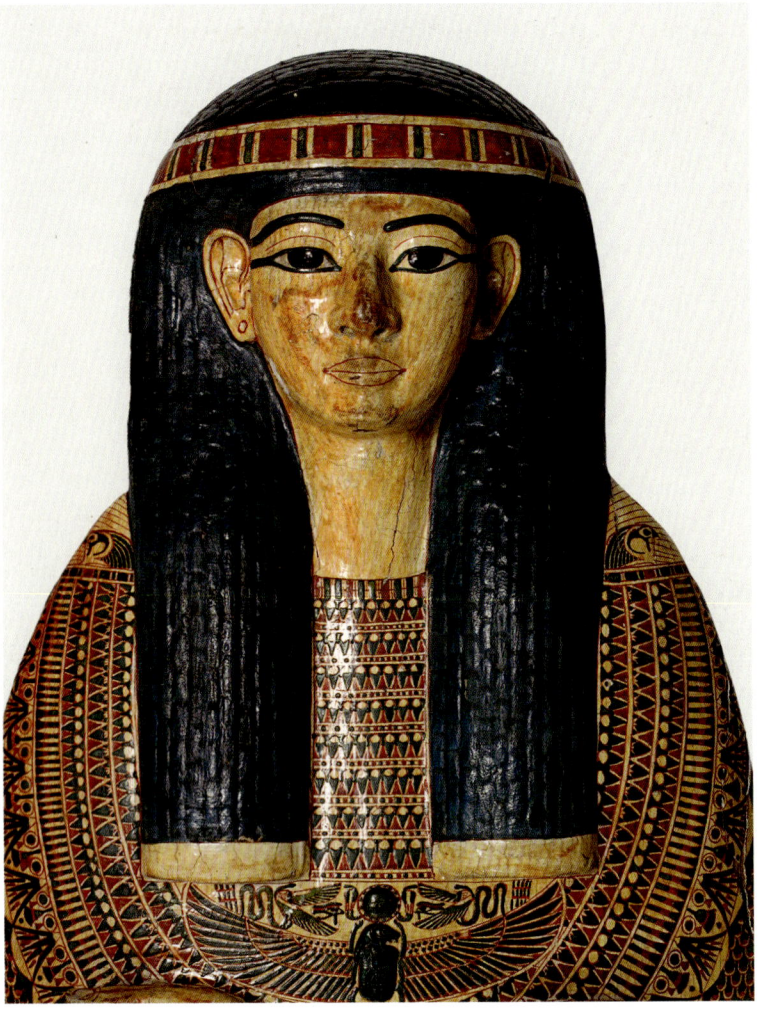

This set of two coffins, fitted one inside the other, with a mummy board which would have lain directly on top of the body inside them, was made for a man called Nespawershefyt. Known as 'yellow coffins' because of the striking background colour of the decoration (cat. 26.1), coffins of this type are typical of the Twenty-first and early Twenty-second Dynasties (around 1070–890 BC).

Nespawershefyt's name means 'The one who belongs to the Great One of the Ram's Head'; in several places, it has been shortened to Nesamun, 'The one who belongs to Amun', because Amun was sometimes referred to as 'the Great One of the Ram's Head' and is occasionally depicted as a man with the head of a ram. Nespawershefyt lived and worked at the vast temple at Karnak dedicated to Amun-Re, 'king of the gods', at a time when that temple was one of the most important institutions in Egypt. He was a supervisor of temple scribes and supervisor of craftsmen's workshops. The importance of these titles to him is clear since they were inscribed more than forty times on his coffins. Patches of darker varnish, even on the inside of the outer coffin, indicate that the titles were changed before Nespawershefyt was buried and probably indicate a promotion (cat. 26.3).

Nespawershefyt's coffins, especially the inner one, are richly decorated. The lids and mummy board have bands of inscriptions alternating with religious scenes and winged gods spread across the body. On the outside of the coffin boxes, Nespawershefyt is shown worshipping various gods. The right side of the box of the inner coffin is decorated with a scene of his being judged before Osiris, including the weighing of his heart; the other side has a striking scene of the earth separated from the sky: the sky goddess Nut appears naked, arched over the god Shu, who represents the air, and a reclining figure of Geb, the god of the earth, painted green (see fig. 38, p. 59). Another version of this scene, but without Geb and with Heka, the god of magic, supporting the figure of Nut, appears on the back of the mummy board (cat. 26.2). Here, the background colour is reddish-brown. Other scenes show the sun's progress through the dark hours of the night. The

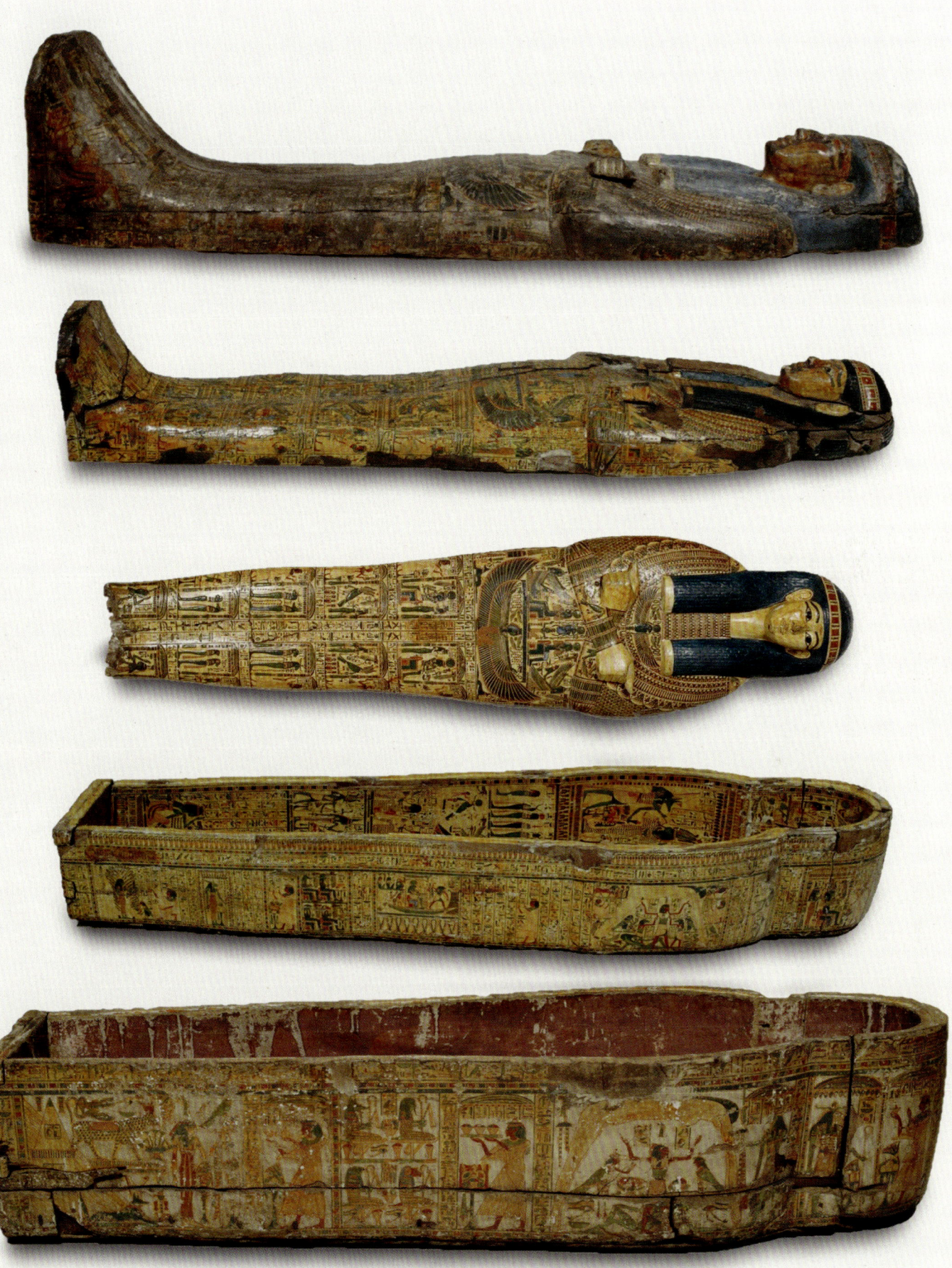

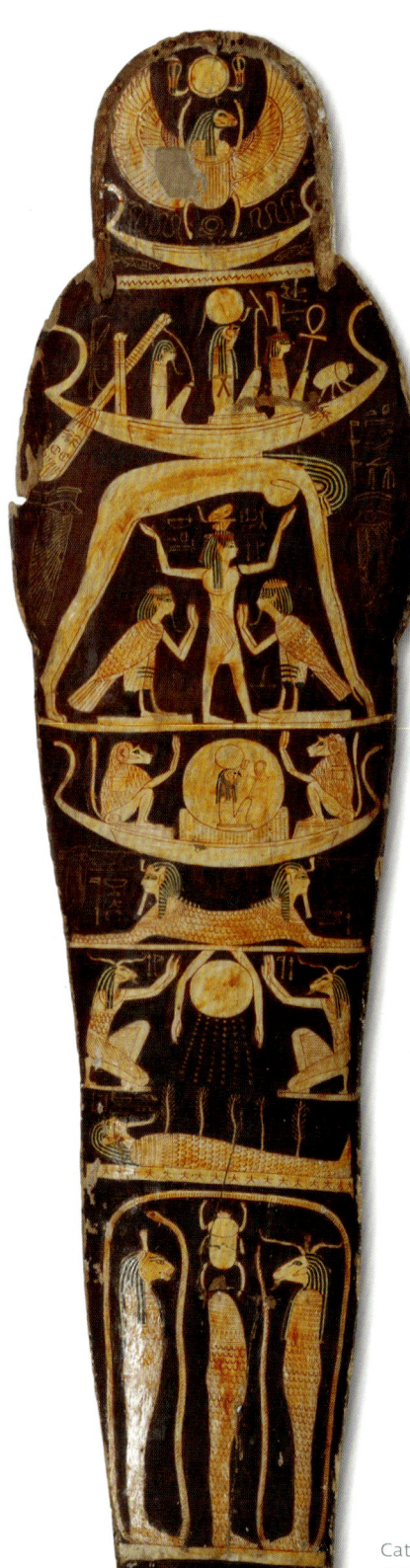

Cat. 26.2
Reverse of the mummy board

Cat. 26.3
Foot end of the inner coffin box. Nespawershefyt makes offerings to the tree-goddess before the tomb. Above, a darker area of varnish indicates where his titles have been changed.

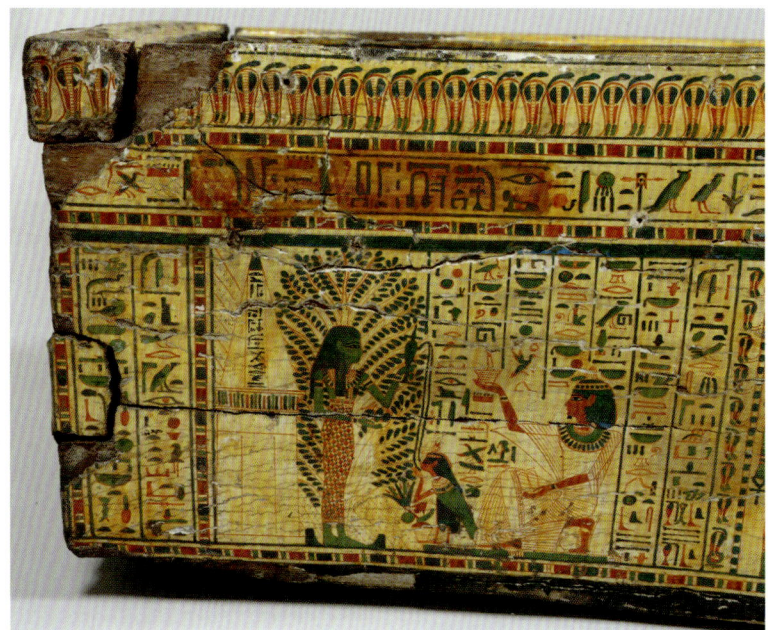

interior of the inner coffin box is dominated by a large figure of the goddess of the West on the base and on the head end by an image of Nespawershefyt's *ba* spirit flying up out of the coffin.

Nespawershefyt's coffins provide a rare opportunity to examine and compare the work of craftsmen across a complete set. They illustrate how, by clever manipulation of resources in construction and decoration, a highly refined, luxury product could be produced from unpromising starting materials.

The mummy board shows the least evidence of compromise. The face is dowelled onto an almost flat board composed of two long fragments held together with loose tenon joints. All the pieces are of sycamore fig. There is no obvious sign of repair and reuse – in contrast to the coffins.

Through CT scanning it has been possible to examine in detail the woodwork beneath the layers of paste and paint of the inner coffin (figs. 95 and 96a). The foundation of the lid is one large plank of sidr with rim pieces of sidr and sycamore fig attached by angled dowels. The feet and footboard are made primarily from a single piece of sycamore fig but completed with numerous small, ill-fitting pieces. The carpenters experienced some difficulties with the big sidr plank: the central section of the legs had to be chopped out (possibly it was damaged) and replaced with two fill pieces. Also, the plank appears to have split, possibly when a dowel hole was drilled to make one of the fixing points for attachment of the face. The two halves were subsequently pinned together with a shallow butterfly cramp (cat. 26.5).

Each long side of the inner coffin box is constructed from two shaped planks of sycamore fig, joined edge to edge with

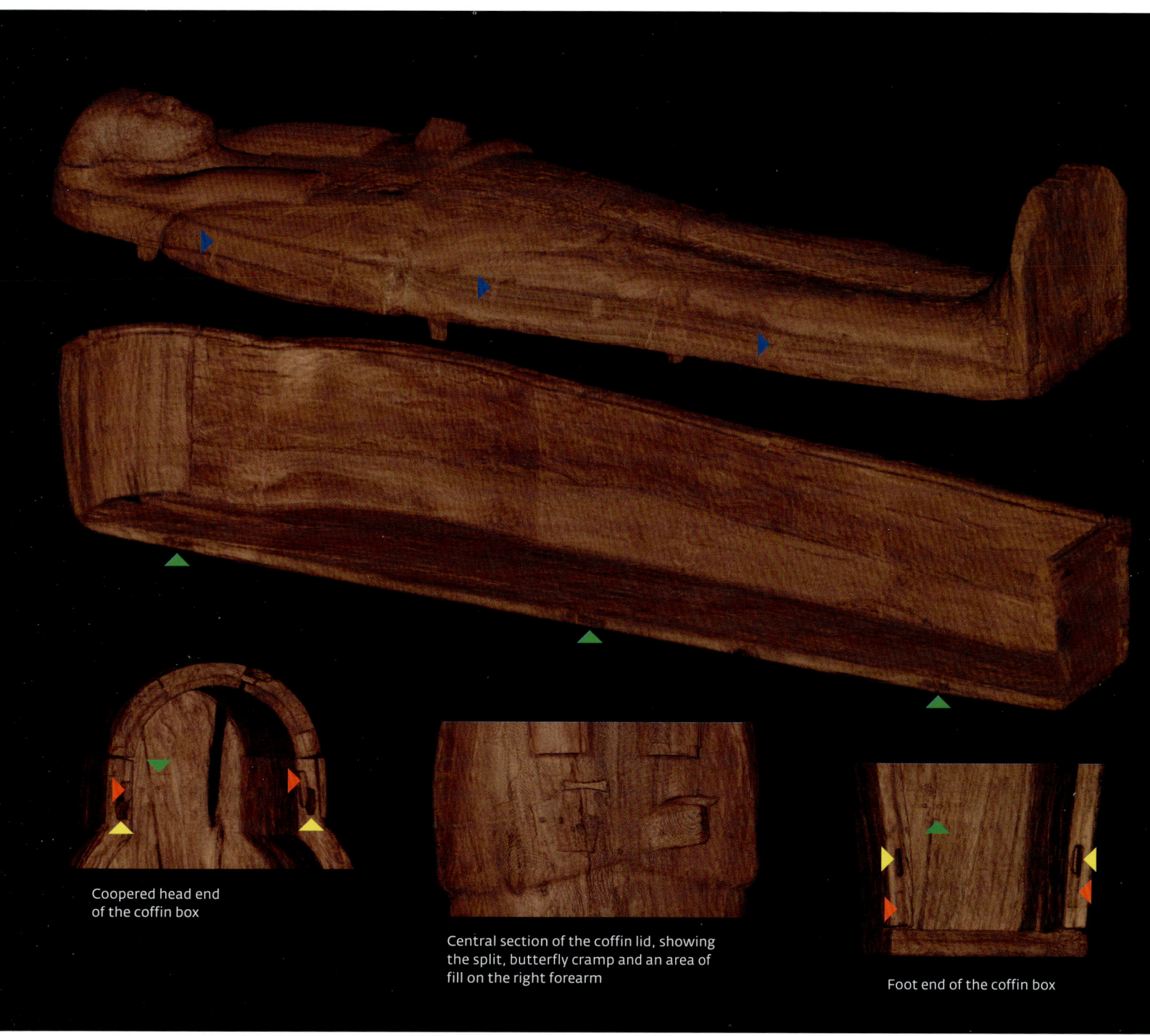

Coopered head end of the coffin box

Central section of the coffin lid, showing the split, butterfly cramp and an area of fill on the right forearm

Foot end of the coffin box

Fig. 95
Images generated from CT scans of the inner coffin of Nespawershefyt, with the coffin base viewed cut in half along its length. These show the wooden carcass beneath the decorative layers. In some places the rendering process leaves fragments of the surface paste visible and in other areas it starts to reveal internal structures: for example, the dowels that pin the lid rim sections to the right hand side of main board can be seen (blue arrows). Mortise and tenon joints holding the baseboards together are also visible (green arrows). On the rim of the box, old mortises have been patched to close them (red arrows) and new ones cut in different positions (yellow arrows).

185

Fig, 96a

These views through the structure of the inner coffin box and lid of Nespawershefyt are generated from CT scans. They reveal the full complexity of the construction and the joining methods, how cleverly pieces of timber have been reused and where small fragments of wood and pastes have been inserted to make good damaged areas. Shown on the scan images are mortise and tenon joints (pink), dowels (green), fill pieces blocking old or recut mortises (brown), paste fills and surface preparation layers (white), decoration sculpted in Egyptian blue and green pigment (pale blue). A metal plate and screw that are part of the nineteenth-century repair are also visible (blue arrows).

For each part of the coffin shown in the photograph to the right, the red spot pinpoints on the coffin surface the region of interest. To the left of the photograph are three CT images, each showing a different section through the coffin structure at that point of interest. The exact position of the each section is indicated by the appropriate coloured spot (magenta, blue or yellow).

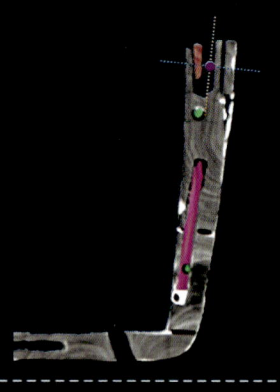 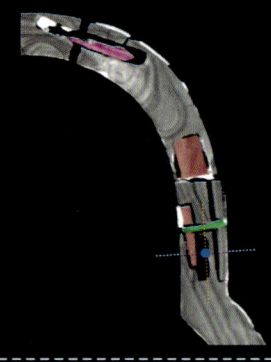 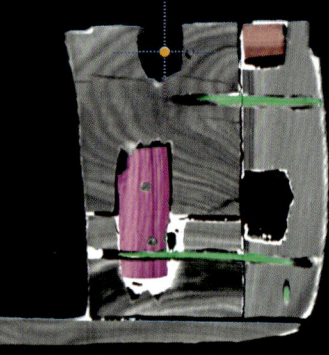 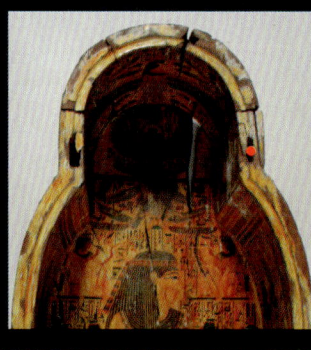

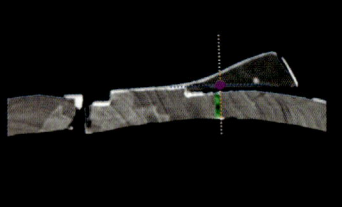 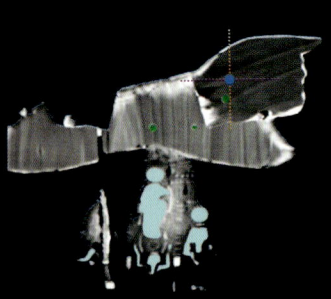 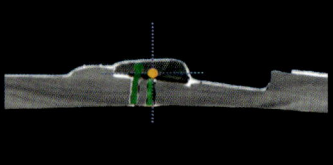 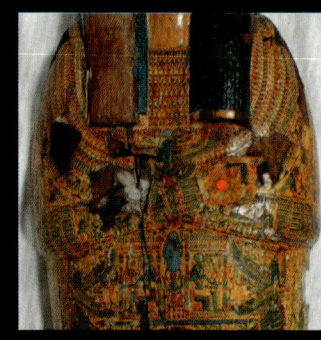

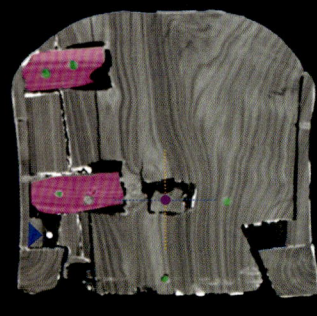 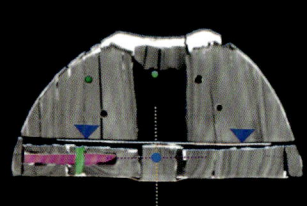 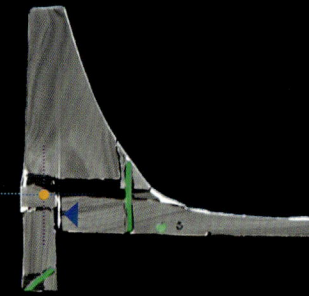 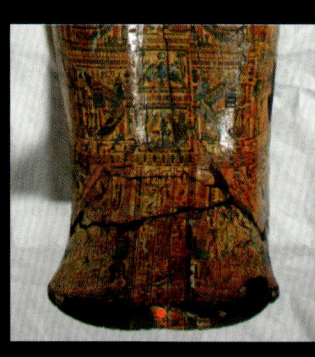

Left to right (transverse) section cut (magenta plane on fig. 96.a and spot on the section)

Front to back (coronal) section cut (blue plane on fig. 96.a and spot on the section)

Head to foot (sagittal) section cut (yellow plane on fig. 96.a and spot on the section)

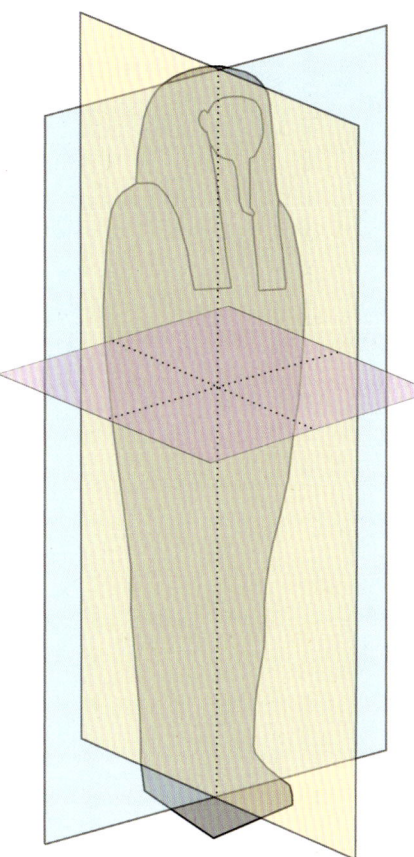

Fig. 96.b
Diagram showing the sections used in fig. 97a: transverse section (magenta), coronal section (blue), sagittal section (yellow)

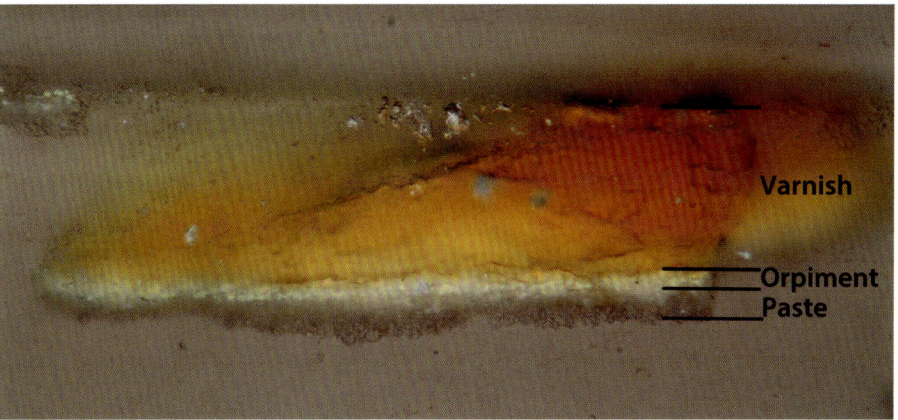

Fig. 97
Cross-section showing thick pistacia resin varnish over a thin orpiment paint layer, which overlies the white preparation layer

massive pegged tenons. A coopered curve of three pieces of wood (sycomore fig and sidr) completes the head end of the box. The sides are fixed to the foot end boards with dovetail joints and to the base boards with angled dowels. The CT scans show the full extent of reworking on the box; the silhouette of an earlier coffin appears to have been changed to reflect new fashions.

The outer coffin has a similar construction pattern: the lid is made of larger pieces of wood (principally sycomore fig, with a tamarisk footboard) which show fewer signs of reuse, while the box is rather a hotchpotch of sycomore fig pieces, with an insert of tamarisk between the base boards. All the edge-to-edge joints are dowelled (rather than mortise and tenon jointed as seen on the inner coffin box). The exterior sides of the head and shoulders have been thickened with thin wood pieces glued and dowelled to the main side panels to ensure that these match the profile of the curved head end, which, in contrast to the inner box, is roughly hewn from a tree trunk.

The three surviving hands on the coffins are each of a different wood: sidr, tamarisk and sycomore fig. Most of the woods available in the workshop seem to have been used to fashion dowels and tenons; acacia, sidr, sycomore fig and cedar have all been identified.

Gaps and flaws in the wood on all parts of the nested set were filled with coarse calcite paste, and most of the inner coffin was covered with a layer of textile, before one or more layers of fine white sparite-type calcite paste were applied across the surface. On the mummy board an additional coarse brown calcite and clay layer was applied to build up the wig.

The inner coffin and mummy board front have similar decoration: a yellow orpiment wash (cat. 26.5) applied across the surface, with figures and hieroglyphs drawn in red earth then painted with Egyptian blue and a copper-based green frit before the final details were added with carbon-based black. The blues and greens are built up proud of the surface, often into three-dimensional, jewel-like figures, especially on the mummy board and the inner coffin lid (see fig. 79, p. 110).

The coffins were covered in a thick pistacia resin varnish (fig. 97) in which there are visible brush strokes and trails.

Cat. 26.4
The outer coffin box, showing Nespawershefyt adoring various divinities. The pistacia resin fluoresces greenish-yellow under ultraviolet light, emphasising the selective varnishing, in contrast to the overall varnish coverage of the inner coffin box.

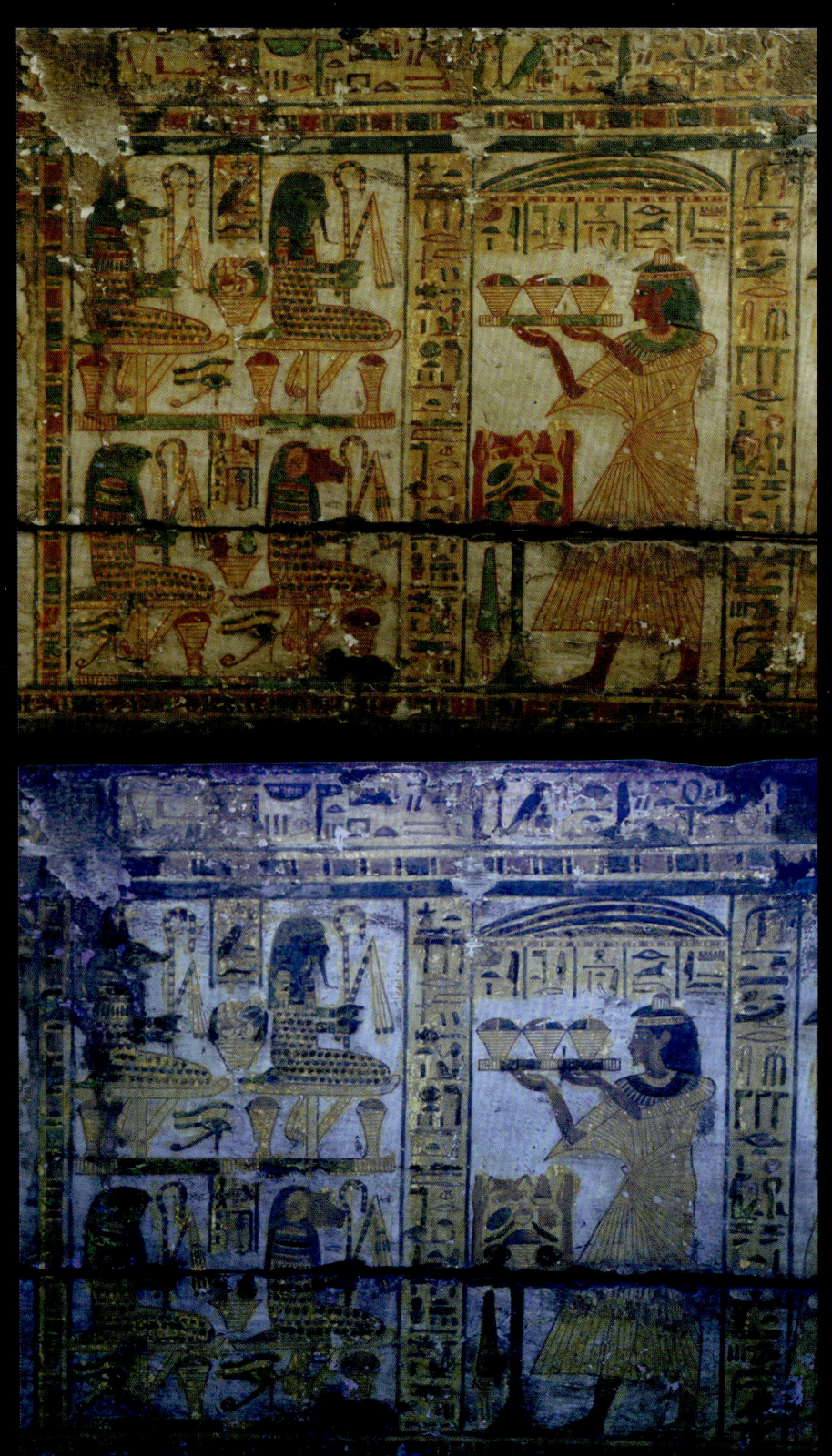

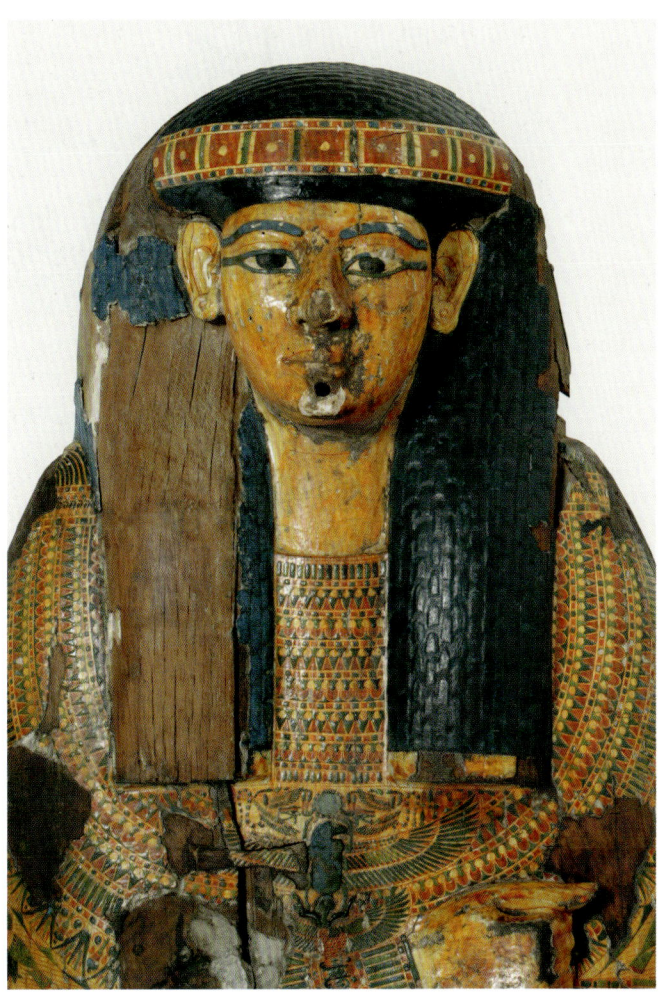

Cat. 26.5
The inner coffin lid. The texture of the wig was created by pressing a shaped tool into the white paste preparation layer. A butterfly cramp is visible below the right-hand wig lappet. This was used to pin together the two parts of the lid after the main plank split.

This layer contributes to the saturation of the colours and their overall yellow colour. The outer coffin differs slightly – here the varnish and the orpiment wash were applied only to the areas of the figures and bands of text, leaving large areas of white preparation layer exposed (cat. 26.4).

The night scene on the underside of the mummy board was painted differently. A yellow orpiment wash was applied to the figures, which were drawn in red earth, with details painted in Egyptian blue. A deep red-brown background (a mixture of earths and carbon-based black) was painted around these figures, with some yellow (orpiment) drawing on top. The lighter areas were varnished, with the edges of the varnish straying messily into the background. The interior of the outer coffin also features a deep red (earth) background. This was painted around a large figure of Osiris as a *djed*-pillar (see fig. 51, p. 81) and left unvarnished. The head of this figure and the exterior surface at the left shoulder both have areas of ancient damage and equally ancient repair where joints between boards opened up, disrupting the decorated surface. These repairs, together with the alteration of Nespawershefyt's job titles, suggest the coffin was made sometime before its owner's death.

Early modern repair work and restoration is still evident on the coffins in the form of a few screws and metal plates and a thin layer of synthetic ultramarine paint over the inner coffin wig.

About 1000 BC
Fitzwilliam Museum, E.1.1822
(given by Barnard Hanbury and George Waddington)
Maximum dimensions:
204.5 × 50.5 × 77 cm

27
Face from a yellow coffin

This face was carved from sycomore fig, with sidr and sycomore fig dowels. The flower on the forehead suggests that this may be from a woman's coffin, although this feature is also found on men's coffins. The chin and nose were heavily restored sometime in the early twentieth century (fig. 98).

The structure and composition of the decorative layers on this face and the following two objects (cat. 28 and cat. 29) are very similar to the inner coffin and mummy board of Nespawershefyt (cat. 26).

About 1070–735 BC
Fitzwilliam Museum, E.GA.507.1947
(given by R. G. Gayer-Anderson)
24.6 × 21.7 × 5.4 cm

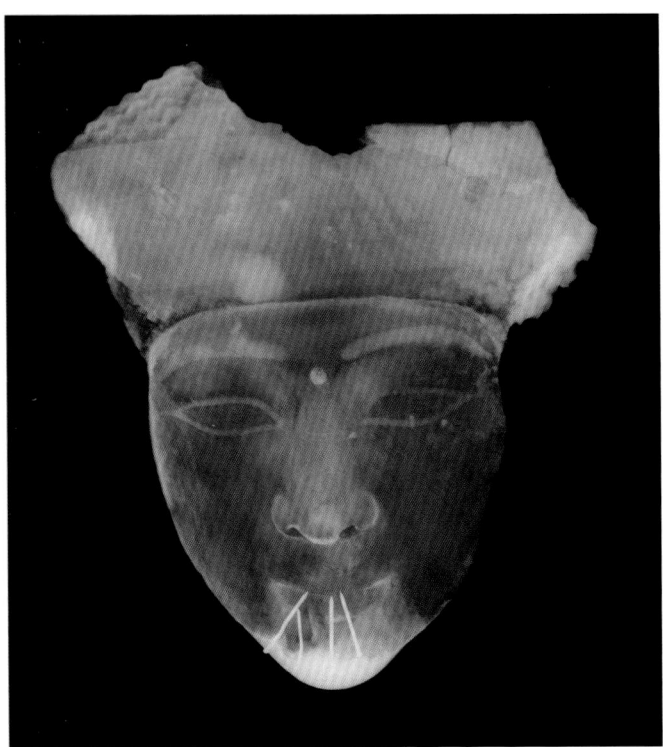

Fig. 98
X-radiograph showing modern nails in the chin; a textile layer on the wig, under the paste ground; and dowels under the nose and on either side of the wig

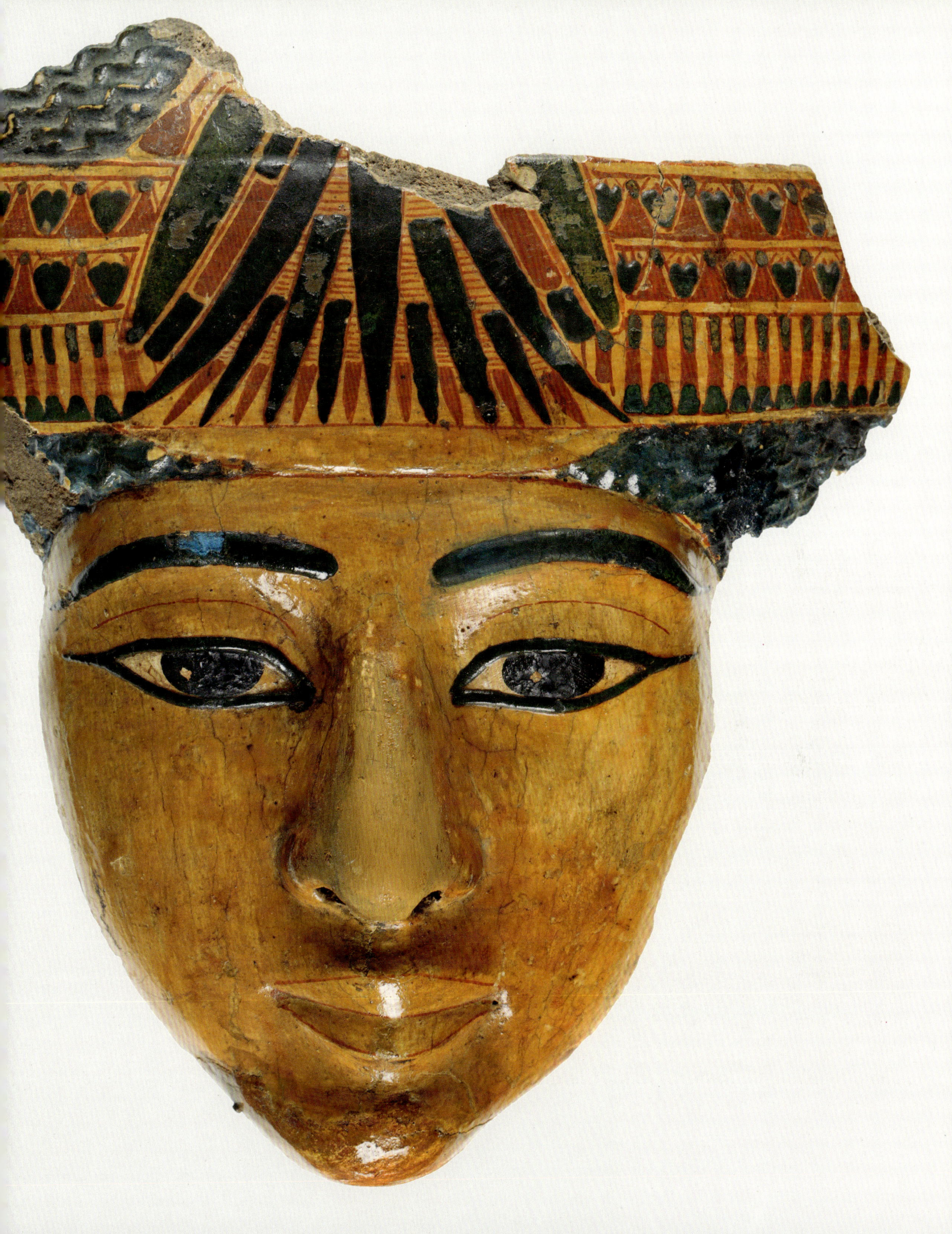

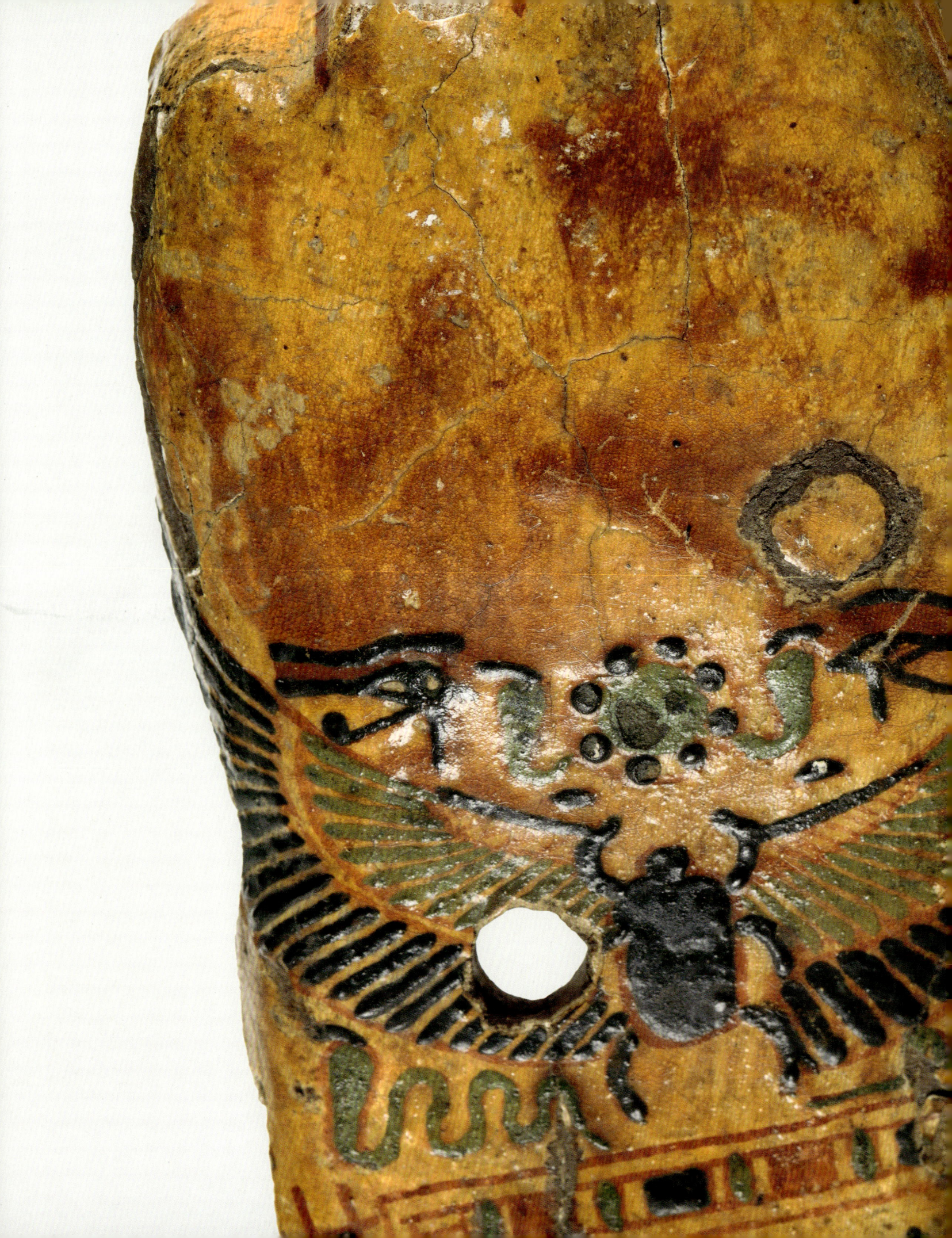

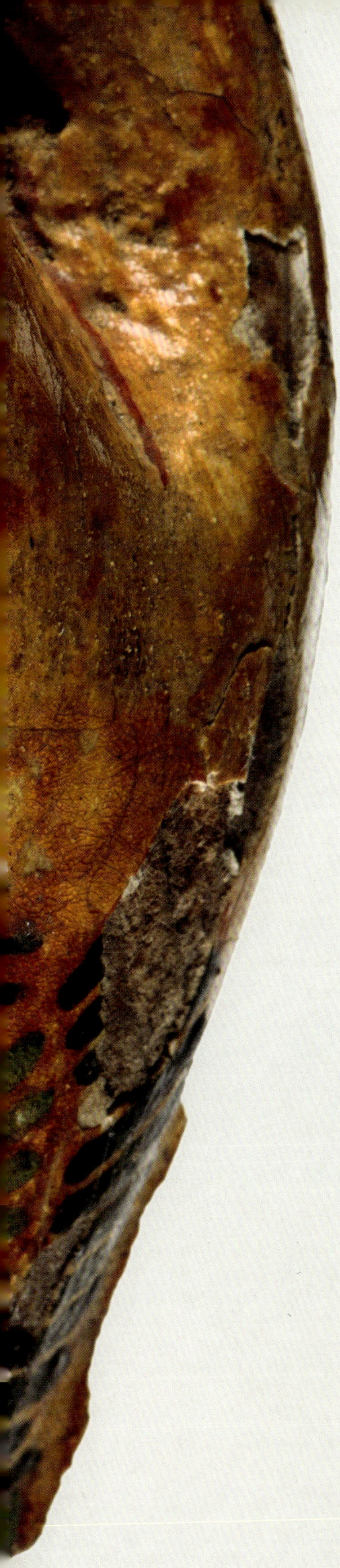

Cat. 28.1

28

Hand from a yellow coffin

This acacia wood hand was fixed to its coffin by two dowels. A hole drilled into the clenched fist signifies that it once held an attachment, perhaps an *ankh*-sign, symbolising life, or a *djed*-pillar, signifying strength and stability.

About 1070–945 BC
Fitzwilliam Museum,
E.GA.2861.1943 (given by
R. G. Gayer-Anderson)
9.5 × 15.9 × 4.1 cm

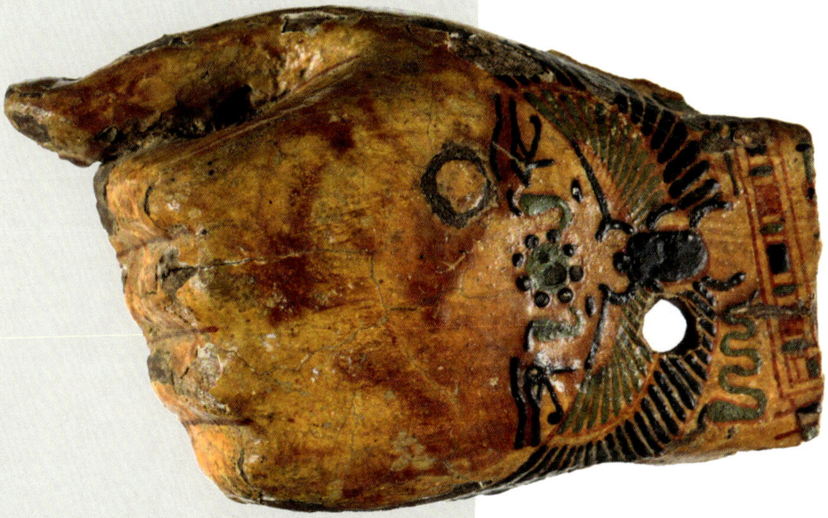

Cat. 28

29

Lotus flower from a coffin

Made from a roughly cut piece of sycomore fig, the flower was originally attached to the elbow of an anthropoid coffin. The lotus, more correctly identified as a water lily, symbolised re-birth due to the way that these plants emerge from water, just as the Egyptians believed the first plants emerged from the primeval waters at the time the world was created.

About 1070–945 BC
Fitzwilliam Museum, E.GA.5851.1943
(given by R. G. Gayer-Anderson)
10.9 × 7.9 × 1.5 cm

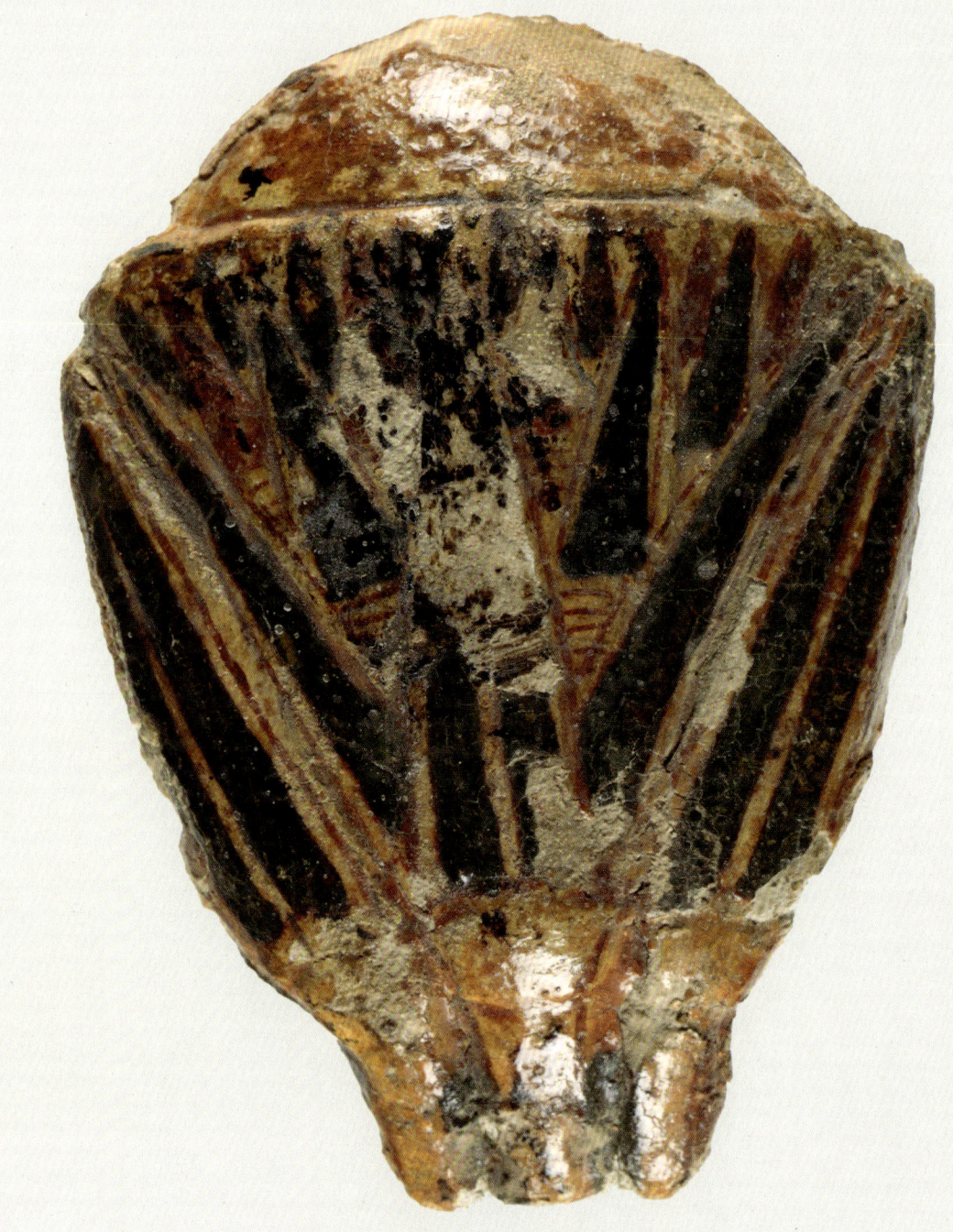

30

Wooden beard from a New Kingdom coffin

Carved channels hold blue glass inlays embedded in a blue paste. The divisions are highlighted with gold leaf.

Between 1550–1070 BC
Fitzwilliam Museum, E.105.1932 (bequeathed by Edward Towry Whyte)
15 × 4 × 3.3 cm

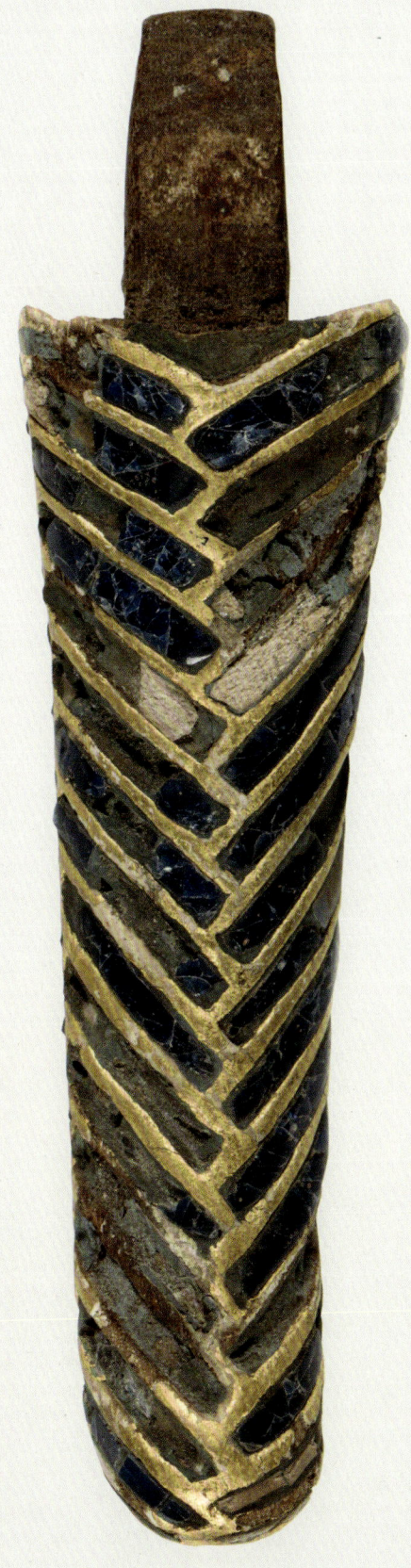

31

Head end of a yellow coffin box

This fragment is roughly fashioned from five pieces of cedar and sycomore fig, joined with sycomore fig dowels. A thick layer of coarse brown paste mixed with chopped vegetable fibres was used to build up the sides and fill insect damage and other deficiencies in the wood. A thin white calcite and calcium sulphate paste was applied over this.

The interior has a red underdrawing, a yellow background, and red, blue (Egyptian blue) and green (severely darkened) paint, with decorative elements outlined in black and red. A pistacia resin varnish has been selectively applied to the surface. The outside is covered with an original (but not fully identified) black coating, making it difficult to see the decoration. Nevertheless, red outlining is visible and VIL images show that there is an intricate design worked in Egyptian blue, including a block border, vertical bands of hieroglyphs and at least one figure.

As on Nespawershefyt's inner coffin (cat. 26), the inside has a depiction of a *ba* spirit flying up from the body.

About 955–735 BC
Fitzwilliam Museum, E.1.2004
(given by Mrs Anne Peers with her brother and sister)
27 × 29 × 32 cm

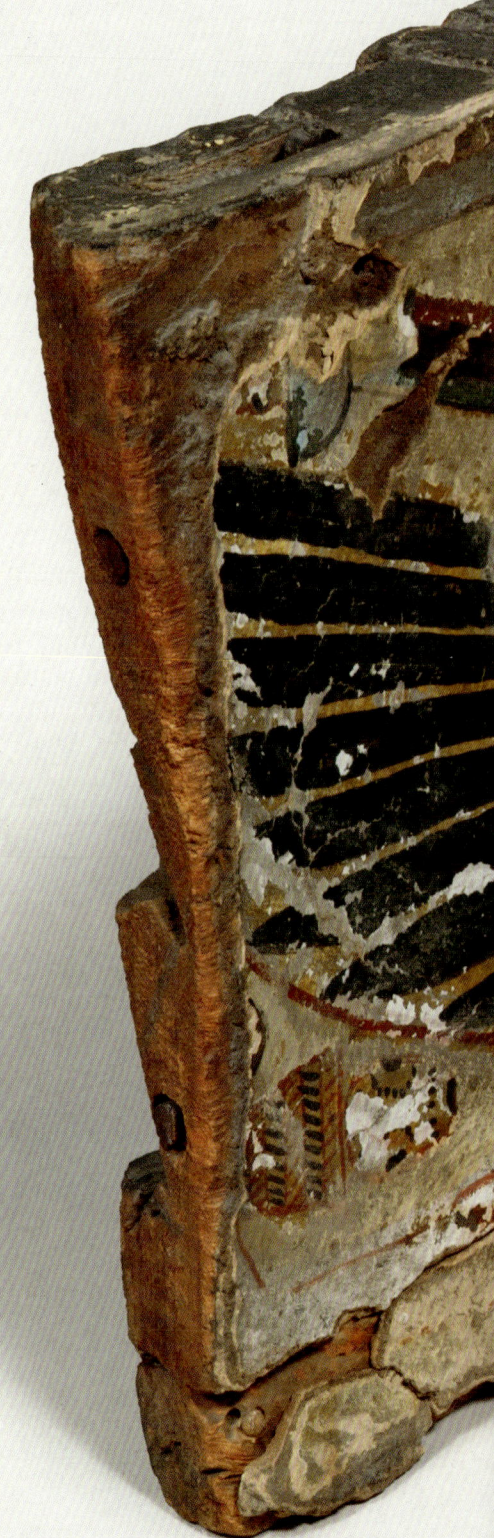

Cat. 31

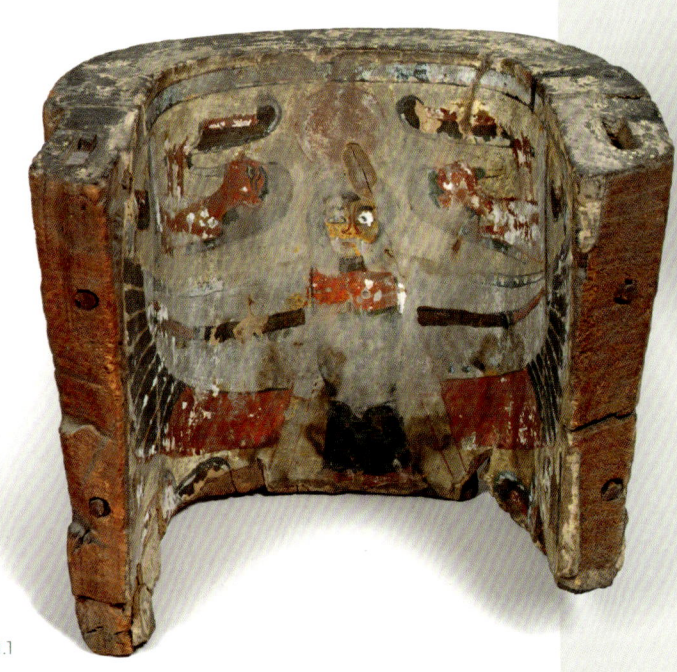

Cat. 31.1

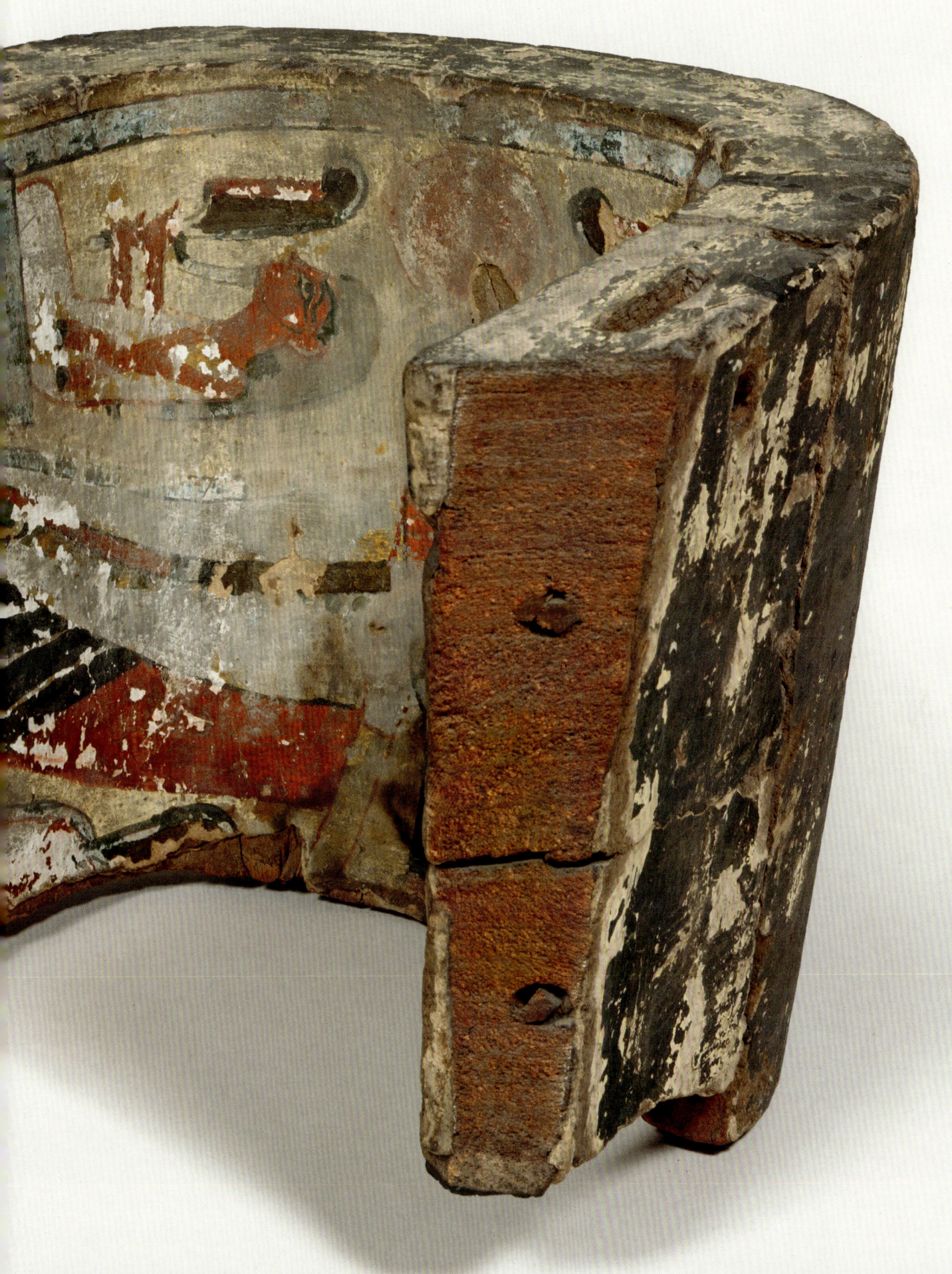

32

Cartonnage coffin of Nakhtefmut

Nakhtefmut's mummy case is made of cartonnage, a material constructed from layers of linen and animal glue and used from about 2100 BC for funerary masks like that of Tjay (cat. 18).

The mummy case was found in an undisturbed burial, inside three wooden coffins. Those coffins have not been preserved, probably because in the Twenty-second Dynasty it was usually only the cartonnage mummy case that was highly decorated; the plain outer coffins were of less interest to early excavators. Objects found with Nakhtefmut bear the name of King Osorkon I (925–890 BC), and dated linen from his mummy indicates that he was buried after year 33 of that king's reign, about 923 BC.

The mummy case is decorated with bands of text and scenes showing winged deities, the Sons of Horus, Osiris and other gods. There is a hieroglyph on each shoulder reading 'east' and 'west', indicating the intended orientation of Nakhtefmut's mummy. The text running down the front of the case records that Nakhtefmut was the 'opener of the two gates of heaven in Karnak', responsible for opening the doors of the shrine that contained the figure of Amun-Re in the innermost sanctuary of the temple. The job obviously ran in the family, because the text also tells us that his father, grandfather and great-grandfather held the same title, while his great-great-grandfather had been a priest in that temple.

The text painted on the back comes from the Book of the Dead (cat. 32.1); it is known as the Negative Confession, which the dead would recite in the Hall of Judgement and which includes a list of misdeeds that they had not done during their lifetimes.

The mummy case is a moulded, hollow shell with a slit up the back. After the mummy was inserted, the slit was laced together and a board inserted under the feet (for more detail, see p. 93, and the Glossary). In 1896 the excavators cut open the back to remove the body. Its fate is a mystery: the excavator recorded that it 'had been soaked in bitumen, which had become much harder than the bones', suggesting that it did not survive the unwrapping process. A subsequent restoration completely sealed the case, but CT scanning reveals the interior surface of the case, including the footboard and remains of the original lacing (fig. 99).

The exterior of the cartonnage is covered with a thick layer of calcium-based paste.

On the wig and the front of the cartonnage, intricate relief decoration was carved into the paste and fine details added with a pointed tool (see fig. 48, p. 77). Some of the decorative elements may have also been built up in paste, creating softer shapes.

Nakhtefmut's beard is made of wood with a tang at the top, which was inserted into the cartonnage chin. The eye outlines, eyebrows, beard strap and beard decoration are blue glass, embedded in a paste made of Egyptian blue pigment and gum. A thin circle of dark material indicates the pupil on each white glass eye.

The surface decoration was drawn in black and red, then painted with copper-based green, Egyptian blue, red earth, orpiment, yellow earth and carbon-based black. The red and blue pigments have been applied in different thicknesses to achieve variations in tonality. Red and black were also used for outlining the block colours before the selective application of pistacia varnish.

A bright white paint (huntite) was applied over the background of the modelled areas, giving a dramatic contrast to the decorative scheme. On the back of the mummy case, mistakes in the decorative scheme have been painted over in white (see fig. 71, p. 103). In some places there appears to have been disagreement between the carver and the painter (see fig. 46, p. 74). The face and other details were gilded after the coffin was painted.

Around 923 BC
Fitzwilliam Museum, E.64.1896 (gift of the Egyptian Research Account)
177.5 × 44 × 33 cm

Cat. 32 (left) and cat. 32.1 (right)

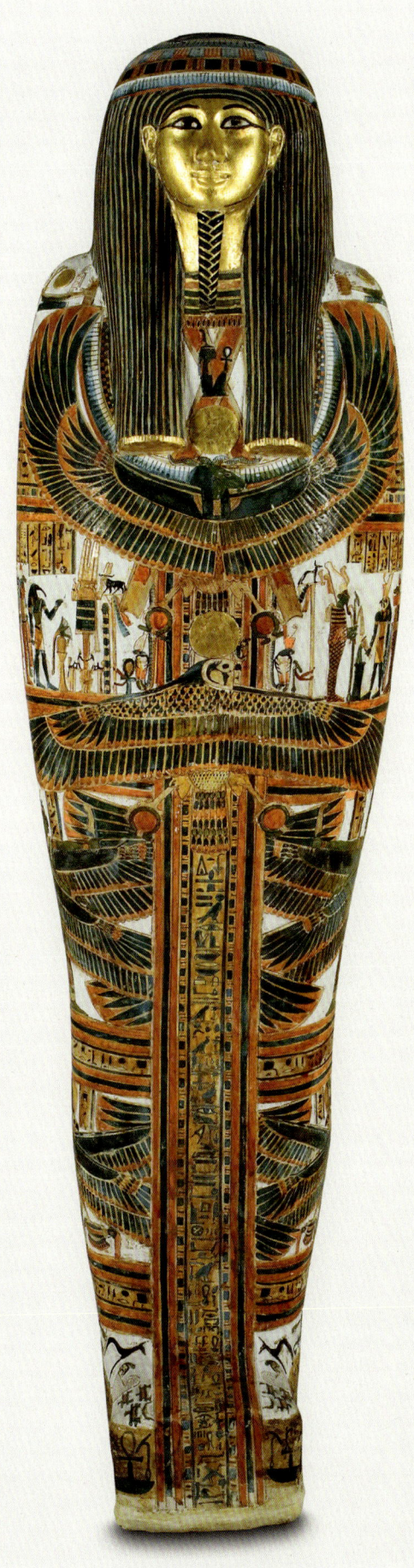
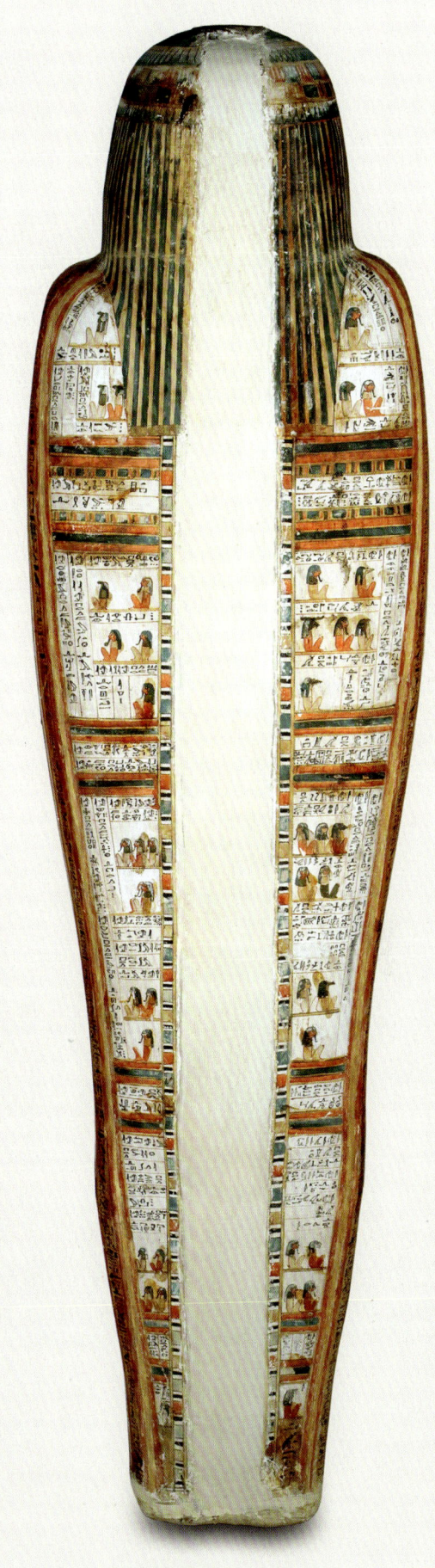

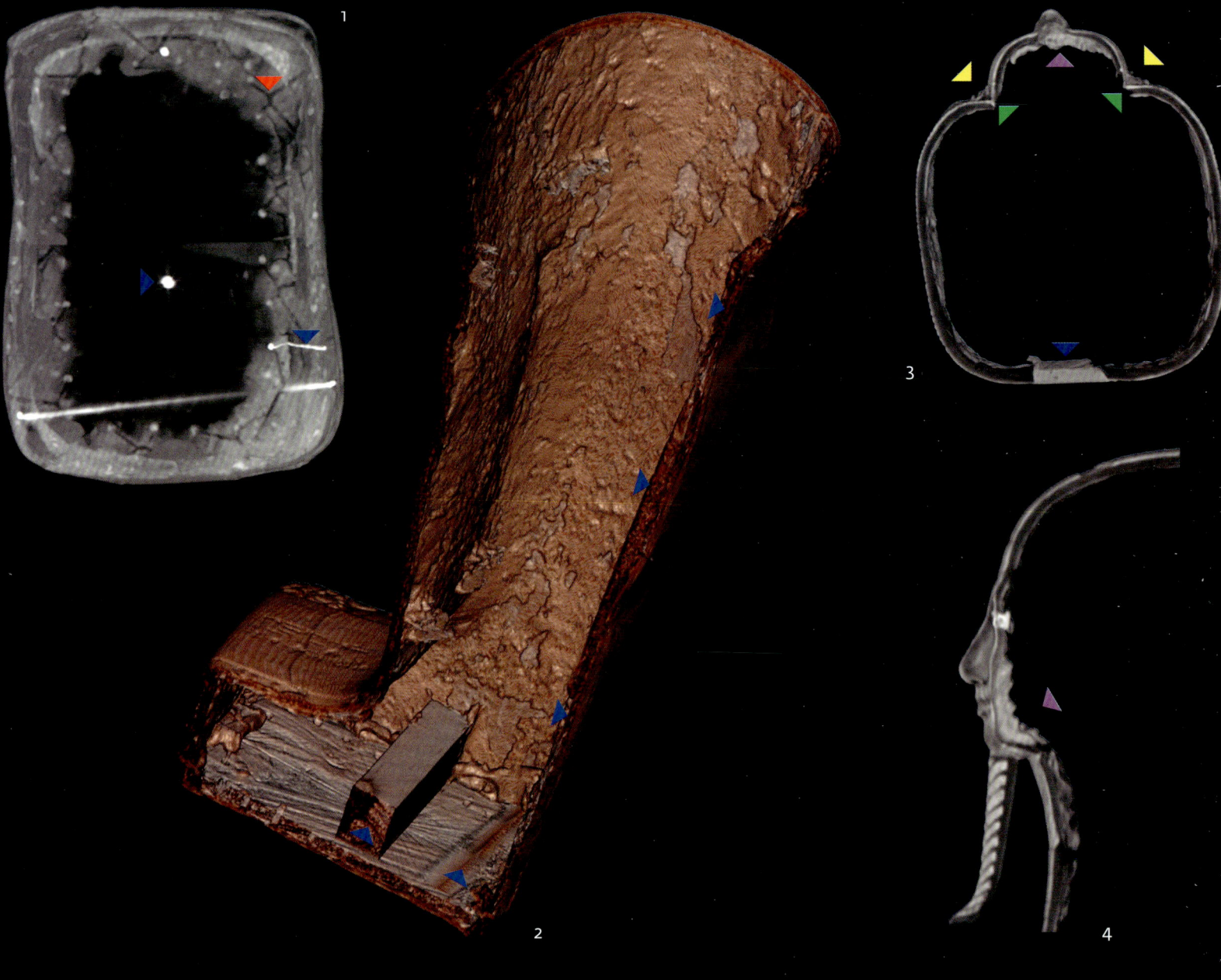

Fig. 99
Images of the structure of the cartonnage mummy case of Nakhtefmut, generated from CT scans:
1. The footboard surrounded by the cartonnage case to which it is attached by lacing (indicated by red arrows) through drilled holes. The two bright white spots and the bright white bars are metal structures that are part of the twentieth-century restoration (blue arrows).
2. Cut-away view through the case. The texture on the internal surface is probably the remains of the inner paste layer and the mud core. The section bisects the original footboard and parts of the restoration structure (indicated by blue arrows).
3. Transverse section through the head of the case, showing that the face is probably a separate structure (green arrows), with cartonnage ears added afterwards (yellow arrows). The external paste and layered linen of the cartonnage can be seen. There are remains of a dense granular material supporting the features of the face (mauve arrow). In the back section of the case is part of the restoration structure (blue arrow).
4. Profile view of the head and neck. The glass eyes and the glass inlays on the beard all set in an Egyptian blue and gum paste, shown as bright white. The supporting material behind the face is visible in the chin (mauve arrow).

33

Sycomore fig footboard from a cartonnage coffin

Nakhtefmut's coffin (cat. 32) has a plain footboard, but about 250 years after his burial, footboards began to be decorated with an image of the Apis bull (the living representative on earth of the god Ptah), sometimes shown carrying the mummy to the tomb.

This footboard was originally attached to a cartonnage coffin with seven angled dowels, unlike Nakhtefmut's, which was laced on. Two layers of white calcite paste (coarse then smooth) were applied to create a background. The bull was finely drawn in carbon-based black, with details added in denser black paint, red ochre and grey (a mixture of carbon-based black and natural chalk).

About 745–655 BC
Fitzwilliam Museum, E.GA.2911.1943
(given by R. G. Gayer-Anderson)
21.2 × 31.7 × 1.8 cm

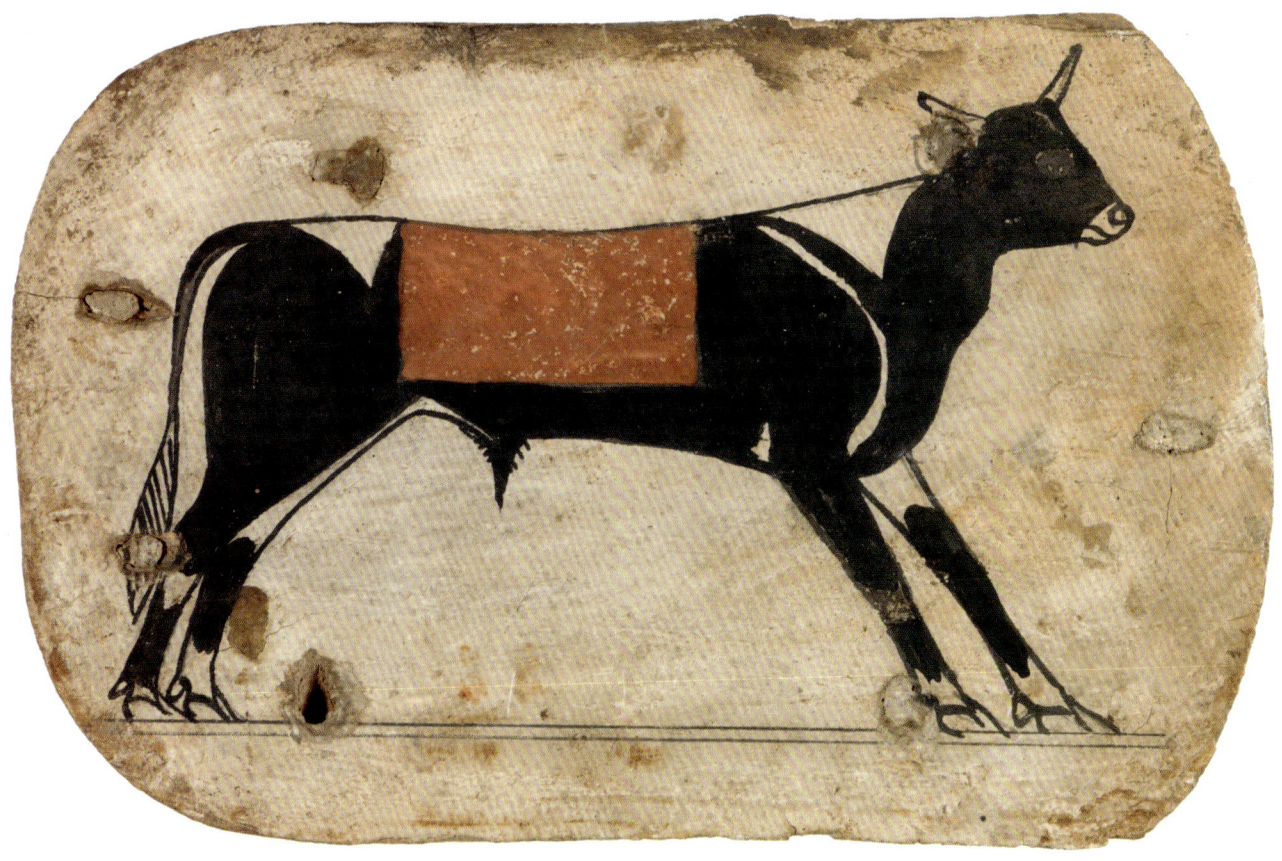

Objects buried with Nakhtefmut

34

Sons of Horus

In this period, the internal organs were placed inside the body cavity, rather than in canopic jars (see fig. 94, p. 179). Since the latter were not needed, burials sometimes included dummy canopics or figures of the Sons of Horus. These examples are made of sycomore fig covered with a black resin.

Fitzwilliam Museum, E.87.1896, E.88.1896, E.89.1896 and E.90.18

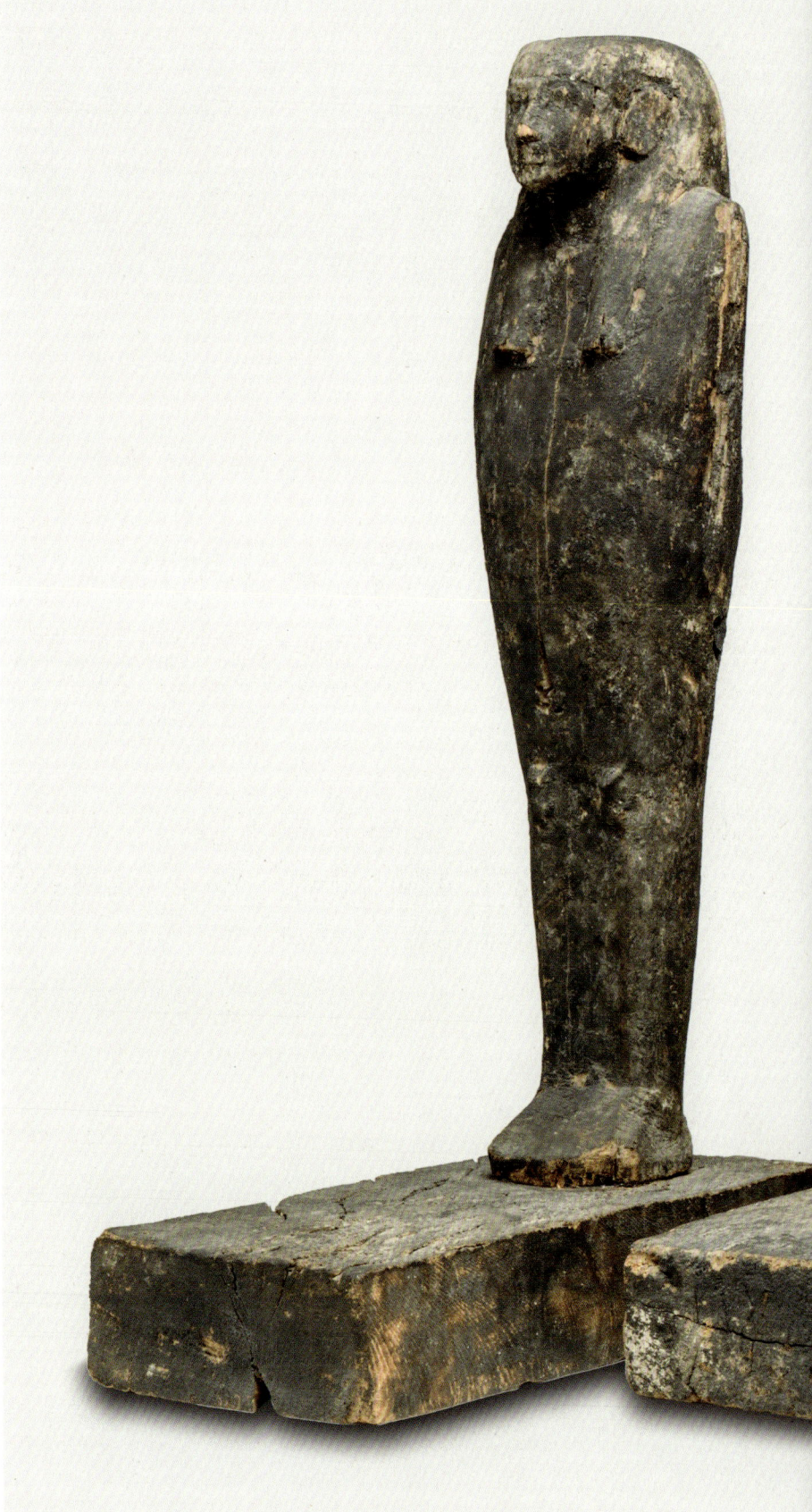

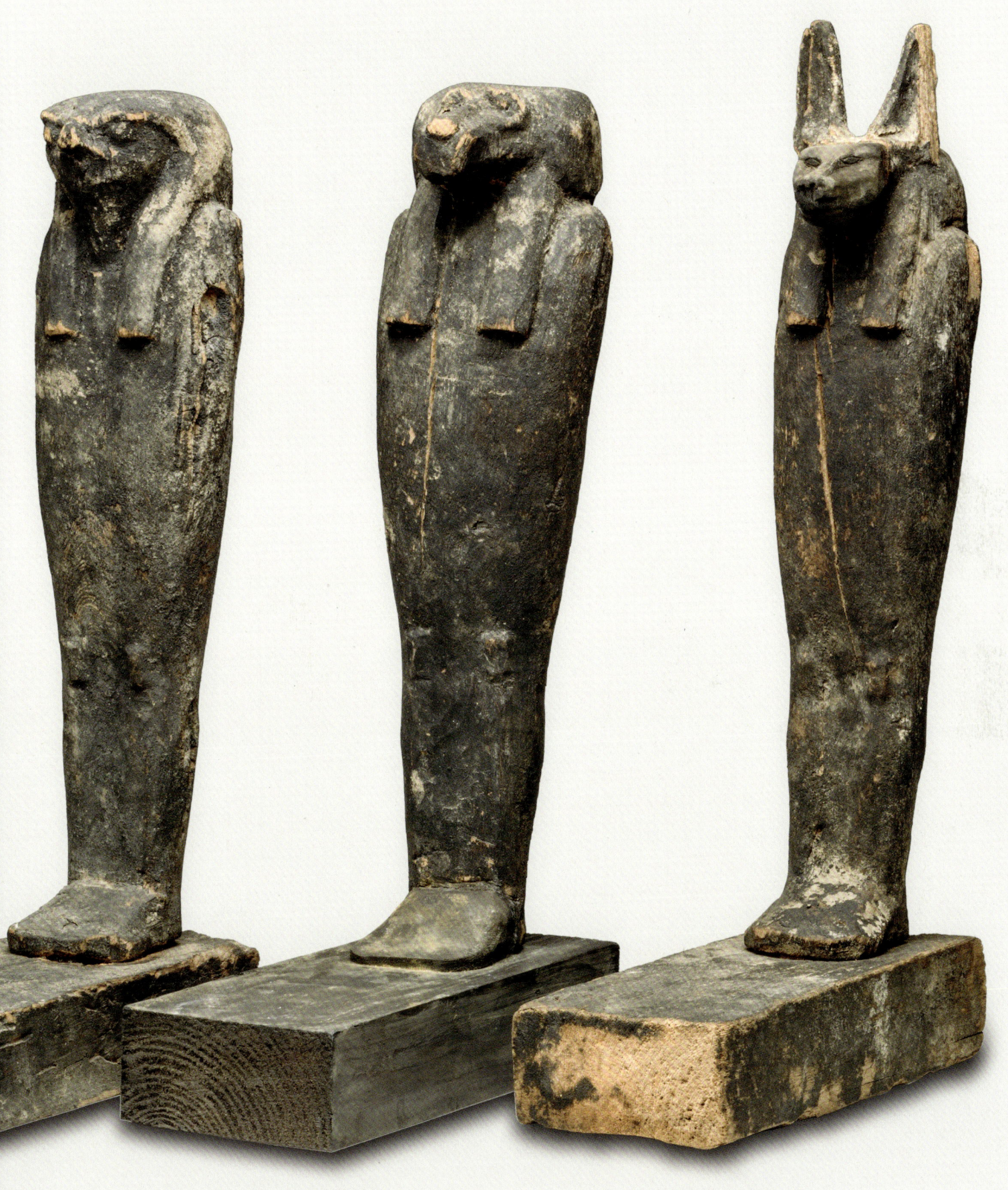

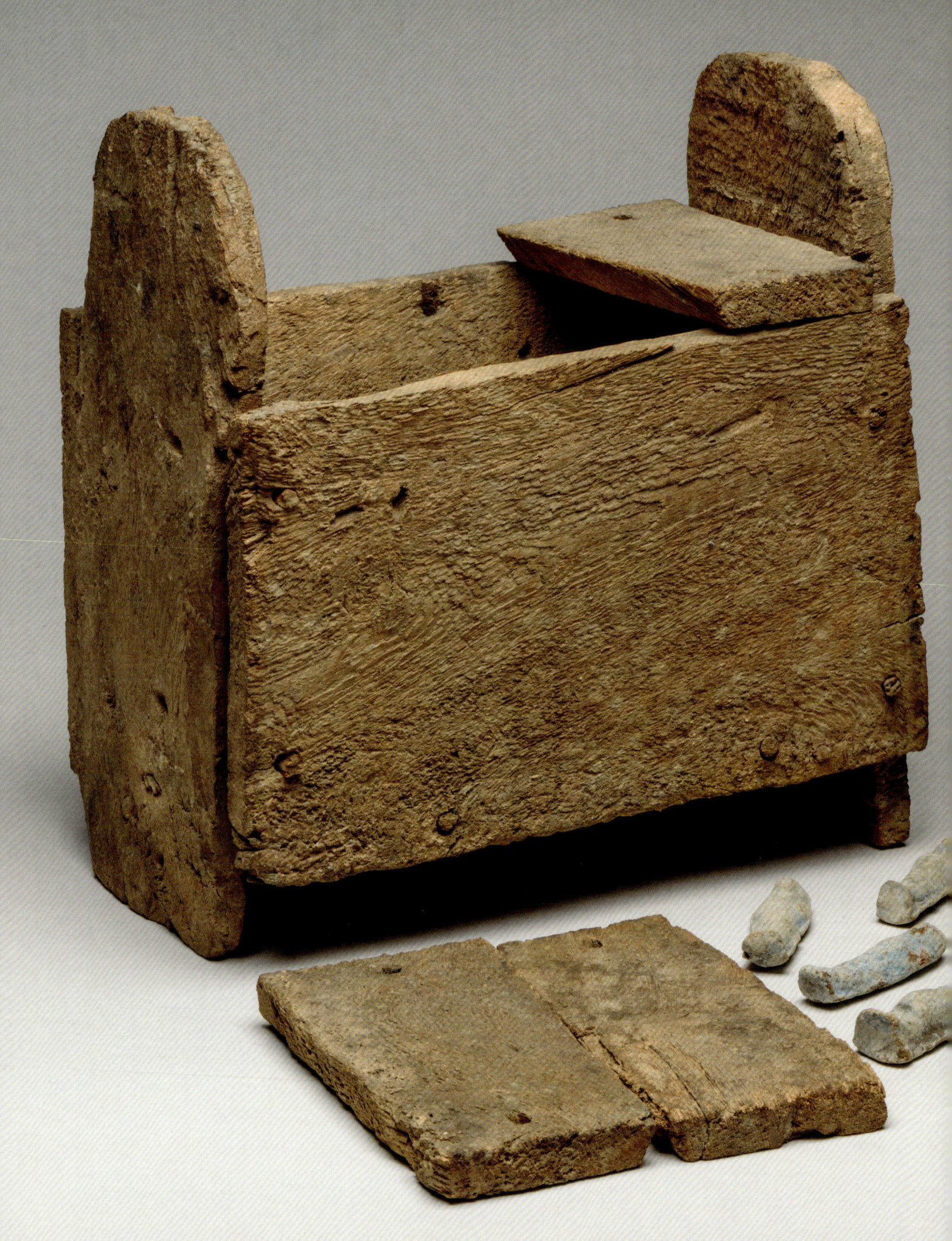

Cat. 35

35

Shabti figures and box

At the time of Nakhtefmut's burial, a full set of funerary figures (later known as *ushabtis*) consisted of 365 ordinary figures, plus 36 'overseers'. The excavator reported that two boxes of *shabtis* were found in this burial; the box that came to the Fitzwilliam Museum contained only 172 ordinary *shabtis* and 18 overseers (cat. 35.1).

The figures are made of lightly fired or sun-dried mud and painted with Egyptian blue. They are in a flimsy sycomore fig box held together with sidr dowels.

Fitzwilliam Museum, E.92a.1896, E.92b.1896 and E.91.1896
Figures: 5.8 × 1.6 × 1 cm; 5.8 × 1.6 × 1.1 cm
Box: 25 × 23.5 × 14.7 cm

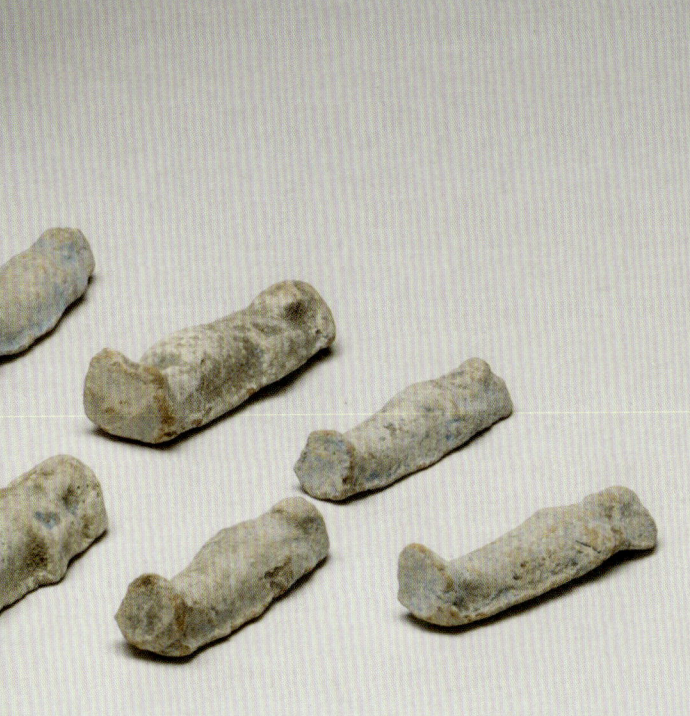

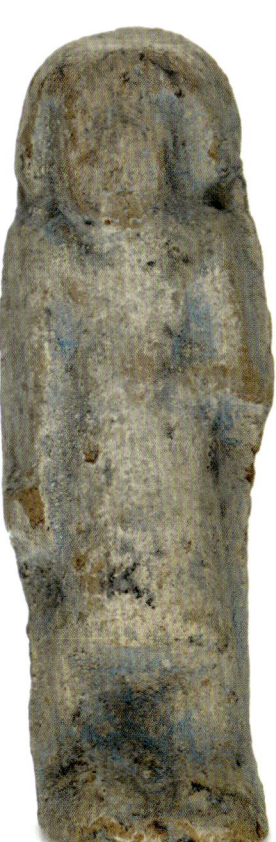

Cat. 35.1
One of Nakhtefmut's shabtis, recognisable as an overseer because it has only one arm across its chest; the other is at its side.

205

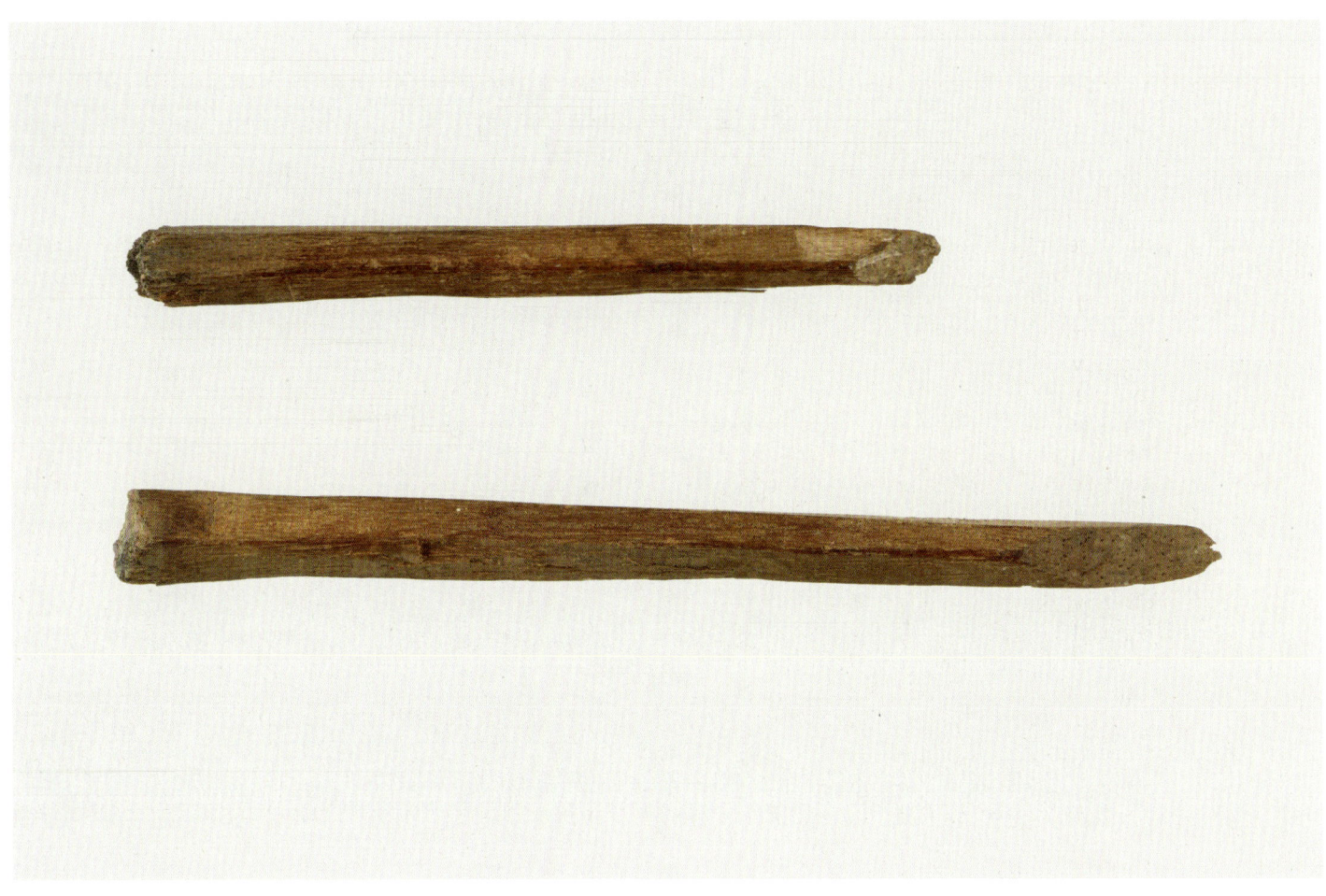

36

Pegs

The excavator concluded that Nakhtefmut's outer coffins must have been assembled inside the burial room, because the access shaft was too small for them to fit down when complete. These sycomore fig pegs, found at the bottom of the shaft, may have been left over from this process.

Fitzwilliam Museum, E.93a–b.1896
7.5 × 0.7 cm (thickness);
5.5 × 0.6 cm (thickness)

Objects found on Nakhtefmut's body

37

Mummy *stola*, *menat* and counterweight

Egyptian gods were sometimes shown with a strip of red fabric, known as a *stola*, around their necks. As the dead became more closely associated with the god Osiris, they were also provided with a *stola*. This took the form of a leather strap which passed around the neck of the mummy and crossed over on its chest. However, by the time of Nakhtefmut, it consisted only of the parts that would be visible, either because the parts hidden by the mummy mask were considered redundant or else it had been forgotten that the *stola* originally continued around the neck. (The *stola* is also depicted on Nakhtefmut's mummy case, crossed over just below his neck and on either side of the legs of the upper winged figure on his chest.)

The *stola* is made of very thin leather, coloured red, with end tabs made of rawhide. Two other rawhide items were found with it: these represent, in miniature, a heavy beaded necklace (*menat*) and a counterweight for the necklace. At specific festivals, people held such items in their hands and shook them. The ends of the *stola* and the counterweight are stamped with the name of Osorkon I.

Fitzwilliam Museum, E.94.1896, E.95.1896, E.96.1896 and E.97.1896
Stola: 43 × 1.8 × 0.2 cm
Menat: 7 × 4.1 × 0.4 cm
Counterweight: 8.1 × 3.2 × 0.4 cm

Cat. 37.a

Cat. 37.b

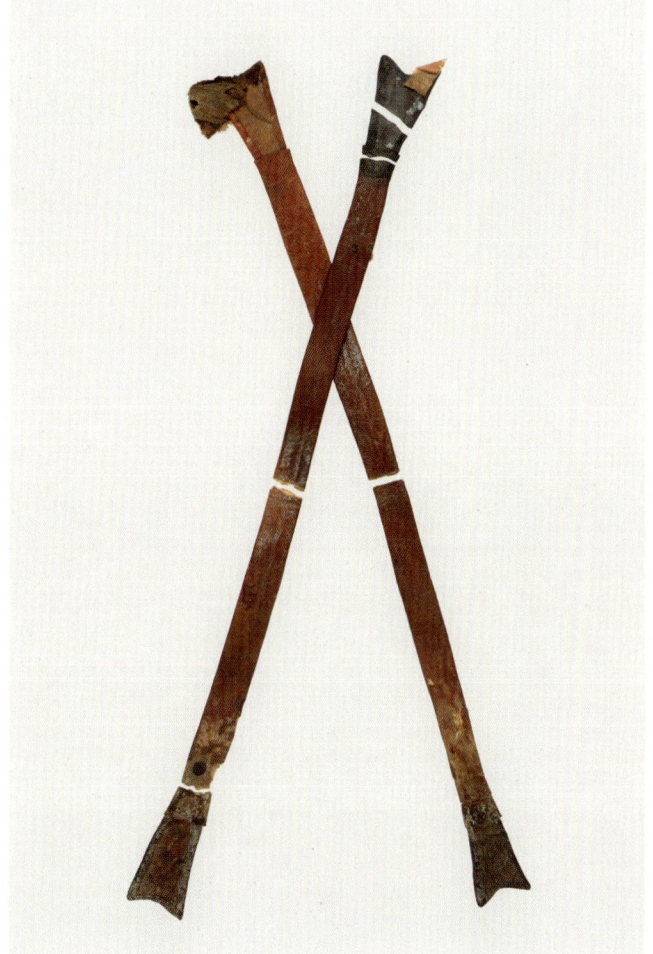

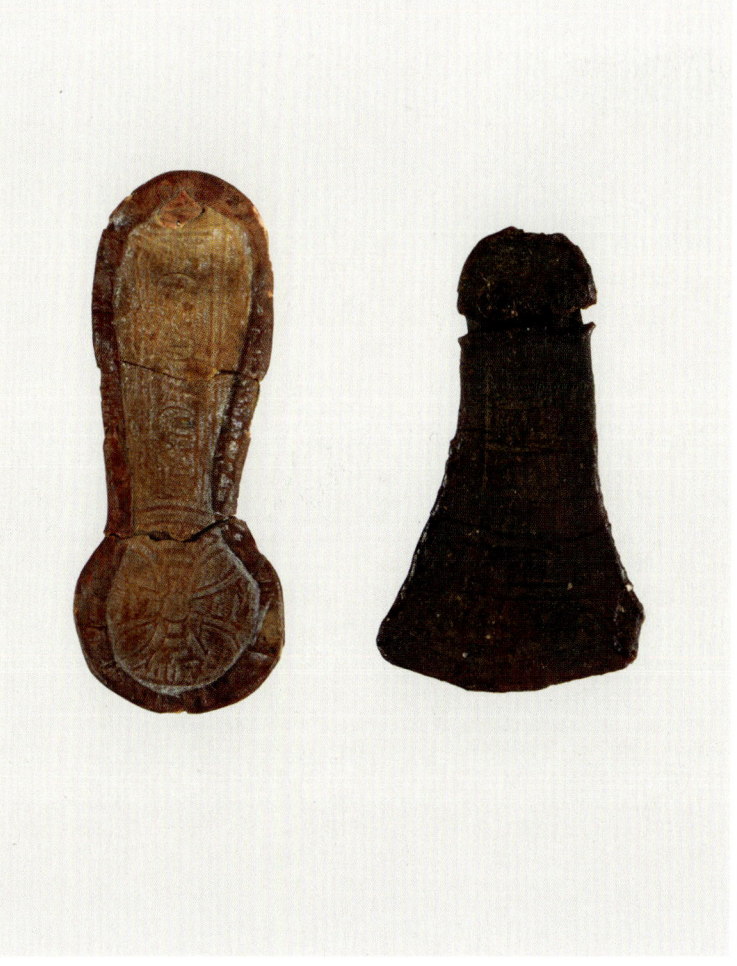

38

'Bouquet'

These plant remains, consisting of a bulb (possibly a spring onion) and garlic cloves threaded onto strips of date palm leaf, were found in the outermost wrappings of Nakhtefmut's body.

Fitzwilliam Museum, E.98.1896
23 cm (approximate length)

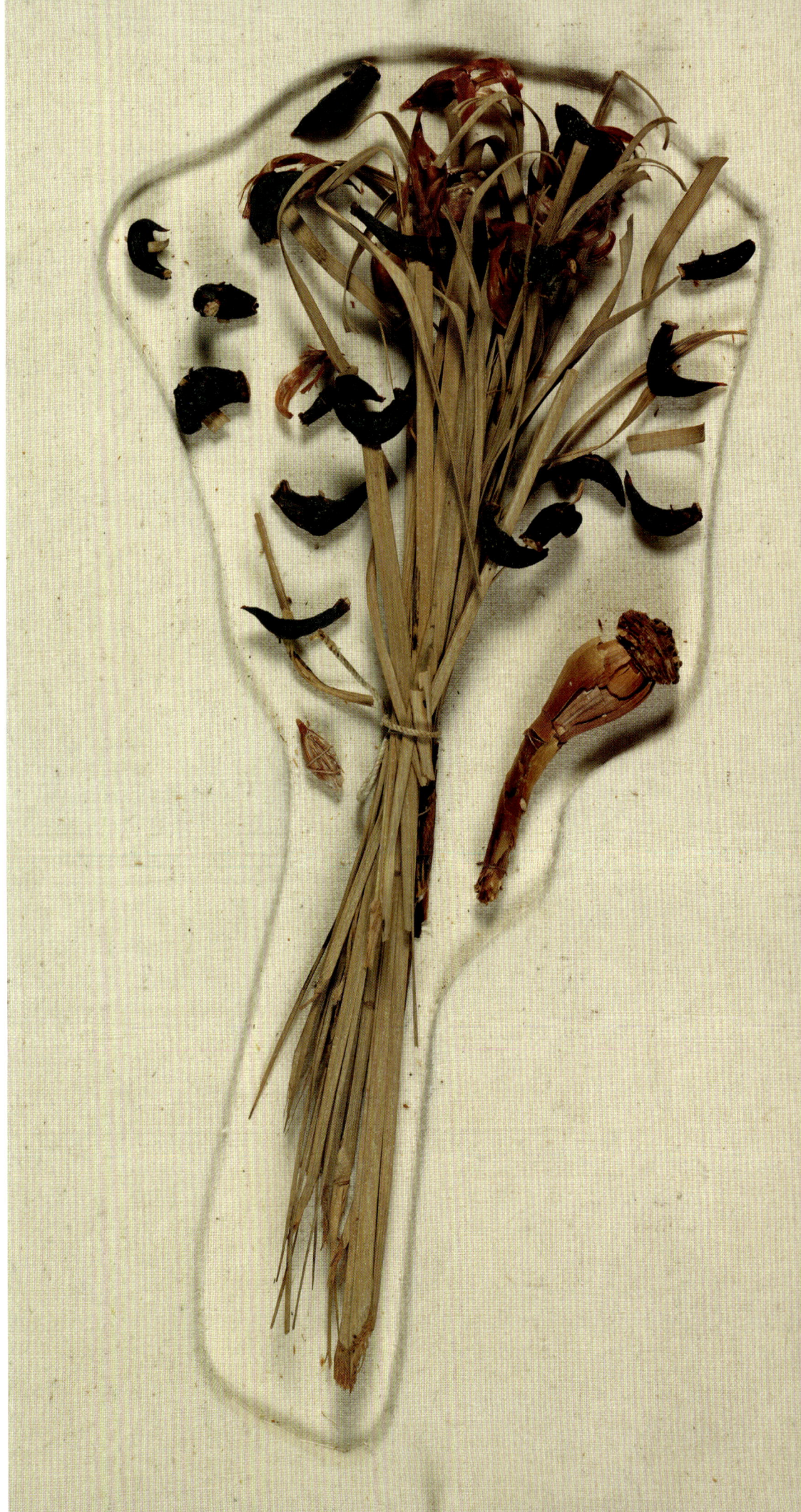

39

Amulets

This set of amulets, made of various materials including faience, frit, glass and lapis lazuli are magical amulets, found under the mummy wrappings near Nakhtefmut's neck.

Fitzwilliam Museum,
E.274.1896 – E.292.1896

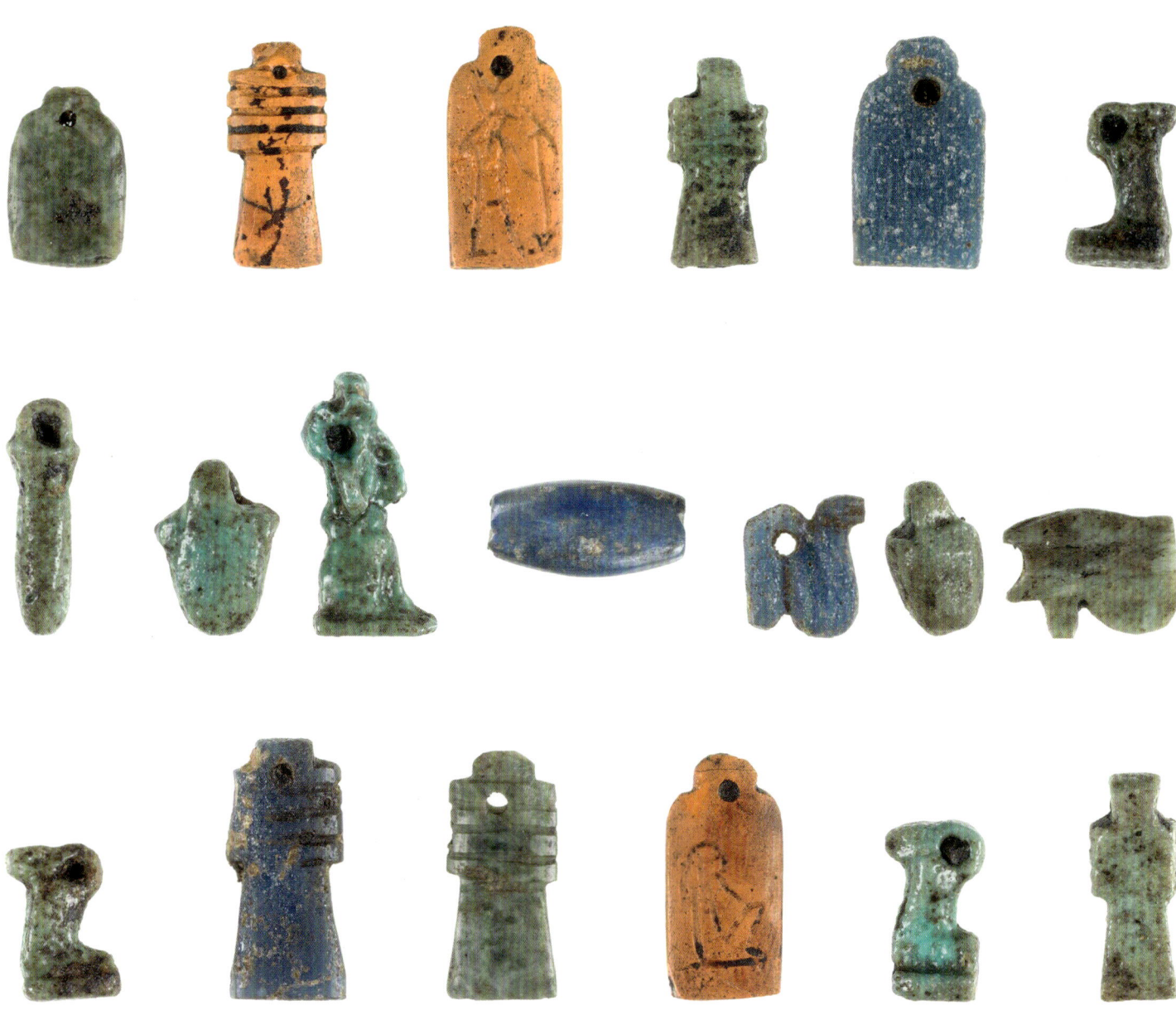

40

Winged scarab

Made of blue glass with wings cut from sheet silver, this scarab lay on Nakhtefmut's chest, under the mummy wrappings. Scarabs signified new life; the verb *kheper* (to come into being) was written with the scarab hieroglyph.

Fitzwilliam Museum, E.294.1896
2.4 × 11.9 × 0.9 cm

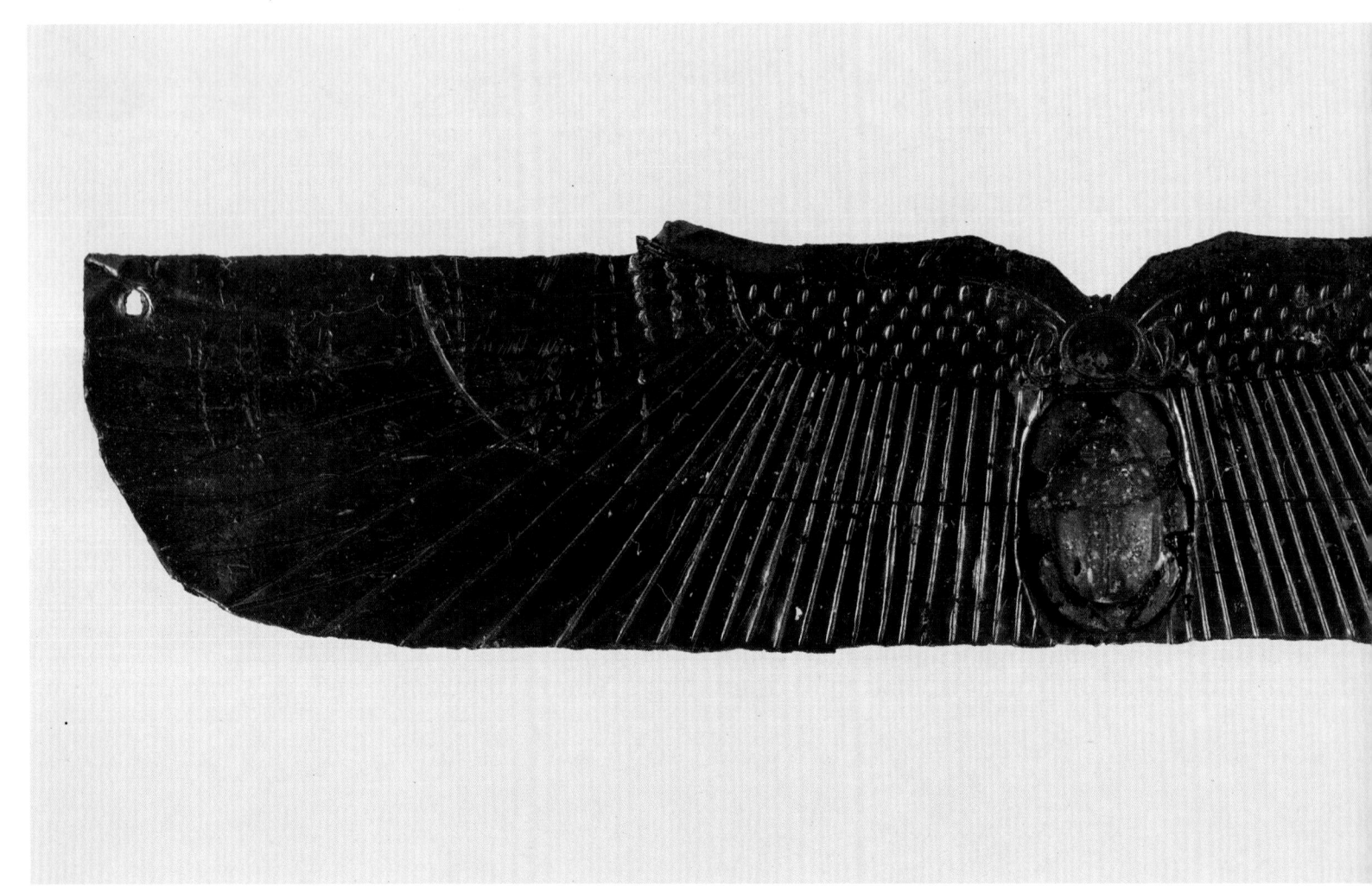

41

Scarab made of metagabbro (greenstone)

This second scarab was found below the winged scarab on Nakhtefmut's chest. Although it has no inscription, it would have functioned as a 'heart scarab', intended to assist at the moment of judgement before Osiris, when Nakhtefmut's heart was weighed to see that it contained only good deeds.

Fitzwilliam Museum, E.293.1896
2.6 × 1.8 × 1.2 cm

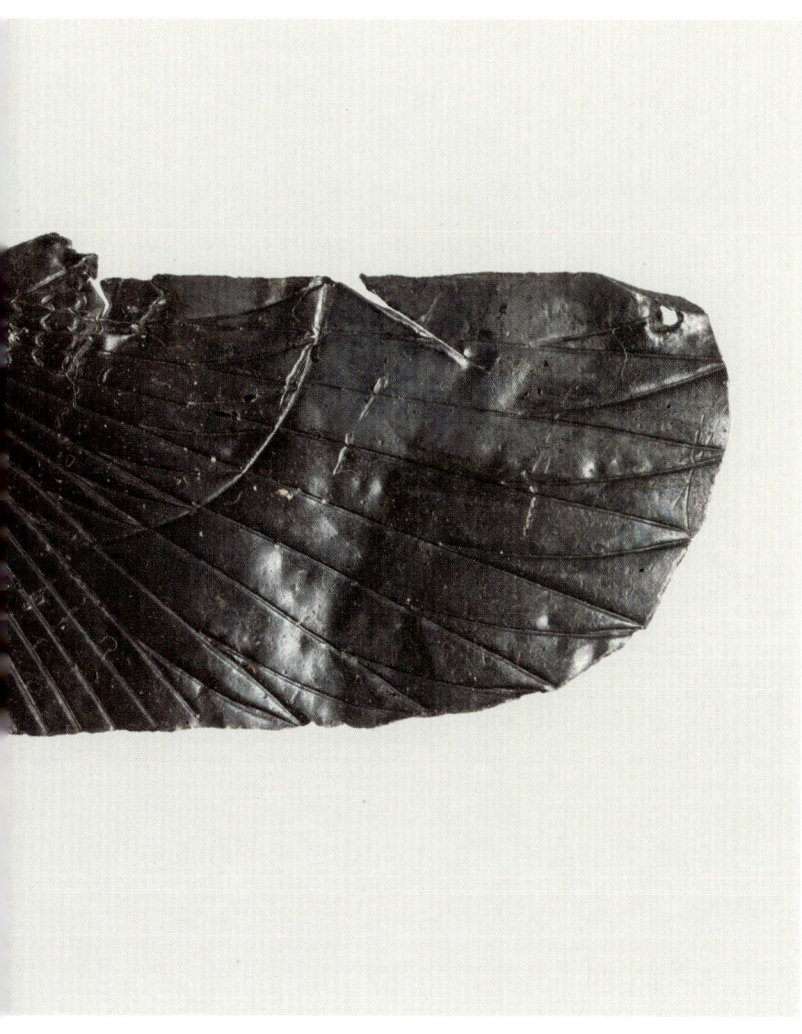
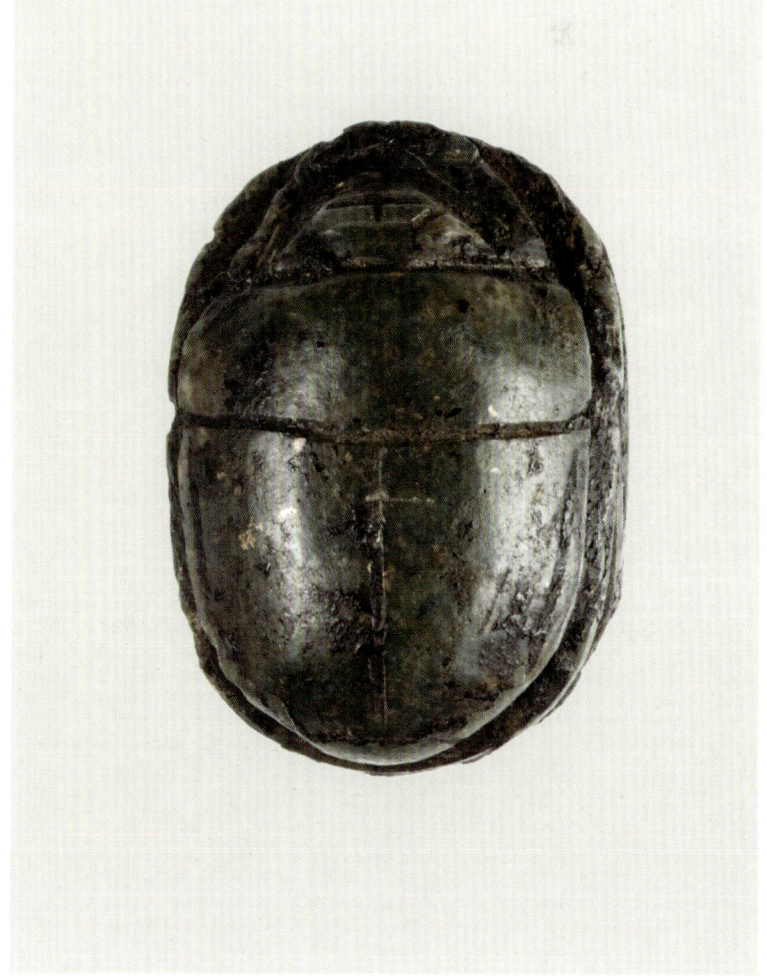

42

Papyrus

Papyri have been found in very few burials of this period. This one was lying on Nakhtefmut's thighs in the innermost mummy wrappings. The text, written on both sides, contains four spells from the Book of the Dead.

Fitzwilliam Museum, E.100.1896
34.5 × 27 × 0.5 cm

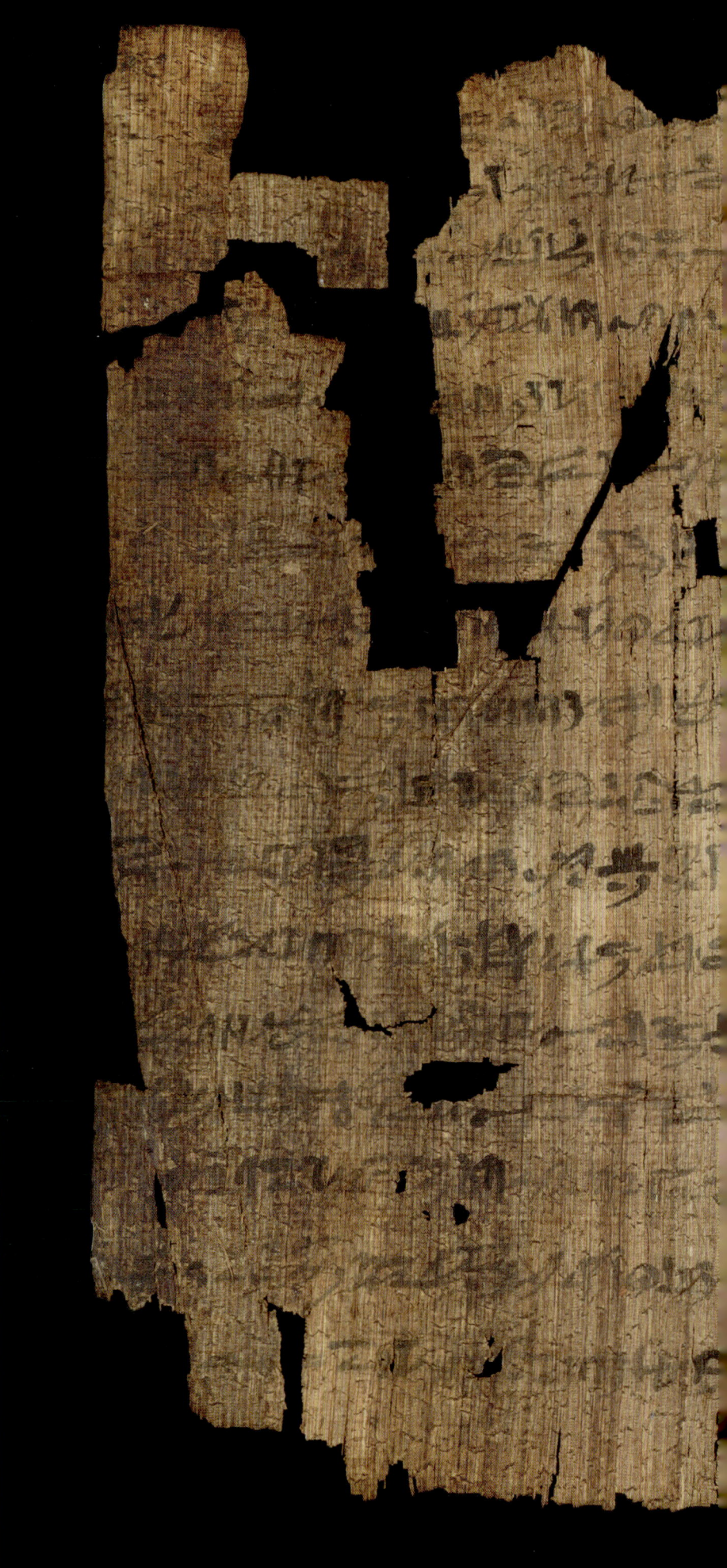

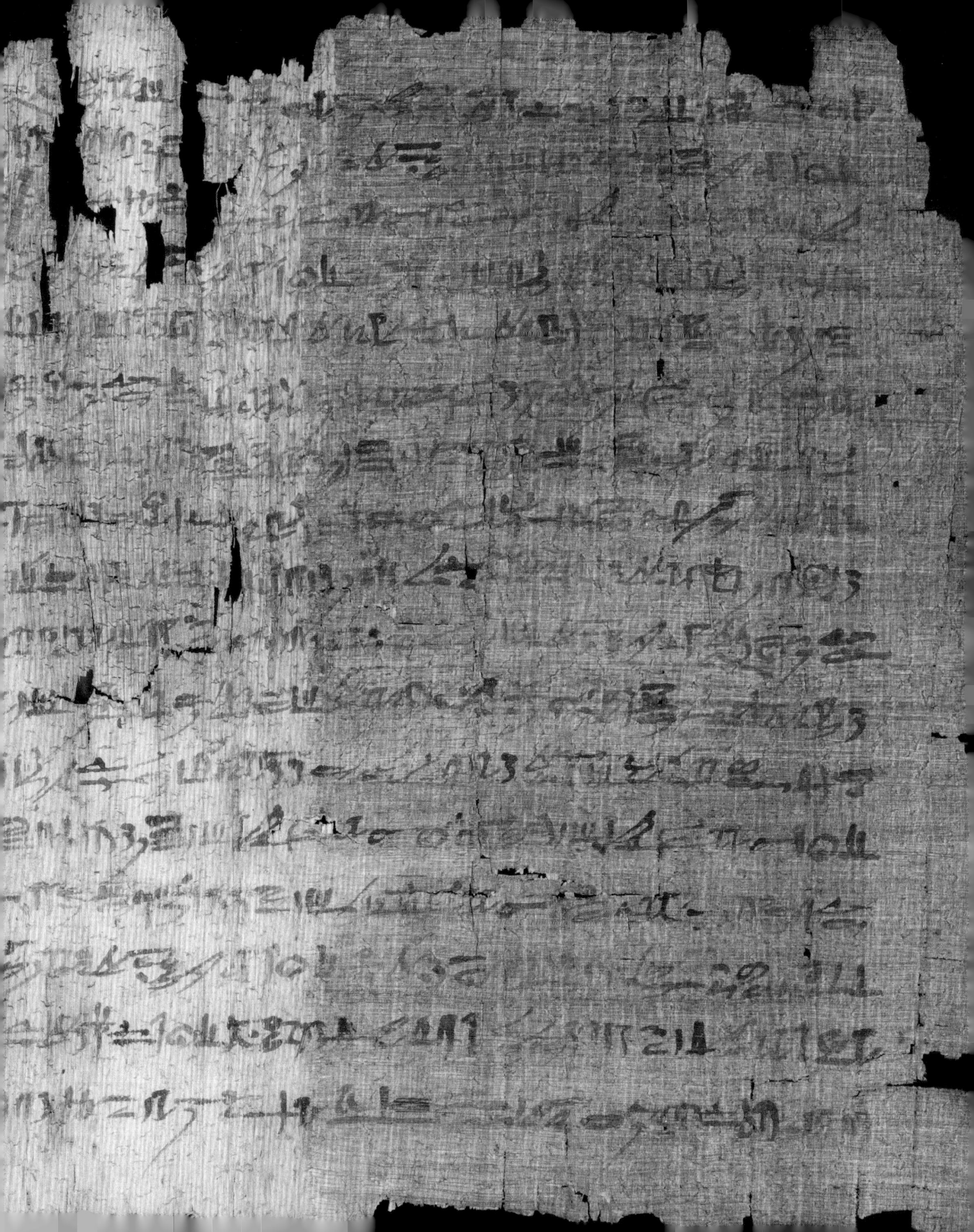

Later nested coffins

From 715 BC, Egypt came under the control of a single king called Shabaka, a Kushite from Nubia; Nubians continued to rule Egypt for the next fifty years. During this period, more highly decorated anthropoid coffins reappeared. Coffins continued to be nested one inside another, but the anthropoid coffins were often placed inside a rectangular outer coffin with vaulted lid and four corner posts, known as a *qersu* coffin (fig. 100). This shape harks back to much earlier stone sarcophagi of the Old Kingdom (about 2700–2170 BC), seen in the hieroglyph for 'coffin' (🗋, *qersu*).

Some mummies from this period have sections of cartonnage over the wrappings, rather than a complete mummy case. Many of them, however, are less tidy on the inside than on the outside, containing only incomplete bodies or bodies with extra limbs, and it appears that the embalmers of the period were less careful with the dead than they had been in the past.

At Thebes, particularly wealthy individuals seem to have been buried in huge tombs, with temple gateways and courtyards, decorated in a style deliberately recalling earlier tomb depictions, particularly from the Old Kingdom. Others were buried in shafts cut into the floors of existing tombs.

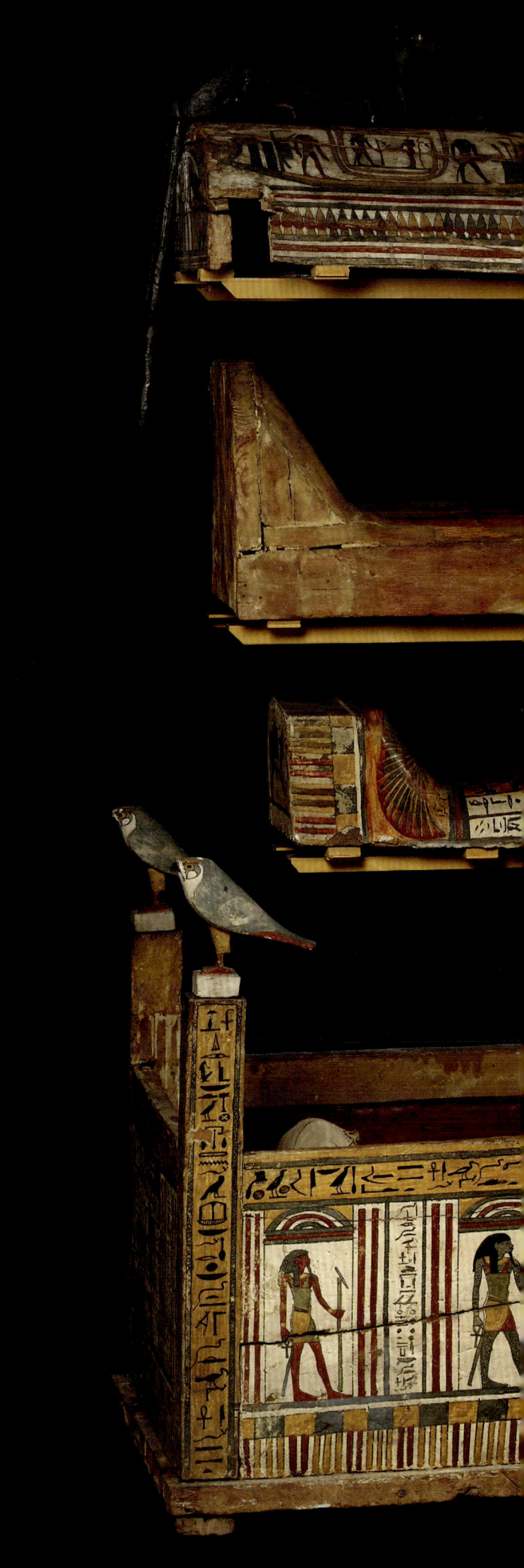

Fig. 100
The coffin set of Djeddjehutefankh, with an inner coffin, an intermediate coffin and an outer *qersu* coffin (The Ashmolean Museum, 1895.153–156)

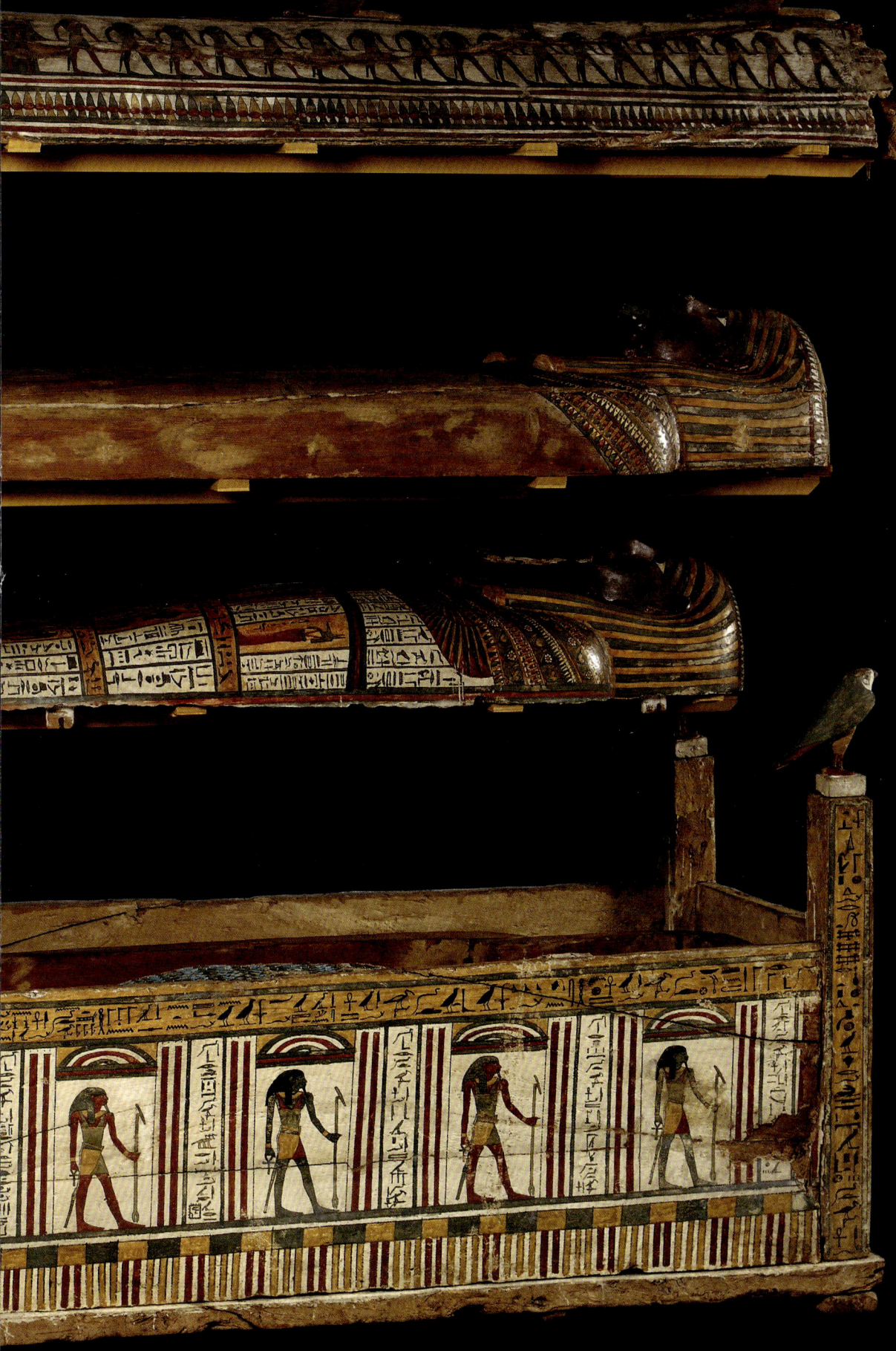

43

Inner and intermediate coffins of Pakepu

These coffins are the inner and intermediate coffins of a man called Pakepu, possibly originally placed within a *qersu* coffin. Both coffins have a flat lid for most of the length of the body, a typical feature of coffins around this date.

There are subtle differences between them: on the intermediate coffin, Pakepu has a short beard, signifying that he is a mortal man, while on the inner one, he has a long beard, usually worn by gods, probably indicating that he is in the form of Osiris. It is clear that the decoration on the inner coffin was applied *after* the body was placed inside, because it runs over the join between the lid and the box and was cut when the coffin was opened (cat. 43.1). It is, in effect, a cartonnage mummy case like Nakhtefmut's (cat. 32), completely encasing the body within but incorporating a wooden structure. This concept is strengthened by the fact that the inner coffin has a substantial plinth under Pakepu's feet, resembling the plinths of cartonnage coffins where the footboard was attached.

Pakepu was a 'water pourer on the west of Thebes'. This title was given to people who were responsible for maintaining the funerary cult of the dead on behalf of their families. In return, they received an income from the produce of land set aside for this purpose. The system of professional water pourers (later known as choachytes) continued until the Roman Period.

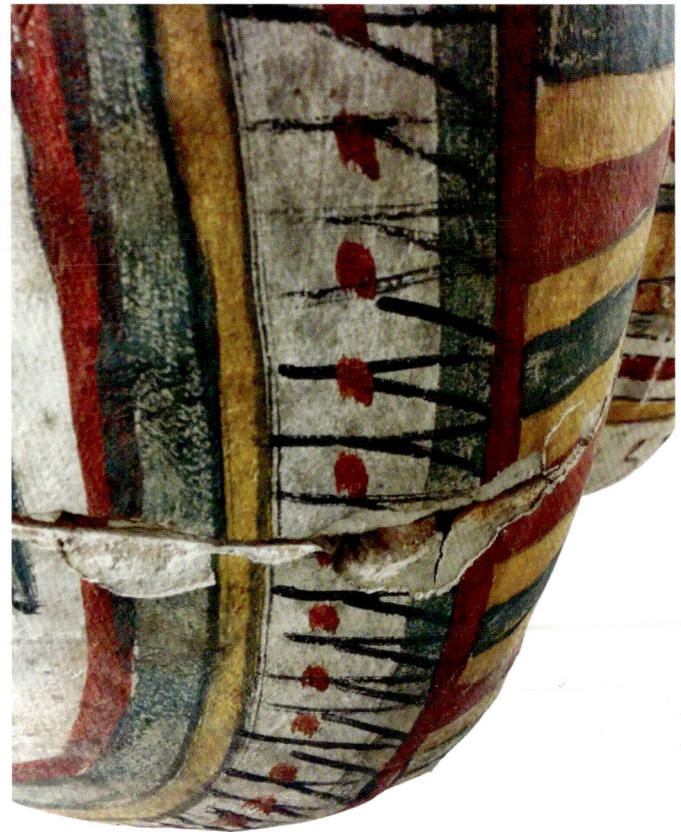

Cat. 43.1

The many inscriptions on the lids of the inner and intermediate coffins are appeals to the gods, especially Osiris, for the provision of food offerings and all good, sweet and delicious things. On the lids of the coffins we see Pakepu's body lying on a bier, attended by Anubis, whose left arm in both examples is strikingly extended – obviously a trait of the artist who decorated this coffin (cat. 43.4).

Both coffins and most of the dowels are made of sycomore fig. The main board in the lid of the intermediate coffin consists of four pieces of timber. Each side rim is made of two long

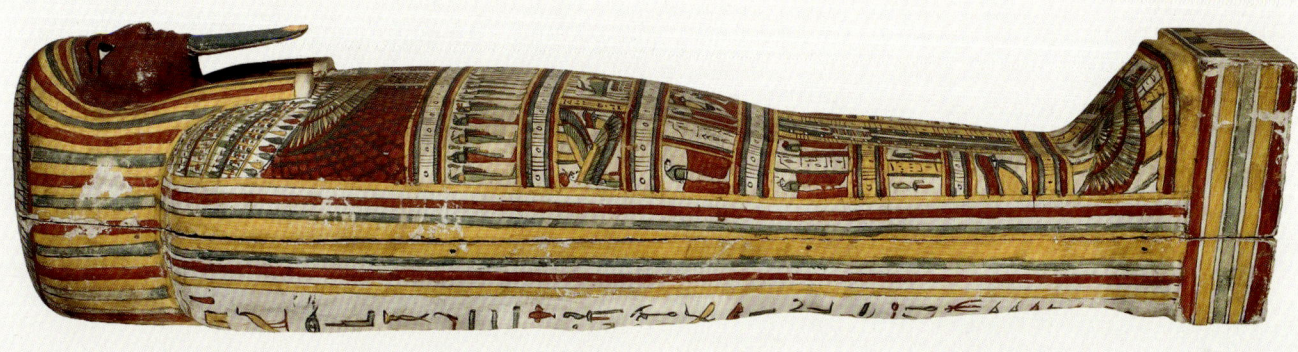
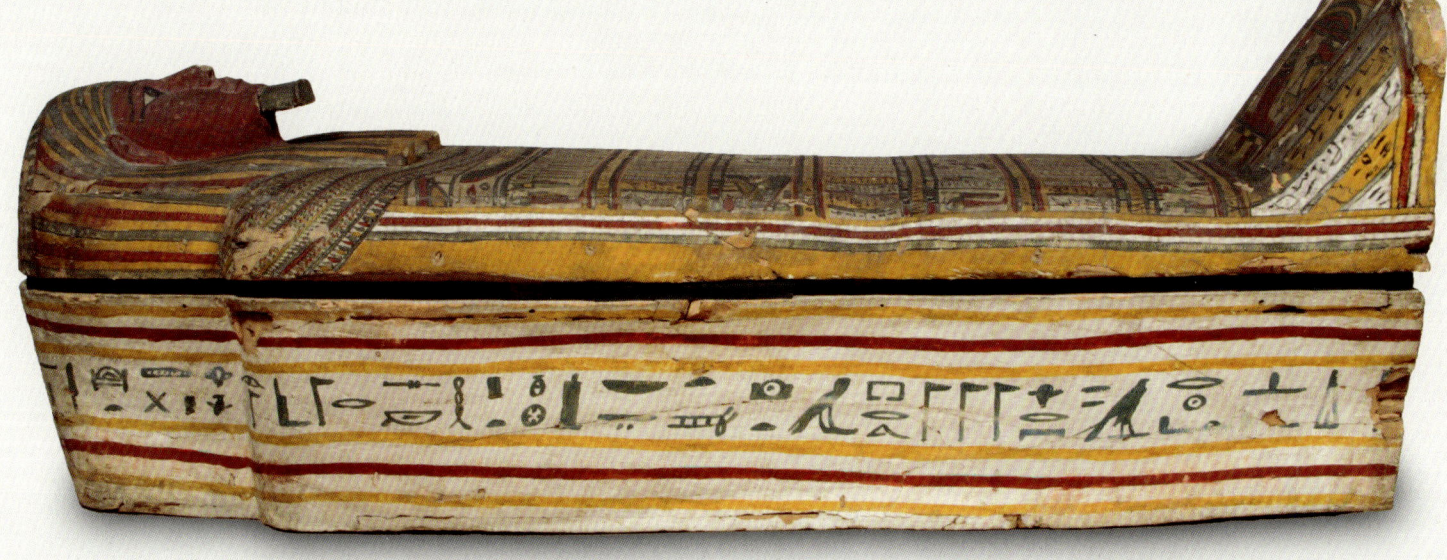

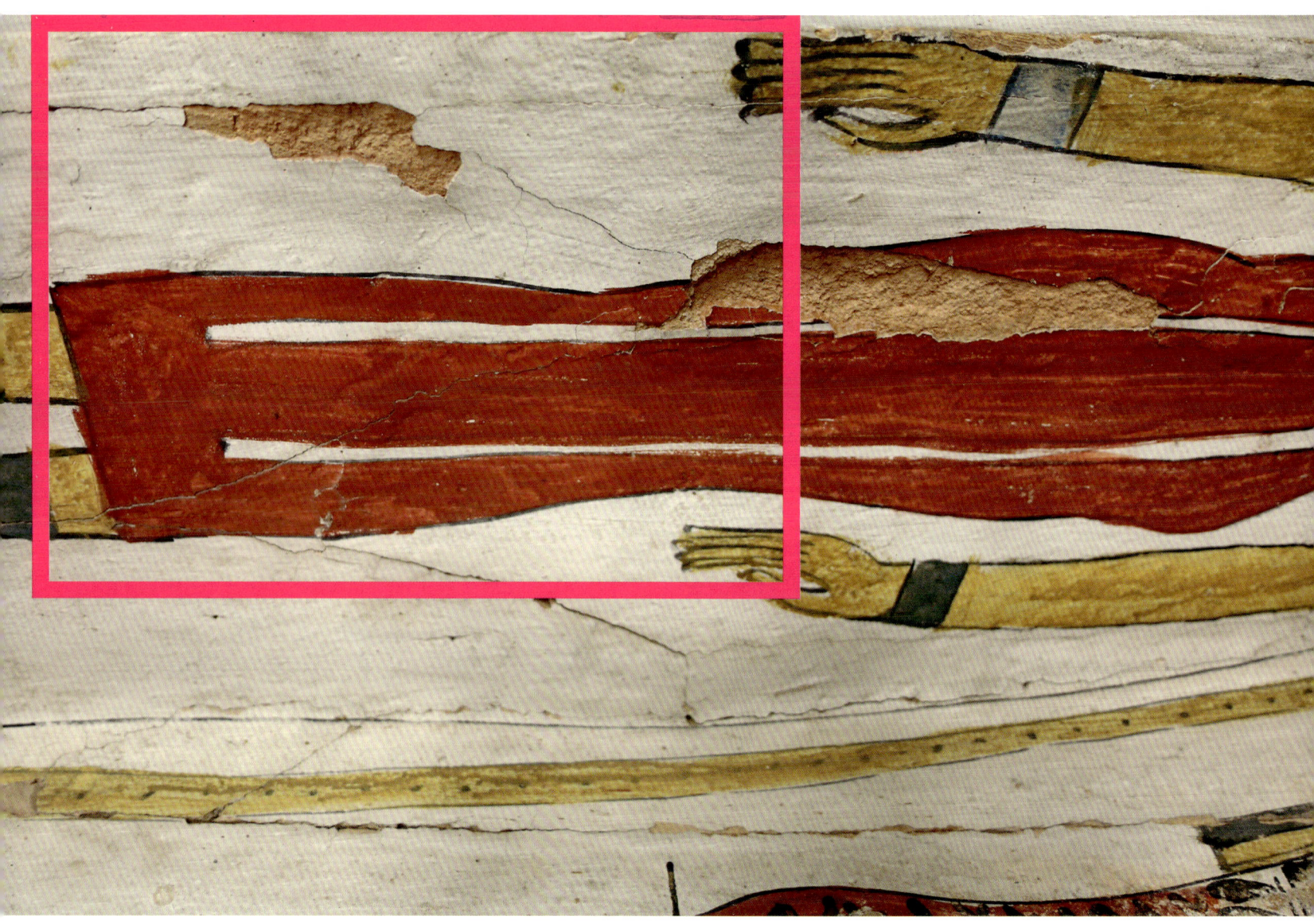

Cat. 43.2
Damage to the interior surface of the intermediate coffin box (right-hand side) reveals the coarse pink paste used to fill in flaws and gaps before the final surface layers were applied.

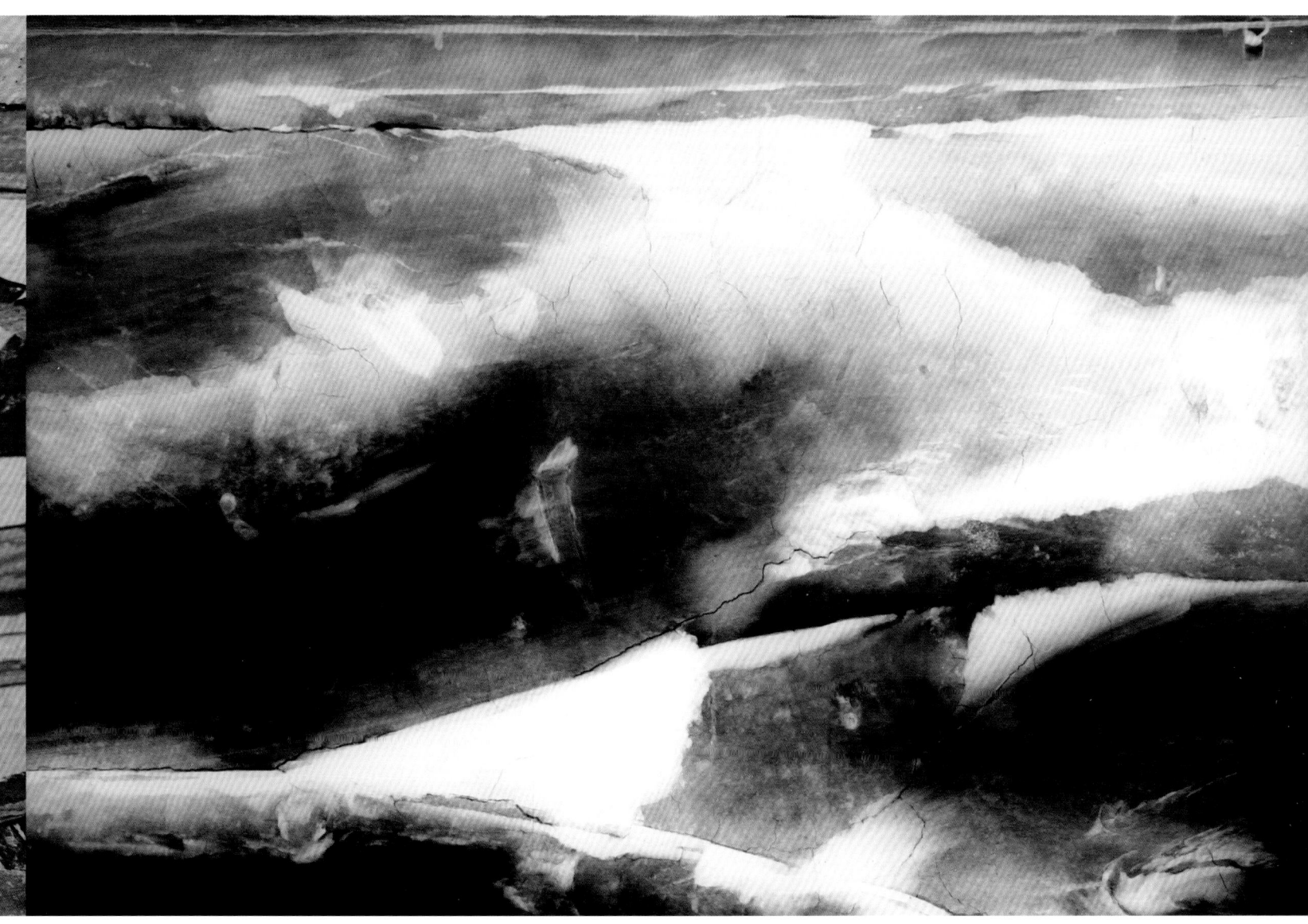

Fig. 101
An X-radiograph of the same area highlighted in cat. 43.2 shows how much pink paste (white areas on the radiograph) was needed.

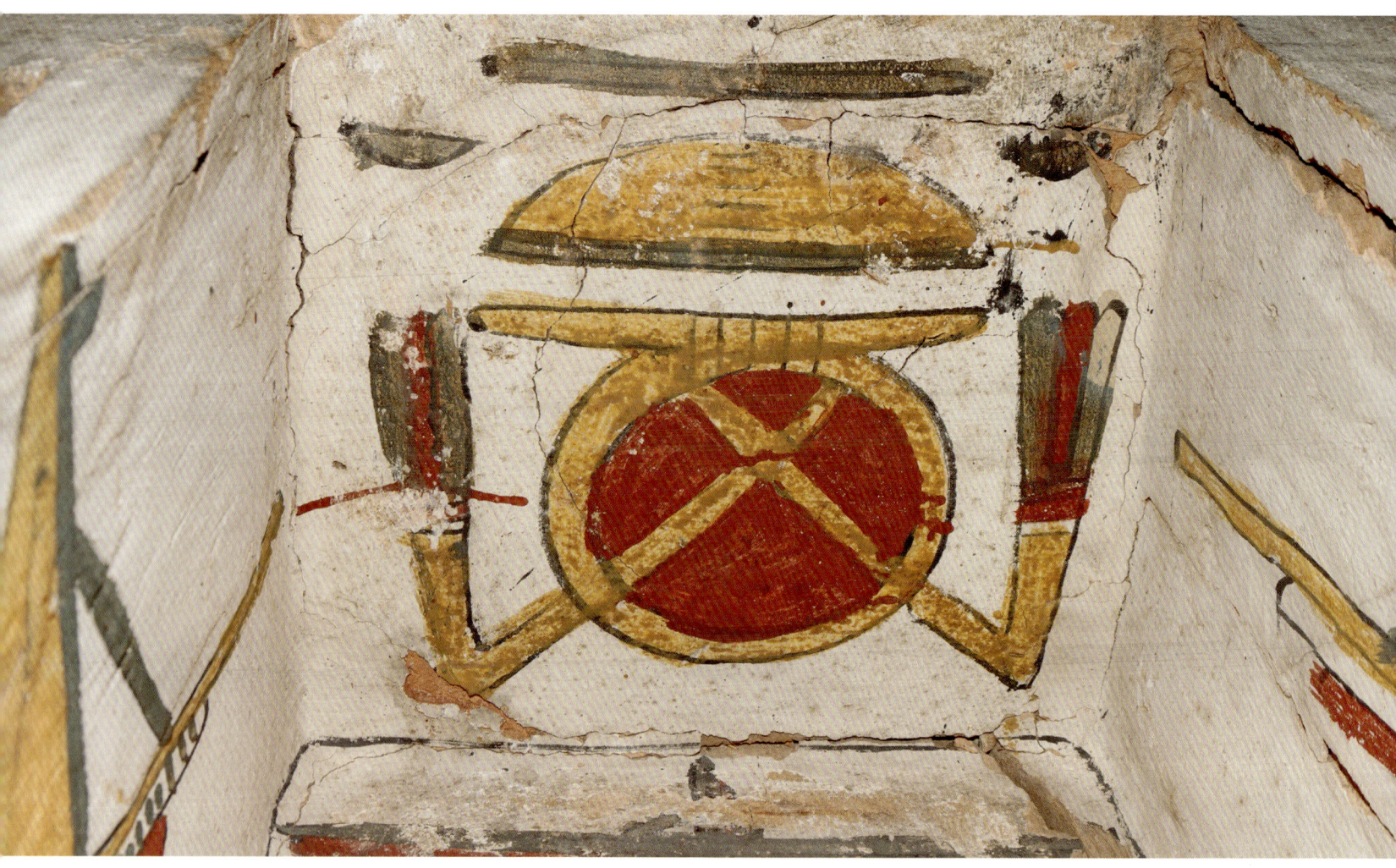

Cat. 43.3
The foot end of the intermediate coffin: large drips of red paint run from left to right, suggesting that the coffin was resting on its right side when painted

pieces attached end-to-end with a variant of a scarf joint. The feet are constructed of five butt-jointed planks, two triangular sidepieces and a footboard made of three pieces of wood. Small slivers have been inserted to fill gaps (fig. 58, p. 88). The wig lappets, face, ears and beard are all separate. The sides and ends of the box are a jigsaw of relatively small, ill-fitting pieces (fig. 56, pp. 86 – 87). Most of the rim has thin planks added to make the box up to the desired height, and possibly to provide a better structure into which to cut the mortises. These mortises held the sycomore fig tenons that locked the box to the lid.

X-radiographs reveal that the wood was damaged by insects before the coffin was made. A large quantity of coarse pink paste (calcite and earth pigments) was pushed into irregularities in the wood and wide gaps between the joints (cat. 43.2; fig. 101); it was also used to build up features of the

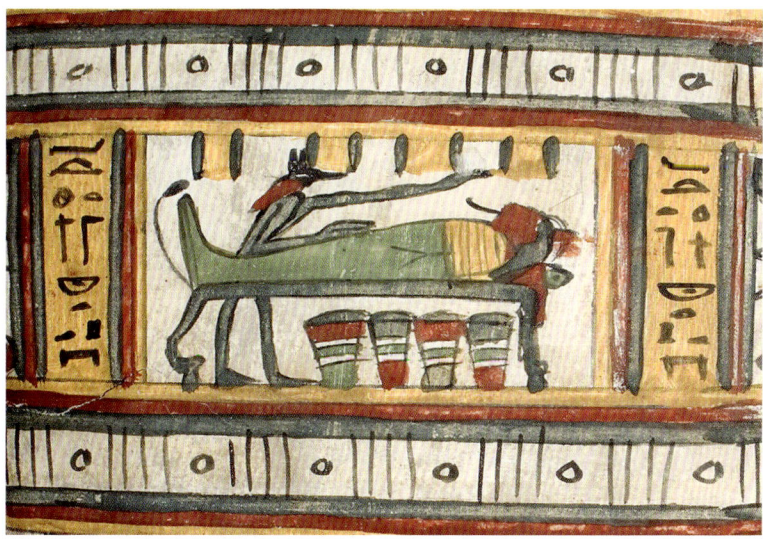

Cat. 43.4
Anubis, with his left arm much extended, tends Pakepu's body on a lion-headed bier, under which are four canopic jars. The greyish background is degraded orpiment, which would originally have been a bright lemon yellow.

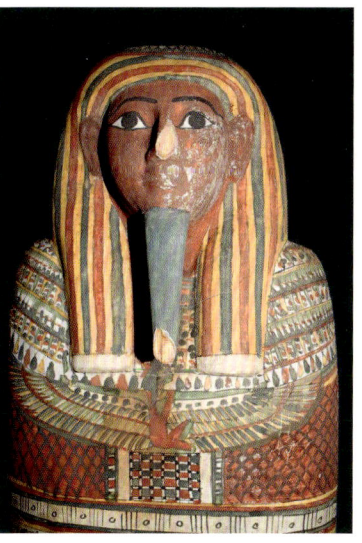

Cat. 43.5
The inner coffin of Pakepu. There are losses on the right-hand side, particularly on the face, which appear to be due to the quality of the paint rather than the result of damage or deterioration.

face. Strips of linen were pasted over the junction of the ears and neck and body. The coffin was then coated with a thick sparitic calcite preparation layer.

The structure of the inner coffin is harder to discern, as multiple preparation layers cover it inside and out. However, X-radiographs show that it is an altogether superior construction to the intermediate coffin. Both lid and box are made of a relatively small number of long, straight boards, which fit together fairly tightly along the dowelled edges. Only a small amount of the coarse pink paste was needed to fill flaws before a cartonnage-like surface was built up from layers of glue, fabric, and micritic and sparitic calcite pastes.

Both coffins are simply and sparsely painted. The use of thin paint has resulted in a matte finish, and the preparation layer was left unpainted in the white areas of background. Underdrawings, where they are present, were executed in carbon-based black paint, with a straight edge used to make the lines. The figures were painted roughly with rapid, clumsy brushstrokes. Some of the colours were applied while the drawing was still wet – there are streaks in some of the drawing lines that coincide with the paint brushstrokes.

The palette consists of red earth, Egyptian blue and copper-based green, with two yellows (orpiment and yellow earth). Orpiment is found in the background of smaller registers, but has degraded to a pale grey colour. Originally, both yellows would have been bright, though slightly different from each other, creating a contrast. Drips in the thick blue paint on the intermediate coffin lid suggest that it was painted whilst standing on its rim; the box, however, was lying on its right-hand side when most of its interior decoration was painted (cat. 43.3).

On the inner coffin, the areas painted with red earth differ in quality. Those on the left-hand side are patchy, with a lot of loss (cat. 43.5). This is quite unlike the surrounding colours and red areas on the right-hand side. Possibly a separate batch of paint was used for each side of the coffin, one less stable than the other.

Around 680–664 BC
Fitzwilliam Museum, E.2.1869
(given by the Prince of Wales [later Edward VII])
209 × 66 × 72 cm

44

Fragments from a *qersu* coffin

Twenty-six fragments of acacia wood from a *qersu* coffin were found in tomb 840 at Abydos. Another piece may have come from an inner, anthropoid coffin.

The owner of the coffins was called Irethereru. As a governor of Abydos, overseer of priests of Osiris at Abydos, and a priest of Hathor, 'mistress of Dendera' (where Hathor's principal temple was located), he was a person of high standing. The texts on the panels include hymns of praise to various deities, asking them to provide Irethereru with food offerings in the afterlife.

The coffin was large, about 265 × 104 cm (fig. 103). The surviving fragments are almost exclusively from text panels, which were originally fixed with dowels to an underlying wooden structure but slightly proud of it, with areas of decoration between them. One corner post survives; it was originally connected to the coffin base by an integral large tenon. The sides of the underlying structure were probably made from a series of planks, the tops and bottoms of which were fixed to the corner post by large pegged tenons (fig. 102). Scribed lines and paint marks were used on the post to position the panels and mortises.

The texts were cut into the wood and filled with white calcite paste or Egyptian blue. Parts of the coffin, especially the decorated surfaces of the underlying structure, were painted with yellow earth, but on most of the fragments the wood is visible; red earth has been rubbed into the surface to enhance the colour.

About 745–650 BC
Fitzwilliam Museum, E.14.1926 (given by the British School of Archaeology)

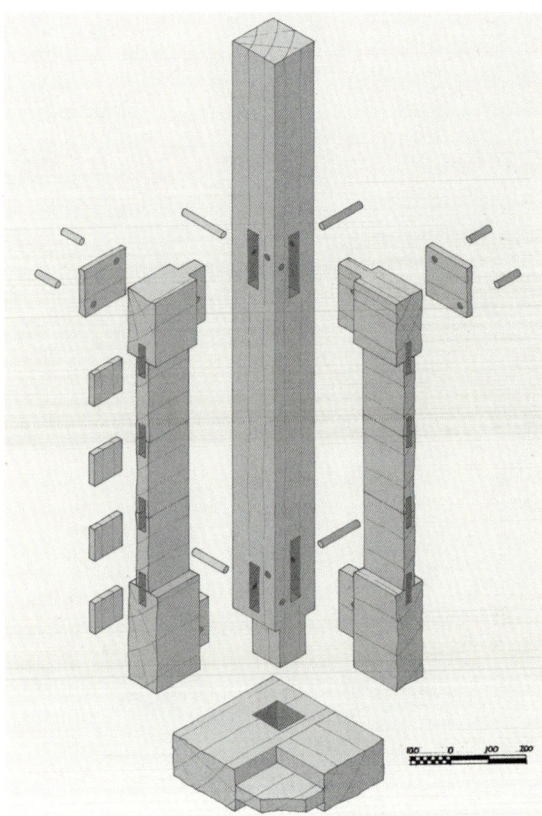

Fig. 102
Components of one corner of the coffin

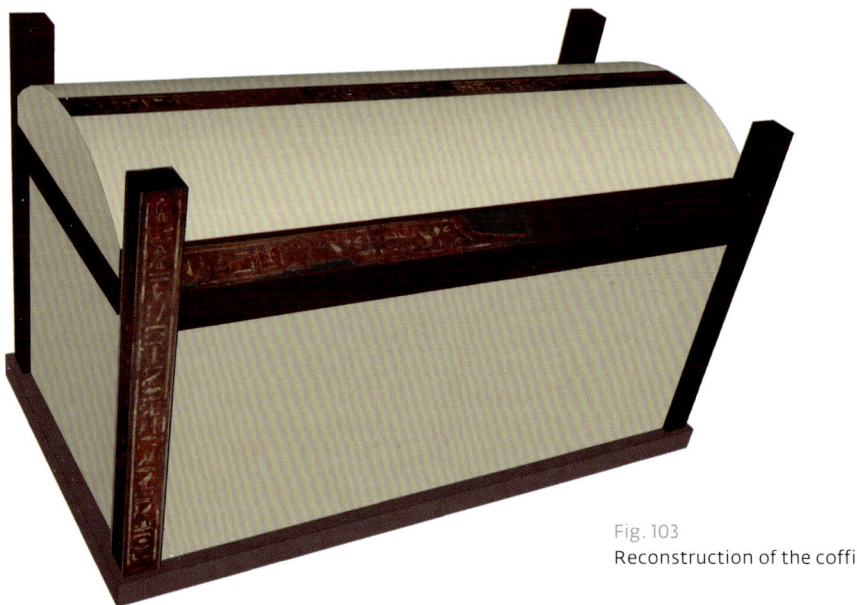

Fig. 103
Reconstruction of the coffin

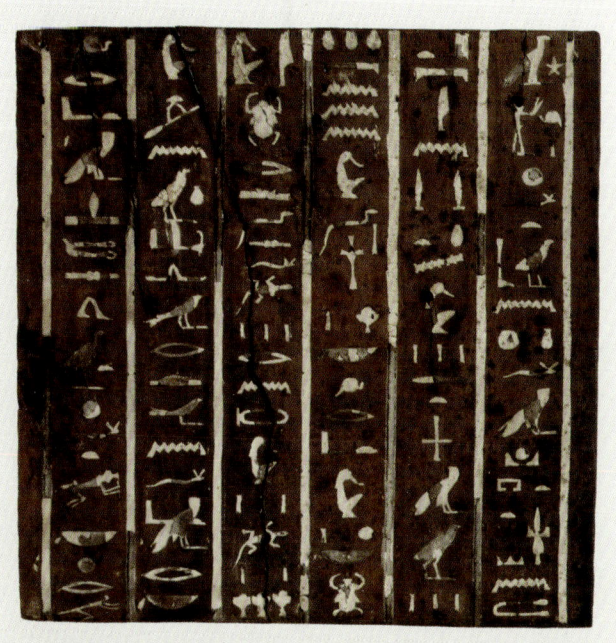
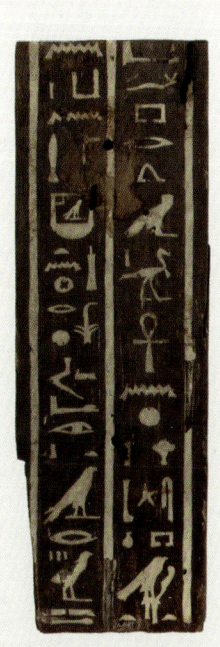
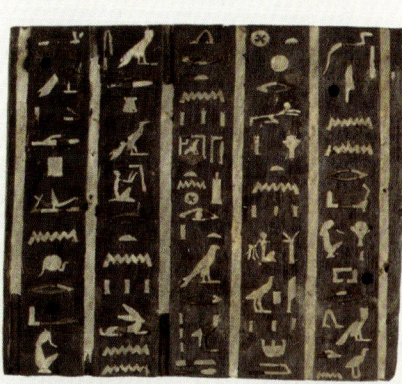
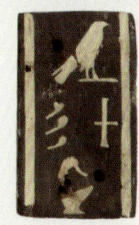
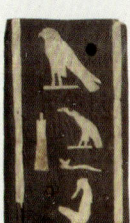
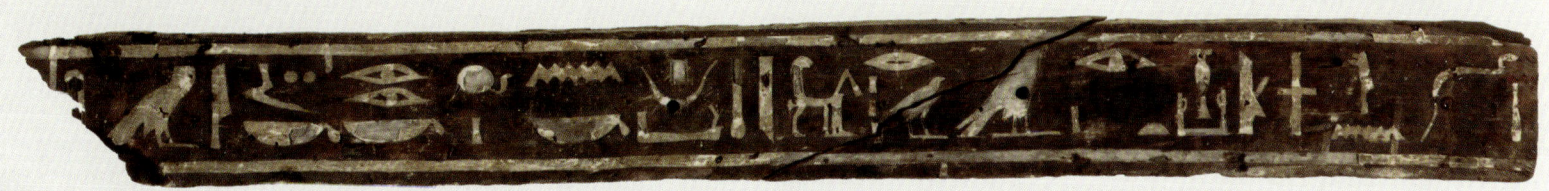

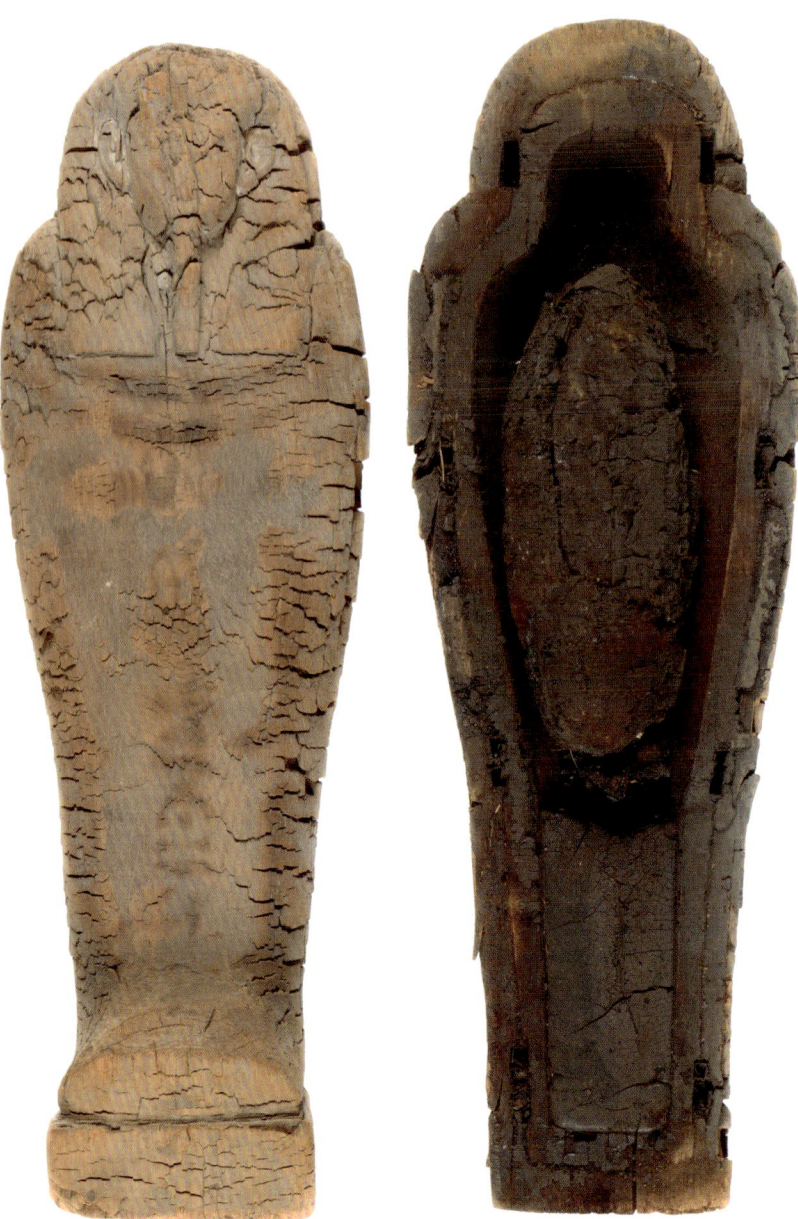

45

Miniature coffin

This miniature coffin was carefully made from two pieces of cedar wood. It originally had painted decoration and an inscription, and was held together with pegged tenons, just like a full-size coffin. The wood is severely deteriorated and no pigment remains. The coffin may originally have been made to hold the internal organs from a mummified body. The contents, surrounded by black resin that has pooled towards the foot end of the coffin, are not yet securely identified but might be the body of an infant.

Probably around 664–525 BC
Fitzwilliam Museum, E.43.1907
(given by the British School of Archaeology)
43.8 × 13.4 × 14.1 cm

46

Box for *shabtis*

This wooden box is inscribed for Pasherienusiraa. Typically for the period, the text is widely spaced (as on the intermediate coffin of Pakepu; cat. 43), except where the owner's name is written, possibly indicating that this box was bought preinscribed but with a space left for the buyer's name to be added.

745–664 BC
Fitzwilliam Museum, E.25.1887
(probably from Thebes)
29.5 × 29 × 16 cm

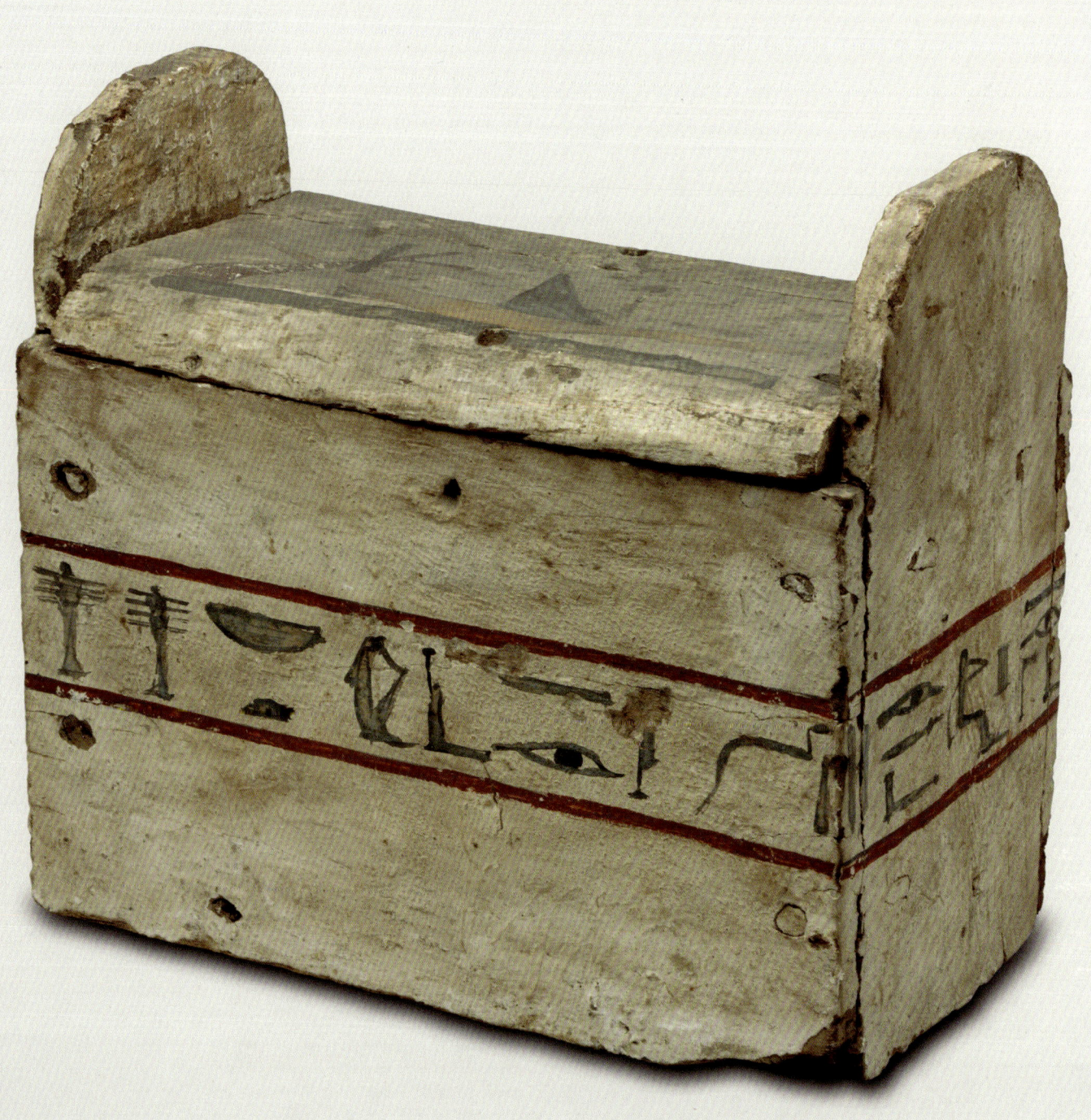

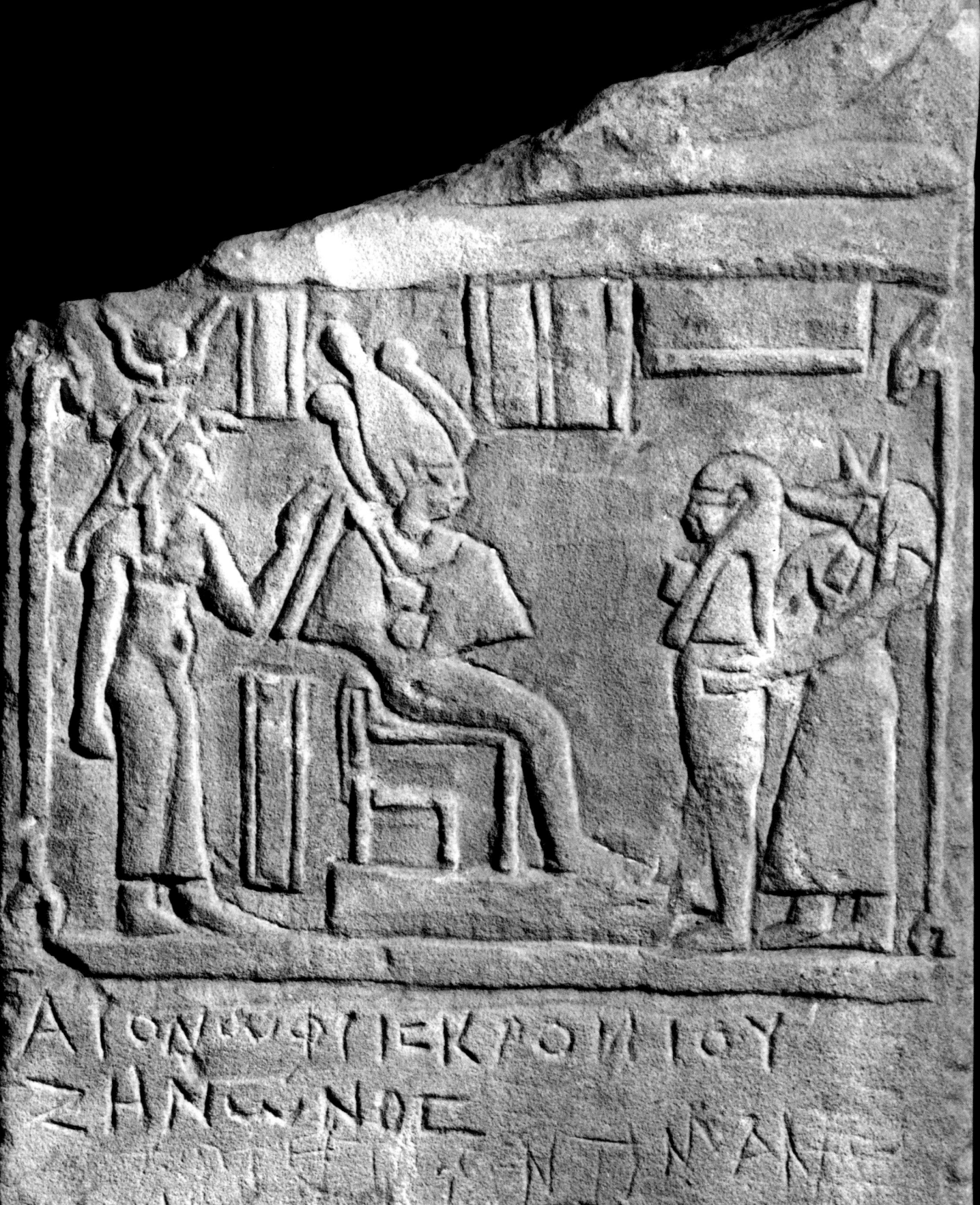

Later coffins

From 525 BC, Egypt came increasingly under the control of foreign rulers, with two periods of Persian occupation, followed by the conquest of Alexander the Great in 332 BC and a series of Greek rulers, before Egypt became part of the Roman Empire in 30 BC. Egyptian burial customs seem to have remained relatively unchanged during this time. Coffins continued to look fairly similar to traditional Egyptian anthropoid coffins of earlier periods, although their shape became broader, with larger decorative collars but with less other decoration and fewer texts.

Even under Roman rule, earlier funerary customs continued and, although the dead might be buried without coffins, examples of Roman coffins do survive. While many are anthropoid, made of wood or cartonnage (very often made using old papyri instead of linen), *qersu* coffins were also used, but the bodies inside were wrapped in decorated linen shrouds rather than placed in inner coffins. It seems that the principal intention of the decoration was to create a closer likeness of the deceased than in previous periods. For example, the red shroud mummy (cat. 54) has no inscriptions identifying the person inside but instead features a lifelike portrait. The decoration on the shroud shows that ancient Egyptian beliefs continued in some form, and it is clear that the ancient gods, such as Osiris, Isis and Anubis, were still seen as important to the continuation of life after death (fig. 104).

Increasing foreign influence also brought some new materials into the coffin-making process, most notably new pigments including pinks and blues based on plant material, lead white, red lead and an array of greens.

Fig. 104
Sandstone stela, Roman Period (Fitzwilliam Museum, E.63.1901), showing a standing mummiform figure supported by Anubis, before Osiris and Isis.

47

Wooden coffin lid of Djeher, son of Psamtek and the mistress of the house, Isetweret

This is lid is very reminiscent of Pakepu's inner coffin (cat. 43), with Djeher shown with a divine beard and a plinth under his feet. Similarly, there is also a depiction of Djeher's mummy lying on a bier with canopic jars underneath. Unlike Pakepu's coffin, however, there is no sign of any cartonnage-like overlay here. Djeher's face and divine beard are gilded and he is shown with a large decorative collar on his chest. Below that is a figure of the goddess Nut (see cat. 16), and texts on Djeher's legs call upon her to protect him. A large ring-shaped *shen* hieroglyph (signifying 'eternity') (see fig. 74, p. 104) appears on the foot end (and continues on the box).

Pale red underdrawing is visible in places, with dense glossy red, green, and pale and dark blues, all outlined in black (cat 47.1). The separately attached face is thickly gilded over a white layer. It appears skewed; this can be seen in the carving, in the size and angle of each eye, and in the painting along the hairline.

About 380–30 BC
British Museum, EA29776
(probably from Akhmim)
181.5 × 32 × 53 cm

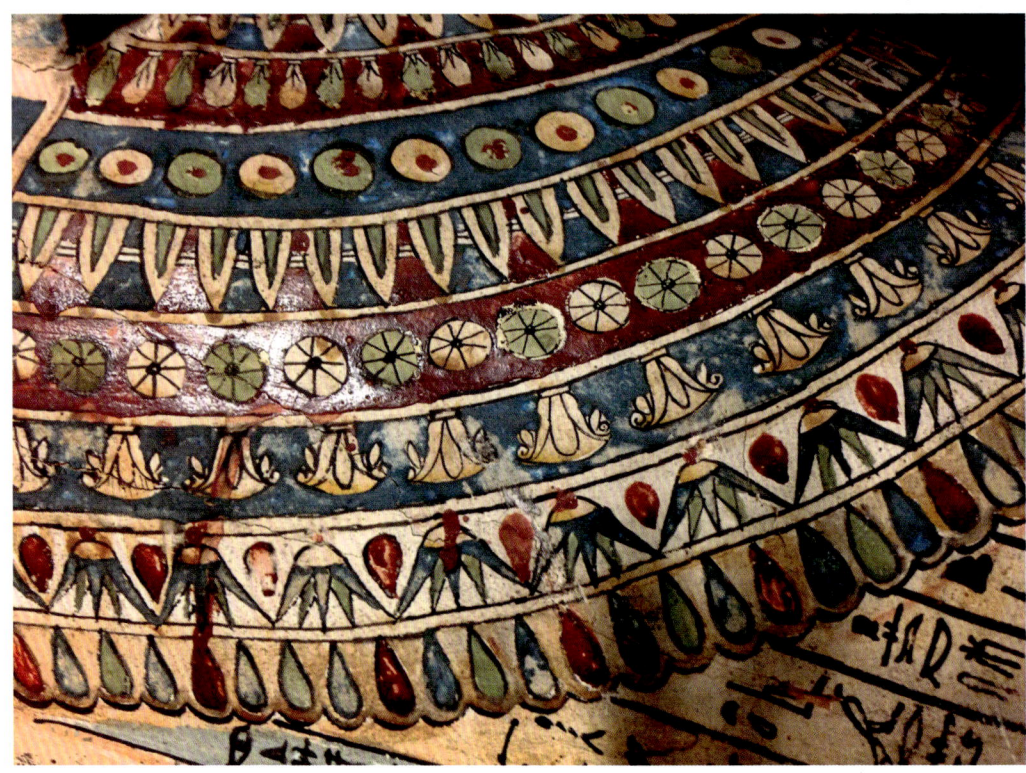

Cat. 47.1
Detail of decoration on Djeher's coffin

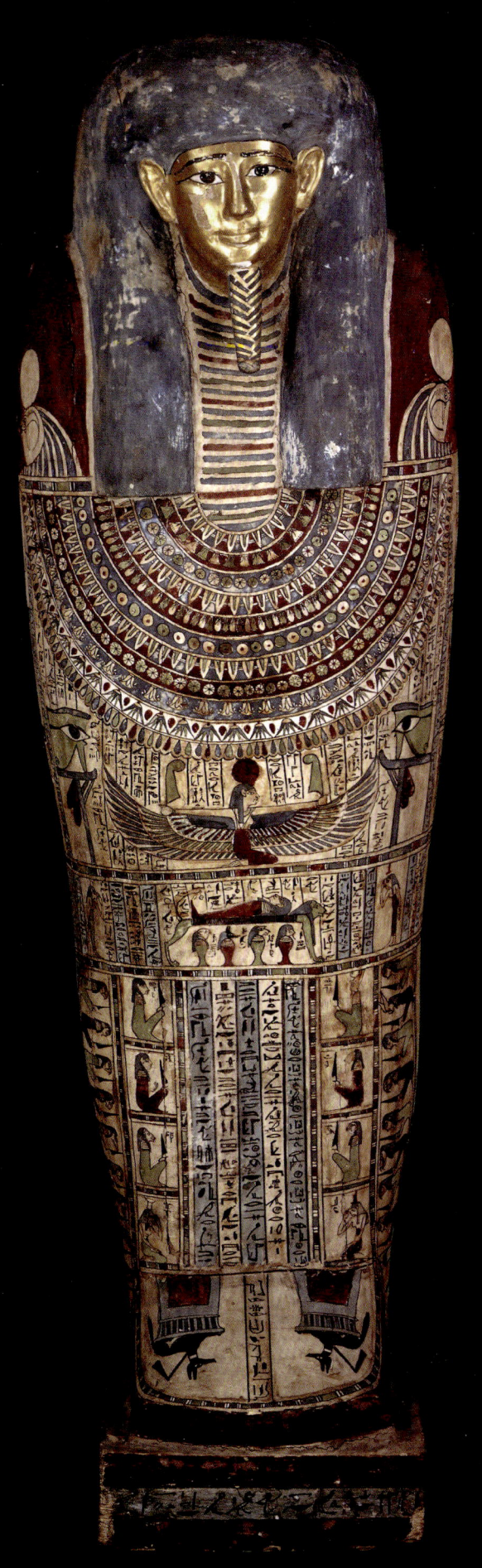

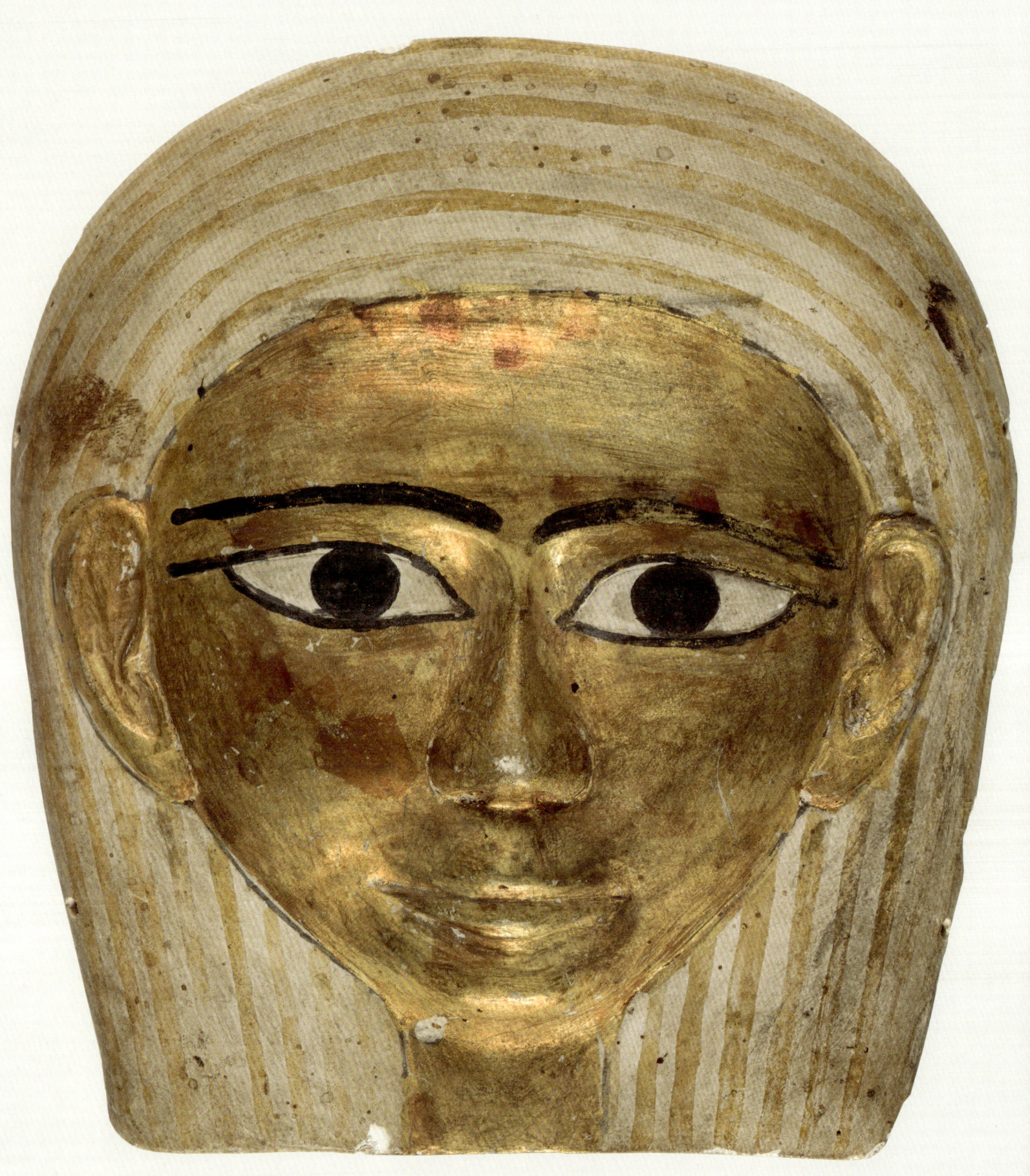

48

Cartonnage mask

This partly gilded mask has a thick white calcite preparation layer; it may have been intended that blue stripes would alternate with the yellow stripes on the wig. The face was outlined in carbon-based black before the yellow (orpiment) stripes were applied to the wig. Next, gold leaf was laid across the skin. The eyes and eyebrows are painted in black and white.

About 380–30 BC
Fitzwilliam Museum, E.GA.290.1949
(given by R. G. Gayer-Anderson)
16 × 15 × 3.1 cm

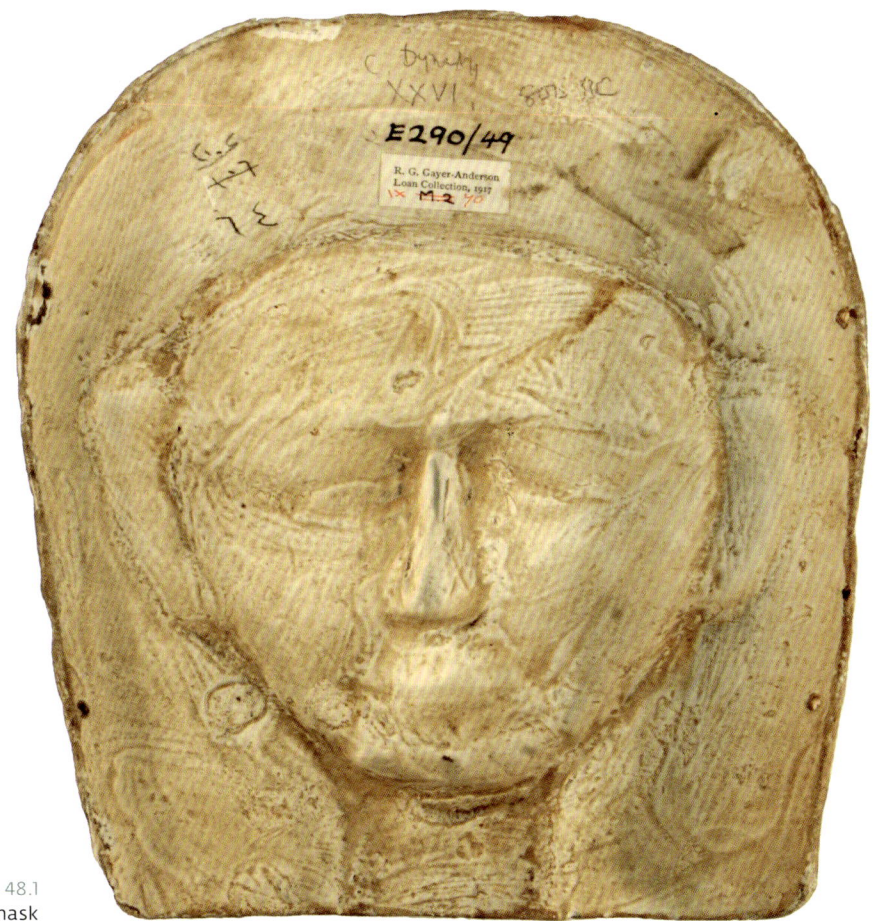

Cat. 48.1
The back of the cartonnage mask

Cat. 49.b (opposite right)

Cat 49.b.1 (opposite left)
On the back of the cartonnage are remains of the outline around which the shape of the figure was cut, as well as a partial layer of black resin

49

Fragments of openwork decoration

These fragments come from overlays that were put directly over mummy wrappings and take the place of a cartonnage mummy case like Nakhtefmut's (cat. 32) or a pseudo-cartonnage like the inner coffin of Pakepu (cat. 43). Here the figures, representing divinities, are separately made and are referred to as openwork.

The figure of Hapy, one of the Sons of Horus, is made of gilded cartonnage, the slight relief effect built up in the white preparation layer (cat. 49.b). The figure of Osiris is cut from a piece of sycomore fig, with dovetails at the top and bottom for connecting it to other pieces of openwork, and was coated with fine white paste over a layer of linen prior to painting.

About 700–30 BC
Fitzwilliam Museum, E.GA.2897.1943 and E.GA.2898.1943 (given by R. G. Gayer-Anderson)
25.5 × 7.7 × 1 cm; 21.3 × 5 × 0.1 cm

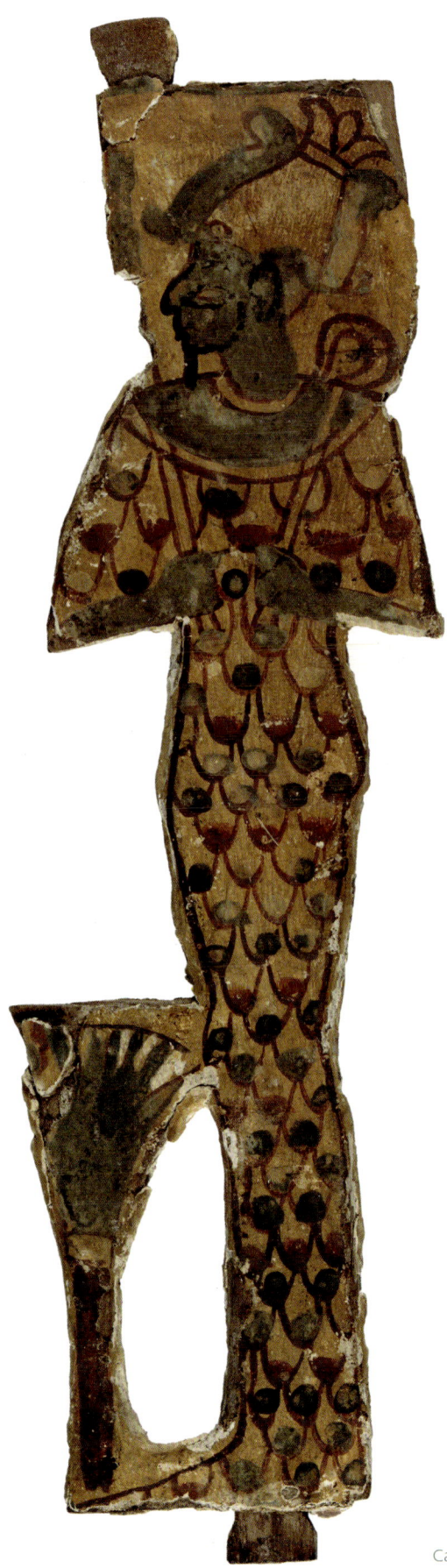

Cat. 49.a

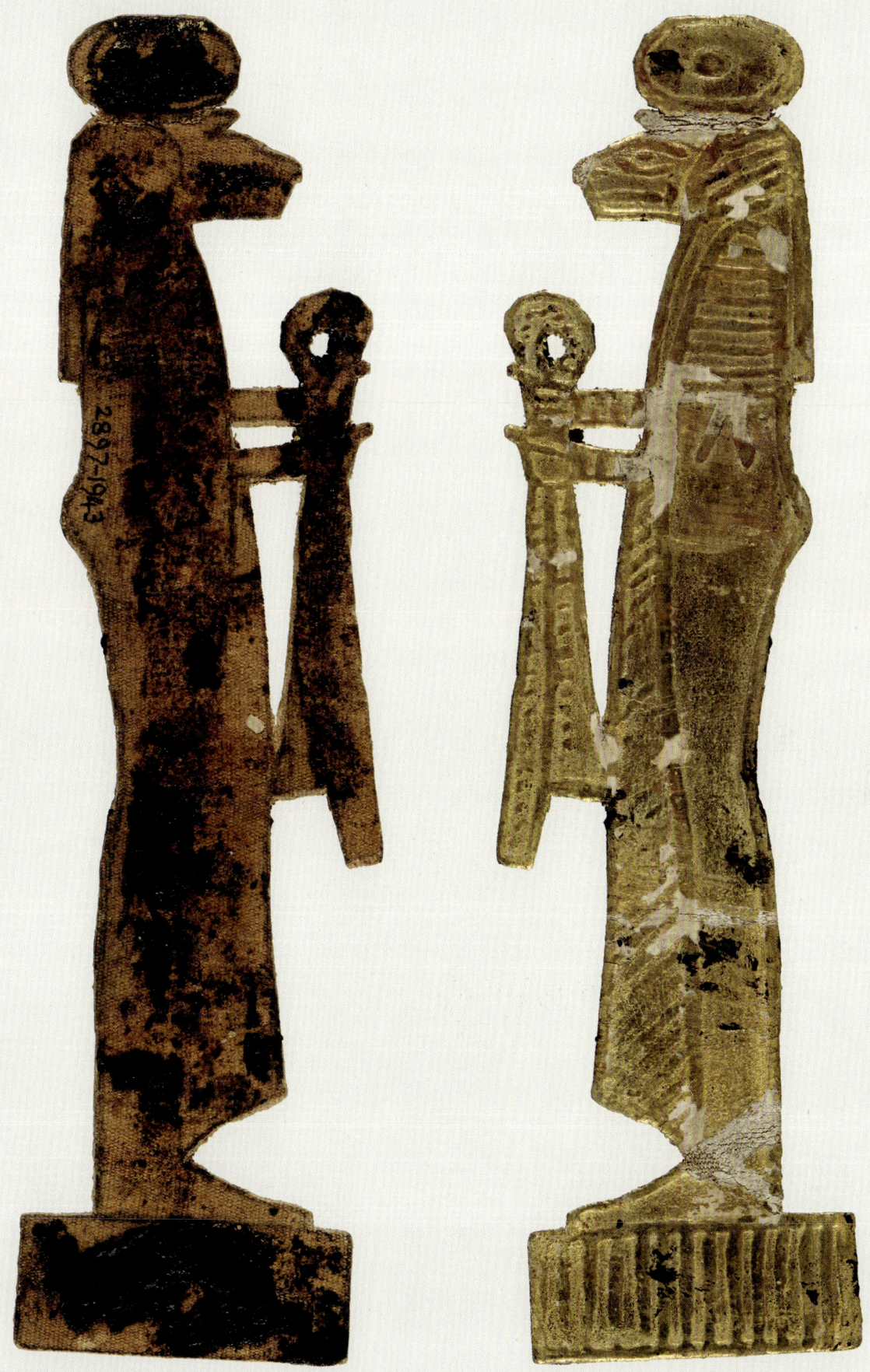

50

Head from a limestone sarcophagus

The shape of this head suggests that it came from a sarcophagus of the Thirtieth Dynasty or early Ptolemaic Period. A white calcite preparation layer was applied to the roughly finished exterior surface to even it out and prepare it for gilding. Gold leaf was applied across the flesh. Black eyebrows, and eye outlines and pupils are just visible. Egyptian blue was used for the wig, but there has been significant surface loss and subsequent restoration (probably carried out in the early twentieth century).

About 380–300 BC
Fitzwilliam Museum, E.27.1973
(given by the Suffolk Building Preservation Trust)
43.9 × 38 × 21.5 cm

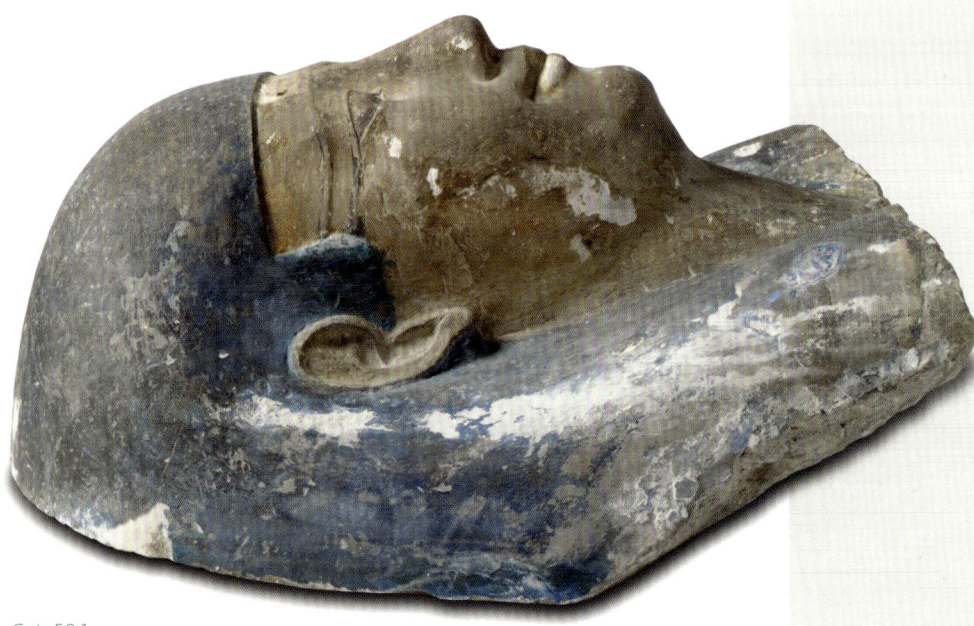

Cat. 50.1

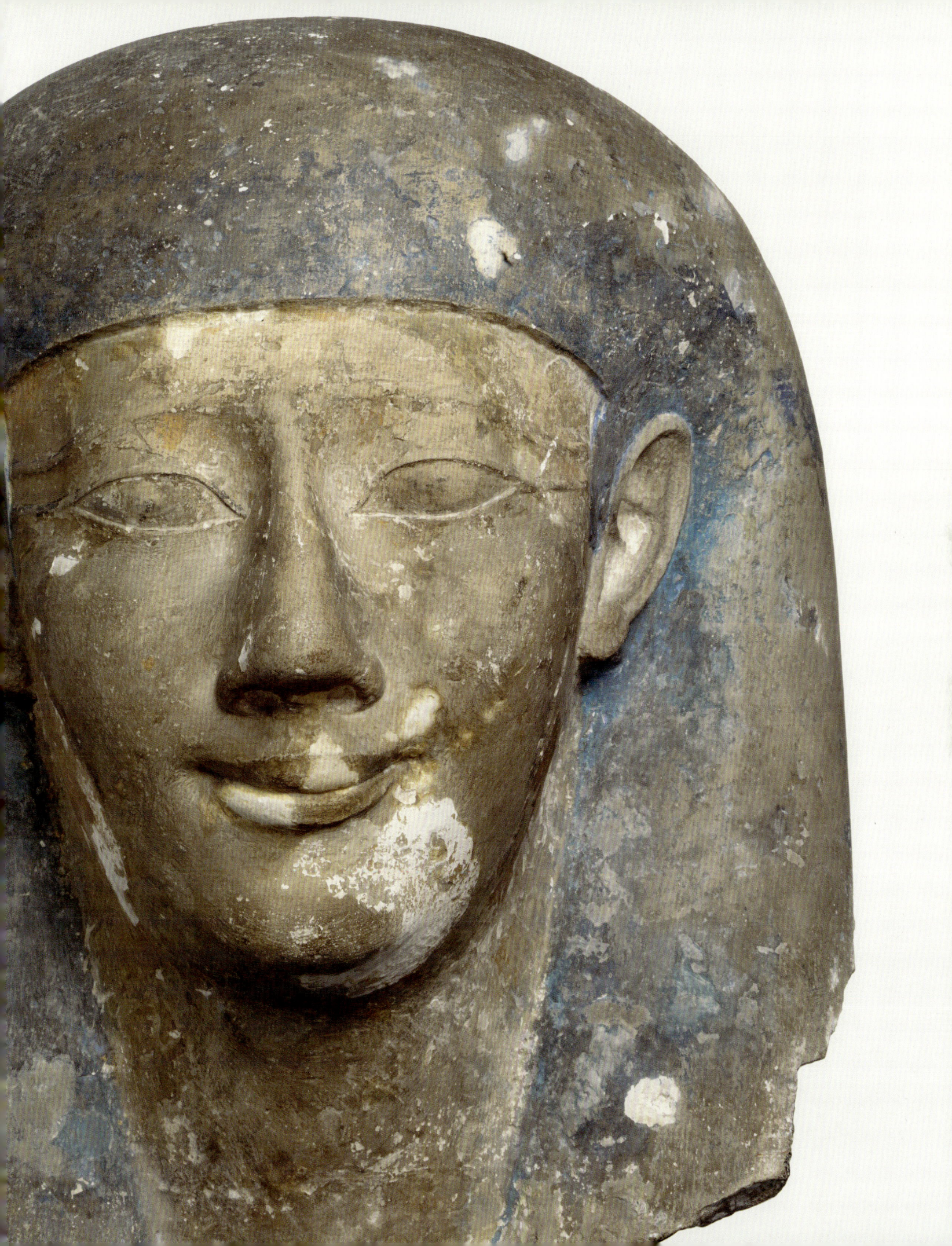

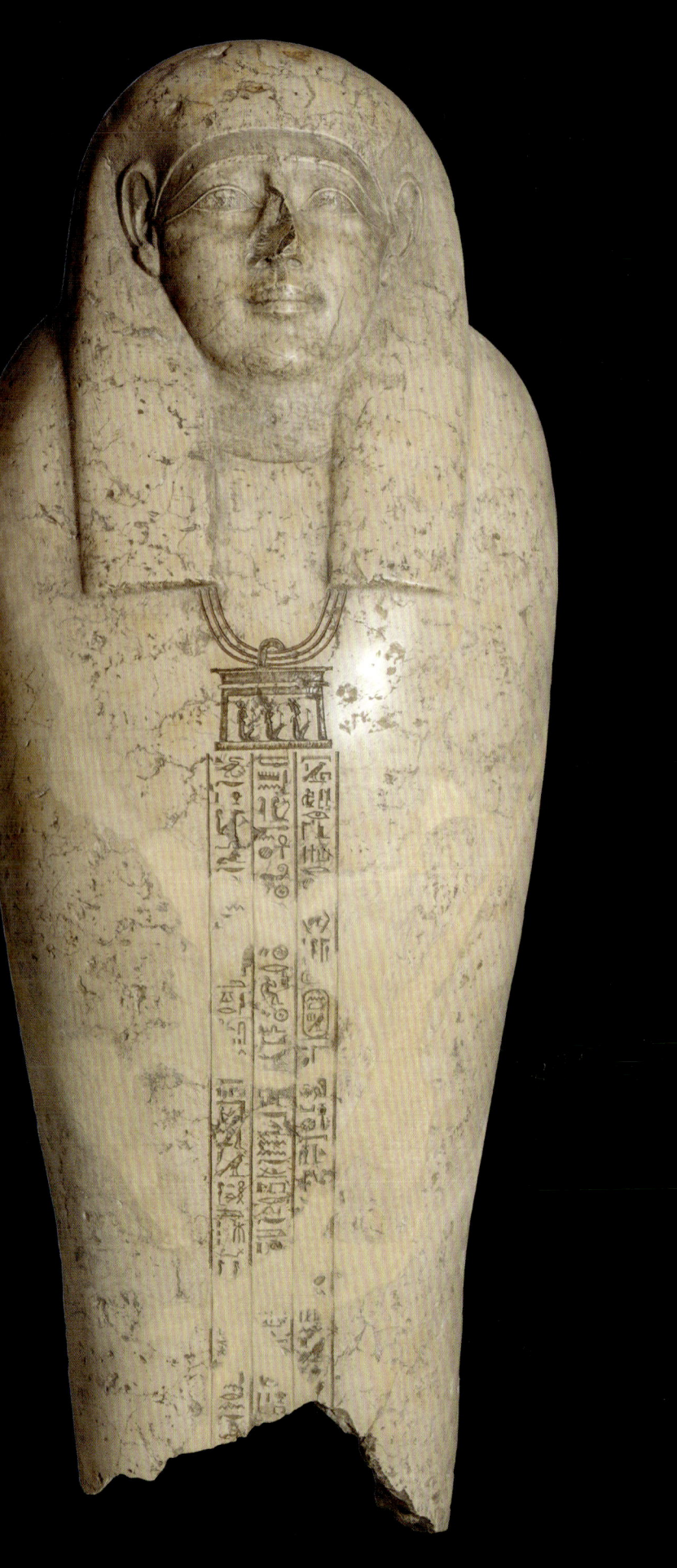

51

Ptolemaic sarcophagus lid

This lid, uncovered during excavations at Abydos, is part of the sarcophagus of a man whose name is lost, but who held many priestly titles. He was associated with royalty as 'overseer of the cool place of the king' and priest of the two statues of king Nectanebo II (360–342 BC). This king's statues continued to be venerated into the early Ptolemaic Period, so it is hard to pinpoint exactly when the owner was alive. The shape of the lid is typical of coffins around this time, with a large, flat head and a broad chest. Coffins had few inscriptions in this period.

The lid is made of highly polished limestone. The eyes are outlined in carbon-based black; the amulet and text column dividers are painted in red earth and the text in a copper-based green pigment. The paint was applied directly to the stone surface.

About 380–300 BC
Fitzwilliam Museum, E.48.1901 (gift of the Egypt Exploration Fund)
27 × 156 × 61 cm

52

Painted shroud

From about 1500 BC, a shroud, inscribed with spells from the Book of the Dead, was sometimes placed over a mummy in its coffin. The spells were later replaced by scenes of the dead person before various gods or sitting in front of an offering table, and, from about 1050 BC, by a large figure of Osiris. This motif continued until Roman times, when a portrait of the dead person might be painted on the shroud.

This shroud is made from a plain-weave linen, coated with a calcite-based preparation layer on which the portrait is executed in carbon-based black, red, brown and yellow earths, an organic pink lake pigment and two different copper-based greens.

AD 200–300
Fitzwilliam Museum, E.GA.5.1943
(given by R. G. Gayer-Anderson)
66 × 44 × 0.1 cm

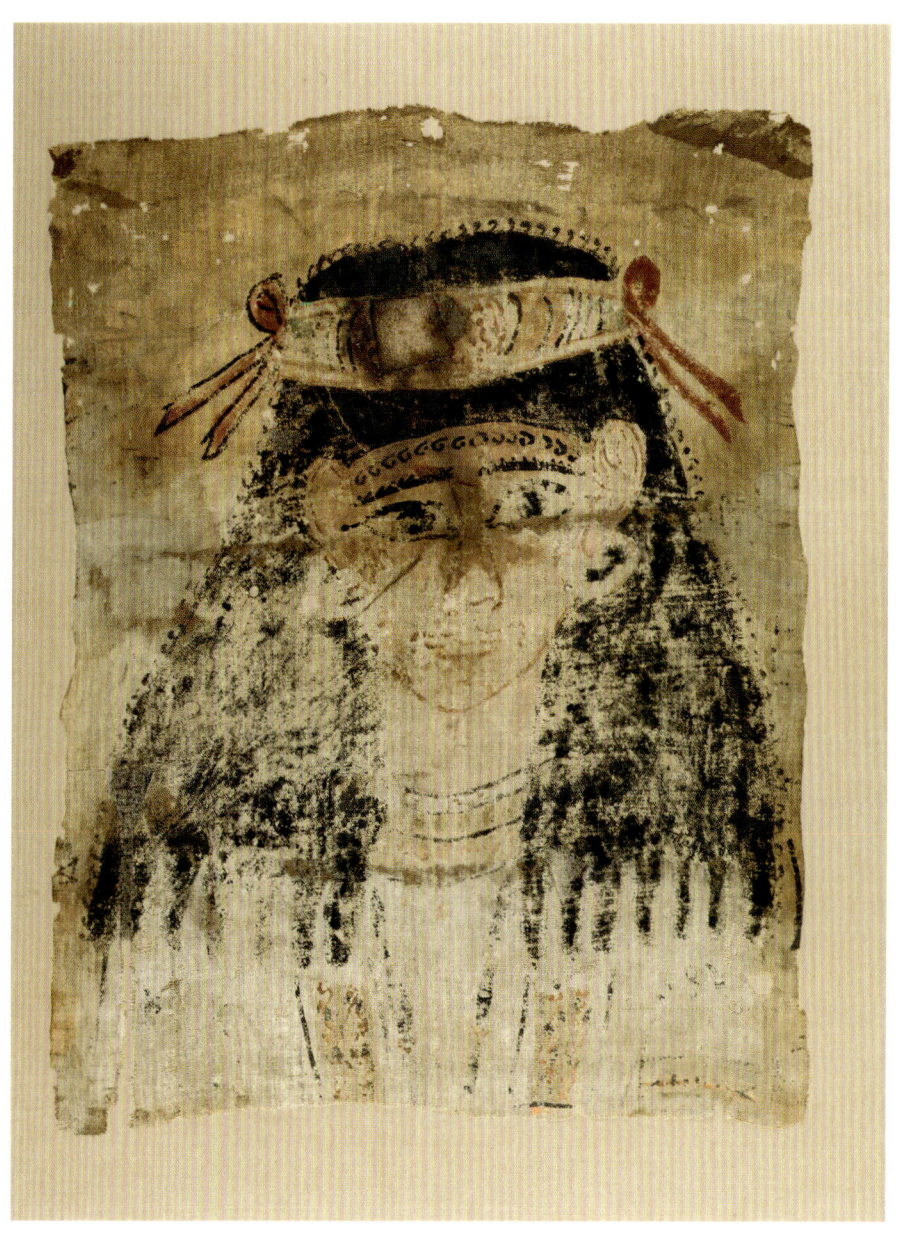

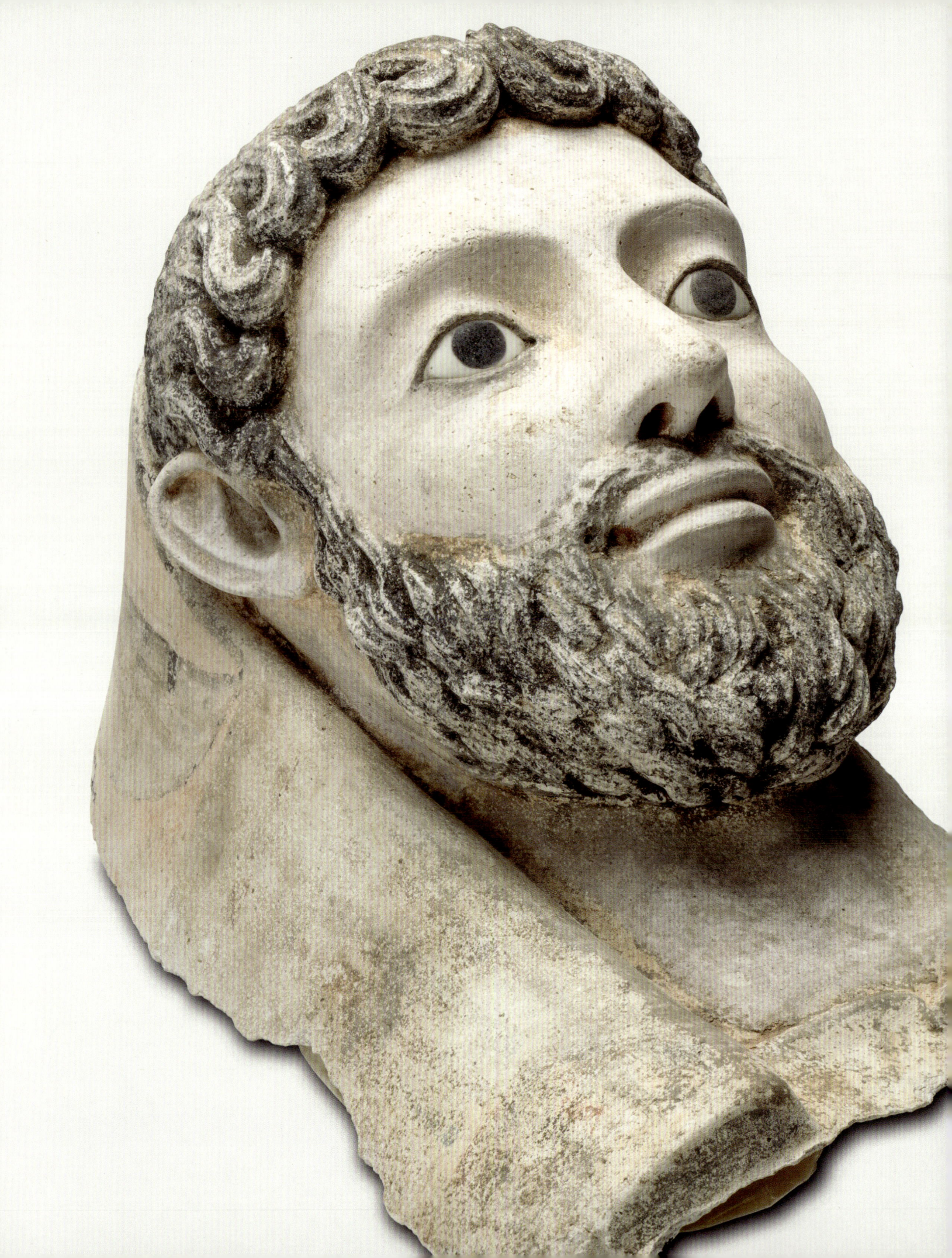

Cat. 53

53

Gypsum plaster mask from a Roman coffin

The plaster face, neck and ears of this mask were cast in moulds, then joined. The hair and beard were modelled separately and applied, giving an individual appearance to the head. The eyes are glass sheets. The mask was painted to give a naturalistic appearance and was set down onto a surround made of layers of plaster and linen placed over the head and shoulders of the mummy. Most of this fragile structure has been lost, but where it survives below the back of the head, faint traces of a painted design can be seen. Other masks from the same mould were apparently made in a workshop near Tuna el-Gebel.

About AD 150
Fitzwilliam Museum, E.3.1906
(uncertain provenance)
34 × 20.2 × 22.2 cm

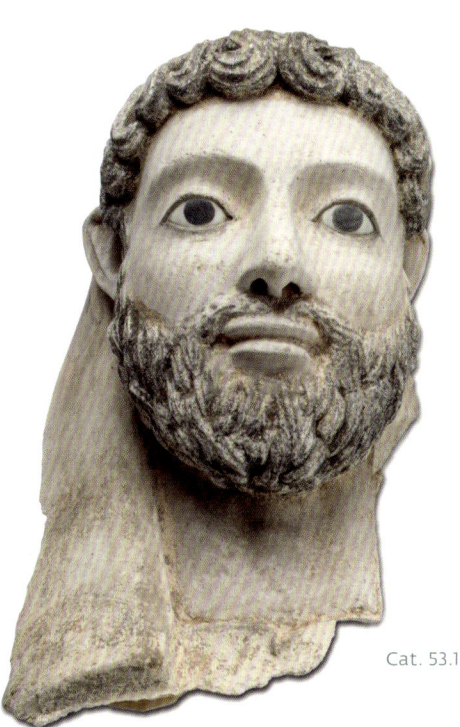

Cat. 53.1

54

Red shroud mummy

The shroud surrounding this mummy is effectively a coffin. The decoration consists of recognisable ancient Egyptian symbols, but there are no inscriptions anywhere to give us the name of the person inside. Instead, in a very un-Egyptian feature, a wooden portrait board provides the means of identifying the dead man.

CT scanning showed that the man was about 174 cm tall and probably in his early twenties, but did not reveal any obvious cause of death. The body is lying with the arms by the sides and hands on the upper thighs, the head pushed forward to rest on the chest. Disruptions to the spine and pelvic area suggest that the brain was removed through the back of the neck and other organs pulled out between the legs. There is considerable crushing and curvature of the spine, and the shoulders are dislocated. All this damage appears to be post-mortem, possibly due to tight wrapping exacerbated by the body's being in a state of decay when it was mummified. By the Roman period, the practice of mummification was in decline, with a greater reliance on large quantities of resin to preserve rather than careful drying and preparation of the body.

The mummy is supported on two narrow wooden planks, which are tied together with bandages (fig. 105). This structure and the mummy were wrapped together in a shroud made of a single piece of plain-weave linen, folded neatly over the feet but gathered more roughly at the top of the head and stuck in place. The shroud is painted in bright scarlet made from a mixture of red lead, chalk/calcite and carbon-based black, and applied in a beeswax medium. The decorative elements are outlined in grey paint (lead white, yellow ochre and carbon-based black in a wax and oil medium) and completed with purple paint (made from carbon-based black, iron oxide red, calcite and lead white), copper-based green frit, and gold leaf, with final detailing in black.

The portrait panel sits in an opening cut into the front of the shroud. The painting was executed in a beeswax medium, using a pigment palette similar to that found in the shroud decoration. The paint was applied with a brush along with a variety of tools to build up texture.

AD 100–150
Fitzwilliam Museum, E.63.1903
(given by the Egypt Exploration Fund)
162 × 34 × 25 cm

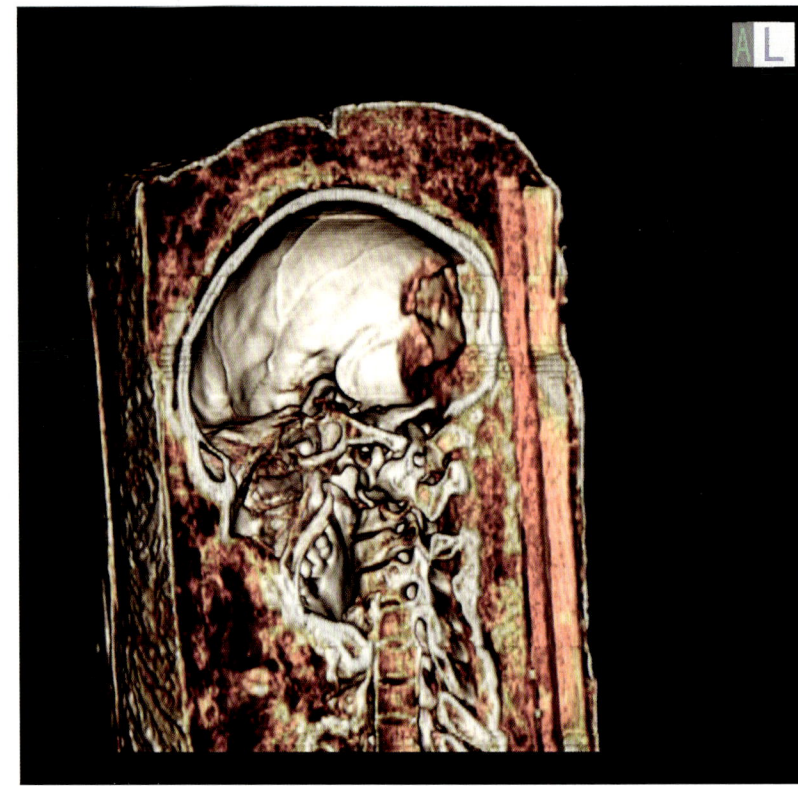

Fig. 105
Image from CT scanning, showing the thin portrait panel in front of the face of the mummy, whose head is pushed down, with disruptions to the vertebrae. Behind his neck, two planks can be seen within the linen wrappings.

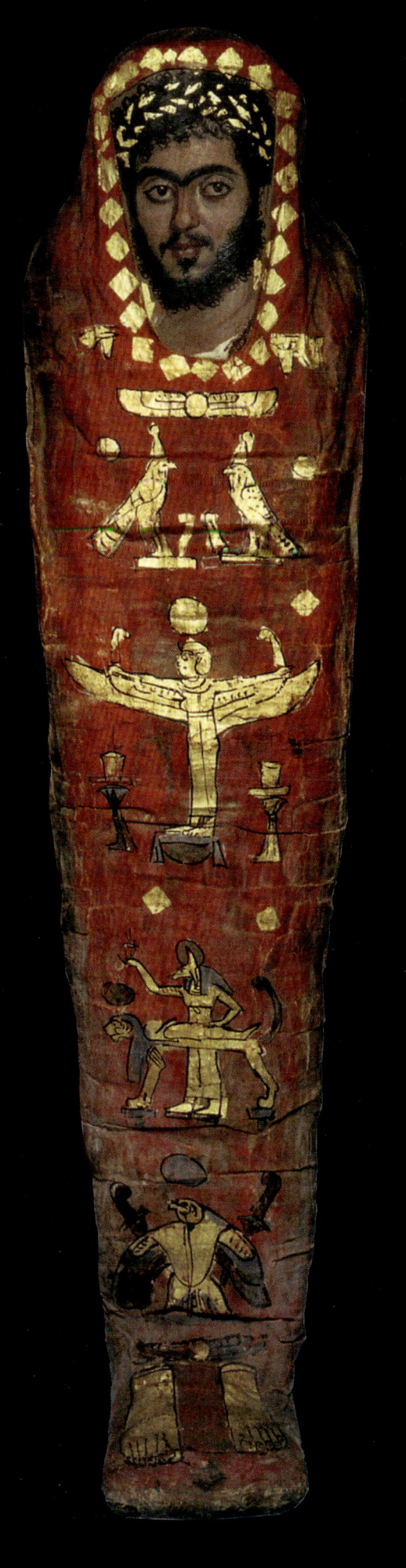

55

Gilded cartonnage Roman mask and footcase

This mask, found on a mummy of a man at Hawara in a room above the ground rather than in a tomb, was inserted into the mummy wrappings; it was originally held in place by linen straps (traces of which remain) threaded through holes punched in the edges. The cartonnage around the head is decorated with traditional funerary motifs. The footcase is decorated on the underside with two bound captives (cat. 55.b.1).

The manufacturing process for these elaborate objects is described briefly on page 94. In addition to the extensive use of gold leaf, decoration was created with both traditional pigments (earths, orpiment, carbon-based black, gypsum and calcite) and newer introductions (red lead, organo-copper greens, lead-white, deep blue indigo and bright pink madder). Although a similar palette of pigments was used on both objects, there is greater sophistication in manipulation, mixing and application on the mask to extend the range of colours and produce more subtle effects in the painting.

The eyes of the mask, now lost, were probably made of glass or stone, and were secured with gypsum plaster, fragments of which remain. X-radiography revealed intricate details beneath the crumpled cartonnage leaves on the forehead – a separately made wreath consisting of a hoop of vegetable fibre to which the leaves were tied, together with small plaster berries on vegetable fibre stalks (cat. 55.a.2 and fig. 106). In the centre of the hoop is a carnelian bead set in plaster.

About 30 BC–AD 100
Fitzwilliam Museum, E.103a.1911 and E.103b.1911 (given by the Egypt Exploration Fund)
Mask: 74 × 42 × 20 cm
Footcase: 14.5 × 24 × 25.3 cm

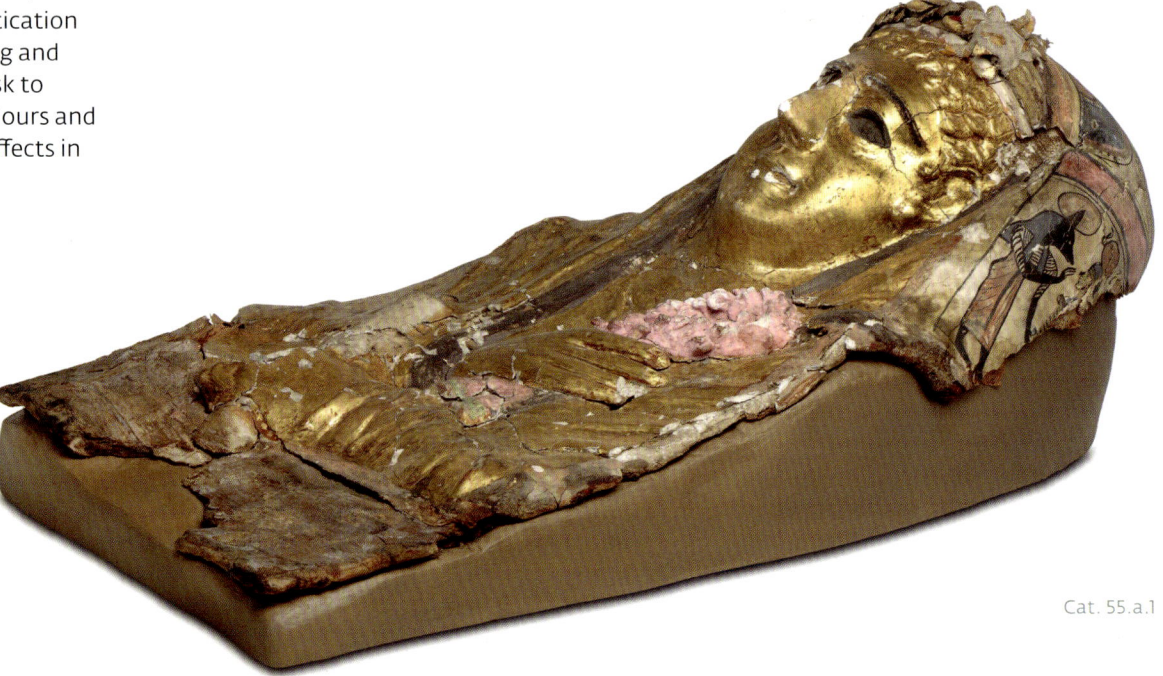

Cat. 55.a.1

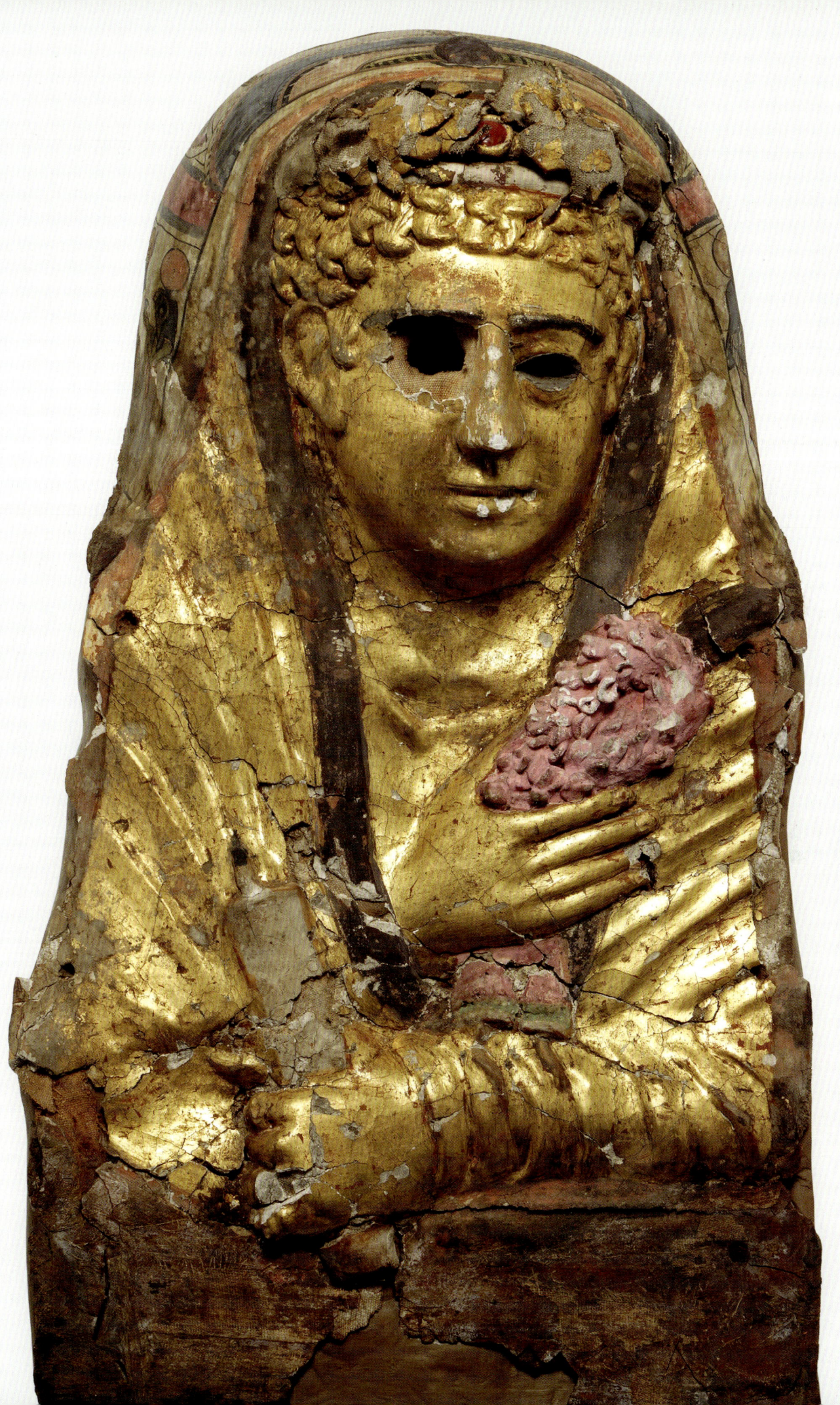

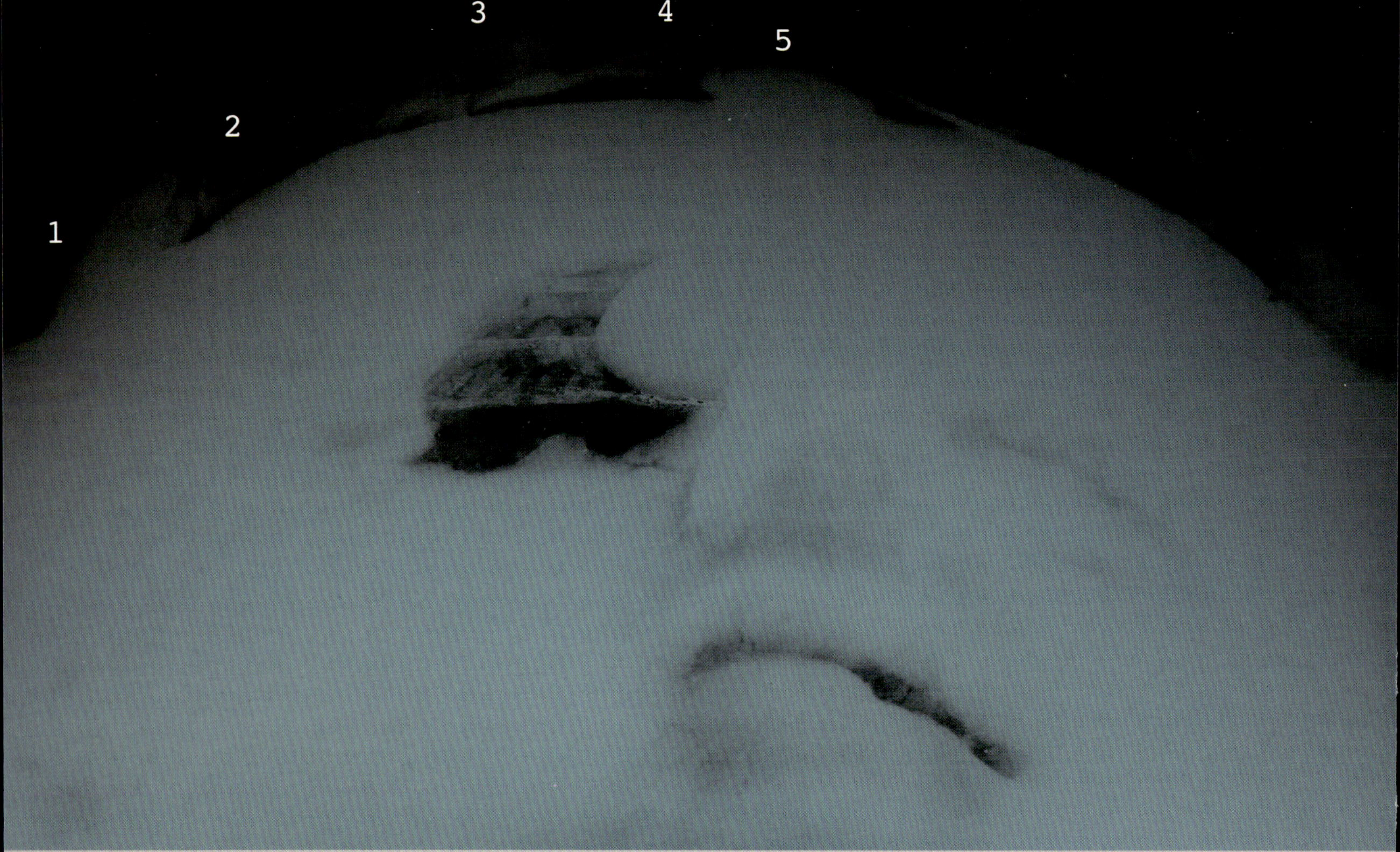

1 2 3 4 5

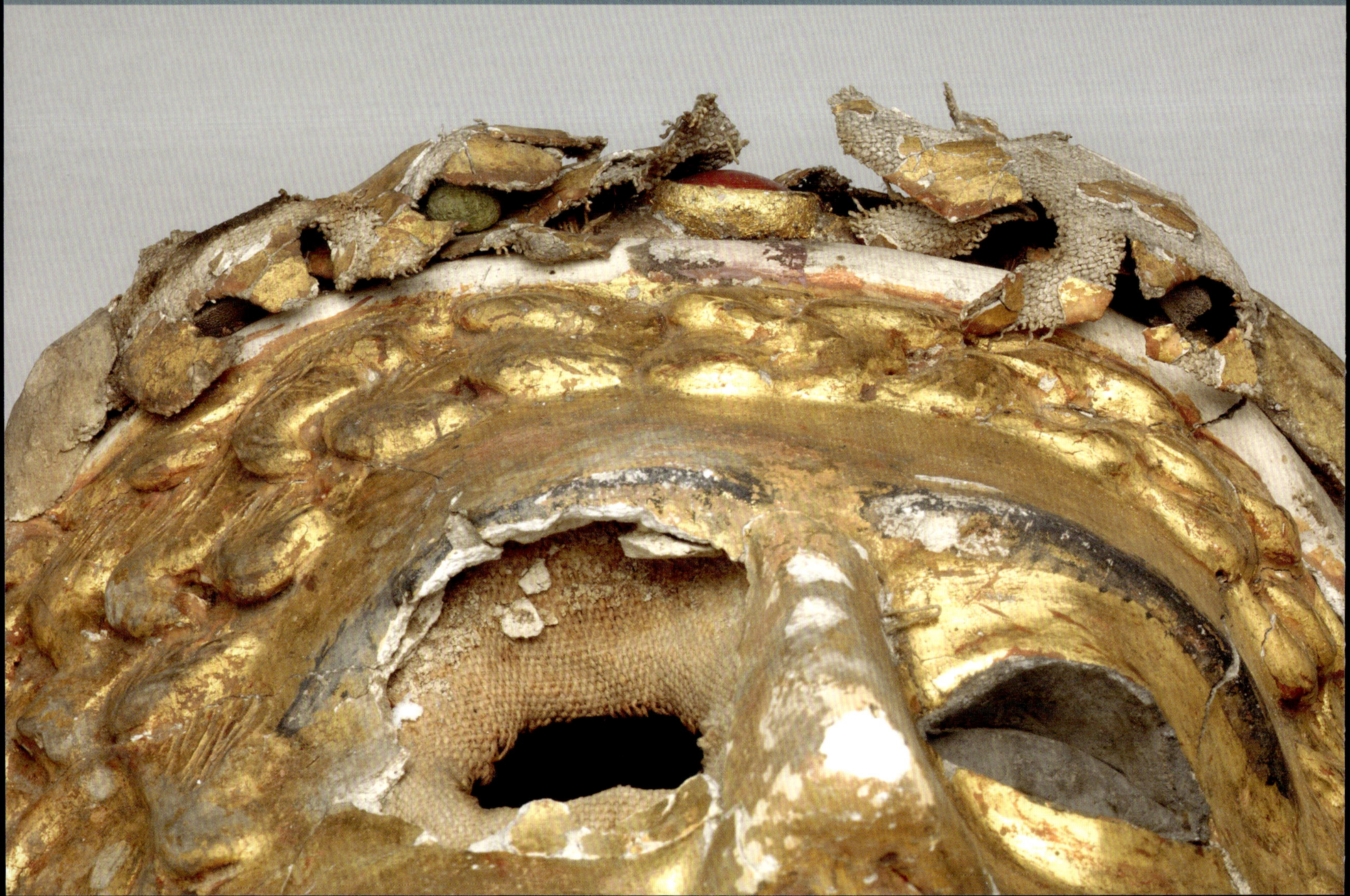

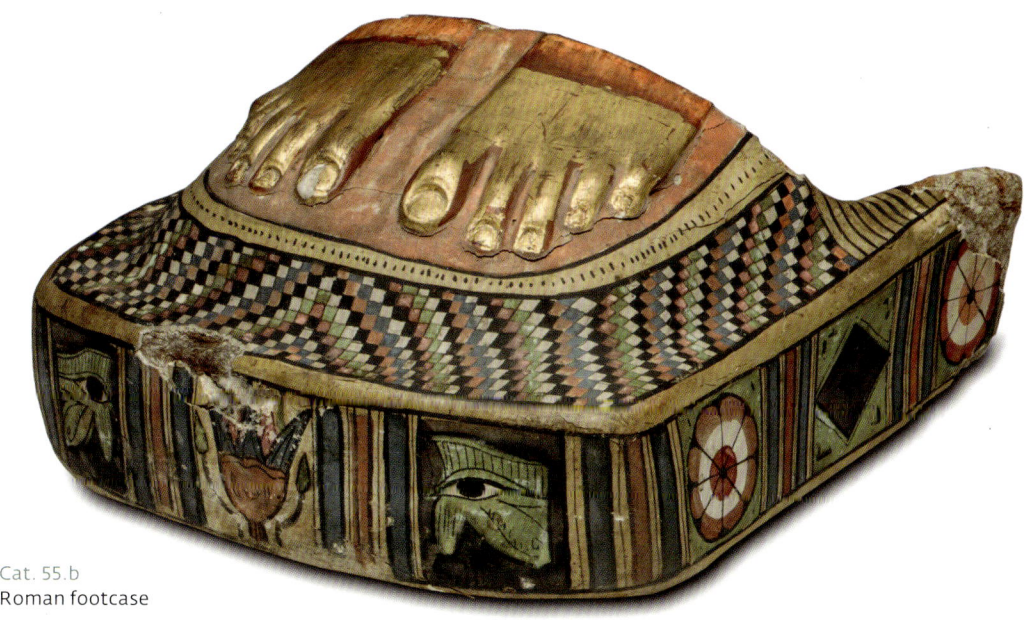

Cat. 55.b
Roman footcase

Cat. 55.b.1
Underside of the footcase. The two figures derive from a traditional ancient Egyptian motif of bound captives, usually shown under the feet of the king, demonstrating his power over his enemies.

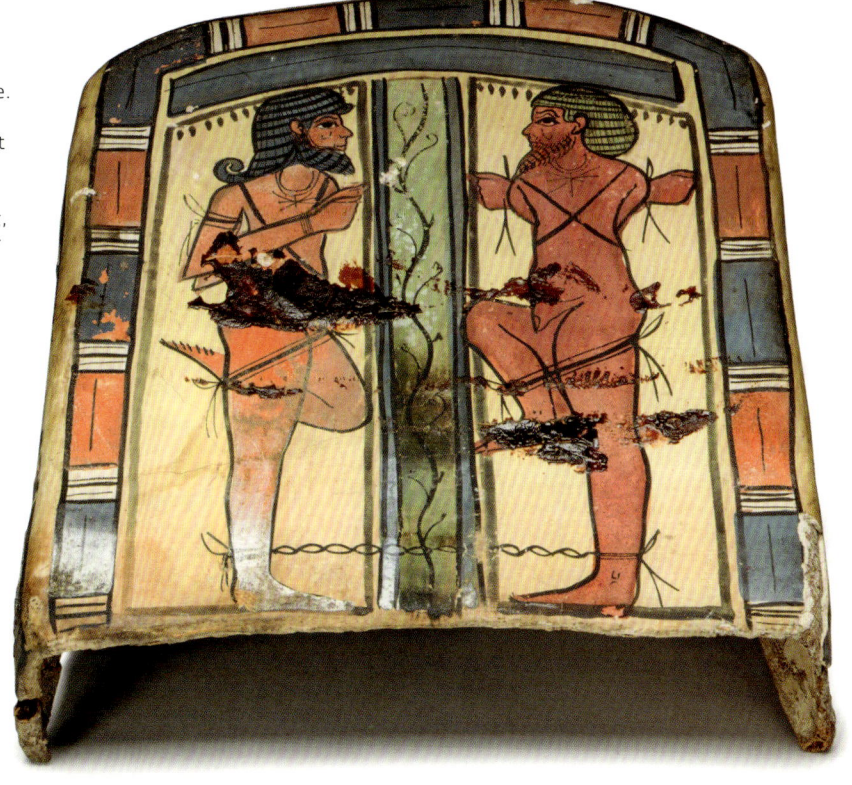

Fig. 106 (opposite top)
An X-radiograph showing details of the construction of the wreath (cat.55.a.2)

1. Paste anchor to hold the wreath in place
2. Fibre hoop onto which the stalks and gilded cartonnage leaves are tied
3. Green paste berry on stalk
4. Stalk on which only a fragment of berry survives
5. Carnelian bead

Cat. 55.a.2 (opposite bottom)
The wreath on the forehead of the mask

Catalogue 245

Fig. 107

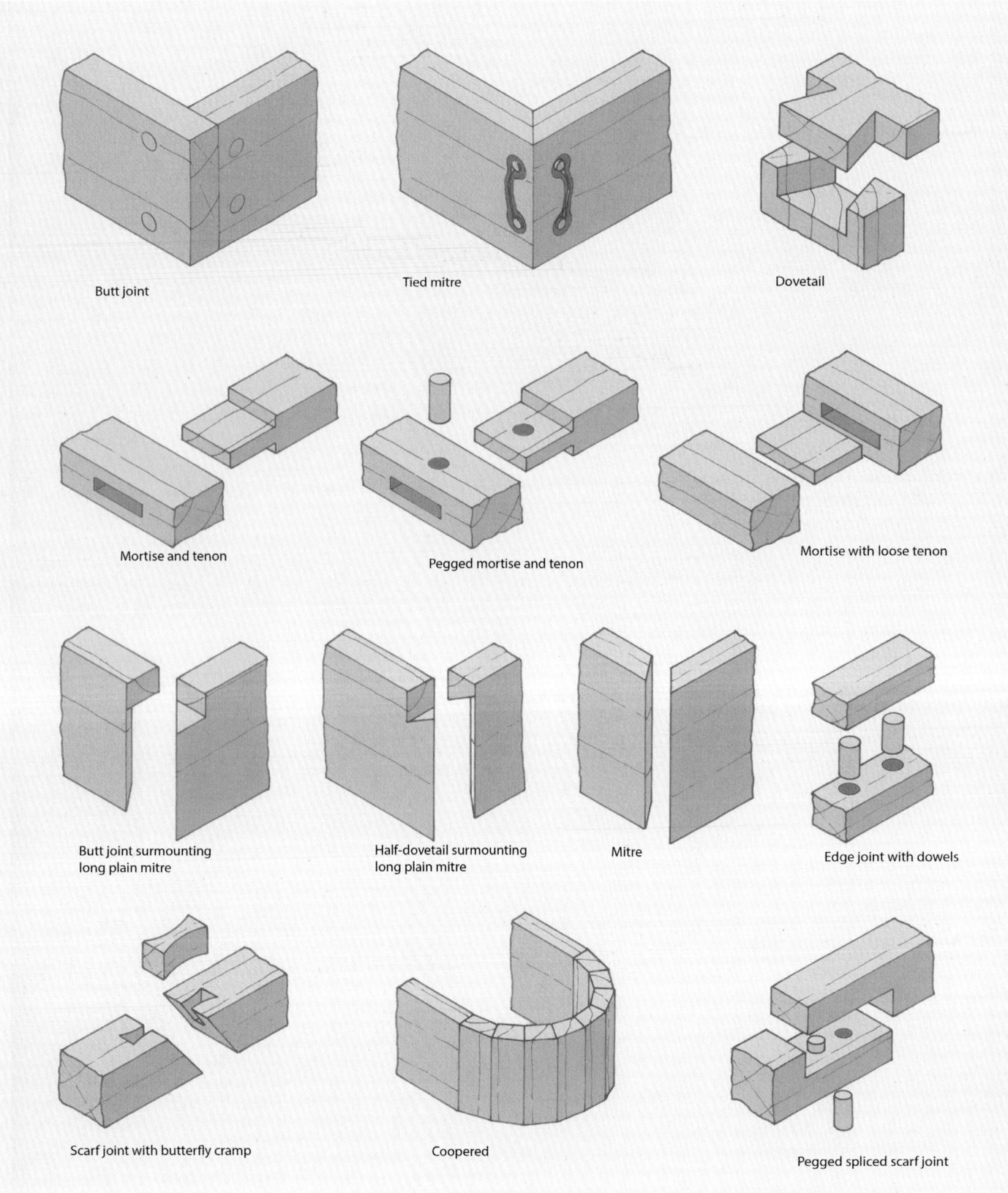

Glossary

Wood working

Joints

Joints mentioned in the text are shown in fig. 107.

Tangential sawing Also known as through-and-through or slash sawing. The trunk or log is sawn down its long axis. Timber cut this way can be recognised by the slash-grain pattern on the planks. It is the most economical way to cut up timber, but the planks are prone to 'cup' because the wood dries and shrinks unevenly across the width of the plank.

Coffin components

Coffin box The part of the coffin in which the body was placed. The term is used here for both rectangular box coffins and anthropoid coffins.

Coffin lid The part of the coffin that was placed on top of the box. In an anthropoid coffin, this would be the part that resembles the front of the head and body of the person.

Coffin base The bottom (long axis) of the coffin box.

Footboard The short panel at the foot end of the coffin box and lid.

Materials

Cartonnage A laminated material constructed of layers of linen or papyrus soaked in glue, with a layer of paste on the internal and on the external surface. For information on how cartonnage was used to make coffins, see pages 92–94.

Papyrus A writing material made from the inner pith of papyrus plant (*Cyperus papyrus*) stems. The term (plural: **papyri**) is used also to describe documents made from this material.

Faience A term that has been used to describe a range of glazed composition materials, but is usually defined as a shaped core made of crushed quartz or sand mixed with small quantities of lime and natron or plant ash, coated with a glaze and fired in a kiln. The glazes usually contain copper, which gives the faience a blue-green colour.

Frit A name commonly applied to Egyptian glassy materials. Frit has the same composition and structure all the way through the material (as opposed to the distinct core and glaze layer of faience). The pigment Egyptian blue is a frit. If it were ground up, mixed to a paste with water, then shaped and refired, an object made of blue frit (e.g., an amulet) could be produced.

Paste In describing Egyptian objects, the term 'plaster' is often used rather loosely to cover both true plasters (made from lime or gypsum cements) and pastes made from a binder (such as animal glue) mixed with calcium sulphate (creating a material often called gesso) or with calcium carbonate (creating a material often called whiting). To avoid confusion and to address the fact that sometimes mixtures of all these materials can be present, together with clay minerals and vegetable fibres, the term 'paste' is used throughout this catalogue as it implies no particular chemistry or technology.

Preparation layer A layer of paste applied across the coffin to provide a smooth, neutral surface to which paint can be applied. Sometimes known as a 'ground' layer.

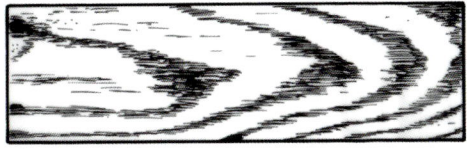

Slash-grain pattern typical of tangential sawing

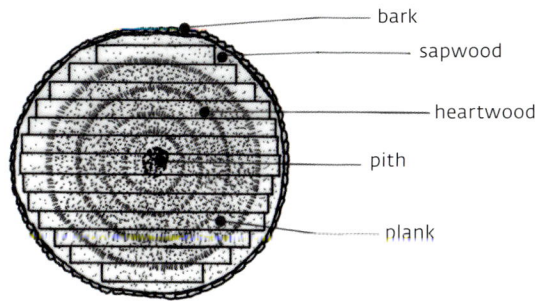

Fig. 108
Diagram showing how planks are cut from a trunk by tangential sawing

Egyptian painting materials
A quick guide to the principal pigments mentioned in the catalogue

When it has not been possible to characterise pigments fully, their elemental make up has been recorded in the catalogue entries: for example, 'calcium-based' or 'copper-based'.

Egyptian blue and **Egyptian green** Manufactured pigments, prepared by firing copper minerals or metal with a calcium compound (like powdered limestone), silica and soda at high temperature. The principal colour component in Egyptian blue is calcium copper tetrasilicate ($CaCuSi_4O_{10}$), and in Egyptian green is cuprowollastonite ($CaSiO_3$ with copper in the structure).

Malachite ($Cu_2CO_3(OH)_2$) A mineral pigment, giving a pale green colour.

Chrysocolla ($Cu_2H_2Si_2O_5(OH)_4$) A mineral pigment with a turquoise blue colour.

Copper-wax, copper-proteinate, copper carbohydrate Green pigments produced from the reaction of copper salts with various organic media.

Verdigris (copper acetate) A copper salt that can be manufactured or found as a corrosion product. Produces a bright green colour.

Earths An umbrella term used to describe a range of pigments derived from naturally occurring deposits containing clay minerals, iron oxides and manganese oxides. They can be found in a range of shades depending on the purity and specific chemical structure of the natural sources, and can include red, yellow, orange and green pigments. The term 'earth' may be confused with ochre, which is a member of the earth pigments group, consisting of earths rich in iron oxide and iron hydroxide. Earths on ancient Egyptian objects may contain one or more of the following:

- **Yellow earths** The iron sulphates jarosite/natrojarosite $KFe_3(OH)_6(SO_4)_2$/$NaFe_3(SO_4)2(OH)_6$, and the iron oxides goethite α-FeO·OH and limonite $FeO(OH)·nH_2O$.

- **Red earths** The iron oxides haematite (Fe_2O_3) and ilmenite ($FeTiO_3$).

- **Green earths** Celadonite and glauconite (iron magnesium silicates belonging to the mica group).

As these pigments arise from naturally occurring deposits, they often occur as a mixture and are not always easily classifiable. Where it has been possible to further identify particular pigments, this has been indicated.

Calcite ($CaCO_3$) Calcium carbonate, a white mineral

- **Micritic calcite** Microscopy term to describe calcite visible as very fine particles, usually originating from **chalk**.

- **Sparitic calcite** Microscopy term to describe calcite that forms into crystals, usually suggesting **limestone** origin.

Huntite ($Mg_3Ca(CO_3)_4$) Magnesium calcium carbonate, a bright white mineral.

Gyspum ($CaSO_4·2H_2O$) Calcium sulphate, a white mineral

- **Bassanite** ($CaSO_4·½H_2O$) Made from roasting gypsum at high temperatures, sometimes found naturally. Modern equivalent is plaster of Paris.

- **Anhydrite** ($CaSO_4$) Completely dehydrated version of gypsum sometimes found naturally, or produced by heating above 200°C (392°F).

Lead white ($PbCO_3Pb(OH)_2$) A lead carbonate, an opaque white pigment produced from the reaction of acid and lead.

Red lead (Pb_3O_4) Lead tetroxide, a bright orange-red pigment that can be a by-product of silver refining.

Cinnabar (HgS) Mercury sulphide, a vivid red mineral pigment.

Orpiment (As_2S_3) Arsenic sulphide, a lemon yellow mineral pigment.

Realgar/pararealgar (As_4S_4) Arsenic sulphide (but different crystal structures), orange mineral pigments. Pararealgar is a degradation product of realgar.

Carbon-based black A group of pigments made mainly of carbon. In Egypt, these are principally soot and charcoal.

Lake pigments Also known as dyestuffs, these are organic pigments that can be made from certain insect or plant matter. The colour is extracted and precipitated onto a metallic salt substrate. Lake pigments found on Egyptian objects include:

- **Madder** Pink dyestuff made from the root of the madder plant *Rubia tinctorum* fixed on a mineral base such as aluminium sulphate.

- **Indigo** Blue dyestuff from plants of the *Indigofera* species fixed on a mineral base.

Imaging and analytical techniques

All the techniques described here are based on examining the interaction of the materials of an object with radiation from various parts of the electromagnetic spectrum (see fig. 109) and recording the results.

The following techniques can be carried out directly on the object: VIL, UV fluorescence, IR reflectography, FORS, XRF, X-radiography and CT scanning.

In contrast, these techniques require a small sample to be removed from the object: PLM, cross-section analysis, SEM-EDX, XRD, Raman spectroscopy, FTIR, GC-MS and wood identification.

Fig. 109
Electromagnetic spectrum

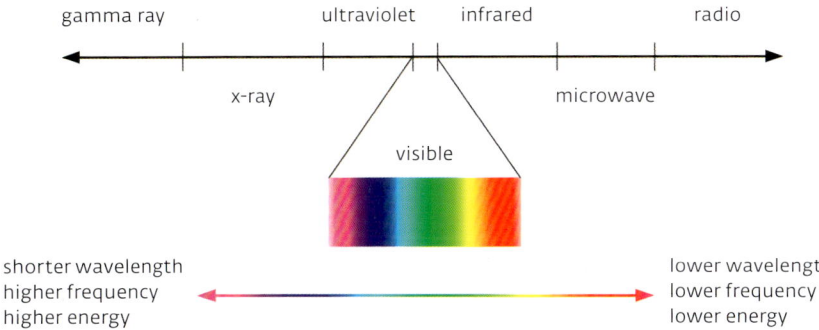

Visible-light induced luminescence (VIL) photography

Egyptian blue pigment emits particular bands of infrared radiation when lit with visible light. VIL photography captures this emission using a sensitive camera filtered to let only those bands of infrared light through. All the Egyptian blue (even minute particles) shows up as bright white on the photograph (fig. 110), enabling detection of lost areas of decoration or traces of inscription.

Fig. 110
Cartonnage fragment (cat. 6) in visible light with a VIL image showing areas of Egyptian blue

Ultraviolet (UV) fluorescence

When subjected to ultraviolet radiation, some materials emit (fluoresce) visible light in characteristic colours. For example, under UV light, pistacia resin varnish fluoresces greenish-yellow and the pink pigment madder fluoresces bright orange. This technique clarifies where these materials are located on the object (see frontispiece) and and also can show up areas of restoration over an original surface (fig. 111).

Fig. 111
Detail from the coffin of Userhet (cat. 20) in visible light and photographed under UV light. The UV fluorescence image shows areas of restoration paint (which appear brown) over the original white paint.

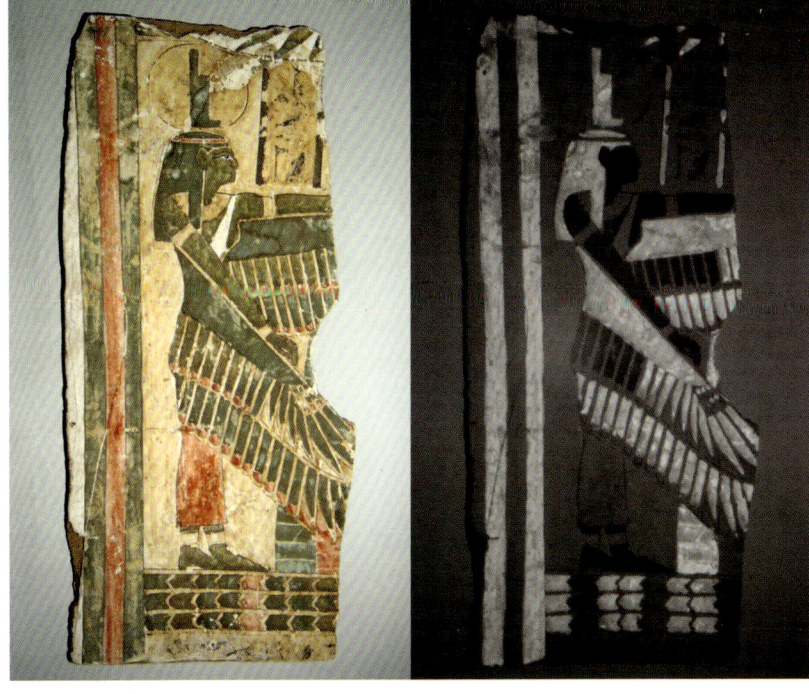

Infrared (IR) reflectography

Infrared radiation is absorbed by certain painting and drawing materials, especially carbon-based black pigments. This type of radiation can penetrate through paint layers and can be captured photographically with a camera sensitive to infrared radiation. Underdrawings executed in carbon-based black show up as black on the image, even when not visible on the surface. It is possible, therefore, to see where they have been used in early drawing stages of the decoration (cat. 21; fig. 93, pp. 170-171).

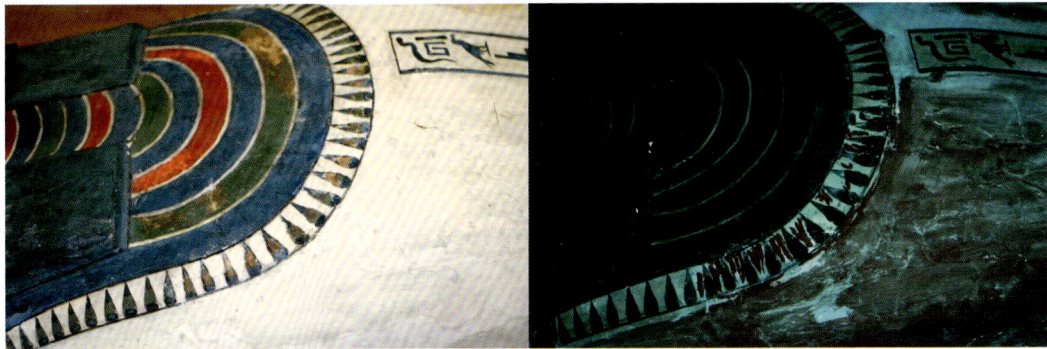

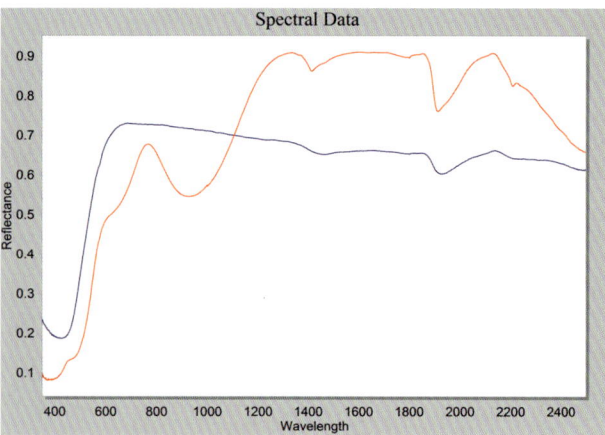

Fig. 112
FORS spectra: yellow earth (red line) and orpiment (blue line).

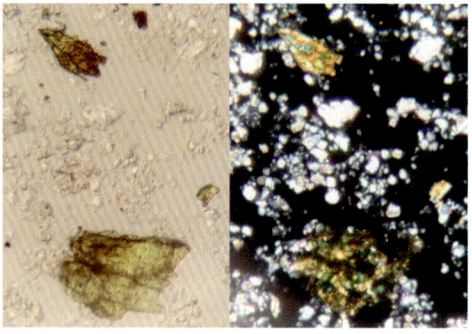

Fig. 113
PLM sample showing orpiment particles. Left: in plane polarised light; right: in cross polarised light.

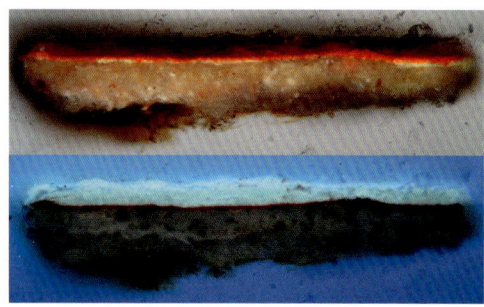

Fig. 114
Cross-section from Nespawershefyt's mummy board (cat. 26) shown in visible light (above) and in ultraviolet (below). The images reveal (from the bottom up) a complicated preparation layer, thin yellow paint, red paint and varnish layer. The pale fluorescence in UV light shows a natural resin varnish in the top layer.

UV-VIS-NIR fibre optic reflectance spectroscopy (FORS) This method measures colour: the paint is illuminated with radiation from the ultraviolet, visible, and near-infrared regions of the electromagnetic spectrum. The light reflected off the surface is captured and the spectrum recorded by a computer. Many pigments produce spectra with key features that are specific to them, allowing the material to be identified through comparison with reference spectra (fig. 112).

X-Ray fluorescence spectrometry (XRF) A small area of the object is bombarded with X-rays. These X-rays excite atoms within the material, causing them to emit secondary X-rays. The energies of these secondary X-rays (fluorescence) are characteristic of the elements present, such as iron or calcium. This is a quick, sensitive method for starting to identify inorganic pigments containing heavy elements (e.g. orpiment, which contains arsenic).

X-radiography X-ray radiation penetrates through matter: the denser a material is, the more difficult it is for the X-rays to penetrate. A sheet of film is placed under the object and records the relative intensity of the X-rays that emerge after they have passed through the object. An X-radiograph shows the internal structure of the object and clarifies the assembly of a coffin (fig. 98, p. 190).

Computed tomography (CT) imaging Conventional X-radiography provides a two-dimensional image of the interior of the object. CT, sometimes known as CAT scanning, is similar to standard X-radiography, but in this technique the data is collected simultaneously in different planes, producing cross-section slices (like the slices in a loaf of bread). Each slice can be examined individually and three-dimensional images of the object can be produced, providing a wealth of detail about internal structure (see fig 96.a, p. 186 and fig. 105, p. 240).

Polarised light microscopy (PLM) A tiny sample of pigment, taken from the coffin surface, is mounted in resin on a microscope slide. Light is passed through the particles, which are viewed down the optical microscope to record features such as size and shape. The use of polarising filters causes the particles to interact with light in different states. All these features can be diagnostic of specific pigments (fig. 113).

Cross-section analysis A minute fragment from the painted surface is embedded in resin, ground and polished. This cross section is viewed in reflected light under an optical microscope. It can reveal information about the materials and techniques used by the artist and show up later restorations (fig. 114).

Scanning electron microscopy–energy-dispersive X-ray spectroscopy (SEM/EDX) A powerful microscope irradiates a sample with a beam of electrons. These particles scatter on the surface and produce a high-magnification image of the sample. The electron beam also causes X-rays to be generated by the elements in the sample. When used on a cross section, this technique can show where inorganic pigments with heavy elements are located within a layer structure.

X-Ray powder diffraction (XRD) When a tiny powdered sample of paint is bombarded with X-rays, the shape of the crystal structure causes the X-rays to change direction and intensity in distinctive patterns. These patterns can help identify pigments and pastes, and can differentiate between materials with similar chemical compositions but different structures (e.g., orpiment and realgar, both made of arsenic and sulphur but with different structures).

Picture Credits

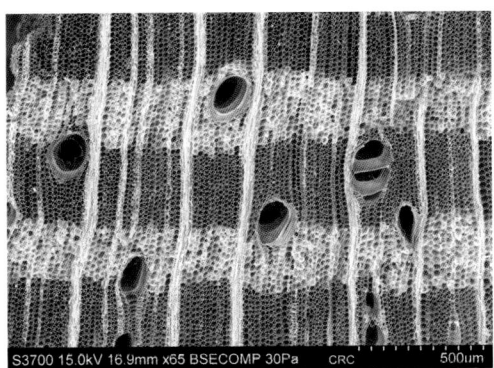

Fig. 115
Scanning electron microscope (SEM) image of a transverse section of Ficus sycomorus (*sycomore* fig) wood

Raman spectroscopy A tiny sample is subjected to a laser beam (wavelengths in the UV, visible or near-infrared parts of the electromagnetic spectrum). The resulting vibration of chemical bonds in the molecules gives information about their structure. It can identify materials and differentiate between certain molecules with similar chemical compositions but different structures.

Fourier transform infrared spectroscopy (FTIR) Molecules in a sample all absorb infrared radiation at specific wavelengths. By measuring the energy absorbed by the movement of the bonds in the molecules, it is possible to identify the class of organic material present (e.g., a plant gum as opposed to a tree resin or animal glue). FTIR can distinguish between organic materials found in the binding media or varnish and identify certain pigments (such as calcite, indigo and lead white) which absorb energy in the infrared.

Gas chromatography–mass spectrometry (GC-MS) Gas chromatography separates out the individual molecules in a complex mixture. Then each of the individual molecular components is identified by mass spectrometry. The technique distinguishes between different species of organic material in the paint binding media or varnish layers: for example, determining whether a natural resin varnish is a pistacia or conifer resin.

Wood identification Tiny samples of ancient Egyptian wood are sectioned to reveal details of the cellular wood anatomy needed for scientific identifications. Transverse, radial longitudinal and tangential longitudinal sections are then examined under high magnifications using the optical microscope in reflected light mode as well as the variable pressure **scanning electron microscope** (fig. 115). Reference specimens and wood anatomy databases are used for comparison.

Director's foreword: © Sandro Vannini/Corbis
Fig. 4: Garstang Archive, University of Liverpool
Figs 14 and 15: Gustave Jéquier, *Tombeaux de particuliers, contemporains de Pepi II* (Cairo 1929), pl. VI and fig. 69 on p. 61
Fig. 16: Cecil M. Firth, Battiscombe Gunn, *Excavations at Saqqara: Teti Pyramid Cemeteries* (Cairo 1926), vol. 2, p. 80
Fig. 17: Garstang Archive, University of Liverpool
Fig. 20: Richard Lepsius, *Denkmäler aus Ägypten und Äthiopien*, (Berlin 1849–59), vol. 2, pl. 147b
Fig. 21: © The Trustees of the British Museum
Fig. 22: © The Trustees of the British Museum
Fig. 23: © The Trustees of the British Museum
Fig. 24: © The Trustees of the British Museum
Fig. 25: © The Trustees of the British Museum
Fig. 28: J. E. Gautier, Gustave Jéquier, *Mémoire sur les fouilles de Licht* (Cairo 1902), pl. XXVII
Fig. 33: © The Trustees of the British Museum
Fig. 34: © The Trustees of the British Museum
Fig. 35: © Gianni Dagli Orti/Corbis
Fig. 36: © The Trustees of the British Museum
Fig. 37: The Metropolitan Museum of Art/Art Resource/Scala, Florence. 2015 © Photo SCALA, Florence.
Fig. 40: © The Trustees of the British Museum
Fig. 41: © The Trustees of the British Museum
Fig. 42: © The Trustees of the British Museum
Fig. 44: © The Trustees of the British Museum
Fig. 45: © The Trustees of the British Museum
Fig. 50: © Gianni Dagli Orti/Corbis
Fig. 62: © The Trustees of the British Museum
Fig. 64: © The Trustees of the British Museum
Fig. 68: © The Trustees of the British Museum
Fig. 71: Garstang Archive, University of Liverpool
Fig. 85: © 2016 Museum of Fine Arts, Boston
Fig. 87: © 2016 Museum of Fine Arts, Boston
Fig. 89: © The Metropolitan Museum of Art
Fig. 91: Photograph courtesy of the University of Liverpool
Fig. 92: © The Trustees of the British Museum
Cats 22 and 22.1: Photo © RMN-Grand Palais (Musée du Louvre) / Les frères Chuzeville
Cat. 24: © The Trustees of the British Museum
Cat. 25: © The Trustees of the British Museum
Cat. 47: © The Trustees of the British Museum
Fig. 100: © The Ashmolean Museum
Fig. 102: Geoffrey Killen
Fig. 103: Geoffrey Killen
Fig. 115: Image: C. R. Cartwright, © The British Museum
All other images copyright © The Fitzwilliam Museum, Cambridge.

MAP AND DATES

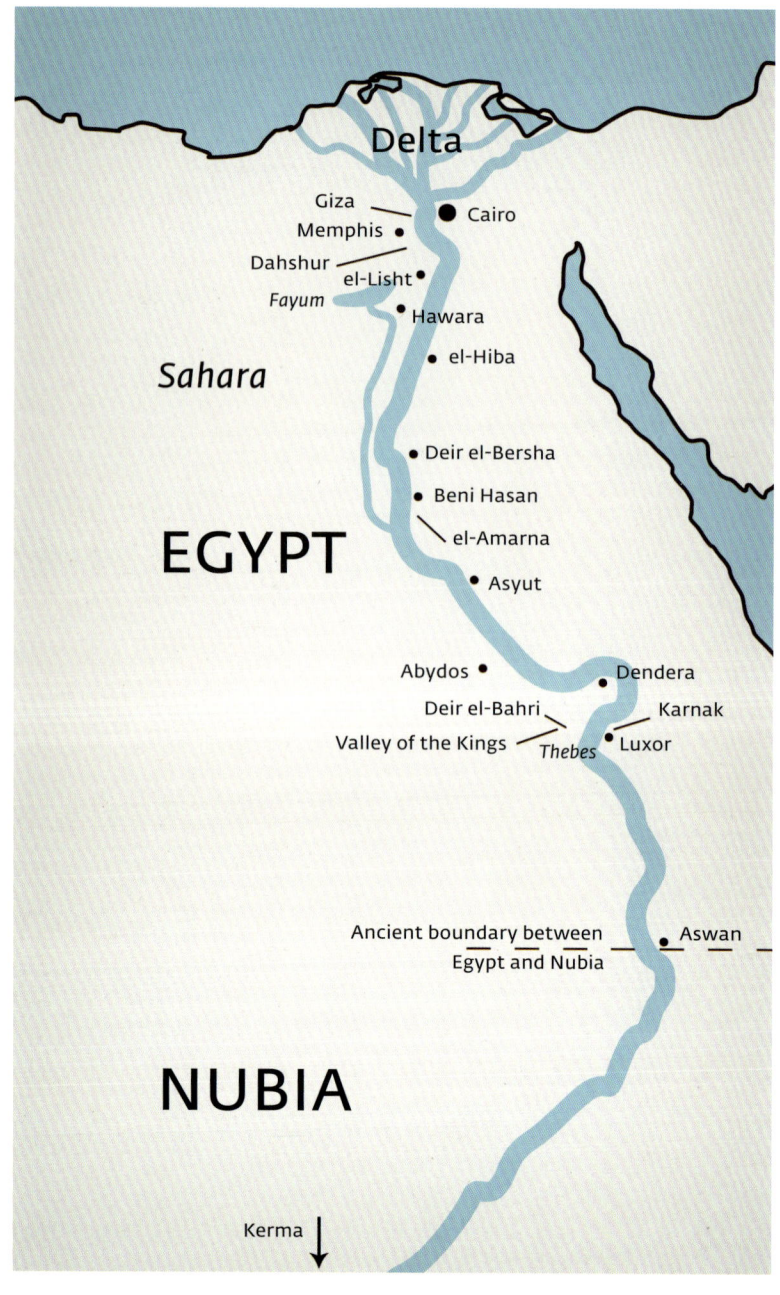

| Predynastic Period | up to 3030 BC |

Archaic period	**3030–2700 BC**
First Dynasty	3030–2850 BC
Second Dynasty	2850–2700 BC

Old Kingdom	**2700–2170 BC**
Third Dynasty	2700–2640 BC
Fourth Dynasty	2640–2505 BC
Fifth Dynasty	2505–2345 BC
Sixth Dynasty	2345–2215 BC

| **First Intermediate Period** | **2170–2010 BC** |

Middle Kingdom	**2010–1790 BC**
Eleventh Dynasty	2120–1975 BC
Twelfth Dynasty	1975–1790 BC
Thirteenth Dynasty	1790–1650 BC

| **Second Intermediate Period** | **1790–1550 BC** |

New Kingdom	**1550–1070 BC**
Eighteenth Dynasty	1550–1290 BC
Nineteenth Dynasty	1290–1185 BC
Twentieth Dynasty	1185–1070 BC

Third Intermediate Period	**1070–715 BC**
Twenty-first Dynasty	1070–945 BC
Twenty-second Dynasty	945–735 BC

Late Period	**715–332 BC**
Twenty-fifth Dynasty	745–664 BC
Twenty-sixth Dynasty	664–525 BC
First Persian Domination	525–401 BC
Thirtieth Dynasty	380–342 BC
Second Persian Domination	342–332 BC

| **Ptolemaic Period** | **332–30 BC** |

| **Roman Period** | **30 BC–AD 395** |

INDEX

Page numbers in *italic* refer to illustrations

A
Abydos 45, 62, 142
  coffins used at 46, *47*, 167, *168*, *170–1*, 222, 236
  excavations 18, 21, *100*, 161, 169, *179*, 222, 236
  royal cemeteries 43
  tombs at *179*, 222
acacia 21, 78–9, *79*, 92, 148, 152, 174, 187, 193, 222
  Acacia nilotica 78–9
administrators, burial of 33
afterlife 29, 30, 32, 35, 36, 37, 40, 41, 49, 50, 51, 53, 55, 58, 59, 65
Ahmose 49
akh 57, 59
Akhenaten 55
Akhmim 64, 69, 72
Alexander the Great 69, 227
el-Amarna 55
amulets *137*, 158, *158–9*, 209, *209*
Amun/Amun-Re 49, 55, 64, 134, 178, 182, 198
  chantress of 55, 134, 180
  priests of 60, 61, 62, 67
anhydrite 98, 248
ankh-sign 192–3
Ankhef, coffin *40*, 41
Ankhwedjes, painted limestone statue *126*, *126*
anklets 35
anthropoid coffins
  construction of 78, 85–7
  decoration of 42–3, 50–1, 52, 55, 67, 92, 108, 167, 194, 227
  development of 42–3, 46, 49, 50–2, 55, 57, 59, 61, 67, 69, 150, 167, 214, 227
  during Nubian rule 214
  Opening of the Mouth and Eyes ritual 53
  reuse and repairs of 85, 91, 178, 180, *186*, 187
  Roman coffins 227
Anubis
  coffin inscriptions 118, 138, 152, 177
  images of 52, *52*, 172, 216, *221*
  view of during Roman rule *226*, 227
  wooden figure of *130*, 131, *131*
Apis bull 201, *201*
Apophis 53
Archaic Period (about 3030–2700 BC) 29, 41, 85
armlets 35

Asasif area 67
Asyut 37, 40–1, 121, 146, 148
Aten 55, 59

B
ba spirits 72, 124, *124–5*, 184, 196, *196*
Bab el-Gasus 61
Bakenmut, outer coffin *48*
bassanite 92, 98, 169, 174, 248
beards 6, *6*, 42, 57–8, 60, 62, 115, 162, 198, *200*, 216, 221, 228, 239
  beard from a New Kingdom coffin *195*, *195*
beliefs 41, 55, 64, 124, 227
Belzoni, Giovanni Battista 13–14
Beni Hasan *20*, 34, 64
  burial pits *20*
  coffin of Khety 138, *138–9*
  coffin of Nakht 21, 152, *152–3*
  coffin of Senuitef 21, *36*
  coffin of Userhet 162, *162–3*
  division of finds 18–21
  excavations 76
  Garstang's excavations 18–19, 21, *22–3*
  mask of Tjay *34*, 160, *160*
  Middle Kingdom box coffins 76
  models from tomb of Khety 142, *142–5*
  tombs at *20*, 34, 160, 162, *166*
Beni Hasan Excavation Committee 18–19
Besenmut, inner bivalve coffin *66*
bitumen 99, 101, 177, 198
bivalve inner coffins 65, *66*, 67
boats, model 34, 36, 78, 142, *144–5*
Book of the Dead 45, 49, 50, 64, 134, 178, 198
  Book of the Dead of Muthetepti *51*
  Book of the Dead of Ramose 45, *132–3*, 134
  The Fields of Iaru in the Papyrus of Ramose *132–3*, 134
  Negative Confession 198
  papyrus found on Nakhtefmut's body 212, *212–13*
  revival of 64
  shrouds 237
  spells *51*, 52, 53, 55, 59, 65, 69, 212, *212–13*, 237, *237*
Book of the Two Ways 37, *39*
Books of the Underworld 49
bouquet, found on Nakhtefmut's body 208, *208*
Bourriau, Janine 14

box coffins/rectangular coffins 43, 76, 121, 136, 150, 162, *166*, 167 172
  construction of 84–5
  boxes/containers for *shabtis* 134, *134–5*, 224, *225*
  shabti figures and box buried with Nakhtefmut 178, *204–5*, 205
British Museum, London 14, 69
British School of Archaeology (BSA) 17, 21
brushes *100*, *101*, 106, *109*, 187, 221, 240
burial chambers 29–30, *31*, 32, *33*, 49, 50, 52, 118
burial customs 29, 30, 32, 43, 45, 46, 49, 50, 53, 59, 67–9, 72, 118, 136, 150, 167, 178, 214, 227
burial pits, Beni Hasan *20*
Butehamun 55

C
Cairo Museum, Egypt 17
calcite
  micritic 98, 221, 248
  paste 91–2, 93, 94, 160, 187, 196, 201, 221, 222, 248
  pigment 92, 104, 106, 152, 240, 242, 248
  in preparation layer 92, 138, 146, 152, 162, 169, 174, 221, 231, 234, *237*
  sparitic calcite 98, 221, 248
Cambridge Chronicle 14
canopic jars 30, 45, 178, *179*, 202, 221, 228
Carnarvon, Lord 22
Carter, Howard 22–3
cartonnage coffins 61–4, 73, 178, 198, 247
  cartonnage coffin of Hor 18, *18*, 92
  cartonnage coffin of Hornedjitef *71*, 72
  cartonnage coffin of Nakhtefmut 17, *61*, 62, *74*, 77, 92, 93, 98, 99, *103*, *108*, 178, 198–201, *199*, *200*, 216
  construction 92–4, *92*
  footboard from a cartonnage coffin 201, *201*
  Roman cartonnage coffins 73, 227
cartonnage footcases 18, 72, 242, 245
cartonnage fragments 102, *103*, 104, 106, 128, *128*, 156, *156–7*, 249
cartonnage masks 35, 42, 72, 94, 178, *230*, 231, *231*

cartonnage mask of Tjay 21, 34, 92, 160, *160*, 198
  development of 35, 42, 178
  gilded cartonnage Roman mask 18, 72, 94, 98, 104, 242, *242*, *243*, 244, *245*
cartonnage mummy trappings 72, 156, 214, 232, *233*
cedar of Lebanon 79, *79*, 84, 92, 119, 152, 187, 196, 224
Champollion, Jean-François 13, 21
chapels 29, 33, 50, 53, 136
choachytes 69, 216
chrysocolla 98, 248
cinnabar 95, *95*, 248
clay pastes 91, 187, 247
Cleopatra, *qersu* coffin 72
Coffin Texts 37, 41, 42, 43, 148
collars 35, 42, 57, 61, 72, 102, 162, 177, 227, 228
  symbolism of 50–1, 55, 177
computed tomography (CT) imaging/CT scan 77, 92, 184, *185*, *186*, 187, 198, *200*, 240, *240*, 250
conifer resins 99
conifer tars 99
copper carbohydrate 98, 248
copper-proteinate 98, 248
copper-wax 98, 248
cost of coffins 58
counterweight, found on Nakhtefmut's body 207, *207*
craftsmen, connecting with 108, 111
cross-section analysis 77, 187, 250

D
Dagi, coffin *37*
Dahshur 45
decoration
  anthropoid coffins 42–3, 46, 49, 50–7, 59, 61, 67, 69–72, 92, 108, 150, 162, 167, 214, 227
  cartonnage cases 74, 77, 93–4, 198
  Coffin Texts 37, 41, 42, 43, 148
  decorating coffins 94–106
  development of decoration 32, 36–7, *38*, *39*, 41, 42–5, 46, 50–3, 55–7, 59–60, 61, 62, 65, 69, 72, 73, 136, 150, 169, 178, 198, 201, 227, 240
  gender markers 32, 57–8, 62, 67, 169, 190
  interior decoration 32, *33*, 37, *38*, *39*, 41, 43, 60, 61, 136
  methods and techniques 101–6,

253

138, 152, 162, 169, 174, 187–9, 196, 198, 216, 221, 222, 228, 240, 242
openwork decoration 57, 93, 232, 232, 233
palace façade 29, 36, 41–2, 150, 152, 155
preparing wooden coffins for 88–92
resins and varnishes 99–101
symmetry 108
wedjat eyes 30, 32, 36, *36*, 46, 52, *121*, 136, *137*, 138, 152, *155*, 162, 169
Deir el-Bahri 61, 67
Deir el-Bersha 37, *38*
Deir el-Medina 58, 172
Dendera 222
Description de l'Égypte 13
division system 17, 18–21, 22–3
djed-pillar 60, 67, 189
Djedameniufankh, cartonnage coffin 93
Djeddjehutefankh, coffin set 214–15
Djeher, coffin lid *104*, 228, *228*, *229*
drawings, preliminary 102, *103*, 106, 108, 169, 174, 196, 221, 228

E
earths 91, 96, 138, 189, 221, 242, 248
 green earth 98, 248
 red earth 92, 95, *95*, 146, 152, 160, 162, 169, 174, 187, 189, 198, 221, 222, 235, 236, 237, 248
 yellow earth 95, *95*, 102, 148, 152, 169, 174, 198, 221, 222, 237, 248, *250*
Edward VII, King 14
Egypt Exploration Fund (EEF) 17, 18
Egypt Exploration Society (EES) 17, 22
Egyptian blue 76, 95, 96, *96*, 104, 106, *106*, *111*, 117, 138, 146, 148, 152, 160, 162, 186, 187, 189, 196, 198, 200, 205, 221, 222, 234, 247, 248, 249, *249*
Egyptian green 95, 96, 104, 106, 146, 162, 174, 248
Egyptian Research Account (ERA) 17, 18, 21
Eighteenth Dynasty (1550–1290 BC) 46, 49–57, 174
Eleventh Dynasty (2120–1975 BC) 80, 92, 96
embalming 29, 99
eye-panel 30, 121, 136, 138, 155, 169

F
faces from coffins *114*, 115, *115*, *116*–*17*, 117, 190, *190*, *191*
 face from a New Kingdom coffin *116*–*17*, 117
 face from a yellow coffin *190*, *190*, *191*
faience 158, *158–9*, 209, 247
false doors *31*, *33*, *36*, *38*, 52

fibre optic reflectance spectroscopy (FORS) 77, 249, 251
Ficus sycomorus see sycomore fig
Fields of Iaru *132–3*, 134
Fifth Dynasty (2505–2345 BC) 29–30
First Intermediate Period (2170–2010 BC) 32, 40, 136, 160
 cartonnage coffins 92
 coffin design 32, 36, 40, 41, 42
 mummy masks 42, 160
First Persian Domination 69, 227
flower motif 61, 64, 190, 194, *194*
food *31*, 32, 36, 118, 136
footboards *104*, 174, *174–5*, *200*, *201*, 216, 247
 footboard, early Eighteenth Dynasty 91, 174, *174–5*
 footboard from a cartonnage coffin *201*, *201*
footcase 18, 72, 98, 242, 245
Fourier transform infrared spectroscopy (FTIR) 77, 251
Fourth Dynasty (2640–2505 BC) 29–30, 96, 118
frit 95, 96, 106, 187, 209, 240, 247
funeral processions 18, 50, 167, 169
funerary gods 124–31
funerary masks *see* masks
funerary rituals 35, 41, 47, 53

G
Garstang, John 18–19, 21, 22–3, 34–5, 169
gas chromatography-mass spectrometry (GC-MS) 77, 251
Geb 59, 60, 182
Getty Conservation Institute 98–9
Giza 118, *119*
Goddess of the West *14*, 60, 184
gods 32, 36, 41, 55, 57, 67, 124, 134, 152, 182, 198, 207, 216, 237
 see also individual gods and goddesses
gold leaf 57, 106, *108*, 195, *230*, *231*, 234, 240, 242
governors 18, 33, 34, 40, 43, 222
granaries *31*, 32, *35*, *38*, 142, 144
Grey, Honourable Mrs William 14, 17
ground *see* preparation layer
group burials 61
Gua, coffin *39*
gypsum 92, 93, 242, 248
gypsum plaster 94, 152, 169, 174, 238, *239*, *239*, 242

H
Hall of Judgement 65, 134, 198
Hanbury, Barnard 13, 14
Hapy 134, 232, *233*
Hathor 60, 62, 222
Hawara 18, 98, 242
headdresses 56, 57
 divine headdress 62
 gender distinction 57, 60, 62

nemes headdress 43, 46, 50
 vulture headdress 62
headrests 35, 37, *37*
heart scarab 211, *211*
Heka 182
Henenu, coffin 84, 85, 121, *121*, *122–3*
Henutmehyt, coffins 52, 54
Herwer 34
el-Hiba 18
hieroglyphic script, Champollion's first theories on 13, 21
Hilton Price, F. G. 21
Hor (British Museum), outer *qersu* coffin 64
Hor (Fitzwilliam Museum), cartonnage coffin 18, *18*, 92
Hor (king), tomb 43
Hornedjitef 69–72, *70–1*
Hornefer 76, 134, *134*, *135*
Horus 30, 62, 65, 136
 see also Sons of Horus
Horus name 42
Hunefer, sarcophagus 14, *16*, 27
huntite 98, 198, 248
Hyksos 45, 49

I
Ineferti, mummy board 56
Ikhtay, coffin 55
imaging techniques 75, 76–7, 249–51
incense 57, 99
indigo 242, 248, 251
infrared (IR) reflectography 76, 249
inlay 99, 106, 117, 195, 200
Ipuky, tomb 53
Ipuy, tomb 6, *6–7*, 7
Irethereru, *qersu* coffin 21, 222, *222–3*
Isetweret 228
Isis
 cartonnage coffin fragment showing the goddess Isis 128, *128*
 foot end depictions 45, 46, 47, 52, 128, 174, *174*
 images of 52, 62, 67, 124, *129*
 reassembles Osiris's body 30, 124
 view of during Roman rule *226*, 227

J
jackals 55, 118, *130*, 131
James, M. R. 19, 21, 26
joints, wood working 78, *80*, 84–7, *88*, *88*, 121, 138, 152, 169, 172, 174, 184, *185*, *186*, 187, 221, 222, 232, *246*

K
ka spirits 124, 126, 152
Karnak 178, 182, 198
Kerma Empire 45
Khety
 coffin 21, 36, 138–41, *138–9*, *140*, *141*, 162
 coffin construction 78, 79, 84–5, *84*, 91

models from the tomb of Khety 21, 35, 142, *142–5*
 tomb of 35–6, *35*
kings
 afterlife 30–2
 burials 14, 29, 30–2, 43, 45, 49, 59, 60, 61
kites 62
Kushite kingdom 64, 214

L
Lahun 64
lake pigments 248
 indigo 242, 248, 251
 madder 98, 242, 248, 249
Late Period (715–332 BC) 64–9, 72, 93, 95, 214
lead white 248
limestone 95, 96, 98, 126, *126*, *127*, 161, *161*, 234, *234*, 235, 236, *236*, 248
linen 38, 57, 126, 142, 160, 172, 198, 242
 cartonnage 61, 92–4, *92*, 160, 198, 200, 239, 242, 247
 for coffin repairs 91, 165
 mummification 29, 30, 35, 92, 150, 161
 on the surface of coffins 94, 162, 180, 221, 232
 shrouds 227, 237, 240, *240*, *241*
el-Lisht 43, 45
lotus flower 194, *194*
Louvre, Paris 14
Luxor 14, 17, 167, 178

M
madder 98, 242, 248, 249
Madja, coffin 85, 172, *172*, *173*, 177
malachite 248
Mariette, Auguste 17
masks 35, 42, 57
 cartonnage 18, 21, 42, 72, 94, 178, *230*, *231*, *231*
 cartonnage mask of Tjay 21, 34, 160, *160*, 198
 mask of Wah 150, *151*
 gilded cartonnage Roman mask 18, 72, 94, 98, 104, 242, *242*, *243*, *244*, *245*
 Greek- and Roman-style 72, 94, 239, 242
 gypsum plaster mask from a Roman coffin 238, *239*, *239*
master physicians 146
mastic 99
 see also pistacia resin
Medinet Habu 67
Meh 126, *127*
Meidum 64
Meketre, tomb of 80, *80*, 82
Memphis 42, 58, 69
Memphis-Fayum region 43
men, coffin designs for 32, 57–8, 60, 62, 67

menat, found on Nakhtefmut's body 207, *207*
Menatkhufu 34
metagabbro, scarab made of 211, *211*
Metropolitan Museum of Art, New York 22
Middle Kingdom (2010–1790 BC) 18, 19, *32*–46, 50, 52, 96, 136, 150, 167
mineral pigments 95, *95*, 96, 98, 248
miniature coffin 224, *224*
models 36, 78, 80, *80*, 136, 138
   boats 34, 36, 78, 142, 144–5
   granaries *31*, 32, *35*, *38*, 78, 142, *144*
   model tools 29, *82*
   models from the tomb of Khety 21, *35*, 142, *142*–5
Montu 64, 67
Montuemhat 67
mourning woman, coffin 18, *19*, 47, 84, 92, *168*–71, *169*, *172*
mud pastes 91
mummies
   position of 30, 32, 43, 46, 53, 65, 118, 121, 136, 167, 169, 198, 240
   red shroud mummy 18, 98–9, 227, 240, *240*, *241*
   representations of 67, 72, 201, 216, 221, *227*, *228*, *229*
   Wah *151*
mummification 29, 30, 32, 35, 118, 150
   during Late Period 214
   during Middle Kingdom 150
   during Roman period 72, 240
   during Third Intermediate Period 178, 202
mummy boards 56, 57, 59, 60, 61
   Nespawershefyt 92, 182, *184*, *184*, 187, 189, 190, *250*
Muthotep, reused coffin lid 180, *180*, *181*

N
Nakht
   coffin 21, 41, 150, 152–5, *152*–*3*, 162, 178
   coffin construction 79, *79*, 84, 85, 88, 92
   coffin decoration 104, *105*, 106, *107*
Nakht from el-Lisht, coffin 43
Nakhtefmut 7
   burial 178
   cartonnage coffin 61, 62, 74, 77, 92, 93, *103*, 178, 198–201, 216
   coffin decoration 98, 99, *103*, *108*
   discovery of 17
   objects buried with *202*–6
   objects found on body *207*–15
Napoleon 13, 14
Nebamun (and Ipuky), tomb 53
Nebty *126*, *127*
Nectanebo II 236
Negative Confession 198
nemes headdress 43, 46, 50

Nephthys 124
   images of 45, 46, 47, 52, 62, 67, 124, *128*, *129*, *129*
Nesmutaatneru, *qersu* coffin *131*
Nespawershefyt 7, 13, 14, 24–5, 26, 182–9
   coffin alterations 75, 185–7
   coffin construction 78, 79, *81*, 87–8, *89*, 92
   coffin decoration 99, 104, 106, 108, *110*, 111, *111*, *112*
   inner coffin *14*, 59, 196
   mummy board *250*
   status of 178, 182, *184*
nested coffins 17, 57, 59, 61, 62–7, 69, 70–1, 182–9, 214
New Kingdom (1550–1070 BC) 46, 49–58, 65, 67, *116*–*17*, *117*, 167, 169, 178, 195, *195*
   coffin construction 85
   coffin decoration 95
   early coffins from 167
   recycling coffins 178
Newberry, Percy 34
Nineteenth Dynasty (1290–1185 BC) 52, 57, 59, 178
Nubia 49, 58, 214
Nut 51, 59, 60, 62, *63*, 65, 67, 69, *103*, 104, *110*, 150, 152, 156, *156*–7, 162, 177, 182, 228

O
officials 33, 34–5, 40, 178
   afterlife 32, 118
   burials 29, *31*, 32, 33, 34–5, 45, 49, 67
Old Kingdom (2700–2170 BC) 29–32, 36, 37, 41, 42, 118, 136, 150, 214
Opening of the Mouth and Eyes ritual 6–7, 53, 65
openwork decoration 57, 93, 232, *232*, *233*
orpiment 95, 96, 98, 102, 104, 146, 160, 169, 187, *187*, 189, 198, 221, *221*, 231, 242, 248, 250
Osiris 30, 32, 36, 124, 227
   Abydos 62, 142, 222
   and Anubis 131, 138, 152, 227
   association with king 30, 31–2, 41, 49
   coffin inscriptions 138, 150, 152, 162, 216
   and colour symbolism 50–1, 162, 177
   dead's association with 41, 42, 50, 52, 55, 58, 59, 61, 62, 65, 150, 152, 207, 216
   fetish 62
   images of 52, 60, 61, 62, 72, 124, 126, *127*, *134*, 172, 182, 189, 198, 216, 232, 237
   judgement 134, 182, 211
   king of Egypt 30, 124
   and Re 49, 59, 62

   ruler of the Underworld 30, 126
   and Sons of Horus 158
   tomb of 64–5
   view of during Roman rule 226, 227
   see also djed-pillar; Ptah-Sokar-Osiris
Osorkon I 61, 198, 207

P
paint 94–9, *97*, 101–2, 104, 106, 248
Pakepu
   coffin construction 78, *82*, 85, 86–7, *87*, *88*, 91, 94, 216–21, *218*–*9*
   coffin decoration 101, 102, *102*, 106, 220, 221, 221
   coffins of 14, *17*, *17*, 67, 68, 69, 216–21, 228, 232
palace façades 29, 36, 41–2, 150, 152, *155*
papyrus 6, 50, 247
   in cartonnage 73, 94, 247
   papyrus found on Nakhtefmut's body 212, *212*–13
   papyrus of Ramose 124–5, *132*–3, 134
   see also Book of the Dead
pararealgar 248
Pasherienusiraa 225
pastes 61, 85, *86*–*7*, *88*, 91–2, 92, 93–4, 98, 121, 138, 152, 160, 162, 164, *165*, 174, 180, *185*, *186*, 187, *189*, 195, 196, 198, *200*, 201, *218*–9, 221, 222, 232, 245, 247, 250
   over body 30
pens 101–2, *104*, 138
Pensenhor, coffin 63
Petrie Flinders, William Matthew 17, 21
pigments 94–9, 101, 102, 106, 169, 227, 250
pistacia resin 57, 99, *100*, 177, *187*, *188*, 196, 198, 249, 251
polarised light microscopy (PLM) 77, 250, *250*
pots, large pots, made of Nile silt, used for burial 120, *120*
preparation layer 85, 92, 93, 98, 101, 102, *103*, 106, 121, 138, 146, 162, 169, 174, *186*, *187*, *189*, *189*, 196, 198, 221, 231, *231*, 232, 234, 237, 247, 250
Prince of Wales (Edward VII) 14, 17
Psamtek 228
Ptah 201
Ptah-Sokar-Osiris 67, 68
Ptahemhat, coffin *33*
Ptolemaic Period (332–30 BC) 69, 236
   coffins 69, 72, 94, 95
   mummy trappings 94, 104, 156, *156*–7
   sarcophagi 234, 236, *236*
Pyramid Texts 30, 37
pyramids 29, 30, 40, 45, 118

Q
qersu coffins 64–5, *64*, 72–3, *72*, 214, 214–15, 222, *222*, *223*, 227
   coffin of Cleopatra 72
   coffin of Hor 64
   coffin of Irethereru 21, 92, 222, *222*–*3*
   coffin of Nesmutaatneru *131*
   construction 85, 92
Quibell, James 17

R
Raman spectroscopy 77, 251
Ramesses II 57
Ramesses III, sarcophagus lid *12*, 13–14, *15*, 26, *27*
Ramesseum, Luxor 17, 62
Ramose, papyrus 124–5, *132*–3, 134
Re 49, 53, 59, 62, 69
realgar 95, 102, 248, 250
rebirth 50–1, 59, 62, 194
recycling coffins and tombs 45, 59, 60–2, 67–9, 152, 178, 180, *185*, 186, 187
red lead 98–9, 227, 240, 242, 248
red shroud mummy 18, 98–9, 227, 240, *240*, *241*
resins 77, 99–101, 187, *188*, 249
resurrection 50, 52, 58, 62, 65, 67
rishi coffins 46, 50, 167
   coffin of Taiuy *167*
rituals
   burial 32, 35, 37, 53, 118, 136
   rituals for the dead 29, *31*, 32, *33*, 35, 41, 52, 53
   mummification 30, 32, 52
   Opening of the Mouth and Eyes 6–7, 53, 65
   temple 57, 67
robberies, tomb 17, 33, 61, 92, 178
Roman Empire 227
Roman Period (30 BC–AD 395) 69, 72
   coffins and decoration 72–3, *72*, 94, 96, 98, *103*, 104, 227, 238–9, *239*
   gilded cartonnage Roman mask and footcase 18, 72, 92, 98, 104, 242, *242*, *243*, *244*, 245
   gypsum plaster mask from a Roman coffin *238*, 239, *239*
   mummification 240
   mummy 18, 240, *240*, *241*
royalty
   afterlife 30–2
   burial chambers 49
   burials 14, 29, 30–2, 43, 45, 49, 59, 60, 118
   recycling coffins 60, 61
   residence 45, 55

S
sah 50, 57, 59, 62, 65, 150, 160
sandals 35, 37
sarcophagi 49, 69, 118, 150, 214

head from a limestone sarcophagus 234, *234*, 235
Hor (king) 43
Hunefer 14, *16*, 27
  limestone sarcophagus head 75, *234*, 234
  Ptolemaic sarcophagus lid 236, *236*
  Ramesses III 12, 13–14, *15*, 26, 27
sawing, tangential 80, *81*, 247, *247*
scanning electron microscope 251, *251*
scanning electron microscopy-energy-dispersive X-ray spectroscopy (SEM/EDX) 77, 250
scarab beetle 59, 69, 72
  found on Nakhtefmut's body 210, *210–11*, 211
Second Intermediate Period (about 1790–1550 BC) 45, 46, 167, 169
Second Persian Domination 69, 227
Sedment 64
Sen, coffin *38*
senetjer 57
Senuitef, coffin 21, *36*
Senumutef, coffin *30*
Service des Antiquités 17, 22
Sesostris III 43
Seth 30, 52, 124
Sety I 57
Shabaka 214
  shabti/ushabti figures 51, 134, 178, 205
  containers 76, 134, *134, 135*, 224, 225, 204–5, *205*
  'overseer' *shabtis* 205, *205*
shen hieroglyphs *104*, 228
shrouds 51, 57, 73, 98–9, 227, *237*, 240, *240*, *241*
Shu 59, 182
Shy *31*
sidr 79, *79*, 116–17, *117*, 138, 148, 152, 169, 174, 184, 187, 190, 205
Society of Antiquaries, London 19, 21
Sons of Horus
  canopic jars *179*
  coffin inscriptions 150, 152, 177
  faience amulets *158*, 158–9
  figures of buried with Nakhtefmut 99, 202, *202–3*
  images of *40*, 41, 52, *52*, 69, 198, 232
spells 37, 42
  Book of the Dead 45, 50, *51*, 52, 53, 59
  shrouds 237
statues 124
  painted limestone statue of a man called Ankhwedjes *126*, 126
stelas
  limestone stela of man and woman before Osiris 126, *127*
  limestone stela of three brothers *161*

Roman Period stela *226*
stereomicroscopes 76, *76*
stola 61, 207, *207*
sun worship 55, 57
surface topography 76
sycomore fig 44, 78, *81*, 84, 121, 138, *138–9*, 142, 146, 148, 162, 169, 172, 174, 184, 187, 190, 194, 196, 201, 202, 205, 206, 216, 221, 232, 251
Syndicate of the Fitzwilliam Museum 26

T
Taiuy, coffin *167*
tamarisk 78, *81*, 187
Tamarix aphylla see tamarisk
Tamyt, coffin *176*, 177, *177*
tangential sawing 80, *81*, 247, *247*
Taqa 76, 134, *134*, 135
Thebes 32, 43, 45, 60, 64
  coffin styles 58, 64, 67
  group burials at 61
  mortuary practices 45, 49, 67, 69
  rishi coffins 46
  ruling elite burials 43, 45, 167, 214
  tombs at 6, *6–7*, 7, 53, 214
Third Intermediate Period (1070–715 BC) 58–9, 178
  coffin decoration 59–64, 95
  mummification 178, 202
  tomb robberies 178
Thirteenth Dynasty (1790–1650 BC) 43, 45
Thirtieth Dynasty (380–342 BC) 69, 234
Thoth 52, 53, 62
Tjay, cartonnage mask 21, *34*, 92, 160, *160*, 198
tombs
  at Abydos *179*, 222
  at Beni Hasan 34, 160, 162, 166
  at Thebes 6, *6–7*, 7, 53, 214
  communal tombs 61
  decoration 29, 30, *31*, 32, *33*, 49, 50, 59, 136, 214
  King Hor 43
  Ipuky 53
  Ipuy 6, *6–7*, 7
  Khety 35–6, *35*
  Meketre 80, *80*, *82*
  Nebamun 53
  officials' tombs 29, 32, 33
  Osiris 64–5
  rock-cut 29, 33, 34, 43
  tomb robberies 33, 178
  Tutankhamun 22–3
tools 80, *80*, *82*, 83, 84, 101
Tuna el-Gebel 239
Tutankhamun 22–3, 49
Tuthmosis III 50
Twelfth Dynasty (1975–1790 BC) 36, 41, 42, 43, 150, 162
Twentieth Dynasty (1290–1070 BC) 57, 178

Twenty-first Dynasty (1070–945 BC) 59–61, 65, 67, 96, 178
  Amun-Re temple 178
  coffin design 65, 96, 182
  yellow coffins 59, 182
Twenty-second Dynasty (945–735 BC) 61–2, 69, 178
  cartonnage cases 61–2, 92, 198
  coffin design 62, 98, 182
  yellow coffins 182
Twenty-fifth Dynasty (745–664 BC) 65, 69, 131
Twenty-sixth Dynasty (664–525 BC) 67, 69

U
ultraviolet (UV) fluorescence 2, 76, 189, 249, *250*
underworld 29, 30, 32, 35, 40, 49, 53, 134, 136
  Book of the Two Ways 37, 39
  Coffin Texts 37, 42
  Books of the underworld 49
Userhet
  coffin 21, 28, 44, 150, 162–7, 172, 249
  coffin construction 85
Userheta, coffin of 91
ushabtis see shabti/ushabti figures
UV-VIS-NIR fibre optic reflectance spectroscopy (FORS) 250, *250*

V
Valley of the Kings 14, 22, 49, 60, 172
varnish 57, 99–101, 106, 111, 177, *187*, *188*, 198
  identification of 77, 249
  yellow coffins 57, 61, 62, 99, 101, 106, 182, *184*, 187, 189, 196
verdigris 98, 248
visible-light induced luminescence (VIL) photography 76, 249, *249*
voice offerings 35
vultures 42, 51, 167, 177, *177*
  vulture headdresses 62

W
Waddington, George 13, 14
Wah, mummy *151*
wall paintings *31*, 49, 53, 55, 65
Warethotep 21
Warti-hetep 152
water pourers see choachytes
weapons 37, *38*, 42
wedjat eyes
  amulets *137*
  anthropoid coffins 52
  coffin of Senuitef 36, *36*
  symbolism and location of 30, 32, 36, 46, 136, 155
  see also eye-panel
Wepwawetemhat
  coffin 42, 146, *146*, 147
  coffin decoration 41, 101, *101*, 106, *109*

Whyte, Edward Towry 21, *22–3*, 23, 26
winged scarab, found on Nakhtefmut's body 210, *210–11*
women
  burial goods 45
  coffin designs 32, 57–8, 60, 62, 67
  coffins 37–40, 72, 148, 152, *167*, 172, 177, 190
  fragment from the coffin of an unknown woman 41, 84, 148, *148*, 149
wood
  preparation of 80–4, 121, 138, 148, 152, 162, 177, 186–7, 216–7
  types used in coffins 60, 78–9, 84, 85–6, 152
wood identification 77, 251
wood working joints see joints, wood working

X
X-radiography 77, 91, 242, 250
  X-radiographs *82*, 85, 162, *165*, *190*, 219, 221, 244, 250
X-ray fluorescence spectrometry (XRF) 77, 250
X-Ray powder diffraction (XRD) 77, 250

Y
yellow coffins 57, 61, 62, 87, 99, 106
  coffin set of Nespawershefyt 182–9
  face from a yellow coffin 190, *190*, *191*
  hand from a yellow coffin *192–3*, 193
  head end of a yellow coffin box 196, *196–7*

Z
Ziziphus spina-christi see sidr